STORIES OF ICE

D1716656

STORIES OF
ICE

*Adventure, Commerce
and Creativity on Canada's Glaciers*

LYNN MARTEL

RMB

Copyright © 2020 by Lynn Martel
Additional photography and artwork copyright © 2020 by the individual contributors
First Edition

For information on purchasing bulk quantities of this book, or to obtain media excerpts or invite the author to speak at an event, please visit rmbooks.com and select the "Contact" tab.

RMB | Rocky Mountain Books Ltd.
rmbooks.com
@rmbooks
facebook.com/rmbooks

Cataloguing data available from Library and Archives Canada
ISBN 9781771603898 (paperback)
ISBN 9781771603904 (electronic)

Printed and bound in China

We would like to also take this opportunity to acknowledge the traditional territories upon which we live and work. In Calgary, Alberta, we acknowledge the Niitsítapi (Blackfoot) and the people of the Treaty 7 region in Southern Alberta, which includes the Siksika, the Piikuni, the Kainai, the Tsuut'ina and the Stoney Nakoda First Nations, including Chiniki, Bearpaw, and Wesley First Nations. The City of Calgary is also home to Métis Nation of Alberta, Region III. In Victoria, British Columbia, we acknowledge the traditional territories of the Lkwungen (Esquimalt, and Songhees), Malahat, Pacheedaht, Scia'new, T'Sou-ke and W̱SÁNEĆ (Pauquachin, Tsartlip, Tsawout, Tseycum) peoples.

All rights reserved. No part of this publication may be reproduced, stored in a retrieval system, or transmitted in any form or by any means – electronic, mechanical, audio recording, or otherwise – without the written permission of the publisher or a photocopying licence from Access Copyright. Permissions and licensing contribute to a secure and vibrant book industry by helping to support writers and publishers through the purchase of authorized editions and excerpts. To obtain an official licence, please visit accesscopyright.ca or call 1-800-893-5777.

We acknowledge the financial support of the Government of Canada through the Canada Book Fund and the Canada Council for the Arts, and of the province of British Columbia through the British Columbia Arts Council and the Book Publishing Tax Credit.

Disclaimer
The views expressed in this book are those of the author and do not necessarily reflect those of the publishing company, its staff or its affiliates.

COVER IMAGE – Jesse Milner ascends the Robson Glacier under moody skies. Photo Paul Zizka

Title Page – While pinned inside their tents for a full week, Charlie Breakey enjoyed a brief respite in the storm to explore the spectacular surroundings on the Rockies' Freshfield Icefield before the storm chased them back into their tents. Photo Phil Tomlinson

To my mom, for sharing with me the perfect space to write this book;

And to my honey, John, for sharing his ear, his shoulder and his heart, and for believing in me to help make it possible for me to write this book.

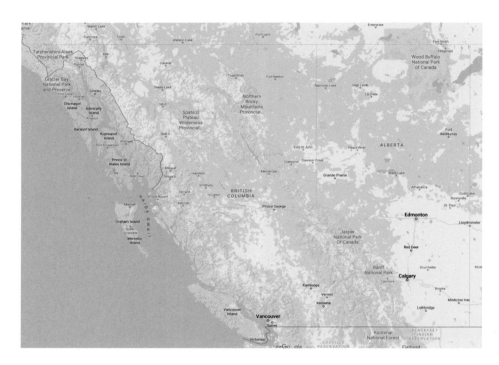

Imagery ©2020 TerraMetrics, Map data ©2020 Google, INEGI

PHOTOGRAPHERS

A picture is worth a thousand words, the saying goes.

Within the pages of this book, I've written many thousands of words with the desire to reveal the glaciers of Alberta and British Columbia as the vibrant, mysterious, multidimensional, fascinating entities they are. But sometimes, words need companions. I owe enormous thanks and gratitude to all these talented professional photographers for sharing their images to help make the story of western Canada's glaciers more fascinating, captivating, intriguing, humbling and downright gorgeous.

John Baldwin
Agathe Bernard
Linda Bily
Anthony Bonello
Bryce Brown
Isabel Budke
Bruno Engler
Nick Fitzhardinge
Martina Halik/Raven Eye
Pam Jenks
Amy Liu
Darcy Monchak
Sam McCoy
Pat Morrow
John Price
Harry Rowed
Scott Rowed
Chic Scott
John Scurlock
Steve Tersmette
Phil Tomlinson
Paul Zizka

Under the warm summer sun, glaciers course with streams filled with their own melting ice.
Photo Lynn Martel

TABLE OF CONTENTS

Like all glaciers in western Canada, those at the fabled Lake of the Hanging Glacier melt more and more every year. Will those lakes retain their stunning turquoise colour as the glaciers diminish over the coming decades? Photo Nick Fitzhardinge

PROLOGUE

CHURNING WIND AND SNOW

The wind was everywhere, a brutal, tangible force pushing my body from all sides at once. With my hood cinched snugly around my face, my eyes focused through rose-tinted ski goggles on the ski tails of my rope-mate just a few metres ahead of me, the wind erasing his tracks like a vigorously shaken Etch-a-Sketch. We skied along in a deliberate procession across the boundless smooth snowfield, connected one to the other by our nylon rope like preschoolers on a field trip. Tilting my eyes up for a moment, I watched a steep charcoal-shaded cliff face materialize through a swirl of cloud directly ahead of me; then in an instant it was gone, as if a remote control had switched the screen back to a scene of churning wind and snow. Feeling isolated inside my own hood despite the rope connecting me to my companions, I realized how on previous mountain trips, when travelling through foul weather I had simply focused on reaching our destination – an alpine hut, a vehicle, eventually home. This time, our destination was whatever place we stopped to set up camp. There and here were the same.

Skiing across a glacier is a thoroughly unique experience. My imagination wandered to previous glacier adventures when I had embraced sunny, windless spring days that granted us time to linger on a summit to soak in the panorama of jagged peaks poking up like rough gemstones displayed on white velvet. A glacier on a sunny, windless day delivers the most sublime experience, mesmerizing quiet in every direction. I remembered skiing back down in a laughing race to the hut before the sun's intensity caused our skis to sink into a surface being reduced to mush.

And that was how I had envisioned our Wapta Icefield traverse. It was April, after all. Reality, however, was accompanied by a soundtrack of howling, frosty wind biting my cheeks, gusting so fiercely that even with a 20-kilogram pack on my back I feared being knocked to my butt. Yup, the very climatic conditions that nourish their existence frequently render glaciers nasty, inhospitable, downright unpleasant places.

And endlessly fascinating.

Soft sunlight highlights a maze of crevasses on Mount King Edward in the Canadian Rockies, with Mounts Columbia and Bryce in the background. Photo Bryce Brown

1 BORN TO MELT

Calving glacial ice,
the blue-green dragon
meets in gravel
lichens breaking the greyness in golden rust,
and south, as the ice-chilled wind warmed,
came soft-spring-green grass
rooting in the till and rotting, forming soil
for hunter to walk upon softly, silently
as great cats walk.

—Jon Whyte, *Mind Over Mountains*

1–1 SNOWFLAKE TO SNOWFIELD

From a Fleck of Dust

The sun creeps above the horizon. A thin curve of its golden dome appears, rising so slowly that motion is barely perceptible. Its pulsing power sends a shimmering radiance fanning outward and upward into the air, and downward, penetrating the soil.

As the gilded orb inches higher, the bushes and trees tremble in its radiance, inviting and absorbing its warmth to feed their leaves and branches and their serpentine roots boring deep underground. Just past midday the sun's heat reaches a crescendo, and the water in the creeks and the lakes and marshy wetlands pulsates, energizing surface molecules so that they break apart and evaporate, the sun's warmth drawing that invisible vapour right up into the atmosphere. When the sun's power is sufficiently intense, it even pulls water right from leaves and dirt.

Pockets of warmer, less-dense air rise, while masses of cooler, denser air sink. When masses of misty air nudge up against the slopes of hills and mountains, the higher terrain forces those masses upward. At the higher altitudes, where the pressure in the atmosphere is less than it is at lower elevations, the vapour expands. As it does, it loses energy and grows cooler. When the air reaches that pressure at which it is saturated with water vapour, in equilibrium with water – water in its gaseous state – it has reached its dew point. This is where water vapour condenses at the same

Fresh snow falls into a crevasse on a stormy day. Photo Lynn Martel

rate at which liquid water evaporates. If the air temperature increases just a fraction of a degree, the gas becomes liquid and rain falls, or sometimes, sleet.

But if that temperature drops just a touch, to below 2 degrees Celsius, then magic happens.

All it takes is a fleck of dirt, or maybe dust, a grain of pollen, or even an airborne micro-speck of a leaf fragment. The cooling temperature causes that vapour to freeze, and those minute ice crystals cohere onto those bits of solid matter.

A snowflake is created.

A second snowflake forms, then another, and zillions more. When so many snowflake crystals gather in one cloud that the cloud grows too heavy to stay aloft in the air currents, snow starts falling from the sky. As it falls, different factors – air temperature and, to a lesser extent, humidity – determine the shape of each snowflake.

Each snowflake forms in a complex shape. Some have long delicate arms, intricate as lace; others short, stocky branches. Some snowflakes are plump and tiny, round and petite; others are slender and elegant as a ballerina's limbs. Since ice crystals have a six-sided structure, the most common shape for snowflakes to assume is that of a six-armed star. Although most snowflakes appear to be perfectly symmetrical, most are not, since each arm grows independently and changes as the air temperature or humidity affect the way water molecules attach to the snowflake. All these factors combine for nature to create exquisite forms, the likes of which inspire humans to create art, which never quite measures up. Changes in the atmospheric conditions can cause snowflakes to undergo numerous changes on their journey as they fall from the sky.

Then they land.

Arms of a Starfish

On the ground, snowflakes continue to change and morph along with rises and drops in the temperature, changes in humidity and movement caused by the capricious forces of wind. When large quantities of snowflakes fall in one area, those flakes accumulate one atop the other. At higher elevations, where – and when – temperatures remain below freezing for extended periods, the snowpack accumulates to

Ancient ice compressed for millennia at the toe of the Illecillewaet Glacier in the Selkirk Mountains resembles polished streaked marble. Photo Agathe Bernard

the point where it begins to compress under the weight of its own mass. As it does this, the delicate arms of the snowflakes break off and the flakes partially melt, devolving into granular snow. As the weight of the snowpack compresses in response to the weight from above, the snow grains are rearranged into a denser pack. Deeper and deeper into the pack, the ice mass coalesces into a solid yet plastic state. Eventually, when the pack reaches a density of about 800 kilograms per cubic metre, any open pores filled with air that remain in the compressing ice are gradually pinched off, and they form bubbles.

Much in the same way an unfathomable number of individual raindrops make up the contents of an ocean, an immeasurable number of snowflakes accumulate to create an icefield spreading hundreds or thousands of square metres, sometimes more than a kilometre in depth. Icefields, and the glaciers that descend from them into valleys and gorges like the arms of a starfish, grow at high elevations in mountainous terrain, and usually at colder latitudes, although not always, since glaciers, or remnants of them, are also found at high elevations in tropical regions. Glaciers exist in mountain ranges on every continent except Australia. Essentially, glaciers grow in places where more snow falls over time than melts during that same period. Snowflakes that fall in cold temperatures are dry, resulting in low-density snow that transforms into ice much more slowly than the moist, dense snow created in warmer temperatures.

After decades, or centuries, pass, the accumulation of ice becomes so heavy and so dense that gravity causes it to respond to the pressure of its own weight lying on the bedrock that supports it. Then it does the thing that makes it a glacier – it crosses from the dormant state of a giant static mass sitting on the landscape, to one of life.

It moves.

Like just about everything on our planet, glaciers are bound by the force of gravity. A glacier moves in much the same way any heavy, thick, gooey substance flows, like lava down a volcano, or corn syrup on a scoop of ice cream. The glacier's contours mirror that of the bed surface supporting it, which is pocked with dips and divots and folds and drops. Seeking the path of least resistance, the body of ice pushes over gentle hills, sinks into troughs and rolls over drops. The thicker the glacier, the subtler these features are – but no matter, they give each glacier its unique form, like wrinkles on a person's face or prints on a fingertip.

When a glacier encounters a sufficiently steep drop, the body of ice is stretched and pulled, and that force causes the ice to fracture and split. The resulting deep gashes are called crevasses, and many a glaciologist or mountain guide has demonstrated this by slowly bending a Mars bar so that the outer chocolate layer cracks apart. Enormous tower blocks or columns of glacial ice, easily as large as a house and often formed where crevasses intersect, are called seracs.

With even the most subtle decline in the land surface, the intense pressure of a glacier's weight upon its own mass causes it to creep downhill. Ice is a much softer substance than the rock or the sediment supporting it, so it is easily made to deform by the pressure of its own weight.

On the underside of the glacier, the friction caused by the ice mass sliding along the bedrock forces it to move at a much slower pace than that of the glacier's surface, whose movement is unhindered. When the base of the glacier is very cold, the movement is extremely slow. When the temperatures of a glacier's underside are warmer, the liquid water acts as a lubricant that speeds up the glacier's movement.

Glaciers creep, glide, flow, slide and shift. They are on the move. It's their purpose, their job. And their fate.

Nordic Glacier in British Columbia's Selkirk Mountains spreads across the landscape with its arms dropping into dips and gullies like a starfish. Photo Lynn Martel

1–2 GLACIERS BLEED BLUE

Sleeping Growth, Lively Demise

The life cycle of a glacier incorporates two main purposes – water storage and water release – but glaciers also serve many other purposes that benefit nature and, by extension, humans.

It may seem contrary, but during the winter months, when glaciers appear dormant, frozen and lifeless – that's when they grow. That happens most at their higher elevations, where temperatures are colder. If more snow accumulates during the winter than melts during the summer, the glacier is nourished.

During the warm summer months, when just about every other living organism in the mountain ecosystem is growing and flourishing, glaciers are diminishing.

Summer, however, is when glaciers appear most alive, springing to life as ice exposed to the sun melts, sending water rushing along the surface, carving creeks that splash and bubble and wind down to the glacier's snout, where they empty, and where lakes often form. Paradoxically, all this lively melting activity is the glacier perishing.

Those running creeks bore holes into depressions in the ice – initiated by cavities below – to create *moulins*, or millwells. These vertical tunnels can begin as tiny as a bathtub drain, but, over time, as firehoses' worth of swirling water pour downward, they can expand to giant bowls large enough to swallow a car. Millwells can drain right to the bottom of the glacier where water slithers between the ice and the bedrock, or sometimes meltwater bores horizontal tunnels that flow furtively metres below the surface. The possibilities are endless; ice is an infinitely malleable substance that can continually be carved and modified by the forces of its own meltwater, forming myriad shapes in the process. Like rock canyons that are made smooth and curved and scooped like potters' bowls in response to the forces of flowing water, glacial ice, too, is nature's sculpting material.

In wintertime, snow-covered glaciers appear smooth and still, as the Rockies' Balfour Glacier does with three extremely tiny skiers slowly ascending lower left of centre. Photo Lynn Martel

On warm summer days meltwater gushes from a glacier's toe, as it does here on the Rockies' President Glacier. Photo Lynn Martel

Sunlight isn't the only force that alters the exposed surface, though, as wind leaves its mark too. In summertime, once all the previous winter's snow has melted away, the exposed surface can be rough, gouged with runnels and potholes and lumpy as a pebble beach or jagged as raw diamonds.

Glacial melt happens through surface melt, evaporation and calving – when chunks and blocks of glacier ice break away from the main ice tongue. Ideally, glaciers will melt and contribute to rivers during the warmest summer months when there is less rainfall. In the Canadian Rockies, glacial melt contributes to just 3 per cent of the Bow River annually; in the month of August, however, when rivers and lakes are at their lowest, as much as 20 per cent of the Bow's flow as it passes through Calgary, where 1.3 million people rely on it, is provided by glacial melt.

In years when accumulation and melting balance out, a glacier is said to be in a state of equilibrium. When more ice melts than is replenished by new snow in the winter, the glacier is in decline. The bulk of a glacier's most visible melting happens at its lowest reaches – the snout, or toe. Glaciers don't retreat, they simply melt. Currently, the vast majority of the estimated 160,000 glaciers worldwide are melting, due to Earth's warming temperatures. And just as sea levels dropped during the ice ages, melting glaciers around the world are now contributing to rising ocean levels.

Home on the Moraine

Why is the ice blue? It's a question that anyone visiting a glacier will ask at least once. In its frozen state, glacial ice is so dense after being super-compacted under its own weight that the ice absorbs every other colour of the spectrum. All that's left is the blue we see.

Then there's the turquoise of glacier lakes and rivers. It can be intense, vivid and concentrated as paint in a can. Beguiling and demanding of attention, this brilliant colour comes from the rock flour that is created by the grinding of the glacier's base over the bedrock as it slowly creeps downhill. The resulting particles that are washed into a lake or river along with the meltwater are so fine and so light that they don't

Fine rock flour created by a glacier scraping the bedrock becomes suspended in outwash lakes, and when sunlight hits the particles this stunning turquoise colour is reflected. Photo Lynn Martel

sink. They become suspended throughout the water column. When sunlight hits the water, it absorbs the long-wave colour – reds, yellows and oranges. The rock flour absorbs the purples and the indigos. That leaves mostly green, with a hint of blue to create the stunning turquoise that reflects back to the viewer. The blue or green tints vary, but they're always exquisite.

Along with rock flour, glacier ice contains a lot more than just water. Glacial snow and ice support unique ecosystems that scientists are only beginning to discover and understand. Among the most obvious organisms living on snow and glaciers – to the fascination of anyone walking or skiing on one – is the pink algae known as watermelon snow, so named because of its scent. One study identified 466 species of organisms living in snow; 77 were fungi, 35 were bacteria and the remainder were algae. When skiing slowly uphill on a low-angled glacier, it's always fascinating to watch small, delicate snow spi-

Where there are glaciers, in summertime wildflowers, such as this river beauty beside Pigeon Fork Glacier in British Columbia's Bugaboos, are nourished by their meltwater. Photo Lynn Martel

ders walking across the surface, or climbing up the side of the trough plowed by the skier ahead. Three species (of 28 worldwide) of Collembola, more commonly known as springtails or snow fleas, have been identified in Canada. And in late 2016, professional adventurer Will Gadd led a team to explore a giant frozen millwell on the Athabasca Glacier. Fifty metres below the surface, Gadd and glaciologist Martin Sharp from the University of Alberta experienced a scientific first when they discovered biofilms colonizing cracks in the ice where water was seeping out. (We will hear more on that discovery in Chapter 4, Study of Ice). In addition to those organisms that live in snow, meltwater from glaciers provides essential nourishment to a wide variety of flowers, plants and animals that inhabit the downstream eco-zone.

1–3 LAND OF ICE AND SNOW

Ages of Ice

Glaciers have formed and melted back many times during Earth's 4.6-billion-year history. The period between 850 million years ago and 635 million years ago hosted a series of severe ice ages whose effects were so nasty the period has been nicknamed Snowball Earth. Scientists believe the glaciation was so extensive it may have reached as far as the equator. Somehow some of the tiny organisms alive at the time managed to survive and evolve. Ice ages have generated mass extinctions and have contributed much to shaping the world we inhabit today, although the mass extinctions happening today are largely a result of human encroachment on natural animal habitat, in addition to our warming climate, much of which is also human caused.

Earthlings are currently enjoying a warm phase of an ice age that began 2.6 million years ago. This warm phase, called an interglacial, began about 11,700 years ago. This period qualifies as an interglacial because the Greenland, Arctic and Antarctic ice sheets still exist today. In North America, the most recent granddaddy of all ice sheets was the Laurentide Ice Sheet, which, at its maximum, covered more than 13 million square kilometres. In some areas it was as thick as 3000 metres, covered nearly all of Canada and extended a bit farther south than Washington, DC, and across sections of Idaho, Montana and Washington State, where it merged into its western counterpart, the Cordilleran Ice Sheet.

Layers upon layers of snow compress to form glacial ice, creating striations showing past events, including forest fires and volcanic eruptions. Photo Lynn Martel

When glaciers melt, they reveal telltale signs of how they scraped on the bedrock that supported the ice mass as it slowly moved downslope. Photo Lynn Martel

When it comes to our planet undergoing fluctuations between warmer and cooler periods, indeed, there have been many changes in Earth's temperatures, and to the life forms that survived during different periods, humans included. One big difference, however, between the ice ages and warmer periods of Earth's lengthy history and the changes that are happening in the 21st century is that changes that previously happened more or less cyclically over periods of thousands or hundreds of thousands of years have now happened in just the 200 years since the start of the Industrial Revolution. Also, the earlier changes happened during a time when there were few humans living on the planet who needed to adapt to those changes, compared to the 7.5 billion – and counting – people who inhabit Earth today.

Currently, glaciers cover about 10 per cent of Earth's surface. The massive ice sheets of the polar regions of the Arctic and Antarctic contain a full 99 per cent of that glacial ice. That ice is much more than just a pretty coating of white as seen from space. Quite simply, glacial ice makes up the largest reservoir of freshwater on Earth. From the alpine glaciers of Alaska and Greenland to the Himalayas and New Zealand's Alps, glaciers store water as ice during the colder months, then release it as meltwater during warmer seasons. Glacier ice is nature's savings account for water, and modern man has structured our way of life by relying on that service nature provides without any help from us, for free.

Canada's Ice

With 200,000 square kilometres of the stuff, Canada proudly boasts more glacial ice than any other country, except for Greenland, which belongs to Denmark, and Antarctica, the continent that doesn't belong to any country. Canada's share of arctic ice is 25 per cent, second only to Greenland. The icefields and glaciers that exist in Canada today are remnants of three ice sheets that stopped advancing some 12,000 years ago. Some of the grooves left by the process of the glaciers' advance are easily visible today in numerous locations, including Kelleys Island in Lake Erie and in Central Park in the middle of New York City. The sea level was so low during much of this glaciated period that land animals, including humans, were able to inhabit the Bering Land Bridge that connects North America and Siberia. Others arrived by boat by following the coastline of that bridge, both of which means allowed for some document-free immigration of some of North America's earliest peoples.

The highest concentration of glacial ice is found in Canada's arctic islands, which together contain 150,000 square kilometres of glacial ice, including some of the largest polar icefields on the planet. Of them, however, only Baffin and Ellesmere have any people living on them. Baffin Island's northeast coastline is ranked as one of Earth's outstanding iceberg galleries, while Auyuittuq (ow-you-we-took) National Park's name translates to "the land that never melts" in the Inuktitut language.

The highest mountains in Canada east of the Rockies, where some of the oldest

From the Rockies to the Coast Mountains and north to Yukon's Saint Elias Mountains, Canada's highest mountains harbour large – and shrinking – glaciers and icefields at higher elevations. Mount Shackleton, 3327 metres, and glacier, Canadian Rockies. Photo John Scurlock

rocks on Earth are found, Labrador's Torngat Mountains still harbour about 40 small glaciers nestled in high-elevation cirque valleys on peaks that rise as high as 1650 metres. The entire landscape of the region displays evidence of the glaciers and ice sheets that once covered the land, carving and plowing their way along, smoothing and polishing wide areas and eroding basins that filled to form lakes. North America's Great Lakes, which form the largest group of freshwater lakes on Earth, were formed around 14,000 years ago by the action of the advancing ice sheets carving basins into the land, which then filled with freshwater.

Glacier sign is a truly Canadian thing.

Ice Jackpot

Canada's west and northwest is where much of the ice lives on, albeit in shrinking measure. Glaciers need cooler temperatures to survive, and in addition to the polar regions, the higher elevations are where those persist. For now.

Running from Mexico to Yukon, the spine of North America is composed of numerous distinct mountain ranges like raised veins on the back of a bony hand. The entire length of British Columbia's west coast is a massive barricade of snow- and ice-capped mountains fencing the Pacific Ocean. Those peaks and the high plateaus connecting them act as a catch basin for moisture carried from the ocean, pouring rain on the lower valleys and, at higher elevations, snow. There are many well-nourished glaciers in the Coast Mountains, which are divided into three sections. The Pacific Ranges stretch from Vancouver to Bella Coola, and the Kitimat Ranges cover the expanse from Bella Coola to north of Terrace. These mountains are lower in elevation and the least glaciated of the Coast Mountains. And then there's the Boundary Ranges of the Alaska Panhandle–British Columbia border region, which extend north to just beyond Skagway. The Pacific Ranges are

Willi Prittie climbs the east ridge of Canada's highest peak, 5959-metre Mount Logan in Kluane National Park, Yukon, with the massive Hubsew Glacier below him stretching more than 50 kilometres to the Pacific Ocean. Photo Bryce Brown

generously glaciated with several major icefields and many glaciers. Together, the south and central coasts of British Columbia contain half of all the ice in western Canada/US, outside of Alaska. Farther north, though, it's the Boundary Ranges where the largest glaciers and icefields are found, including the southernmost tidewater glaciers in the northern hemisphere.

In Yukon stand the Saint Elias Mountains, where the immense Donjek Glacier is 56 kilometres long. Covering five times the area of Grand Canyon National Park, Kaskawulsh Glacier bloats to 6 kilometres across at its widest. The Hubbard Glacier flows a whopping 122 kilometres - equivalent to 2,000 hockey rinks - from near Mount Logan across the Alaska border to empty into Yakutat Bay. Glaciologists have determined it takes 400 years for ice to travel its entire length. Blanketing a gargantuan 40,570 square kilometres - 25 per cent larger than Vancouver Island - the largest non-polar icefield in the world is found in Yukon's Kluane National Park and Reserve, and adjacent Wrangell–Saint Elias National Park and Preserve in Alaska. In places a kilometre deep and feeding dozens of glaciers that descend both sides of its serpentine spine like giant centipede legs, it is a UNESCO World Heritage Site and Biosphere Reserve.

Moving inland, mountain ranges continue to poke into the clouds. Forming a section of the Yukon–Northwest Territories boundary, the Selwyn Mountains harbour a number of glaciers today, including some of the oldest impressions left by glaciers on the planet. Across northern British Columbia, two-thirds of the province is creased with a labyrinth of valleys and slopes and peaks forming the Continental Divide.

In the bottom half of the province, the four ranges of the Columbia Mountains rise on the west side of the Rocky Mountain Trench, while the Canadian Rockies rise on

A skier tows his sled down the immense Hubbard Glacier, which flows 122 kilometres down from near Mount Walsh to Alaska's Disenchantment Bay. At the spot in this photo, the skiers saw a duck resting on the glacier ice. Photo John Baldwin

the east side. Icefields and glaciers crown the peaks and plateaus on both sides of the Rocky Mountain Trench like giant whipped meringue. Comprising a section of one continuous chain of mountains running the length of North America from Mexico to Yukon, the Canadian Rockies are home to 16 major icefields with hundreds of glaciers descending from them. According to the most recent satellite surveys (2018), Alberta holds approximately 1160 glaciers in total (the vast majority of which are smaller than 1 square kilometre). British Columbia's mountain ranges harbour about 50 major icefields and as many smaller ones, and more than 17,000 glaciers which combined cover about 2.5 per cent of that province's land mass.

Never the Same Ice Twice

Along the Pacific edge of British Columbia stretches a coastal temperate rainforest zone where old-growth trees gain tremendous heights and girths (when allowed, as current forestry practices are perpetually reducing their numbers) and bushes flourish to create impenetrable valleys and lower mountain slopes. Concealed from view by the dense canopy, at high elevations glaciers and icefields persist not only on the mainland but on Vancouver Island too – 16 per cent of the region is covered by glacier ice. Rivers in this region that gush from the higher-elevation icefields to empty into the ocean maintain a steadier and cooler flow of glacial meltwater than rivers that are nourished only by rain and seasonal snowfall. This cooler water helps support seven species of salmon, as well as other cold-water fish, a wide variety of alpine plants, and even Pacific plankton.

While these glaciers are rarely visible from valley bottom today, archeological evidence stretching back 14,000 years shows that the people living in this region did visit the glaciers near their snouts to pick berries and even to use the expansive icefields as travel corridors. In 1999, hunters in Tatshenshini-Alsek Provincial Park, in the province's northwest corner, discovered the naturally mummified 550-year-old remains of Kwäday Dän Ts'ìnchi – the name means Long Ago Person Found in the language of the region's Southern Tutchone. Exposed by recently melted glacial ice, he was found through DNA testing to be connected to 17 descendants living today.

In the interior mountains too, the Selkirks and Purcells and Rockies, the Indigenous Peoples knew the glaciers. They knew when the avalanche – or glacier – lilies would emerge. They knew where the ice line was. They knew how to walk across or avoid glaciers to travel from one place to another to hunt or trade. They knew that mountain goats frequented cliffsides bordering glaciers and the moraines created by them. No doubt they knew wolverines and grizzly bears sometimes crossed glaciers to access the next valley, as they still do.

Large boulders that fall from nearby mountains to land on glaciers are often left behind when the glacier melts. Photo Lynn Martel

Markedly more than picturesque decorations on the mountain scape, those glaciers are alive. For those who

John McIsaac stands near the entrance of an ice cave naturally formed at the toe of Bow Glacier, Banff National Park. Photo Lynn Martel

recreate, work, run businesses, study and create art on and around glaciers, they are living, growing, moving and endlessly interesting elements of our planet. Like the ocean to a sailor, a surfer, a fisherman or a marine biologist, glaciers are unique environments that reveal themselves to those who choose to experience them through different means. Sounds, smells, ever-evolving shapes, formations – they are constantly changing. At the same time, those who return repeatedly to a particular glacier become acquainted with its defining features. It becomes familiar, like a cliff to a rock climber, a river to a paddler, a trail to a hiker.

Western Canada's glaciers are many things to many people: picture-perfect postcard images, mountaineers' playground, scientific research sites, profitable tourist attractions and backcountry skiing getaways. They are spiritually inspiring landscapes for painters, photographers, writers and thinkers. Infinitely more substantial than static masses of ice melting on a landscape, many glaciers of Alberta and British Columbia's mountain ranges – which this book focuses on – are the places of dynamic experiences shared and preserved in stories lived by people who have explored their surfaces – and every so often, and sometimes inadvertently, the passages and cavities inside their masses – leaving them cold, sacred, amazed and, as they melt and shrink before our eyes, somewhat saddened.

Jesse Milner climbs above crevasses toward the summit of Mount Robson, at 3954 metres the Canadian Rockies' highest peak. Photo Paul Zizka

2 ADVENTURE ON ICE

In the end, to ski is to travel fast and free – free over the untouched snow covered country. To be bound to one slope, even to one mountain by a lift may be convenient but it robs us of the greatest pleasure that skiing can give, that is, to travel through the wide, wintery country: to follow the lure of the peaks which tempt on the horizon and to be alone for a few days or even a few hours in clear, mysterious surroundings.

—Hans Gmoser

2–1 WIND–SCULPTED AND FROZEN MERINGUE

Schools of Swimming Fish

The eight of us skied on, following Lars, our guide on this adventure organized by the Alpine Club of Canada. Except for my acquaintance with Lars and John, our camp manager, for the most part we were strangers from Canada, the United States and Germany who'd come together to experience skiing and living amidst glaciers high above treeline for a week, knowing the Canadian Rockies are one of few places on the planet where such an adventure is possible. Travelling the Bow-Yoho route was a first for us all except Lars and John. As the only woman with seven men, I was by far the smallest, lightest person on the team, yet I carried a multi-day pack that weighed only a smidge less than any of the men's packs. Glacier camping, unfortunately, demands a lot more gear than backpacking in summer: heavy four-season tent; winter-weight (heavy) sleeping bag; winter-thick sleeping pad; extra clothes; and extra fuel for melting snow, plus the standard shovel, probe and avalanche transceiver, stove and food. Six inches shorter and weighing a third less than most of the men, I was well aware that 20-plus kilograms on my five-foot, three-inch frame demanded a lot from me.

Despite the load, I was determined not to be the slowest, and was relieved to learn half the group had never skied across a glacier before; one had never skied carrying a big pack. I had winter camped once, below treeline where we had enjoyed a luxurious campfire. There would be no such comfort this time, camping on the glacier midway between Bow Hut, on the eastern edge of the Wapta Icefield, and Stanley Mitchell Hut in the Little Yoho Valley – a 20-kilometre distance with 2000 metres' elevation gain.

Reaching a flat plateau, we slipped off our packs and pulled out our avalanche shovels to dig a large, round hip-deep pit as the wind pushed and tugged at us from all sides. John pulled out a tent fly, and with each of us holding onto one of the loops of cord threaded through eyelets at the corners, we wrestled the nylon sheet as the relentless wind attempted to send it airborne to become snagged on some tree several valleys away. Threading ski poles, ice axes and skis through the loops, we staked the fly securely to the wind-stiffened snow around the perimeter of the pit. Once we were inside, an upright ski made an excellent centre pole, and we all huddled next to one another savouring the relative luxury of our makeshift shelter, sipping hot tea from our thermoses.

Back into the storm, Lars and John stopped every 15 minutes to take compass and GPS readings, since all we could see was each other's clothing. Our original plan to make a ski ascent of Mount Collie was unceremoniously abandoned as our focus shifted to locating an even marginally sheltered place to camp on the icefield.

Leaning into the irrepressible wind that swirled and howled around me, I watched the powdery top layer of snow blowing around on the surface like schools of fish swimming at top speed in one direction then abruptly turning and darting off in another. Mesmerized by it, I had to check myself from focusing on the action for too long before I lost my sense of balance and toppled over.

Reaching a steep slope whose bottom was barely perceptible in the featureless

Christina Brodribb skis up Vulture Glacier in a whiteout during a hut-based tour of the Rockies' Wapta Icefields area. Photo Lynn Martel

light, Lars skied down a bit then side-stepped back up to ask Brian and Tony how they felt about slowly skiing to the flat glacier somewhere below. The two strongest skiers after Lars and John, they asked him how bad it was.

"Shit," he replied, "as bad as can be."

They shrugged and slowly skied down, their ski edges scratching on the icy slope like nails on a blackboard. Wrapping slings around a table-sided rock, Lars set up a belay station to lower the rest of us with the security of a rope.

Tied in just a few metres apart, Norbert and Jim descended slowly, their skis grating on the wind-blasted surface until they reached John waiting below, faint ghostly shadows from our stance above.

"You're going to move down this quickly, right? You don't have anything to worry about, you're on the rope," Lars instructed Dave and me. "No problem," I replied. The surface was hard as marble, and even with the added weight of my pack my edges wouldn't hold. I let my skis run, awkwardly tugging on Dave above me, both of us fighting to stay on our feet. Though we couldn't see the change, gradually the slope eased off under our skis until we were on low-angle terrain where the snow was just soft enough for us to make survival turns. The light was so flat I felt nauseous.

Seven hours after leaving Bow Hut, we were shovelling out tent sites and stomping the plots flat by walking over them in our skis. By dusk Tony was sitting on a bench hewn from compacted snow in the vestibule of the tent he was sharing with me and Brian, boiling snow for our dehydrated chili dinner. After the commotion of Bow Hut, which we'd shared the previous night with a dozen other skiers, we felt somewhat isolated as the wind engulfed any sound from our companions' two tents.

We could have been on the moon.

How I Learned to Stop Worrying and Love the Wind

Having imagined our spring ski traverse on the Wapta Icefield much the same way I had, Tony had packed a small, summer-weight sleeping bag. He spent the entire night in the tent shivering and hugging close beside my body, which was wrapped in a bulky minus 40-degree bag, with Brian doing the same on my other side. Thankfully, I hadn't shivered, but now that it was morning, I was in no hurry to leave the toasty comforts of my down-filled cocoon. Overnight, fine snow grains had filled every possible nook and crease of our packs, plastic boot shells, pots and food bags stored in the back and front vestibules. I dreaded shoving my feet into cold boots and decided I didn't love winter camping at 2500 metres on a wind-blasted field of ice five kilometres from shelter in the nearest grove of trees.

Lars ducked under our tent fly with

Ski mountaineers' tents are protected from howling winds by snow walls high on the Columbia Icefield below the heavily glaciated slopes of Mount Columbia, at 3747 metres Alberta's highest peak. Photo Bryce Brown

his toothbrush sticking out of his mouth. Just anther glacier camping trip for him. Via satellite phone he'd learned the weather was expected to improve that afternoon, then worsen by nightfall. We wouldn't climb nearby Mount Des Poilus that day; we'd ski straight to Stanley Mitchell Hut. I didn't state aloud how that had been my wish all along, but I felt better that Tony and Brian weren't objecting either. We methodically struck camp and soon were carrying all its contents again on our backs.

Moving got the blood flowing and, one by one, cold body parts warmed up. The routine of skinning along, stopping for a bite and a sip from our thermoses and moving on again had become just that, a comfortable routine. We'd become a nomadic band of skiers, travelling as a unit. Less than an hour into our morning's journey we looked up toward Isolated Col, a constricted notch between two jagged peaks whose tips were obscured by clouds. Lars explained the options of skiing up the steep slope to the col then down the other side to the hut, or the longer, safer way around via a flat-topped ridge known as the Whaleback.

"That looks like fun," Tony said, eyeing the col with anticipation. I thought it looked intimidating. Lars decided the notch presented too many potential dangers with us being slowed by the heavy packs we carried, plus an uncertain forecast. We'd ski the Whaleback. I was disappointed and relieved at the same time. Skiing away from under the col, we heard a rumble and turned to watch an avalanche tumble down from the cliffs of Whaleback Mountain.

"I guess we made the right decision," Lars commented casually.

The ascent up the broad bench of the Whaleback at the upper reaches of treeline was slow and laborious. My pack felt heavy, pushing on my shoulders and my back like a sack of sand. My skis felt heavy, my legs felt heavy, even the snowflakes clinging to my toque felt heavy. I lagged behind. I was tired. Skiing downhill through tight forest on old, hard lumpy snow was anything but fun.

It would be years before I clearly understood that, while many of my mountain partners could always be keen to chase back-to-back days of continuous adventure, I need to stop and rest and absorb my surroundings to alleviate the stress that builds within me during periods of sensory overload, like the wind needing to rest between gusts. For me, constant moving dulls my vision, inhibits me from seeing the small details that open up the mountains' magic to me. Like the glaciers in winter, I need rest time, so I will have energy to spend on later days.

But then, on this trip, I would also learn how travelling on glaciers in winter often renders resting impossible, or at least impractical. Cold, wind and isolation make the glacial environment one where a body can freeze to death quickly with little ceremony. I learned to accept that moving was essential to survival. I learned to embrace and persevere through the cold gnawing at my bones. I learned how to stop worrying and love the wind.

After six hours of strenuous travel, we arrived at the hut, a splendid log cabin with spacious living room and kitchen on the main floor and an upstairs sleeping area large enough for 18, delighted to find a fire being tended by skiers already there. I missed the solitude of the glacier already, but as I curled up in a well-worn wooden armchair beside the crackling wood stove, listening as John gently strummed the hut guitar, I was completely and utterly content.

With Lars eager to show our group the best adventure possible, right after breakfast we re-applied our climbing skins and set off toward the nearby President Glacier. Shuffling along into the wind again, I could barely remember any other way to start the day, and a big part of me wanted to be sipping tea by the wood stove. We pushed forward determinedly for 45 minutes, the wind slamming into our faces.

"Can we camp here?" Jim asked with a wry grin. "We know how."

We were being pummelled, beaten by a nasty snowstorm, and we were laughing. We'd gelled, our group members becoming cohesive layers of our own snowpack. We turned west, down the moraine, and skied toward Kiwetinok Pass, straight into a headwind. Wrong way. Satisfied that we'd at least made an effort, we retreated to the hut in record time. That chair by the wood stove had my name on it.

Undeterred, we launched out again the following morning. Before long we reached the previous morning's turnaround point on the moraine and decided conditions would allow us to continue upward. The glacier surface was wind scoured with ridges and ripples like meringue frozen solid. Lars skied directly uphill to the snow-filled bergschrund – the gaping space where gravity pulls the upper edge of the glacier away from the mountain face – then stopped. In summer, the gap formed a single-lane-wide cavity whose bottom dropped into darkness, but now the hole was stuffed with snow. Lars laid his skis down horizontally on the steep wall of glacier ice in front of him, leaned into the shelf they created and started kicking steps. At the top of the two-storey slope he cut away the overhanging cornice (shelf of wind-stiffened snow that extends beyond the ridge) for us to climb though to the col separating The President and Vice President peaks.

Skiers braces themselves against typically fierce winds as they ski on the Rockies' Wapta Icefields. Photo Lynn Martel

With a chilling wind swooping up the south side from Emerald Glacier, we left our skis and headed up The President in our boots. Ski pole in one hand, ice axe in the other, I followed Brian on the rope, the others behind me. Progress was intermittent, a dozen solid steps followed by two dozen lousy ones in sugary snow that had collected around the bases of discontinuous rock bands with all the cohesiveness of ball bearings. Stopping and starting kept my fingers painfully cold, and maybe it was because I'd already climbed The President one balmy summer morning a few years prior that I silently decided I didn't love winter alpine climbing. We had no views, but thankfully, no sense of exposure either. The conditions were terrible, dangerous even. We retreated; my mind fixated on the moment we'd be low enough on the glacier that warmer temperatures would ease the stinging in my fingers.

But first we had to get there.

The ski run back down the glacier was crap. Awful. Boot deep, heavy and dense as dirt, and my thighs screamed as I pushed my skis through cardboard-stiff snow. Down, down, the snow surface mutated into partially frozen wind-scoured patches interrupted by soft sections, the abrupt changes in conditions causing us to lurch awkwardly. Every metre descended was worse than the last. Lars appeared to cruise along, as did Brian and John, but Tony cursed his telemark skis, which were softer and less responsive than our alpine touring gear. Despite my reasonably stiff skis, I struggled to stay on my feet, frequently resting. At its best, glacier skiing is a gift of downy, flowing turns through snow as welcoming as the finest talc, or in springtime smooth, tantalizing creamy butter. This was glacier skiing at its absolute worst.

Exhausted, we finally reached the cozy hut, shed our wet clothes and feasted on rehydrated chili dinner, passing around a plastic salad dressing bottle filled with whisky.

I hit the trail first the next morning to begin our full-day ski to the trailhead through spruce-scented forest that intermittently opened into tranquil meadows. My skis glided silently in ten centimetres of fluffy new powder, the track offering just enough decline that I coasted effortlessly, watching the scenery scroll by. Patchy clouds let shimmering light beams touch the rocky summits. Warm and comfortable with my pack lightened of all my food, I allowed my mind to wander back to the swirling wind and wild unfettered space of the icefield.

Maybe next time I would camp on a glacier for two nights.

2-2 THE SHINING MOUNTAINS

Glacier-Carved Landscape

Comprising hundreds of peaks, including some 400 that nudge the clouds above 3000 metres, that part of North America's Rocky Mountains that extends into Canada is 1500 kilometres long – longer than California. The Canadian Rockies run from Marias Pass in northern Montana (an hour's drive south of the Canada–US border) to the Liard River in far northern British Columbia. At its widest, the range elbows its way 150 kilometres across, petering into foothills on the east, and dropping more abruptly to the Columbia River valley on the west. The lofty elevations of the entire range create conditions that result in several expansive icefields and a high concentration of glaciers. Currently, some 28 per cent of the Rockies (as of 2017, and decreasing) are glaciated. All along the range branching upward from both the east and west perimeters, many dozens of valleys lead upward into dead end cirques and lofty passes choked with glacial ice that is many hundreds of years old.

The first written accounts to mention glaciers in western Canada were penned by explorers and traders, often in the employ of the voracious fur trade, who visited the Rockies from the east, and the northern British Columbia and Alaska coast by ship in the 18th century.

To those European fur traders who muscled across the Prairies in canoe brigades from the ports of Montreal and Quebec City during the 18th and 19th centuries, the Canadian Rockies posed a formidable hurdle to reaching the west coast, and beyond there, the Orient.

Not so for the local Indigenous tribes. Immediately prior to the arrival of any Europeans, at least a dozen different First Nations peoples inhabited the Rockies and surrounding ranges; evidence dates back nearly 12,000 years to seasonal hunting sites just a few kilometres from the present-day town of Banff. On the British Columbia coast, the glaciers began melting back about 17,000 years ago, and evidence of human activity there dates back 14,000 years.

Athabasca Glacier 1917, courtesy Mountain Legacy Project

The glaciers that advanced, then filled and later melted back, helped create the giant U-shaped Bow Valley where the towns of Banff and Canmore now thrive. As the ice melted, Indigenous Peoples came from the plains on the east, pushing deeper into the mountains to hunt the game animals that were attracted to the plants that grew in soil recently exposed and nourished by melting ice. They also came to cut lodgepole pine for tipi poles. Barely 15 minutes' drive west from Banff, these hunters left behind tools of their relentless quest for food – flaky rocks scraped and shaped into sharp points and then attached with sinews to hardwood poles. Along with fragments of these tools, in 1984 archeologists found ash, pieces of bone and broken stones – evidence of ancient camps inhabited by small groups of people living in the heart of a region that now draws more than four million visitors annually.

As the glaciers continued melting over the ensuing centuries, generations of Assiniboine, Blackfoot and the Ktunaxa tribes travelled the handful of wind-blasted passes that weren't buried in snow and ice, regularly crossing the Continental Divide to trade goods and hunt bison on the plains. They guarded their routes over ice-free passes protectively, and when Europeans showed up being guided by members of eastern tribes, they weren't eager to reveal those passages.

Nevertheless, in 1807, under the employ of the fur trading North West Company, David Thompson – who would become greatly admired for exploring some 90,000 kilometres across North America and mapping 4.9 million square kilometres along the way – set off from the foothills with his Métis wife, Charlotte, their three children and a small party of men. Following the North Saskatchewan River around gently rolling hills, they penetrated a landscape of huge rocky peaks with glistening glaciers tumbling from their flanks. Passing under towering cliff bands and buttresses, the group crossed over Howse Pass and followed the Blaeberry River to reach the Columbia River. The first European to travel the route, Thompson noted, "The Heights of the Mountains still present that cold clear shining white Snow…. Some have about 2000 ft perpend of greenish Ice, which seemingly never thaws."

While it was certainly navigable, the Piegan didn't want Thompson trading with the Ktunaxa, who were their enemies, a situation that eliminated Howse Pass as a fur trading route. So, in late October 1810, Thompson departed Rocky Mountain House again. It was January, and a vicious minus 35 Celsius when he crossed Athabasca Pass, 120 kilometres north as the raven flies from Howse Pass – the first European to do so. His 13 men included his guide, Thomas the Iroquois (an eastern First Nation now called the Haudenosaunee), who had travelled that route before. The trail they followed over Athabasca Pass would reign as the main fur trade route to the Columbia River, and the Pacific, for the ensuing half-century. Recording some of the earliest observations of western Canada's glaciers on paper, Thompson wrote, "On our right about one third of a mile from us lay an enormous Glacier, the eastern face of which quite steep, of about two thousand feet in height, was of a clean fine green colour, which I much admired."

Athabasca Glacier 2011, courtesy Mountain Legacy Project

While Thompson admired the Rockies' glaciers, others weren't so enamoured. One Gabriel Franchère, who crossed Athabasca Pass just four years later, described how the sun cast a "chilling brightness over the chaotic mass of rocks, ice and snow" and the "rumbling noise of a descending avalanche ... burst with a frightful crash."

"I'll take oath, my dear friends," Franchère declared, "that God Almighty never made such a place."

As traders over the following years travelled the route while witnessing the glaciers from a respectable distance, it took a botanist named David Douglas to be the first recorded person to climb a glaciated peak in western Canada. Camped near Athabasca Pass in 1827, Douglas laced up his snowshoes after breakfast and set off alone to climb the closest mountain on the west side of the pass.

"The labour of ascending ... is great beyond description.... Half-way up vegetation ceases entirely.... One third from the summit it becomes a mountain of pure ice." Five hours after setting out, Douglas stood on the broad, rounded summit now named Mount Brown, from where he admired his surroundings for 20 minutes.

"The sensation I felt is beyond what I can give utterance to," he wrote. "Nothing, as far as the eye could perceive, but mountains such as I was on and many higher, some rugged beyond description.... The aerial tints of the snow, the heavenly azure of the solid glaciers, the rainbow-like hues of their thick broken fragments...." The first known person to bag a glaciated summit in the Canadian Rockies, Douglas described in his journal the rapture that has enticed countless mountaineers to ascend lofty peaks ever since.

By the mid-19th century, mountaineering had evolved into a popular sport in Europe's mountain ranges, particularly in the Alps of Switzerland, Austria and France. Glaciers were crossed as a matter of course to access peaks, and over time the historical perception of them as entities to be feared and avoided – they were sometimes depicted as giant dragons eager to swallow men and livestock whole – morphed into natural curiosities that could be explored by "civilized" man. The British upper class, who had the means and the leisure time to travel – and luckily for history, respectable writing skills – formed a substantial number of the young sport's devotees. In Switzerland, goat and sheep herders who spent their lives literally running up and down mountains as a requisite of tending their flocks found they could supplement their incomes by leading British flatlanders up convoluted icefalls and crevasse-split glaciers to sky-scraping summits in the Alps. Thus, the mountain guiding profession was born. In Britain, the Alpine Club was founded in 1857, the world's first organization to advocate for the sport of mountaineering, giving shape to activities by fostering a culture that included exploration. As explorers journeyed along the trails penetrating Canada's Rocky Mountains, journals were published describing the peaks, the forests, the lakes, rivers and wildlife. And the glaciers.

Preserve, Protect, Profit

According to popular accounts, the idea behind creating Canada's first, and the world's fourth, national park began in 1883 with a trio of 20-something railway workers, Frank McCabe and the brothers William and Thomas McCardell.

One condition of Canada's founding in 1867 was the promise of building a railway to connect the young country from the Atlantic to the Pacific, not only for reasons of commerce but also to keep British Columbia from being absorbed by the United States. Building a railroad spanning nearly 5000 kilometres from Montreal to the west coast was a mammoth process that was accomplished in an impressively speedy four years. It employed thousands, many of them immigrants, and many of whom did not survive abysmal working conditions.

A full-page ad from a 1938 issue of *Fortune* magazine touted the splendours of the Rockies' Banff and Lake Louise with its sapphire waters reflecting Victoria Glacier. Image Lynn Martel Collection

Overwintering in the area while railroad construction was on hiatus due to the cold of the season, McCabe and the McCardells took a day off from their fur trapping endeavours to build a crude raft. Poling across the winter-shallow Bow River, they landed on the north side of Terrace Mountain (now Sulphur Mountain) and, following their noses, they discovered pools of warm sulphur water steaming amidst spongy bogs.

That's one version. The First Nations peoples in the region had not only known for hundreds, probably thousands of years about the underground pools and caverns that vented steam up through the earth, they considered the site sacred and practised spiritual ceremonies there. By some accounts, it was several natives who brought the three railway workers to the site – an act for which they were admonished. Either way, none of that mattered to McCabe and the McCardells. The young country was a land of opportunity, and to them the acrid stench of sulphur smelled of money. They built a rough shack at the springs and invited other railway workers – no doubt in need of a bath – to come have a soak. Although they didn't immediately register a formal claim on their little hot springs, they finally applied for legal title in early 1885. A few days later, a second claimant applied for the rights to another spring nearby. More claims followed.

The cat was out of the cave.

Hot springs rich with mineral water were all the rage among people looking to cure a raft of ailments, and government officials knew a cash cow when they smelled one. A former member of Canada's Parliament visited the springs and recommended to Prime Minister Macdonald that the valuable site be controlled and administered by the federal government. He suggested creating a national reserve similar to one that had recently been set aside to preserve a hot spring in the United States. In late 1885, just a few weeks after the railway's final spike was driven into the ground, 26 square kilometres were formally designated as Canada's first national park reserve, rendering the land off-limits to private development – except for those with the right connections. In 1887, Rocky Mountains Park was officially expanded to encompass 673 square kilometres, "set apart as a public park and pleasure ground for the benefit, advantage and enjoyment of the people of Canada."

The town of Banff was designed and built, and businesses sprang up to serve the needs of the tourists, with the Canadian Pacific Railway-owned Banff Springs Hotel and the superstar hot springs in principal roles. The debate over whether preservation should take priority over profit in Canada's flagship national park, Banff, and adjacent Jasper park, has bounced back and forth like tennis balls on the hotels' courts ever since.

Many management decisions adopted in the decades to come would have long-lasting negative effects that spilled beyond the park boundaries, including the destruction of "vermin" such as wolves, lynxes, eagles and porcupines. Done for the benefit of tourists, and tourism, these acts were anything but beneficial to the natural ecological processes of the mountain and prairie landscapes. Suppression of naturally occurring wildfires, essential to natural regenerative processes, didn't do any good either. Canada's first national park had much to learn, and the process is ongoing.

Some decisions, however, did provide long-lasting benefits.

Over the following decades the margins of the park were expanded, contracted, expanded and adjusted some more. Today, the combined area of the Magnificent Seven – the contiguous Banff, Yoho, Kootenay and Jasper national parks, plus Mount Robson, Mount Assiniboine and Hamber provincial parks – make up the UNESCO Rocky Mountain Parks World Heritage Site. Nearly 23,000 square kilometres of spruce and pine forest, home to grizzly bears, wolverines, marmot, osprey, beaver and myriad other wild creatures, remain, for the most part, protected and undeveloped. Slightly larger than New Jersey, the area contains 44 rivers and nearly 300 lakes. Within its 27 individual mountain ranges spiked with hundreds of prominent peaks sprout the headwaters of four of the continent's major rivers. Beyond the defined town boundaries of Banff and Jasper, and the tiny hamlets of Lake Louise and Field, there are no towns, no farming villages, no industrial enterprises, no resource extraction operations. And cradled in those lofty cirques and high plateaus lie a dozen major icefields and some 740 (for now) glaciers.

If You Build It, They Will Come

With the railway fully completed in 1885, adventuring on Canada's great glaciers became an accessible, and even justifiable, pastime. Passengers crossed the country from Montreal's port in comfort and style in a short journey of a few days, shorter still from Vancouver. Building the railway had been a very costly affair, so filling it with passengers was essential. The timing could not have been more serendipitous.

Several decades of mountain climbing in Europe's Alps had left all the major peaks already climbed many times over. While a number of western Canada's mountains offer steep but walkable routes to their summits, many of them – massive, glaciated, complicated, spectacular and remote – presented irresistible virgin challenges to serious mountaineers. And while surveyors had for decades routinely climbed up mountain slopes and ridges on the job, usually lugging heavy, awkward equipment, it was mapping the mountains, not recreation, that had motivated them.

A pair of British clergymen would change that.

The Reverend William Spotswood Green was an Alpine Club member, a fellow of the Royal Geographic Society and a very keen climber. His cousin, the Reverend Henry Swanzy, had toured the Rockies in 1884 with the British Association for the Advancement of Science. Lured by Swanzy's tales of rough travel in wild country, the two men returned four years later.

They came prepared. Green had a tent specially made following a design proposed by Britain's most revered climber, Edward Whymper. They packed surveying instruments, sketchbooks and watercolours for painting, plus cameras and film. Complete with free first-class passage aboard the railway from Montreal to Vancouver, theirs was a proper Victorian-era, generously sponsored climbing expedition in search of first ascents.

They disembarked at Glacier House, where they settled into their upscale base camp, a Swiss chalet-style jewel-in-the-wilderness constructed by the railway near Rogers Pass in British Columbia's Selkirk Mountains. Wasting no time, they eagerly threaded their way through dense forest of cedar and skin-slashing devil's club. They lumbered up steep terrain for several hours carrying a plane table on their shoulders to reach Glacier Crest, the steep forested ridge that separates the Illecillewaet and Asulkan glaciers. The survey observations they conducted would lead to the creation of the area's first hiking and climbing guide map.

Over the course of their stay they named quite a few more mountains than they climbed. Most notable was their ascent of Mount Bonney, draped with thick, plush glaciers. Equipped with supplies for a week, including their state-of-the-art tent, they endured miserable bushwhacking to reach the mountain's base, from where they made their way onto the Lily Glacier, but retreated. Days later they crossed Bonney Glacier, making it as far as a steep-sided ridge. Between adventures they returned to the luxury of Glacier House, where they took advantage of optimal conditions in the wine cellar to develop their photographs.

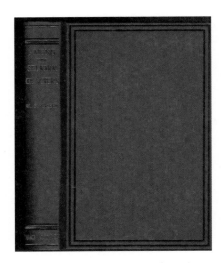

Reverend William Spotswood Green's book, *Among the Selkirk Glaciers*, published in 1890, inspired many to embark on their own visits to western Canada's big glaciated mountains.

"This great field of undulating and in some cases much broken ice, divided itself into no less than seven distinct glaciers separated by moraines; beyond these, in a hollow of its own, was the glacier descending from the col I have called Ross pass, and this with the Lily glacier on our left made nine glaciers all converging to the narrow canon through which we had attempted to make our way, and through which the combined streams roared and swirled. It was a grand amphitheatre paved with ice."

Once home, Green wrote his book, *Among the Selkirk Glaciers: Being the Account of a Rough Survey in the Rocky Mountain Regions of British Columbia*. Published in 1890, it remains a classic of the Victorian adventure genre. And as such books do, it inspired generations to launch their own explorations of Canada's mountain wilderness. No doubt this pleased the Canadian Pacific Railway too.

An Accidental Course

While Rogers Pass would remain a popular climbing destination for decades to come, the summer of 1894 saw the glacier-cloaked peaks of the Rockies' Lake Louise evolve into the next hot spot for mountaineers. The pursuit of the day was all about first ascents, a perk of which included being allowed to name the peak one climbed, an activity that involved more than a bit of nepotism and cronyism, and, occasionally, some geographic or native cultural relativity.

It was just such a group that arrived in Laggan (as the Lake Louise hamlet was then called) in 1895 intent on making some new ascents. While the main valleys of the Canadian Rockies have been glacier-free since 6000 BC, allowing easy travel for the Indigenous inhabitants and Europeans alike, with steep ridges, vertical cliffs and crevasse-riddled glaciers on their upper flanks, hundreds of the Rockies' summits were – and are still – inaccessible without technical mountain climbing equipment and experience. This group arrived prepared with the latest in hemp ropes and leather boots with nails fixed into their soles to provide traction on hard, icy slopes.

They were led by Charles Fay, president of the Appalachian Mountain Club and the founding president of the American Alpine Club. Fay organized the expedition with Charles Thompson and Philip Stanley Abbot, a 28-year-old lawyer with a substantial resumé of successful climbs in the Alps. That summer they made the first ascent of Mount Hector, one of the 58 Rockies peaks higher than 3353 metres (11,000 feet), by climbing its gradually tilted north glacier. The route remains popular today, particularly for ski mountaineers keen on savouring four kilometres of continuous turns down that north glacier.

Sunrise illuminates the north face of Mount Fay, and its famous "bulge" (top right of centre) where the glacier hangs at a seemingly impossible degree between rock ridges. The bulge is a test-piece route for skilled alpine climbers in Banff National Park. Photo Nick Fitzhardinge

Chuffed by their success, the following summer the trio returned with Professor George T. Little and set off to climb Mount Lefroy rising at the west end of Lake Louise. To reach its base they boarded a small boat to cross Lake Louise, sparkling with turquoise glacier meltwater, then hiked over undulating hills of moraine rubble to reach the steep tongue of fractured and creased glacier ice poking down a chasm walled by vertical rock on both sides.

After they had successfully skirted the gaping crevasses of the corridor professional Swiss mountain guides would a few years later dub the "Death Trap," the real climbing began. Even in their nail boots, the steepness of the slope and the firmness of the snow and ice meant that they had to swing their ice axes like scythes to cut steps. Climbing the final stretch to the summit, Abbot decided to untie from the rope so that he could climb unrestricted. Minutes later, Little realized the object that had just fallen swiftly past him was, in fact, Abbot. North America had just experienced its first climbing fatality, and the climbing community was forced to defend their sport to a public that thought it should be banned.

Fay and his companions would have none of it, and the following summer they returned prepared to vigorously defend their passion by climbing Mount Lefroy in honour of their friend. This time, they brought with them a professional Swiss mountain guide named Peter Sarbach. The climb was successful and the precedent set; prudent climbers would employ the expertise of Swiss guides to lead them safely to Canadian Rockies summits, and back down to dinner and a well-earned beverage.

Two years later, following the urging of hotel visitors who were familiar with the practice in Europe, and in light of Sarbach's excellent performance on Mount Lefroy, the Canadian Pacific Railway launched their program to employ Swiss mountain guides at Glacier House in Rogers Pass, and not long afterward, at their Chateau Lake Louise. Having professional guides stationed at the ready to guide their hotel guests up and down the surrounding peaks was the start of a tradition that would continue in the Rockies for the next half-century. And it created the foundation for Canada's mountain guiding and rescue professions that continue at a world-class level today.

Into the Gaping Hole

Fay and Thompson weren't done yet, though, and following their success on Mount Lefroy, followed by the first ascent of its neighbour, Mount Green (which they promptly renamed Mount Victoria in honour of the Queen's Jubilee Year) they set off with J. Norman Collie – one of the most skilled mountaineers of the era – and several companions. Led by wily, seasoned Rockies outfitter Bill Peyto, they journeyed north following the Bow River with a large team of horses, men and provisions. From the summit of Lefroy, the climbers had spied a large snow-capped peak rising from the Wapta Icefields. Covering about 600 square kilometres – the size of the Greater Toronto Area – the Wapta Icefields are made up of two distinct icefields, the Wapta and Waputik. More than a dozen notable peaks hedge the perimeter of the snowfields, and an equal number of individual glaciers creep down the valleys like fat white octopus arms slithering between high ridges and chiselled peaks.

Highly motivated to add that peak to their list, they endured boot-sucking marshland, ferocious mosquitos and deadfall piled upon deadfall, and laboured to extricate a stuck packhorse from deep mud. That was just their first day. Exhausted from their ordeal, they camped at Lower Bow Lake (now Hector Lake). The next day, a seven-hour march brought them to the shore of Upper Bow Lake, which is now the Rockies' iconic Bow Lake, an essential tourist bus stop just 30 minutes' drive from Lake Louise.

The following morning, they walked right onto Bow Glacier, which at that time descended nearly to its outlet lake. Today that glacier's terminus trickles into small, brilliant aqua-green Iceberg Lake, hidden 400 metres higher and nearly four kilometres in distance up-valley.

Ascending the glacier, they walked for an hour or so up easy slopes to the broad, flat summit of a snowy peak. There they discovered they weren't standing on their intended prize – it rose some six kilometres to the south, with a large icefield between. "Still it had been a most delightful climb over a hitherto untrodden piece of icefield; and certainly no one had been to the summit of Mount Gordon before," wrote Collie in *Climbs & Exploration in the Canadian Rockies.*

Lured by another summit about a third of a mile to the west, several of the group struck off in that direction. That's where things got interesting. Not far from this dome-shaped summit was a large crevasse that was partially covered with snow. One after the other the mountaineers crossed over it without incident, but Thompson, bringing up the rear, broke through and quite unexpectedly "disappeared headlong into the great crack that ran perpendicularly down into the depths of the glacier."

With their packs at maximum weight after picking up supplies at the Kingsbury Hut midway through their nine-day Bugaboos to Rogers Pass ski traverse, Christine Mireault (out front, left) and Matthew Breakey navigate a route through large, gaping crevasses on the north side of Sugarloaf Mountain. Photo Phil Tomlinson

Despite having been swallowed quite far into the void, Thompson called loudly for help. Miraculously, he was uninjured, despite having come to a stop by jamming his body head first like a cork between the two ice walls.

Realizing they had no time to waste,

his companions tied a section of rope to make a stirrup, and decided that Collie, who was not only the lightest member of the party, but unmarried, should be the one lowered down. With the rope snugly tied around his waist, Collie was then unceremoniously pushed over the lip of the chasm, where he dangled, swinging in mid-air.

"I was then lowered into the gaping hole," Collie wrote. "On one side the ice fell sheer, on the other it was rather undercut, but again bulged outwards about eighteen feet below the surface, making the crevasse at that point not much more than two feet wide. Then it widened again and went down into dim twilight. It was not till I had descended 60 feet, almost the whole available length of an 80-foot rope, that at last I became tightly wedged between two walls of the crevasse, and was absolutely incapable of moving my body."

Face downward and covered with snow, Thompson couldn't see Collie. Shouting for another rope, Collie threw one end down to Thompson's waving left hand until he caught it. But when Collie pulled on it, it slipped free. So, still upside-down, Collie manoeuvred into a position that enabled him to reach his arms beyond his head as close to Thompson as he could get, and he tied the rope into a noose.

"With this I lassoed that poor pathetic arm which was the only part of Thompson that could be seen. Then came a tug-of-war. If he refused to move, I could do nothing more to help him; moreover, I was afraid that at any moment he might faint." Slowly, as the men on the surface began pulling, Collie's ears filled with the thumping sound of his own heart in the "ghastly stillness of the place."

Eventually, Thompson's body was loosened a little from the icy vise, and before too long he was yanked and wiggled into an upright position next to Collie. Still unable to get a rope around Thompson's body, Collie shifted and squirmed and pulled on his own rope until he was in position to tie a tight knot around Thompson's arm, just above the elbow. The extra leverage made the difference.

"A shout to the rest of the party, and Thompson went rapidly upwards till he disappeared round the bulge of ice forty feet or more above. I can well remember the feeling of dread that came over me lest the rope should slip or his arm give way under the strain, and he should come thundering down on the top of me; but he got out all right, and a moment later I followed."

Unbelievably, neither man was injured, but they were far from comfortable. Both were wet to the skin and nearly frozen after spending the entire time with the glacier dripping icy water on them. On top of that, in his desire to be as little encumbered as possible, Collie had been lowered into the crevasse wearing only a flannel shirt and knickerbockers.

All's well that ends well, and after the party reached their campsite at Bow Lake and warmed themselves by the fire, they did find humour in their close call, with Thompson emphatically declaring that whatever scientific exploration or observations were carried out in the Rockies in the future, "investigations made alone, 60 feet below the surface of the ice, in an inverted position, were extremely dangerous and even unworthy of record."

2–3 OCEAN OF SNOW

The Great Snowfield

Just as it had been by Mount Lefroy, J. Norman Collie's craving for climbing Rockies' peaks had been whetted again by the sight of higher summits to the north that he'd spied from the top of Mount Gordon. So, it was a fine day in August 1898 when he and Herman Woolley hoisted canvas backpacks and set off on a climb that would prove significant beyond their wildest expectations.

Their party, which included a third fellow-Brit, Hugh Stutfield, and a large string of pack horses, was again led by outfitter Bill Peyto. The journey from Laggan had taken 19 demanding days, and they pitched camp at the height of land that separates the North Saskatchewan and Athabasca River drainages.

"Immediately opposite our camp, to the southwest, rose a noble snow-crowned peak, about 12,000 feet in height, with splendid rock precipices and hanging glaciers; and on its right the tongue of a fine glacier descended in serpentine sinuosities to the bottom of the valley. We named them Athabasca Peak and Glacier, respectively. The spirits of us three climbers rose high, and our blood was stirred within us at the thought of being once more on the ice and snow." The party, however, was low on food. They had set out, Collie wrote, "with an insufficient stock, our appetites were healthy, and the dogs had eaten a great deal more of our bacon than was good either for them or for us." With flour for five days, only enough bacon for two and a roaring appetite for two or three weeks of climbing, they decided Stutfield, who, fortuitously, was a crack shot, would stay behind to hunt for sheep while Collie and Woolley headed up Athabasca.

After spending the first part of the morning stalking and killing two ptarmigans with stones, the pair soon reached a small glacier on the east side of the mountain. Cutting steps in a frozen slope with their ice axes for two continuous hours, then climbing some of the rotten, crumbly limestone for which the Canadian Rockies are notorious, they clambered up a narrow chimney. Surmounting a five-metre overhanging rock wall, they saw their trials rewarded.

"The view that lay before us in the evening light was one that does not often fall

The author savours the view despite bone-chilling temperatures above 3000 metres on the Columba Icefield. Photo Gail Crowe-swords

to the lot of modern mountaineers," Collie wrote. "A new world was spread at our feet: to the westward stretched a vast ice-field probably never before seen by human eye, and surrounded by entirely unknown, unnamed and un-climbed peaks."

Measuring their elevation by mer-curial barometer, they recorded the summit at 11,900 feet; today's more ac-curate GPS technology registers Mount Athabasca at 11,454 feet/3491 metres. Their journals correctly noted the mas-sive icefield before them as the origin of the Saskatchewan Glacier a few kilometres to the south, as well as the Athabasca River, which flows to the north. "Far away to the west bending over in those un-known valleys glowing with the evening light, the level snows stretched to finally melt and flow down more than one channel into the Columbia River, and thence to the Pacific Ocean."

While they were credited with the "discovery" of the Columbia Icefield, it's most unlikely the Indigenous inhabitants who'd travelled in the area for centuries weren't fully aware that a massive field of ice filled that high plateau and fed the glaciers descending from it. From Wilcox Pass, the view to the west reveals the Athabasca and Dome glaciers descending from an ice plateau. The pass is not the high point, though; Wilcox Peak is easily ascended via its rubbly south ridge, and Nigel Peak, while higher, is also easy to hike up and, since it's farther back, provides an even bet-ter view. What self-respecting young Indigenous traveller wouldn't have hiked up higher to take a look?

Nevertheless, with a solid appreciation for the significance of their ascent of Athabasca, which, covered in glacial ice, had most likely never been climbed, Collie and his rope-mates were a whole lot more excited by the prospect of the treasure chest of untouched peaks that ringed the icefield. They settled their gaze on a pair of "magnificent peaks" that they excitedly over-estimated to reach 13,000 or 14,000 feet. "A little to the north ... and directly to the westward of Peak Athabasca, rose probably the highest summit in this region of the Rocky Mountains. Chisel-shaped at the head, covered with glaciers and snow, it stood alone, and I at once recognized the great peak I was in search of."

They were in lust.

Two days later, Stutfield joined Collie and Woolley for an attempt on that prominent peak, which, at 3747 metres, is the Canadian Rockies' second highest. It had already been christened Mount Columbia in 1792 by US merchant sea captain Robert Gray, the first European to navigate the river of the same name, who had viewed it from the west. Collie, Stutfield and Woolley marched onto the Athabasca Glacier – which then descended to the valley floor some three kilometres lower than it does today, many times thicker and wider – and pitched a higher camp along its right flank. Setting off at 3:00 a.m. they navigated through and around "many zig-zags between seracs, ice pinnacles, and yawning chasms of immense depth." By daylight they were mere specks exploring the immense icefield, but eventually after several hours they came to the same conclusion many mountaineers have for decades since: "That great glacier-clad, chisel-headed peak ... was farther off than we imagined, for it lay on the opposite shore of this frozen ocean." Mount Columbia would wait four more years to be climbed.

While impressively high, Columbia wasn't the only desirable objective around. The Rockies were a smorgasbord of magnificent unclimbed glaciated peaks, and Collie and his crew weren't going to let a little detail like running low on protein keep them from bagging new summits. Hunting skills were an advantage their party enjoyed over modern climbers' limited supply of dehydrated dinners, and they would stay as long as they could manage.

And they weren't alone. Over the following decades mountaineers, many British, Swiss, Austrian or American, but also a few Canadians, would not only explore dozens of side valleys and high alpine passes in pursuit of tantalizing first ascents but in the course of doing so would contribute a lot to the mapping of the wild region. Conveniently, glaciers often provided accessible onramps to reach those summits. And

Climbers ascend a ridge bordered by crevasses on Gilgit Mountain in the Rockies' Freshfield Icefield area. Photo Bryce Brown

they weren't all men: Mary Schäffer, Caroline Hinman, Mary Jobe Akeley, Katie Gardiner are just a few who explored valleys and glacier-fed lakes and climbed up ancient ice to lofty summits. Today, climbers not only continue to retrace the old standard routes – many of which have changed considerably due to glacier melt – but are still forging new routes up steeper and more challenging and dangerous terrain all year round.

And while SUVs and pickup trucks, and not pack horses, are now the means by which climbers arrive to chase summits in the mountain parks, one thing that hasn't changed is how, since most of the Rockies' highest peaks are protected within park boundaries, travel beyond the trailheads is still as it was in Collie's time – by boots or by skis, carrying a backpack filled with stove, fuel, food, sleeping bag, rope and climbing equipment. With 11 of the Rockies' 58 highest peaks in the immediate vicinity, plus several more just beyond, the Columbia Icefield has lost none of its allure for enthusiastic mountain adventurers.

The Alpine Club of Canada

With the railway providing ready access, tourists travelled to soak in the splendour of the rugged Rocky Mountains. While many were content to gaze upon the lofty peaks and ancient glaciers from the comfort of first-class hotel dining rooms, others came intent on being the first to stand on those summits.

ACC GMC 1906 camp – The Alpine Club of Canada hosted its first camp in 1906, just months after it was formed. The camp continues to run annually for six consecutive weeks in a different location each year. Photo ACC Collection

Among them were members of Britain's Alpine Club and American mountaineers – many with summits in the Alps already under their boots – who created their own clubs.

When Charles Fay proposed that a Canadian chapter of the American club should suit the needs of their northern neighbours, a woman columnist at the *Manitoba* (now Winnipeg) *Free Press* named Elizabeth Parker, who was an ardent Rockies fan, picked up her pen in disgust.

In her response to Arthur Oliver Wheeler, a respected Canadian surveyor and keen mountaineer who supported

Fay's proposal, Parker wrote, "It knocks me speechless and fills me with shame for young Canada. Surely, between Halifax and Victoria, there can be found at least a dozen persons who are made of the stuff, and care enough about our mountain heritage to redeem Canadian apathy and indifference."

As a result, Wheeler co-founded the Alpine Club of Canada in Winnipeg in March 1906 with Elizabeth Parker, he serving as president, she as secretary.

Just four months later, in July 1906, one hundred members each paid $1 per day to congregate in a tent village at Yoho Pass. Arriving in Field aboard the train, the next morning they continued to Emerald Lake on foot. The procession included dozens of horses and wagons carrying food, cooking equipment, 40 canvas tents, bedding, climbing ropes and personal luggage – including "proper" dining attire. Donations from the Dominion and Alberta governments, the CPR (who loaned tents, canopies, cooks and the services of two of their Swiss guides) and the North West Mounted Police (who also loaned tents), along with the voluntary services of four local outfitters, all helped create the grand event.

The camp was divided into Residence Park, Official Square and the horse paddock, with tenting areas subdivided into male, female and married quarters. The massive dining tent accommodated everyone at once, with meals served from early morning to late at night. A bulletin board announced the daily programs. In the Square, a robust fire burned unceasingly.

From the main camp, participants embarked on overnight trips to climb distant peaks and to explore Yoho Glacier, where a row of metal plates was placed across the ice tongue to mark its rate of flow, and rocks marked its advance or retreat. The varied rock, snow and ice route up 3066-metre Vice President was selected as the official climb, and by camp's end 44 members had graduated to active status. Fifteen of them were women. Inclusive from the beginning, Canada's Alpine Club embraced women as full members at a time when no other national climbing club would.

Mountaineers at the Alpine Club of Canada's 2017 General Mountaineering Camp weave a route through crevasses on Justice Glacier at British Columbia's Albert Icefield area. Photo Amy Liu

In addition to advocating for and celebrating the activity of mountain climbing, the first listed objective of the Club was "the promotion of scientific study and exploration of Canadian alpine and glacial regions."

The annual General Mountaineering Camp continues to flourish. Now running for six consecutive weeks every summer,

Participants at the Alpine Club of Canada's 2018 General Mountaineering Camp enjoyed the spectacular scenery and numerous climbing objectives of the Hallam Glacier area in British Columbia's Monashee Mountains.
Photo Lynn Martel

it changes location from year to year, but one constant is that it takes place in a glaciated area with climbing objectives of easy to moderate difficulty for 30 participants each week. The campers sleep comfortably two to a four-person, high-quality expedition tent, skilled cooks prepare scrumptious meals on full-size propane ranges in a large kitchen tent that is attached to a larger dining tent. The camp includes tents for reading and self-serve tea and coffee, drying gear and storing food, solar power, well-designed outhouses and even hot showers. Professional guides and skilled amateur leaders safely lead the attendees up glaciers to stand on lofty summits. Everything is flown to the site by helicopter and skilfully set up in one week, then dismantled and every possible trace removed – including temporary bridges spanning rowdy creeks gushing with glacial meltwater – over a tear-down week.

More than a mountaineering organization, the Club set high aesthetic and environmental standards for its activities that went far beyond summit bagging. In the early 20th century it advocated for conservation of precious wilderness that led to the establishment of the mountain parks, actions that continue through public support of creating new parks and protected areas. For decades, the *Canadian Alpine Journal* included scientific observations of mountain environments, including glaciers. In 2011, the Club published the first *State of the Mountains Report*, written by Meghan J. Ward. Compiled and published annually since 2018, the report provides accessible, current and accurate information about the forces that affect Canadian mountain places, ecosystems and communities, including those caused by climate change, through essays submitted by experts.

Today, with 25 local sections from Newfoundland and Labrador to Vancouver Island and Yukon, the Club's 15,000 members continue to passionately explore, celebrate and advocate for Canada's mountains and glaciers.

The Glorious Thrill of the Descent

Two hours' drive north of the Columbia Icefield, Mount Robson is the unmistakable king of the Canadian Rockies. Heaving its bulk into the clouds at 3954 metres, just a smidge under 13,000 feet, and noticeably the highest in the range, the immense mountain imposes an inescapable presence on anyone and everything for kilometres in every direction.

Prior to its being named Robson in 1863, the Texqakallt, a nomadic Shuswap people who were the earliest known inhabitants of the region, called it Yuh-hai-has-kun, or Mountain of the Spiral Road, aptly describing the multi-coloured layers of sedimentary rock piled one atop the other from base to pyramid summit.

The route over the low pass near its base had been travelled by local tribes for generations before 1913, when railroad cars began rumbling by. The mountain had enticed several climbers to attempt its first ascent by the time the Alpine Club of Canada hosted its 1913 camp there. With no tolerance for failure on a peak with no easy way up, the organizers brought in a ringer, Austrian-born mountain guide Conrad Kain. Revered to this day as a bold, visionary climber ahead of his time for this and other difficult ascents, Kain guided Albert MacCarthy and Billy Foster through near-impossible obstacles to be the first to stand on its summit.

Despite some ten routes up its various airy ridges and jumbled icefalls today, Robson remains a difficult mountain to climb, and some years pass without successful ascents. It is, however, a spectacular and popular destination for hikers and backpackers, with seven campsites providing tenting sites between the trailhead and Robson Pass. Camping at Berg Lake is a treat. Like a giant tongue reaching down to lap up aquamarine nectar from the basin, Berg Glacier sporadically calves off car-sized chunks of ancient ice with a thunder-like crack, which is reliably followed by a booming splash as they land in the water. Then, after a few moments of quiet, interrupted only by the chatter of chickadees and alarmed squirrels, the waves reach the north shore, slapping the pebbly beach just metres from the hiking trail and campers' tents. It's an experience well worth carrying overnight gear for seven hours up the steep trail.

Mount Robson's north face glacier glows in late day sunlight. Photo Lynn Martel

That trail, which wanders through lush, enchanted old-growth cedar forest, then wraps around turquoise Kinney Lake nourished by glacier melt, and up steep slopes of willow and spruce through the Valley of a Thousand Falls, had already been well-tramped by the time Jasper area mountaineers Rex Gibson and Joe Weiss set off on a new kind of adventure in 1931.

Winding down around the east

side of Robson's smaller companion, Rearguard Mountain, and descending 1800 metres from Mount Resplendent, in those days Robson Glacier pushed some 12 kilometres downslope right to Berg Lake. The extensive tongue of glacial ice coated with late-winter snow promised the sort of long, long glacier run that lures skiers like pirates to a chest spilling with gold. For Weiss and Gibson, early adoptees of the new-to-the-Rockies sport of skiing, Robson Glacier was the motherlode. And while it is not often skied nowadays due to the requisite long approach from valley bottom, and the relative accessibility of other glacier runs more easily reached from the Icefields Parkway, it remains a worthy prize for those who make the effort.

"Resplendent is an ideal peak for a winter climb, as it is a snow and ice proposition from base to summit," wrote Gibson in the 1931 volume of the *Canadian Alpine Journal*. "In fact I would go so far as to assert that it is an easier, safer and far more enjoyable climb under good winter conditions than in the summer."

Following a breath-stealing climb on a rugged trail whose highlight was a wooden walkway called the Flying Trestle just below the colossal Emperor Falls (a trail which, now improved, serves many hundreds of hikers every summer), the duo reached the cozy log cabin on the shore of Berg Lake. Unrolling their sleeping bags after a long day's march, they settled in for a well-earned snooze. Setting off after breakfast, before long they easily skied right onto Robson Glacier.

Excellent snow conditions provided them rapid progress to the foot of the main icefall below the Resplendent-Robson Col. Their route thus far had taken them through a maze of seracs, some of the columns of ice leaning and threatening to topple over. With a healthy snowpack, they deemed the glacier's crevasses to be solidly bridged and safe to cross. Before tackling the steeper snow slopes ahead, they applied climbing skins made of seal pelts to their ski bases. Like modern synthetic climbing skins, the one-directional nap of the seal fur allowed for the skis to glide forward uphill while preventing any backsliding. Once the skins were removed at their high point, the skiers would freely swoosh and schuss downslope.

Though much smaller and thinner than it was when the first men ventured onto its surface a century ago, Robson Glacier pushes its way down the east side of the Canadian Rockies' highest peak. Photo Lynn Martel

Before they topped out, however, Weiss and Gibson were greeted by 60-kilometre winds. Staking their skis solidly into the firm snowpack, they climbed the final section with the aid of steel crampons strapped to their boots. Summitting by mid-afternoon, they found taking photos required some delicate manoeuvring.

"Here we experienced the full force of the wind and it was such that we could not stand upright on the knife edge of snow that forms the highest point. Beautiful cornices overhung the north face and in order to obtain a photo, Joe was obliged to lie prone and wriggle out to the edge."

The views were magnificent, revealing a panorama of diamond-sharp peaks all around them, interrupted by the Fraser River snaking toward the Pacific.

The wind, however, was relentless, and after five minutes they'd had enough. For them, though, the summit was just half their goal.

"Then came the great moment of the day – off came our crampons and on went our skis for the glorious thrill of the descent of nearly 5000 feet of glacier under perfect snow conditions.... The best route passes close beneath the Extinguisher and this stretch comprises some two miles of very fast downhill running which can be 'taken straight' by those who have an urge for speed. Lower down the glacier levels off until the tongue is reached where there is another rapid descent of 500 feet. As we turned the corner below Rearguard we saw the beauteous rosy afterglow on the snowy spire of Whitehorn and the moon came out in all its glory as we reached our cozy little cabin at 6.10 p.m. or 2 hours and 25 minutes total elapsed time since leaving the summit."

While they would have been pleased to have made a first descent, they knew before they started out that morning that they'd been scooped. A note on the cabin wall announced a P.L. Parsons had climbed and skied Resplendent – a decidedly bold and risky feat for a man travelling alone.

"Be it hereby recorded that I this day, February 28th, 1930, went up along Robson glacier to

Malcolm Sangster skis the Canadian Rockies' North Twin, with the Columbia Glacier in the background. Photo Bryce Brown

the top of the divide on skis, to where I could look down in the Fraser valley,
about 10,000 feet elevation. Here I left the skis because of hard snow and ice
and continued to the summit of Mt. Resplendent on foot; it was blowing hard
and 5 below zero F. in the bright sunshine on top, so I just ate a bit of lunch
and took some pictures, and then came back down to the skis in 35 minutes
and then coasted down to the flat in 40 minutes more. It took me 5½ hours to
climb up to the top. A beautiful day and sure had some sport."

(Signed) "P. L. Parsons"
Mt. Robson, B.C.

"All honor to this intrepid young ski-er who made this, the first major winter as-cent by himself," Gibson graciously wrote, adding, "He has unfortunately lost his life by drowning while running some rapids in the Peace river."

Ski Turns on Ice

Weiss and Gibson knew they were on to a good thing, and skiing Robson Glacier was just the beginning.

That same winter, with Russell Bennett and Cliff White, Weiss made the first ski as-cent – and descent – of Snow Dome. From valley bottom the trio skied up the gentle incline of the Athabasca Glacier to gain the massive Columbia Icefield, then steered north to ascend to Snow Dome's broad summit. Despite the teetering seracs perched menacingly above the narrow strip of smooth glacier that leads to the upper icefield, a strip which is bordered on both sides by gaping crevasses, that route remains popu-lar today. Skiers on day trips up Snow Dome or Mount Andromeda, or those carry-ing big multi-day packs in the hopes of bagging summits ringing the icefield, follow that route all winter long every year, right into May and June when the flowers begin to sprout up through thawing soil in the valley bottom. For nearly a century now, from the Rockies to the Columbia Mountains of interior British Columbia to the Coast Mountain range, springtime remains glacier skiing season.

Weiss, who immigrated to Canada from his native Switzerland in 1921, was a pro-lific pioneer of ski mountaineering in the Jasper area, and while he became a respected guide during the summer months, he spent his winters exploring the region on skis, capturing the quiet meditative stillness of the snowy, glaciated landscapes with his camera. Gibson, too, made numerous first ski descents on Rockies glaciers. Operating a farm near Edmonton, he managed a mountaineer's ideal schedule – climbing through the summer until harvest time, and skiing to his heart's content during the winter.

Skiers are dwarfed by seracs high above them as they ski on the Columbia Icefield. Photo Bryce Brown

In the 1930s, as skiing became more familiar to Canadians, others were also drawn to explore glaciers that way, as A.A. "Mac" McCoubrey and friends did in Yoho Park and on the Wapta Icefields. Setting out from the railway town of Field in 1932 with Campbell Secord and brothers Roger and Ferris Neave – all members of the Alpine Club of Canada's Winnipeg section – they overnighted at the bungalow camp at Takakkaw Falls, then skied on to Twin Falls Chalet the next day. From there they embarked on some impressive ski tours, venturing up the Little Yoho Valley to make a ski ascent of The President Glacier, at the top of which they removed their skis to kick steps in stiff wind-blasted snow to climb to its summit. They enjoyed a long run down the glacier, and it was dark by the time they returned to the chalet.

A couple of days later, they made their way from the chalet up a steep forested headwall and into the hanging valley above that led them straight onto the Des Poilus Glacier, which they followed to climb Mount Collie. After McCoubrey left to return to Winnipeg, the others skied farther up the Yoho Valley to the north and onto the Yoho Glacier on approach to ascend Mount Gordon. The route back to the chalet provided a long, long ski back down the glacier. Today, Yoho Glacier has receded so far back it is rarely visited by anyone. With a campground and the Alpine Club of Canada's Stanley Mitchell Hut less than an hour's walk from its toe, the much-diminished President Glacier is regularly skied in winter and ascended by mountaineers in summer. Mount Gordon, meanwhile, is a popular ski ascent more commonly approached from the east, either as a day trip from the Bow Lake parking lot, or for those overnighting at Bow Hut a few kilometres from the peak.

The Rockies' glaciers, though, weren't the only ones being explored by skis in the early 20th century. While climbers had been walking up the glaciers of Rogers Pass in the Selkirk Mountains en route to the towering summits since Spotswood Green's adventures, skiers were lured to explore those glaciers in winter too. No doubt the lower-angled glacier slopes offered safer skiing than the steep, avalanche-prone slopes that caused the railroad track to be buried regularly, more than once fatally burying the men charged with clearing it. The Swiss guides who were stationed at Glacier House to lead guests during the summer season were skiers as well as climbers, so, naturally, it was one of them, Edward Feuz Jr., who made the first ski ascent of Asulkan Pass in the winter of 1906/07. Reaching the pass then meant gaining the Asulkan Glacier just above a place known today as the Mouse Trap, a tight pinch where steep avalanche-prone slopes rise like funnel walls. Today the glacier ice isn't reached for another two or more hours of uphill travel, and the Alpine Club of Canada–run Asulkan Hut is perched on the crest of the moraine just below where the ice reached a century ago.

While travel to Rogers Pass dwindled after Glacier House was permanently shut down in 1925, once the Trans-Canada Highway was completed through the area in 1962 the glaciers of Rogers Pass and the aptly named Glacier National Park (established in 1886, 24 years before the US park of the same name) began seeing more traffic. And while relatively small numbers of summer visitors hike the steep trails to see the glaciers up close or climb the spectacular peaks, in winter the Asulkan, Bonney, Illecillewaet, Lily, Uto, Hermit, Tupper and other glaciers of Rogers Pass are well tracked by backcountry skiers from November into May.

Pacific Ice

In British Columbia's Coast Mountains, passionate climbers were exploring their own nearby peaks as the Pacific Great Eastern Railway made them increasingly accessible. Accessible is a relative term, however, when speaking of glaciers in the Coast Mountains, where great distances between sea-level valley bottoms and summits are obstructed by leg-piercing devil's club and a profuse understory, rendering coastal rainforests a lot less penetrable to hikers or skiers than the comparatively thin Rockies subalpine ecoregion. Even today, many Coast Mountain glaciers remain so far beyond the nearest gravel forestry roads that they are rarely visited by anyone approaching on foot (after a boat ride), and only by small numbers who hire expensive helicopters to drop them off in remote wilderness.

Recognizing the sublime beauty of the glacier-wrapped volcanic peaks, aquamarine lakes and alpine meadows profuse with lupine, Indian paintbrush and other wildflowers, after the British Columbia Mountaineering Club hosted camps in the area in 1910, 1911 and 1912, C. Chapman wrote an article in the 1917 *Canadian Alpine Journal* pleading the case for the establishment of Garibaldi Park.

"The physical and mental value of the weekly climb on Grouse Mountain and the nearby hills cannot be over-emphasized," Chapman wrote. "But the case is a little different as regards the proposed Garibaldi Park with its wide solitudes, its snowy plateaus, and numerous glaciers. The stimulus, both mental and physical, which belongs to an alpine district, is altogether different from that afforded by the mountains which we of Vancouver see from our northern windows. The air is more bracing in a marked degree, and the variety and interest of the landscape are immensely greater."

Chapman described the various approaches to climb Mount Garibaldi – which saw its first ascent in 1907 by a team of Vancouver mountaineers – its two peaks ringed by seven glaciers that then extended well below timber line, which had been christened Garibaldi, Lava, Pyramid, Pitt, Sentinel, Phoenix and Warren glaciers. He also recounted moments from the first recorded ascent of Mamquam Mountain in 1911, from where "our first glimpse of the vast snowfield at the top almost justified the remark of our leading man that it was 'as big as England.'" Crossing it, he said, was a five-kilometre walk.

"If our government does not recognize the value of the district soon, it is probable that some of the syndicates which are always on the lookout for such things will discover it and make arrangements to exploit it for their own benefit." With the support of the Alpine Club of Canada and the British Columbia Mountaineering Club, by 1920 a park reserve was established, a designation that evolved into the 1946.5-square-kilometre Garibaldi Provincial Park seven years later.

Garibaldi is a special mountain in that it is a volcano that erupted both under and over a glacier. As the ice melted away at the end of the last glaciation, it collapsed and formed what is now the Cheekye Fan. Garibaldi Lake was formed about 9,000 years ago when large lava flows emanating from the west shoulder of the double summits of mounts Price and Clinker flowed toward the Cheakamus River valley. With the valley filled by glacial ice at that time, the lava flow was stopped by the ice and ponded. When the ice melted, the lava flow that had been cooled by the ice formed a steep cliff. The water that ponded behind the lava dam formed Garibaldi Lake.

Cradled by Wedgemount and Armchair glaciers, Wedgemount Lake is a popular destination for hikers and mountaineers. In 1973 the glacier was floating on the lake; by 1994 the glacier no longer touched the water. It continued to melt, exposing a minor bedrock ridge called a riegel. A second, bigger riegel was soon exposed, and recently an ice cave with a small pond developed at the glacier's toe behind the larger riegel. The glacier's terminus continues to retreat. Photo Isabel Budke

More than 150 glaciers exist in Garibaldi Provincial Park, with Garibaldi Névé, Misty and Mamquam icefields being the largest, each covering more than ten square kilometres. These glaciers have behaved similarly to those in the other mountain areas of western Canada, undergoing standstills and periods of minor growth during the first two decades of the 1900s, followed by slow retreat. Since the 1980s, the melting of glaciers across western Canada has been particularly pronounced; while about 13 per cent of Garibaldi Park remains covered by glacial ice, those glaciers are retreating rapidly, and if present warming trends continue, scientists expect some of them to vanish altogether by 2100.

Prior to construction of the Sea to Sky Highway – which didn't link Vancouver to Squamish until 1959 and didn't extend to Pemberton until 1966 – members of the fabled University of British Columbia Varsity Outdoor Club (VOC) travelled from the city to Squamish by Union steamship. From there, those headed to the Garibaldi Névé and Diamond Head region hitched a ride with members of the Brandvold family, who finished building their Diamond Head Lodge in 1947, riding aboard a jeep, truck or snowcat up to Elfin Lakes. Those intent on reaching the Garibaldi Lakes area boarded a train from Squamish to the now decommissioned Garibaldi Station and shouldered their gear for the six-kilometre hike up the Barrier. The trip was finally made easier in 1956 when the Pacific Great Eastern rail line connected North Vancouver with Squamish.

While Eric Brooks had travelled through the area on skis in the early 1920s, legendary Coast mountaineers Phyl and Don Munday followed in the 1930s. In 1944 it was the Mundays – who would become well known for the many years they spent exploring the nearly impenetrable heavily glaciated terrain of the Mount Waddington area, some 240 mainly roadless kilometres to the north – who made the first recorded tracks on the Sphinx Glacier. Don Munday's article in the 1944–45 volume of the *Canadian Alpine Journal* described skiing in Garibaldi Park, and mentions how access to the area was made easier by logging roads pushing closer to the park boundary. In 1945 eminent Canadian geologist and polar explorer Fred Roots, then VOC president, established a spring ski camp at Garibaldi Lake. The tradition continued for decades, later becoming known as Sphinx Camp.

Mountaineers stand outside the Jim Haberl Hut in the Coast Mountains' Tantalus Range. Photo Lynn Martel

Many have schussed in their tracks since and continue to today. Linking Garibaldi Park's Diamond Head area in the south to the Rubble Creek parking lot in the north, the 40-kilometre Garibaldi Névé Traverse was first skied in 1946 by a crew of VOCers known as the "Dirty Nine," four of whom were women. Usually skied from south to north – which offers more downhill turns than climbing – the route crosses small glaciers and high cols over two or three days, with nights often spent at Elfin Lakes Shelter, Burton Hut or the Sentinel Bay Glaciology Huts. In summertime Garibaldi's glacial ice, including the Sentinel and Sphinx glaciers and the expansive Garibaldi Névé, attract climbers too, as they offer relatively straightforward approaches on the east side of the 2678-metre peak, which is guarded on the west by steep ridges and cliffs of loose, rotten lava.

Across the valley, high above Squamish to the west, the steep, broken and jumbled glaciers of the Tantalus Range are spectacularly visible from the designated Highway 99 viewpoint. They dominate the view from the higher elevations of the Garibaldi area and are another popular destination for climbers in the summertime and a few ski mountaineers in winter. Not as easily accessed, however, they require the young, the hardy or light of wallet to make the arduous long day's journey on foot, beginning with a crossing of Squamish River by boat or by an exhilarating zipline via the water survey cable. Those with more money than time or energy book a helicopter flight from Squamish to arrive in mere minutes at the Tantalus or Jim Haberl huts, run by the Alpine Club of Canada's Vancouver section, savouring a brief opportunity to peer right down into countless crevasses lined up like accordion folds on the glacier right before landing.

John Clarke, Mountain Goat

If the name Munday is synonymous with the Coast Mountains through the first half of the 20th century, then John Clarke is the name that evokes the least-explored treasures of the range for the second half of the century.

Unlike the Mundays, Clarke was not primarily a climber or seeker of the highest, most elusive and difficult summits. He was, in the purest sense, an explorer and true lover of utterly remote wilderness, a commodity that sadly shrinks every day in every corner of the globe. With this awareness, Clarke was also a devoted conservationist. In the course of his expeditions amongst the peaks of the Coast range – many of them unnamed – he managed to explore some 10,000 square kilometres of wilderness, much of it never-before-visited territory. He did like to climb, though, and along the way he made some 600 first ascents over the course of 39 years, quite likely more than any other person, ever.

What defined Clarke was his low-budget, no-fanfare style of expeditions. He made many of his arduous trips solo, increasing the amount of weight on his back without a partner to share the tent or stove – or the decision making. The reason was simple: with his trips often lasting a full month, partners who could take that much time off were hard

John Clarke enjoys the summit views amidst the big glaciers of the Coast Mountains above South Bentinck Arm. Photo John Baldwin

to find. He travelled light and eschewed modern technology and its sweat-shedding fleece and processed energy foods, choosing instead to wear cotton long underwear and eat homemade granola. He sought no sponsorships or media attention and worked odd jobs to earn just enough to finance his next season's adventure.

To prepare for a trip he'd cover the floor with maps and aerial photos and sometimes commandeer his sister's basement to pack up his food-drop parcels, which also contained gas for cooking, matches, candles, socks, books, summit cairn tubes, foot tape, soap and sunscreen. On one trip he boarded a bus from Vancouver to Williams Lake with his bulging pack and skis, then waited in Nimpo Lake for nine weeks before the weather cleared for the pilot to deliver him to his starting point. During the wait he camped in the woods and stored everything in a friend's shed.

Accounts of his multi-week expeditions, shared on the pages of the *Canadian Alpine Journal* through the 1970s, '80s and '90s, gained him legendary status. They entertained many a reader as he shared rich descriptions of places more often visited by grizzlies, mountain goats and marmots than by humans. He also recorded many glacier observations in places scientists have no manpower or budget to access.

"I spent the early morning exploring around the intricacies of the pass, having a wake up swim and photographing the waterfalls. Later on I hiked up the Wave Glacier and climbed Breaker and Comber at its head. To the south across the Little Toba there was a stupendous scene. The broad névé of the Terrific Glacier narrowed to less than half a mile wide at about 6200 ft and plunged dagger like in a wildly broken icefall for 4000 ft. The moraines at the steep snout have well established slide alder right up to the ice and there seems to have been either a recent advance or very little overall recession since maximum extent over a hundred years ago." (Quoted in Lisa Baile's *John Clarke: Explorer of the Coast Mountains.*)

Fortunately, Clarke carried a camera on his trips. In some photos the glaciers are stupendously large, sprawling across entire valleys, sometimes completely overtaking all but a few tiny rock points. One image captures gaping crevasses in the foreground dwarfing a substantial peak in the distance. Another shows a giant teardrop-shaped mass of glacial ice tucked inside an overhanging rock scoop, like a gargantuan ice diamond set inside a black volcanic pendant. Clearly, he was aware he was witnessing very special phenomena, and he framed his images perfectly.

Clarke knew how to use his spectacular photos for good, too, by sharing them in his talks. Liked and admired for his balanced views, unique sense of humour and well-researched presentations, he used his captivating imagery to help share his message of conservation. His efforts contributed substantially toward the preservation of the Randy Stoltmann Wilderness Area (Stoltmann was a friend who was killed in an avalanche during a multi-week trip with Clarke, a life-changing event that inspired Clarke to devote more energy to conservation projects), which led to the creation of the Clendinning and Upper Lillooet provincial parks, and later, the Upper Elaho Valley Conservancy and the Sims Creek Valley Wildland. Clarke was also a key member of the Wilderness Education Program founded in 1996 by a small group of individuals who recognized and acted upon a need to educate youth about the vital importance of British Columbia's wilderness, and its valuable role in Canadians' heritage.

He also teamed up with Chief Bill Williams, hereditary chief of the Squamish First Nation, and photographer Nancy Bleck to create the Witness Project, creating a successful partnership between artists, First Nations, conservationists and the general public to raise awareness of one of the few remaining – and dwindling – ancient forests on the British Columbia coast. In recognition of his efforts, Clark was inducted into the Squamish First Nation and endowed with his Coast Salish name, Xwexwsélken. It means Mountain Goat.

For all his work, in 2002 Clarke was invested into the Order of Canada. Sadly, the following year he succumbed to a brain tumour, with his wife, Annette Clarke, and their son, Nicholas "Skookum" by his side. After his death the British Columbia government named Mount John Clarke (formerly known as Sun Peak), a glaciated summit in the Pacific ranges of the Coast Mountains, in his honour. His story is also preserved in *John Clarke: Explorer of the Coast Mountains*, by his friend and Wilderness Education Program co-founder, Lisa Baile.

New, Mysterious and Tempting

There are few places in the world where ski mountaineers can travel for weeks at a time crossing glaciers, descending to valley bottom and skinning back up onto the next glacier, camping night after night after night, carrying the necessary equipment and enthusiasm. Canada's Rockies, Columbia and Coast Mountains harbour just such places. While professional guides can be hired to manage complicated route finding across featureless terrain in stormy conditions, and through chaotic icefalls, these adventures cannot be bought. Only muscle and sweat and determination can deliver these experiences. Your sweat.

When it came to brute determination and limitless sweat, nobody was more motivated than Hans Gmoser. He and his friend, Leo Grillmair, arrived in the Rockies in 1951 as young men seeking better fortunes than available in their home country of Austria in the wake of the Second World War. Gmoser dreamed big. He also delivered. By 1960 he had established himself as the top professional mountain guide in Canada. While Swiss-born mountain guides had broken trail up and down valleys and across glaciers to lofty peaks all over the Rockies through the first half of the 20th century, they mostly chose the easiest routes, albeit often while undertaking the relentless labour necessary to build approach trails. With all the major peaks having been climbed many times over by popular routes, though, Gmoser, inspired by his fellow Austrian Conrad Kain who guided the first ascent of Mount Robson, sought out bigger challenges. He repeatedly set new difficulty standards on rock climbs up vertical cliffs, and on technically challenging, highly complex new routes on giant, remote glaciated peaks, including Canada's highest, Yukon's glacier-swathed 5959-metre Mount Logan.

And Gmoser had a grand plan.

He and five companions would travel on skis carrying knee-buckling 35-kilogram packs across 300 kilometres of isolated wilderness following the crest of the Great Divide from Wapta Lake in Yoho National Park to emerge from the backcountry near Jasper townsite. Their route would cross eight major icefields, including the largest, the Columbia. They would live for weeks between 1200 and 3350 metres' elevation. They carried with them two small tents, and their dehydrated food was packaged in daily rations. Seven food caches were dropped by airplane at intervals along their intended route, each of them securely packed in case a grizzly or wolverine wandering across the ice – as they sometimes do en route to the next valley – should sniff them out. Ravens, too, they knew, wouldn't hesitate to tear into a poorly packed food cache. They planned to complete their adventure in 30 days.

The 1960 Great Divide Traverse team, led by Hans Gmoser, far left, succeeded in skiing about half the distance from Lake Louise to Jasper by crossing glaciers and icefields. Photo Bruno Engler

Gmoser was not the first to dream up the trip. J. Monroe Thorington wrote an article in the 1932 *American Alpine Journal* titled "A High Level Route from Jasper to Lake Louise," in which he explored the possibility of walking the route across the firm surface afforded by bare glacier ice in summertime. With the glaciers being thick and fat and descending quite far down to the valley bottoms, in his day this was an entirely plausible idea.

In 1954, a group of skiers from Ontario mapped out the route and launched their attempt. Most of them, however, possessed very little high-alpine experience. Their highly publicized effort only lasted a few days when post-storm avalanches drove home to them the seriousness of their undertaking, and the seriousness of their inexperience. Gmoser, however, had followed the media accounts of their trip with more than armchair curiosity. He was confident it could be accomplished safely, and that he and his friends should be the ones to do it.

"The purpose of our trip was to explore and prove the feasibility of such a ski route," he wrote in the 1961 *Canadian Alpine Journal*. "Of course, you can get plenty of skiing by going to one of our modern ski resorts, but this gets dull after a while. In the end, to ski is to travel fast and free – free over the untouched, snow-covered country. To be bound to one slope, even to one mountain, by a lift may be convenient but it robs us of the greatest pleasure that skiing can give, that is, to travel through the wide, wintry country; to follow the lure of the peaks which tempt on the horizon and to be alone for a few days or even a few hours in clear, mysterious surroundings." ("High Level Ski Route from Lake Louise to Jasper," p. 11.)

Alone they would be. For the duration of their expedition they would not pass through any towns. There were no ski lodges, not even any climbers' huts. They would not cross any paved roads, and any hiking trails or gravel forestry roads within a day's travel would likely be buried in snow for weeks to come. Their route involved many unknowns, including long stretches when they would be more than a day's travel from the Icefields Parkway on the east. There are no paved roads on the Columbia River side of the range. They did not know which side valleys were even navigable on skis. For great sections of their route, they would be fully committed.

On Top of the World

On April 2, 1960, the six men skinned up from Wapta Lake in thick wet snow and settled in under the nagging weight of their huge backpacks. Several days later, the sun appeared. By then they had skied steadily upward onto the Wapta Icefield. After pitching their fourth camp, Gmoser and Pat Boswell skied with empty packs to retrieve their first food cache. Climbing over a small rise, they quickly spied the two red flags marking the site. The cache was buried under six feet of snow, so the act of digging up the contents generated an even greater appetite than they'd started with. The following morning was clear and cold as they climbed to a high col, and progress was

Mountaineers enjoy the views from their cozy glacier camp while climbing Mount Fairweather in Tatshenshini-Alsek Provincial Park, British Columbia. Photo Bryce Brown

slow under their newly weighted packs digging into their shoulders. They could taste the respite the ten-kilometre downhill that awaited them would bring.

"Even though you can almost imagine the impressive panorama that awaits you on the other side, it always takes your breath away when mountain range upon mountain range unfolds before you – hundreds of peaks, many of them old friends, many of them strange, new, mysterious and tempting. Below us stretched the Baker Glacier and further down, the green forest along Wildcat Creek. It was a swift ride. The snow was so good that even with our heavy loads we could make nice linked turns and long schusses across the three miles of glacier. Then we were among the trees. It was a wonderful feeling to be back in a living world after five days on the glaciers."

Camping at an open area cradled in valley timber next to a sparkling creek with a campfire to warm them, they stripped off their shirts, enjoying a brief respite from the cold. While springtime is when flowers bloom in the valley bottoms, winter doesn't give up easily above treeline. The following days brought them thick fog, fierce winds and biting cold. Added to that, the terrain was difficult. They relied on strong legs and years of experience to keep their skis under control on a steep slope that dropped like a 500-metre ice slide. Then they had to zigzag uphill through a maze of crevasses and seracs and narrow snow bridges.

"Then there was just a large ice wall ahead of us. It started to snow hard and a strong wind drove the snow like needles into our faces," Gmoser wrote. "We tried to find a way but there was always either a vertical ice cliff or a huge crevasse which stopped our progress."

Eventually they skied down into a large crevasse and followed along on a solid snow bridge. Then, removing their skis, they climbed up the equivalent of three storeys. They were relieved to have reached the crest of Cairns Icefall, which they had rightly anticipated to present one of the most difficult sections of the trip, and with renewed energy they charged across the upper part of the glacier. Reaching a col, they stopped in their tracks, puzzled. It was the wrong col.

Mistakes on a glacier traverse can bring serious consequences, and they knew it.

Travelling eats up energy, and food is limited to what you can carry. There are no crit-ters to hunt on glaciers, and no plants to eat. Water is available only as long as stove fuel lasts. Glaciers are no place to make a wrong turn.

With no other choice, they skied back down, then flat for a kilometre, and then climbed up a much steeper slope than the previous one. Worse, they each made the trip twice, first kicking steps up the hard snow carrying their skis, then climbing back up lugging their hefty packs.

"To say the least, we were exhausted," Gmoser wrote. "When we looked over the other side, however, our enthusiasm returned. Six miles before us stretched the Freshfield Icefield and in less than an hour we had coasted across it, pitched our camp and fallen wearily into our sleeping bags."

Swirling World of White

The long day behind them had gifted them what would be the best ski run of their en-tire journey. It also delivered some tense moments when Kurt Lukas kicked steps to surmount a large cornice and a section broke off, sending him hurtling downhill for 20 metres. While he was miraculously unhurt, he was justifiably annoyed at having to climb up again.

Enthusiasm on long trips peaks and wanes along with the dips and rises in terrain. A ferocious storm pinned them in their tents for three days, reducing their activity to reading and sleeping. And, as if being continuously cold wasn't bad enough, they were hungry. With their supplies running out, food occupied their thoughts inces-santly. Adding to their frustration, with the storm upon them they had pitched their camp not even two kilometres – 20 minutes' ski – from their next food cache.

Eventually Gmoser and Lukas couldn't take it any longer. Dressed in all their lay-ers, they launched a desperate attempt to ski to their cache. Within minutes they lost sight of their bright yellow tents, with only the black tips of their skis breaking the swirling world of white. Frightened, they retreated. Finally, a break in the storm was their salvation, but not because they located their food cache, which was hopelessly buried. Two friends from Banff, including pilot Jim Davies, who had placed their food caches, flew over to check on the team. After they signalled that they needed food by stomping out letters in the snow, Davies soon flew back and dropped them some supplies, leaving them to feast on pork chops and chocolate Easter bunnies.

The challenges of the trip, however, didn't ease up. Climbing to a notch between two of the Lyell peaks, they began an 1800-metre descent in dense cloud and fog. On their way down, they came within a ski length of launching off a drop higher than the World Trade Centre.

A skier breaks a fresh trail through intermittent clouds on the Mamquam Icefield in the Coast Mountains. Photo Isabel Budke

"Groping our way down a steep ridge which dropped off suddenly on both sides was just part of the game, but when a huge avalanche thundered down, stopping just short of us, it became rather uncomfortable," Gmoser wrote. "The final blow came when I found myself 100 feet down in a crevasse, standing practically on my head with my pack driven so hard into the snowbridge that I was almost unable to free it. With the help of my friends, I was able to get out. Life felt pretty wonderful when we finally dumped our packs in the valley and pitched our tent on a patch of dry ground."

While the snowpack piled up higher and deeper, morale within the group sank in equal measure. They had endured 12 continuously snowy days. Hunger gnawed relentlessly. First one member skied out, following a long side valley to the Icefields Parkway, then a second called it quits. Soon the others acquiesced. Not accustomed to giving up, in his trip report Gmoser outlined a long list of factors that contributed to their difficulties. Chief among them, he suggested, was the absence of high alpine huts on the Rockies' glaciers, as existed in Europe's Alps.

"I can speak for all of us in saying that we are firmly convinced that this is a trip that can afford a great deal of pleasure to many, many people, especially in our day and age when there is need of such adventure and intimate contact with nature. I feel that since we have all this fine country right in our backyard, it is our duty to do everything within our power to develop the ski route between Lake Louise and Jasper to such a point that the average skier who desires to travel this route or portions of it, will be able to do so."

A handful of huts would later be built, but only in the Wapta area. But before that would happen, inspired by Gmoser, a few years later four skiers from Calgary, their average age just 22½, would prove him right, and wrong. Meanwhile, Gmoser would go on to gain success and fortune using a helicopter as a lift to guide skiers down sparkling slopes on British Columbia's wild and mysterious glaciers.

A Magical Experience

"What unfolded over the next three weeks was a magical experience."

So wrote Rockies adventurer and historian Chic Scott in his book *Powder Pioneers*.

Scott and his companions, Don Gardner, Neil Liske and Charlie Locke, were the first to ski the route Gmoser had dreamed of completing. Beginning at Moab Lake just south of Jasper, they travelled north to south. They accomplished their adventure in May 1967, and linking the high glacier route was their way of celebrating Canada's centennial.

Over 21 days they crossed nine icefields, pristine snow glinting in sunlight. They shared deep conversations under ebony skies profuse with stars. They broke trail through deep powder, shoulders aching under their loads. They waited out two storms, each lasting three days. They navigated the previously untravelled north section of the Great Divide route across unknown glaciers and icefields in 14 days without a mishap. A week later they skied down to the Sherbrooke Lake trailhead.

"There had been no avalanches, no crevasse falls, no heroics and no epics," wrote Scott. "All in all, it was a pretty boring story."

And a really inspiring one.

Since then, barely 20 parties have completed the entire 300-kilometre Great Divide Traverse, which involves 10,000 metres of elevation gain; it took 20 years before the second group succeeded, also in 21 days. In 2005, Catherine Barrett became the first woman to ski the entire route; in 2007 Janez Ales completed the traverse solo in a remarkable 17 days. He'd planned his trip carefully, waiting for a deep snow year so the crevasses would be well plugged, alleviating some of the danger of travelling alone with nobody to help him out should he fall into one. Many other parties have skied sections of the Great Divide, some of them purposefully exploring the most remote legs, others aborting trips they intended to run longer.

In 1967, the young team of (from left) Don Gardner, Chic Scott, Charlie Locke and Neil Liske skied the first Great Divide Traverse, linking glaciers and icefields from Jasper to Lake Louise, over 21 days, succeeding on the difficult journey where other more experienced teams had not. Photo Chic Scott

With nearly the entire distance located within the boundaries of protected Jasper, Banff and Yoho national parks, the extensive hut and trail system Gmoser envisioned never came to fruition. Skiing the Great Divide remains a true wilderness adventure very much as it was for Gmoser and his crew, and for Scott and the others who've followed. Helicopter landings are prohibited in the national parks, so most food caches are placed by skiing up side valleys in advance. Except for a handful of Alpine Club of Canada huts in the Wapta Icefield area and one at the north end, and two privately owned ones in the Lyell area, nights are spent sleeping in tents, and days spent navigating icefalls and crevasses, forcing feet into frozen boots every morning and breaking trail under demanding heavy loads. They are also spent in glorious solitude high above treeline, where on a windless day the silence is profound. More than a half-century and numerous long-distance ski adventures later, Scott remains smitten by the magic of his and his companions' Great Divide Traverse. It's still his favourite trip.

"One of the most wonderful things about the Great Divide Traverse is that it has not changed over the years like so many other adventures," Scott explained over a glass of wine. "Going to the South Pole today is not what it was when Amundsen and Scott went in 1911–12. Climbing Mount Everest is not the same thing today as it was when Hillary and Tenzing climbed it. The Great Divide Traverse is one of the greatest ski adventures in the world, and I think it's just as wild and difficult today as it was 50 years ago. No one does it any faster than we did it. No one has an easier time. It still beats people."

Even better, he added, for Canadians, it's a full-blown wilderness adventure right in their backyard. The route follows a logical line, from start to finish. And while more than 4,800 people had climbed Everest by the end of 2018, fewer than a hundred had skied the Great Divide Traverse.

But for all that hasn't changed on the traverse, Scott laments how one thing has altered the nature of the adventure – the availability, and pervasiveness, of high-tech communication devices.

"I am pleased to have been able to experience an old-style expedition," he said. "When you were gone, you were gone. We registered out with the wardens for 35 days. If we didn't show up at Lake Louise in 35 days, we were somewhere out there. But now, no one cuts the ties with the city. They are getting weather reports and snow stability reports and sending InReach messages, etcetera. Too bad."

"On some sections of the traverse, you are way back in there. I remember standing beside the tent on the Chaba Icefield and looking west toward the

From front, Don Gardner, Charlie Locke and Chic Scott ski toward the Scott Glacier. Photo Neil Liske

Selkirks and feeling so far away from civilization. It is really wild out there. It's not like the Wapta. You won't run into anyone else out there."

For now, the route remains viable, yet every party that repeats it – fewer than one group per year – reports changes in how and where the glaciers carpet the landscape and provide climbable ramps up steep cols. Younger adventurers often contact Scott before and after their trips to gain information and compare notes, particularly since his *Summit and Icefields* guidebook for the Canadian Rockies, co-authored with ACMG (Association of Canadian Mountain Guides) mountain guide Mark Klassen, provides practical descriptions for those interested in skiing the route. A slide show Scott shared at Banff's Whyte Museum of the Canadian Rockies in the spring of 2017 – 50 years after their original trip – filled the house with skiers and armchair adventurers who feel the allure of long wilderness ski traverses.

Lately, however, Scott has begun calling the Great Divide Traverse "Canada's Great Disappearing Adventure."

"The ice is going, and in 100 years will be gone," he said. "I think the 2,000-metre-high climb from the Alexandra River to the Lyell 2-3 Col will become increasingly difficult with the shrinking of the glacier. It would be hard to find a way around this section if it were impassable. I think it's a shame that the trip may be so altered in coming years."

"I had the greatest adventure of my life 50 years ago along the Great Divide. Part of me will always be out there with the wind and the snow."

Bugaboos Teen Climbing Camp

When Pat Morrow was just 17, a group of experienced climbers invited him to join them for a climbing camp in British Columbia's fabled Bugaboos. As a novice climber Morrow appreciated the chance to climb easier routes while he watched some of Canada's top climbers of the day attempt more serious objectives. The experience made a lifelong impact.

Since then, Morrow has returned to the iconic area numerous times, climbing many of its world-renowned granite spires that rise like formidable pillars from crinkled glaciers.

And since 2009, Morrow has returned to the area every summer with ten Columbia and Kootenay valley teenagers and three professional ACMG mountain guides to run the Bugaboos Teen Climbing Camp. Created and organized by the Conrad Kain Centennial Society, the camp honours the memory and the accomplishments of the Austrian-born mountain guide who arrived in Canada in 1909, and who is revered for many impressive first ascents, including Bugaboo Spire and Mount Robson, as well as his conservationist philosophy.

Participants of the Conrad Kain Teen Camp follow behind on ropes led by ACMG mountain guides Tim McAllister and Jen Olson as they ascend Pigeon Fork Glacier. Photo Lynn Martel

ACMG mountain guide Tim McAllister celebrates with teen climbers on the summit of Hounds Tooth Spire, wedged between Bugaboo and Pigeon Fork glaciers. Photo Pat Morrow

Open to grade 10 and 11 students, the camp aims to introduce teens to the excitement of climbing in a spectacular setting, and to the wonder of being in remote wilderness amidst towering peaks and picturesque glaciers. The participants benefit from the generosity of several sponsors, including staff at Canadian Mountain Holidays' Bugaboo Lodge, who kit them out with free rentals of harnesses, crampons, helmets and ice axes, and British Columbia Parks and the Alpine Club of Canada, which runs Conrad Kain Hut. Over the course of their adventure they practise self-arrest skills and ascend a glacier en route to climbing to a rocky summit.

"I came here when I was 17 and was blown away," said Morrow, who is Conrad Kain Society chair. "The aim of the camp is to expose the teens to as many people as we can – CMH Bugaboo Lodge housekeeping staff, cooks, guides, the Conrad Kain hut custodian – people who are making a living in the outdoors doing what they love to do."

An impressive role model himself, Invermere-born Morrow became the second Canadian to summit Everest in 1982, two days after his teammate, Laurie Skreslet, made national history. In 1986, Morrow became the first person to climb the Seven Summits, the highest mountain on each of Earth's seven continents. He and his wife, Baiba, have spent decades photographing and filming cultures in mountain regions around the world. Since settling in Wilmer in 2007, they've become passionately involved with Columbia Valley environmental and conservation efforts.

The youths, aged 15 to 17 and now numbering more than 100 who have participated in the program since its inception, have not only shared their enthusiasm for the camp with their classmates every fall, but in several cases have embarked on outdoor-related careers, including photography, river guiding and working at backcountry lodges.

Expressing gratitude to the program's generous sponsors, Morrow said turning teenagers on to the mountains by visiting an undeveloped place via self-propelled, non-mechanized means is a way of paying it forward to the land itself.

"I hope to instill a sense of vulnerability of the land," Morrow said. "Their generation is going to become stewards of the land. Maybe they'll do a better job than we have."

2–4 EAT, SLEEP, SKI

The Grand Traverses

For mountaineers, glaciers are often one component of a route to a summit. Sometimes vertical seracs and steep glacier features, such as the Bulge on Mount Fay in the Rockies, become routes unto themselves for highly skilled and motivated ice climbers. Beginning in the 1960s, improvements in equipment helped ice climbers to ascend increasingly steep ice, and the sport of waterfall ice climbing evolved from what was originally a necessary mountaineering skill for reaching summits on glaciated peaks. In the 1990s, the practice of climbing steep and often overhanging cliffs of mixed rock and ice developed into the hybrid sport of mixed climbing.

For skiers, though, glaciers can make up the route, or much of it. They are the medium for travel. Glaciers often are the destination, the goal, the prize.

Western Canada's first long-distance ski traverse – one of several that are known as the Grand Traverses – was accomplished in 1958 by four young American men from Dartmouth College. The adventure of their desire was to ski 130 kilometres by linking glaciers and icefields from the Bugaboos, in British Columbia's Purcell Mountains, north to Rogers Pass in the Selkirks. Despite not having maps for much of the terrain they would cross, they were well prepared and were blessed with favourable weather for all but the last day. The ropes they carried allowed them to safely rappel (lower themselves down) some unavoidable steep cliffs. While April and May traditionally offer the best conditions for multi-day or multi-week traverses with long daylight hours, plus supportive snow right down to most valley bottoms and well-filled crevasses on the glaciers, their choice to travel in June left them negotiating some gruelling bushwhacking down low and some terrifying crossings of dangerous rivers raging with spring snowmelt. Still, they completed their route without mishaps in an impressive nine days.

Sixty years later, the Bugaboos to Rogers Pass Traverse is the most popular of western Canada's long-distance glacier ski routes. In 1989, the first all-female team, consisting of sisters Kathy Calvert and Sylvia Forest, and Lin Heidt and Martha McCallum, skied the route in 16 days. In April 2005, Troy Jungen, Douglas Sproul and Jon Walsh skied the entire route in a blistering 80 hours.

Rising on the west of the Rocky Mountain Trench, the Purcell, Selkirk, Cariboo and Monashee mountain ranges are all capped with massive icefields and glaciers. In 1973 Chic Scott and three friends, Don Gardner, Dave Smith and Ron Robinson, repeated the Bugaboos to Rogers Pass Traverse, travelling north to south. Two years later the same team pioneered the Northern Selkirks Traverse, skiing 200 kilometres from Mica Creek to Rogers Pass, crossing immense icefields and Windy, Haworth and Goat glaciers, among many others, over 15 days. Through the 1970s and '80s, the Grand Traverses were repeated by a young group from Calgary, key among them being an explorer of boundless energy and enthusiasm named Steve Smith. Over a period of seven years, Smith and his strong, determined companions would ski all the major traverses and pioneer several new ones. Today, every spring, after months of studying maps, dehydrating food for dinners, lunches and snacks and organizing food drops, several parties excitedly embark on wilderness ski traverses that link glaciers and icefields across the mountain ranges. Short ones can be completed in three days, others take three weeks. Some take longer.

In 1998, Dan Clark and Chris Gooliaff broke new ground by skiing the length of the Columbia Mountains, crossing glaciers, descending into forest valleys and then skinning – or sometimes carrying their skis while bushwhacking - back up onto glaciers and icefields. Over 61 days they skied 700 kilometres, beginning from McBride, British Columbia, and completing their adventure in Kimberley, in the south of the province. Along the way they traversed massive, remote glaciers and icefields of the Northern and Southern Cariboos, Northern Selkirks, Rogers Pass to Bugaboos and the Southern Purcell Mountains, resupplying with food caches along the way. It was a remarkable achievement for a team of just two men to share all the trail breaking.

In what was considered the last of the Grand Traverses, in 2004, Revelstoke's Greg Hill, Ian Bissonette and Aaron Chance spent three weeks skiing the 210-kilometre-length of the Monashee Range, with Jeff Volp and Dave Sproule joining them for the first week. It was not their first long traverse, and not their last either. Hill has excelled at long days travelling on glaciers. In 2006 he set a world record, skiing one million self-propelled vertical feet in a single calendar year. He bested that feat in 2010, skiing two million vertical feet that year. Many of those feet ascended and descended were on glaciers, some accomplished during long-distance traverses.

"These traverses remind me of the simplicity of life, with no concerns but the fundamentals of staying alive," Hill described. "Our group must act cohesively to safely move through the hazardous mountain terrain, which develops strong friendships,

Madeleine Martin-Preney surveys massive glaciers in the Sir Sandford area during her and her companions' 36-day, 520-kilometre first complete traverse of the Selkirk Mountains. Photo Sam McKoy

and the sharing of amazing moments. I have always been mesmerized by the timelessness of glaciers, and when travelling them I am transported back in time."

Season after season, keen adventurers continue to seek out new areas to explore. In the Coast Mountains, Vancouver adventurer Dave Williams, accompanied by an equally intrepid roster of friends, has, since the early 1990s, embarked on multi-week ski traverses and summer explorations of the range, recounting his travels on the remote and often unexplored glaciers and icefields in the *Canadian Alpine Journal*. In British Columbia's interior, over a period of 36 days in the spring of 2016, a determined team of five – Madeleine Martin-Preney, Stephen Senecal, Mark Grist, Sam McKoy and Douglas Noblet – skied more than 520 kilometres, with 42,000 metres of vertical gain, from Kootenay Pass near the US border to north of Mica Dam. By linking previously skied sections, they accomplished the first complete traverse of the Selkirk Mountains. Waking at midnight to avoid daytime warming that weakened snow slopes which threatened to bury them, they endured rain and fog in the valley bottoms, even becoming separated while fighting through twisted alders between steep raging creeks and canyons. The rewards were many, though, including an open-air camp high on Pyrite Ridge where they savoured views of the sunrise glow on the heavily glaciated giant of the range, Sir Sandford, from the comfort of their sleeping bags.

Those with bigger ambitions head north to Yukon to ski around Mount Logan – not only Canada's highest mountain, but the one with the largest base circumference of any non-volcanic mountain in the world. It takes a week to ten days to ski around Logan – if you're fit and the weather is good. The region's Saint Elias Mountains harbour numerous glaciers that have maintained gargantuan masses into the 21st century. Riding the Canada–US border, the Saint Elias–Wrangell Icefield is larger than the entire country of Belgium. The potential for long-distance glacier and icefield traverses is boundless.

The Purcell Traverse

Their first glacier crossing came on day one, right after lunch.

Steve Tersmette and Shawn Emmett, both residents of the East Kootenay mountain town of Kimberley, were at the beginning of a three-week backpacking trip to traverse the Purcell Mountains. By the end of 24 days, they would travel 271 kilometres on foot from Dewar Creek, at the southern boundary of the Purcell Wilderness Conservancy, hiking north until they stepped on the hard asphalt of the Trans-Canada Highway a few kilometres east of Rogers Pass at the Beaver Valley trailhead.

The adventure had been on Tersmette's mind for a decade, ever since he read an account by Dave Quinn in the book *The Purcell Suite* detailing his own 2002 attempt on the route, the only time it had been tried in summer. Knowing it had been twice completed on skis and that it began practically in his backyard motivated Tersmette to invite his good friend on board. For three years they planned, studying topographical maps and eventually committing to dates and arranging three food drops along the way.

On August 25, 2017, they heaved their 27-kilogram packs onto their backs and ascended a familiar overgrown outfitters' trail, climbing a gruelling 1800 metres from valley bottom to the summit of Radiant Peak, where a small remnant glacier hugs the steep north face. From there they would encounter few established trails in the undeveloped wilderness. And as they elected to avoid dropping down into valley bottoms – where one day thick alder ground their progress to a soul-crushing three hours to travel a single kilometre – they crossed 19 glaciers over the course of their journey. Most of those were small and were crossed in just an hour or two, but some, including the Conrad Icefield, Toby and Starbird/Stockdale glaciers, were significant and each took a full day to traverse.

Though small, even that first glacier proved a bit different from what the maps and satellite imagery showed, as it was steeper than expected and the ice was tricky for them to access.

"The ice was well below the lateral moraine and it was a steep/loose/exposed little downclimb to set foot on the snow," Tersmette described. "We were surprised nearly every time we stepped foot on a glacier. The most common theme was not only how far they had retreated from their position on topographic maps, but even the retreat from their positions shown in more recent satellite imagery."

Shawn Emmett, carrying a heavy multi-day pack, peers into a deep crevasse on the Toby Glacier, which is covered in pink algae commonly known as watermelon snow – because that's exactly what it smells like. Photo Steve Tersmette

Toby Glacier, for example, had melted back more than a kilometre from where it was marked on the most recent 1:20 000 TRM map. In the Bugaboos area, Howser Glacier was nearly three kilometres back from some rock cairns marked by BC Parks just a couple of decades ago. For the hikers, the melting of glaciers repeatedly left them to navigate unexpected terrain challenges such as steep or slabby headwalls, creeks and even lakes.

"We'd set out expecting to travel for so much time and distance on the snow and ice at a more rapid pace and instead find ourselves picking away at the debris left behind," Tersmette said. "On other occasions, we found it difficult to gain access to or exit from the glaciers as they had lost volume, making it harder to access the terrain above glaciers – such as moraines and ridges."

The hot, dry summer, however, aided their travel; most glaciers had shed the majority of the previous winter's snowfall, enabling them to walk on hard ice rather than post-holing in soft snow. It also meant water levels in creeks and streams were lower, making them easier and safer to cross.

"With the crevasses exposed and snow bridges melted out, the routes around the glaciers tended to wander a little bit, but it also meant you could see most of the hazards right in front of you," Tersmette said.

While their four days fighting through thick lower-elevation bush were demoralizing and often led to difficulties staying hydrated, the best moments, he said, were usually arriving at their camping spot.

"Most of the places we camped were spectacular – high in an alpine meadow, alongside a lake at the toe of a glacier, on a headwall with nothing but air below, at the base of a waterfall," he said. "After ten to twelve hours of grinding away the kilometres under the load of an expedition pack, getting into camp and getting our boots off, starting a pot of soup, having a drink of water and soaking in the scenery was always the best part of the day."

Shawn Emmett tends to camp chores under smoky skies with icebergs floating in the meltwater pond formed at the toe of the Vowell Glacier. Photo Steve Tersmette

Surprises were frequent; one day they found themselves looking at a massive crater scooped into a glacier's surface.

"I couldn't even offer an explanation as to its existence," he said. "We called it the alien ice circle. Our guess was 100 feet deep and 500 feet across."

While physically gruelling, spending three weeks amidst the glaciers of the Purcells was a highly rewarding and unforgettable experience.

"I love the remote and raw landscape of the glaciers," Tersmette said. "They have a very unique way of making human beings seem even smaller and more insignificant than we already are. Their ability to forge and shape landscapes is beyond compare. I love returning to the same glaciers and seeing how the earth has been altered by their retreat, which is very obvious in the summertime. The carnage left in their wake never ceases to amaze.

"In wintertime," he said, "glaciers seem quiet, serene and completely at peace; the world blanketed in white. The change of the seasons in these high places are incredible and while not as obvious as the change in the valleys or the meadows, the mutation of the ice and snow is far more surreal."

"I return to the glaciers to keep my world in perspective. It becomes too small if I'm not out exploring it. I love to be feeling alone and minuscule in these vast environments and to watch the planet alter itself rather than to see humanity force its change."

A Whole Other League

Then there's the Coast Mountains ski traverse.

The granddaddy of Canadian mountain ranges, the Coast Mountains extend a commanding 1600 kilometres from the Fraser River in southern British Columbia all the way to the Yukon–Alaska boundary. So vast that hundreds of major peaks don't even have names, the range lunges into the sky, in places rising above 3500 metres just 12 kilometres from the Pacific to form a veritable dumping zone for frequent and generous maritime storms. The constant inundation of snow and rain makes the range one of the world's most heavily glaciated. From the Misty Icefields just beyond Vancouver's northern city limits to the boundary with the Saint Elias Mountains, the Coast Mountains are home to a hundred expansive icefields and thousands of glaciers. Among them, the largest glacier found entirely within British Columbia is the Klinaklini, which spreads 470 square kilometres – an area larger than Winnipeg.

While most skiers who embark on long glacier traverses are satisfied by the end of two or three weeks of dehydrated meals, heavy packs and damp sleeping bags, in February 2001 Guy Edwards, John Millar and Dan Clark began walking on muddy, bush-choked forestry roads just beyond earshot of Vancouver's urban din. For months, day and night, they had planned their adventure. They had organized logistics with bush pilots and ski partners who would join them for segments. They had collected every crucial piece of equipment. They'd shopped, measured, packed and delivered two dozen food caches, some on foot, others by air drops. After all that, theirs was a rather uninspiring start as they slogged along under 39-kilogram packs – the heaviest they would be the entire trip – in a torrential downpour. Within minutes they were soaked to the skin.

Thus began a wilderness journey that would last five and a half months. It's been called, and with good reason, the most ambitious ski traverse ever. Before this group accomplished it, many hardcore mountain adventurers had declared it impossible due to the extreme distance, risks from avalanches, crevasse falls and severe storms busting off the Pacific. The team had two advantages: experience and youth.

Enthusiasm was essential, too, as more than once rain poured from dense skies, confining them to their tents for days. When the clouds finally parted, they'd pack up all their soggy gear and continue. When travel conditions improved, they covered 150 kilometres in just ten days. Hitting their stride, they adjusted from the frenetic pace of urban life to that of long-distance self-propelled travel in an environment untouched by man.

"The longer I'm out there, the calmer my mind gets," Edwards explained in a post-trip interview. "You get stuck in such a meditative and reflective mindset for so long, you become much more open and aware of the world around you. If you're a week-end warrior, you never get to get out of your daily regular workday mindset."

A fourth skier, Vance Culbert, joined them in Pemberton. Adhering to their trip ethos of non-motorized travel, he rode his bicycle the 153 kilometres from Vancouver. They crossed the Lillooet and Bridge glacier systems under blue skies and then began traversing over the massive Homathko Icefield, covering in just two weeks a distance they had estimated would take a month and a half. Speedy conditions meant that they had extra food to eat, an unusual and enjoyable luxury on a type of trip that more often demands times of rationing and constraint. They even had extra choco-late. Life was good.

Then, while they were camped on the Homathko, roiling charcoal clouds des-cended. Hunkered in their tents, which they fortified with walls built of snow bricks

Martina Halik skis down an icefield between the Iskut and Stikine rivers during her and her mother Tania's five-month ski traverse of the Coast Mountains. Photo Tania Halik

encircling their camp, they sat and listened. Snow fell incessantly, pil-ing deeper and deeper around their tents, forcing them to repeatedly ven-ture into the gale with shovels to excav-ate and re-excavate their canvas home. Attempting to walk beyond the snow walls, Culbert was soon pushing his way through chest-deep snow.

"The swirling snow in the air was in-distinguishable from the snow on the ground," Culbert wrote in the 2002

Canadian Alpine Journal. "After just a few metres, the camp was out of sight, leaving my track as the only feature to be seen. In this completely white world, with strong winds and no visibility, one's sense of orientation is severely challenged. Noting how quickly my track was filling in, I resigned myself to returning to our tiny world, crawling back into my damp sleeping bag and snuggling up with my snow-filled water bottle." (Quoted in Guy Edwards, "The Traverse—The First Complete Coast Mountain Ski," at p. 6.)

With just a few days' supply left, they used body heat to melt snow in their water bottles to conserve fuel. When the storm finally eased, they eagerly broke camp and began skiing. Their enthusiasm was quickly tempered by deep trail breaking, as it took them six hours to ski three measly kilometres – a distance usually covered in about 45 minutes. Finally topping out on a col, they were relieved to discover that the shallower snowpack on the north side granted them pleasurable turns all the way to the snow-covered logging roads of the Homathko River valley. It was there, far below the dangers of severe cold and vicious storms high on the icefield, that the team suffered the most serious accident of their trip when Dan Clark skied over a patch of exposed gravel protruding like a scab on the smooth snowy road. The abrupt change in surface sent him airborne. His fall was stopped by the force of his head crashing into gravel with his heavy pack still on his back.

Fighting the urge to lie down and be still – a choice he understood would be his last – he fished out extra clothing from his pack and put the layers on to counter the inevitable symptoms of shock. With blood pouring from the wound on his head, he applied a bandage and tied his pack to the plastic crazy carpet he'd used up on the flat glaciers to tow his heavy load. Worried that his head injury might cause him to lose clarity, he denied himself any painkillers. Then he began walking down the dark road to catch up to his companions.

An hour later, Edwards and Culbert were walking back up the road searching for Clark when they found him. Together they walked five more kilometres, his two friends encouraging and coaxing him every step of the way to the logging camp where their food cache was waiting. From there they arranged for him to be flown to Campbell River, a community of 35,000 on Vancouver Island, where he was diagnosed with severe fractures to his C1 and C2 vertebrae. The surgeon bluntly told him most people with this injury "end up in the morgue." While for him the ski trip was over, he was fortunate, after many months, to fully recover.

Linking One Place to Another

As they absorbed the sudden absence of their friend, Edwards, Millar and Culbert found their spirits were soon buoyed by the pre-arranged arrival of another friend, Kari Medig. Rendezvousing at Knight Inlet at the mouth of the Klinaklini River, he joined them for several weeks. Sixty kilometres north, another storm imprisoned them in their tents for four days as the raging tempest buried their camp deeper and deeper. The timing was lousy; they were only one day's travel from their next food cache.

"We started running out of food and fuel, and our sleeping bags and insulating jackets were getting wet," Edwards wrote. "Everybody's patience was wearing thin. Our card games had become too competitive, and we had started snapping at each other."

Just before their cabin fever exploded, the clouds parted enough to lure them from their tents and, over one long, tiring day, reach their next cache.

Bella Coola, home to fewer than 2,000 residents, was the first community they encountered after nearly two months of travelling. Nestled at the foot of domed hills swathed in cedar forest at the cul-de-sac of a 100-kilometre-long fjord reaching inland from the Pacific, the valley is one of just three coastal land areas with roads connecting them to the interior of the province. For the skiers, it was a hub of activity, with fresh food, new faces and conversations that energized them for the next leg of their journey.

Since the 270-kilometre (as the raven flies) section between Bella Coola and Terrace – the Kitimat ranges of the Coast Mountains – had never been skied, a sense of uncertainty increased the exploratory nature of their days. For much of that month-long leg, the mountains were lower with less glaciation, and fewer and smaller glaciers meant more work, as they had to carry their packs up passes and down into valleys several times a day, rather than towing their loads behind them on their lightweight plastic sleds. Manned by a crew of shift workers, the hydroelectric station at Kemano provided a comparatively luxurious one-day rest stop. Adapting to the new rhythm was just par for the course of their routine.

The most elusive of alpine travellers, a wolverine sprints across a glacier near the skiers' camp on the remote Andrei Icefield in the northern Coast Mountains. Photo Linda Bily

"I love that aspect of having a daily purpose – the main purpose is to cover ground," Medig shared in a post-trip interview. "I just love waking up and knowing that. You have to get back to the basics. You have to streamline and analyze every detail, try to make your days easier. Linking one place to another, by foot, day after day."

After 1080 kilometres, Terrace marked the halfway point of their adventure, where they said goodbye to Medig and welcomed Lena Rowat. A tireless explorer whose parents embraced outdoor adventure as an unmatched teacher of life skills, Rowat was among those few who believed the traverse to be possible. In fact, she'd been dreaming of skiing it for years. When she had learned of the men's plans, she had asked Edwards if she might join them. He had turned her down, however, since their preparations were too far advanced to incorporate a fifth person. Undeterred, Lena enlisted her sister, Ruby, to ski the traverse with her. So that spring, not one, but two teams had embarked on the "impossible" ski traverse. They launched a few weeks after the men, and skied the Vancouver to Bella Coola section in 54 days.

And then, serendipity, of sorts, intervened. When the two women were in the throes of the lowest moment of their journey, storm-bound in their tent for several days, low on food and with Lena battling a stomach bug, a satellite phone call to their father changed their fortunes, as he relayed to them the story of Clark's injury, and Edward's invitation that Lena join their team for the Terrace to Skagway leg. Hugging her sister goodbye, Lena hitchhiked the 1260-kilometre circuitous route from Bella Coola inland, then north and back toward the coast again to Terrace.

Skinny Dipping in Glacial Tarns

While team dynamics can be a delicate balance at the best of times on such a long and arduous journey, Rowat's presence was a positive addition to the male-dominated team, as she tempered the competitive natures. She was tall, strong and infinitely capable, and her delight in skiing in a flowery dress and swimming naked in glacial tarns went a distance toward keeping morale high, too.

John Baldwin skirts the edge of a sapphire-blue glacial tarn. The next day the glacier had shifted and the pool was gone. Photo Linda Bily

Beyond Terrace, warmer springtime temperatures necessitated that they travel during the morning to take advantage of snow slopes that had been frozen firm overnight to avoid avalanches caused by midday heat. Leaving the glaciers to descend steep, forested valley slopes, they endured arduous bushwhacking and negotiated creeks that had swelled with snowmelt to raging torrents. There they delighted in spotting wildlife and the vibrant colours of spring leaves and wildflowers, such a bold contrast to the white world of ice higher up.

Crossing the Canada–US border as the wild, rugged terrain, not politics, dictated, they passed through Stewart, British Columbia, a rustic village called home by about 400 – much reduced from its peak of 10,000 during its mining heyday in the years before the First World War.

Crossing vast tracts of ancient ice, they skied to the doors of the active Eskay Mine, as well as some abandoned mines and two extremely remote homes where they stayed overnight visiting the friendly and generous locals.

While their pre-trip planning involved amassing a sizeable collection of 1:50 000-scale topographic maps, they didn't have one for the area around the Choquette Glacier. Travelling in pitiful visibility caused by stormy weather, the skier in front would toss a red stuff sack attached to a cord onto the snow several metres ahead – to determine which way was up – employing an essential technique for skiing a glacier in flat light. After climbing onto the glacier, they began skiing down the icefall on the other side. Without a proper map, they hadn't realized how fractured and crevasse-riddled the ice was, but as soon as they did, they tied into their glacier rope so that if one of them fell in, they could be rescued.

"We skied back and forth lots, searching for a route, finally going over to the north side and steeply down below threatening seracs," Edwards wrote. "I was ahead, trying to cross over a bergschrund [large crevasse/slot in the glacier], when the edges collapsed into the slot! Me too. I fell into the slot!"

Falling ten metres before the rope attached to his partners caught him, he realized he was upside down in a "worm hole."

"Then a large block of ice fell from above and crashed into me. It pummelled me five feet lower, knocking my skis, poles and sunglasses off and grinding me into a little sub-slot." While his first instinct was to accept the fact he would be injured, he was relieved to find he wasn't at all. He was able to climb out of the crevasse by himself, but the rest of the crew opted to rappel over the bergschrund rather than follow his route.

Sun-Weathered, Hairy and Happy

Keen climbers as well as skiers, the team was excited when their route delivered them to the bases of some of the region's most enticing peaks. Chief among them was the Devil's Thumb, a dramatic granite spire that juts into the clouds like, well, a sharp-sided giant thumb poking up from the glacier floor. Setting up camp, they were joined by Culbert's girlfriend, Cecelia Mortenson – a skilled climber on her way to becoming an internationally certified mountain guide – to attempt the difficult climb. With meagre route information and minimal gear, since they would have to carry their heavy metal climbing hardware for the rest of the traverse, they made four unsuccessful attempts.

Their climbing interlude concluded, they carried on to the powerful Taku River, which they canoed across, and then made their way back up into the alpine for the final leg of their journey – crossing the enormous Juneau Icefield.

For five days they described their travel as "life in a milk bottle" as the snowy glacier surface blended seamlessly with the white of the sky. Or was that the ground? A mountain? Fortunately, the skies cleared to grant them views of British Columbia's highest peak, 4671-metre Mount Fairweather, and other hulking glacier-capped peaks of the largely roadless Saint Elias Mountains.

Then, on a foggy July morning, with Culbert's sister Heather joining them, the group executed their final "knee jarring" descent on a trail that led them right into the Alaska town of Skagway. They had skied, climbed or bushwhacked 2015 kilometres. And while the charming town is home to only 1,000, and its streets are lined with wooden boardwalks and restored Gold Rush-era buildings, after months of solitude high on remote icefields the bustle of tourists disembarking from a flotilla of cruise ships was too much for them. Switching snow for dirt trails, they hiked the fabled three-day Chilkoot Pass trail to the headwaters of the Yukon River.

"After five and a half months of skiing – travelling through winter, spring and summer – our bodies were tired, and our minds were frazzled. We were sun-weathered and hairy, but very happy. We had ski traversed the entire length of the Coast Mountains from Vancouver, BC, to Skagway, Alaska, and to the headwaters of the Yukon River. It had been one of the longest alpine ski traverses ever completed, along one of the wildest mountain ranges in the world."

But the story didn't completely end there. By the end of the traverse, romance was in the air between Rowat and Millar. Maintaining a relationship was a challenge for both, who were continuously embarking on their own independent adventures. In spring 2003, Lena and her father, Peter, returned to the Devil's Thumb with plans to climb it by its standard route, while Millar and Edwards attempted the more diffi-cult, unclimbed northwest face. As the Rowats were stymied by stormy weather low on the mountain, a long week later they faced the grim realization that the men had disappeared, likely during the same storm. Millar and Edwards were extremely tal-ented climbers, well liked, admired and respected. Their loss reverberated through-out the mountain community, and their names maintain their place among Canada's bold and visionary adventurers.

Rowat continued skiing the sections of the Coast traverse she had missed. The year before Millar died, with Kari Medig, Jacqui Hudson and Merrie-Beth Board, she skied a route she'd dreamed of as an extension of the Coast Mountains traverse – cross-ing the Saint Elias Mountains from Haines, Alaska, inland to Mount Logan, then re-turning to the coast at Cordova.

Writing in the 2003 *Canadian Alpine Journal*, Rowat recounted, "Our days stretched into fine lengths of meditation as we took in the vast beauty that con-tinually changed around us." Naturally, their journey included consecutive days of whiteouts too. "For a number of days, we zigzagged along a path behind our compass and GPS, careful not to lose our minds in the milk." After five weeks they reached Logan, where the East Ridge climbers' base camp provided a social highlight. After two weeks of gradual climbing they accomplished a team high point of 5640 metres, savouring sunny-day views across endless peaks and icefields before the thin air and dwindling energy turned them around; three days later Medig and Board climbed to within a few metres of Canada's highest point. Heading back west, they laboured for four days to cross the 123-kilometre length of Alaska's ten kilometre–wide Bagley Icefield, and suffered a major scare when Hudson fell into a crevasse. Continuing de-spite her injures, they finally reached the coast and hot showers after skiing 675 kilo-metres over 55 days.

Over the ensuing years, Rowat skied the sections she had missed when she hitch-hiked from Bella Coola to Terrace, completing the final 200-kilometre leg with her father in 2009. Now a midwife, she continues to explore the region, and remains the only person to have skied the extended 2700 kilometres of the astounding Coast and Saint Elias traverse.

John Baldwin

He's known by some as the King of the Coast Mountains. While it's a grand label for a humble person, there are plenty of reasons John Baldwin has earned this moniker.

Baldwin began exploring his backyard mountain wilderness as a teenager. As an engineering student at the University of British Columbia in his hometown of Vancouver, he joined the renowned Varsity Outdoor Club. Having read articles in the *Canadian Alpine Journal* describing others' trips in the Coast Mountains, he was familiar with John Clarke's exploits when Clarke was invited to share a presentation at a VOC banquet in 1977. Inspired, Baldwin launched out on longer and more ambitious adventures with his friends. When Clarke read about Baldwin and his friends' remarkable 220-kilometre ski traverse from Ape Lake, southeast of Bella Coola across the Monarch and Ha-Iltzuk icefields to their exit at Knight Inlet, Clarke knew he had to meet him. They connected as kindred souls and began embarking on long adventures exploring the remote corners of the Coast Mountains together.

Over more than four decades, Baldwin has climbed more than 700 mountains, many of them first ascents, and completed perhaps 100 multi-week, long-distance forays across the icefields and along the ridges of what is one of the last true wilderness areas on Earth.

"Shunning the easy path, John has forged his own way through some of the most rugged geography on the planet," said Canada's premier mountain historian, Chic Scott in his biography of Baldwin, *A Life in the Wild*. "He is a mountaineer and an explorer of the first order."

Through his adventures, Baldwin has shared his enthusiasm and his passion for wild places, through several publications. A researcher in civil engineering, he made time to write the backcountry skier's indispensable guidebook, *Exploring the Coast Mountains on Skis*, now in its third edition. He's produced eight custom topographic route maps for skiers and hikers looking to venture into different regions of the Coast Mountains.

A skier pulls a sled down the massive Grand Pacific Glacier, which flows 40 kilometres from the Saint Elias Mountains to the Pacific Ocean in northwest British Columbia. The group journeyed up the long glacier reaching up right of centre. Photo John Baldwin

But it's in the sublime photography and thoughtfully written essays and personal impressions expressed in his two coffee-table books, *Mountains of the Coast* and *Soul of Wilderness*, co-written with his wife and adventure partner, Linda Bily, where Baldwin's passion and reverence for the beauty and the magic of high, wild glaciated landscapes illuminate the peace and the powerful emotions found in those experiences.

"Icefields adorn the Coast Mountains like a string of pearls laid along the spine of the range, in some places

John Baldwin soaks in the stunning view of seracs on the Bute Glacier tucked at the end of Bute Inlet in a rarely visited area of the Coast Mountains. Photo Linda Bily

drowning all but the highest summits," he writes in *Soul of Wilderness*. "These icefields form the core of some of the largest remaining areas of wilderness left in North America. Every year in May, as the winter storms start to wind down with a shift to calmer spring weather, we head up into one of these remote, icy places.... Our usual objective is to traverse an icefield but the real goal is to spend time in wilderness regions. These trips combine our love of wilderness with our love of skiing."

Like Clarke, Baldwin is actively involved in conservation issues, including sharing awareness of climate change and how glacial loss is happening in western Canada, and how our ecosystem as well as the lifestyles of skiers and climbers are being affected. With this, he encourages others to live more earth-friendly lives by buying less, flying less and changing everyday habits such as driving more fuel-efficient vehicles, using transit, buying green power and carbon offsets and spending more time at travel destinations per the amount of time it takes to travel there. His books are printed on environmentally friendly paper and he donates a percentage of revenues to the backcountry ski community and to environmental organizations. (Read more about his books on page 314.) For his part, Baldwin explains his passion for wilderness as having two sides.

"They say home is where your heart is, and that is one side," he said. "And the other side is the earth is our home. And then for me I think that when you are coming home that is sort of combining the two. So, it's when you are in a landscape that makes your heart sing, you just feel alive and speechless at how incredible it is. And for me that landscape is mountains, that part of the earth that is the Coast Mountains and just being in it I feel at home and alive and in awe at how incredible it is."

Daring, Determination and Danger

The potential for injury, or worse, is a fact of mountaineering accepted by those who pursue alpine adventures. Rockfall from above can maim or kill a person on impact, while crumbling rock underfoot can send a person hurtling down a slope, off a cliff or a knife-edged ridge. Avalanches on snow slopes – including sufficiently steep glacier slopes – sometimes triggered naturally but often by a skier or climber, can fatally entomb a person in less than a minute. Cornices – shelves of snow created by strong, persistent winds that extend into thin air beyond a summit or ridgeline – can break off to send a person plummeting down, or land on a hapless party travelling underneath. These hazards are appreciated by mountaineers as challenges to be recognized and evaluated to the best of one's ability, and to be mitigated by safe route selection, protective equipment and diligence when moving through potentially dangerous terrain.

Knowing how to identify potential crevasses lurking under a glacier's surface by detecting the subtlest of depressions, and how to extricate a person who has fallen into one as well as how to rescue oneself, are all skills anyone setting off on a long glacier traverse on foot or skis will have mastered during an apprenticeship on numerous day trips and shorter expeditions.

Awareness and preparedness for all those risks, as well as some less expected ones, were on the minds of two women who spent half of 2017 skiing the Coast Mountain traverse from Squamish to Skagway. To tackle such a massive adventure as just a team of two was a bold enterprise – just as it had been for Lena and Ruby Rowat. Martina Halik and her mother, Tania – who was 60 years old that year – were both veterans of wilderness adventures and had both worked many seasons as professional ski patrollers. Tania, whose resume includes working as an avalanche forecaster and paramedic, grew up rock climbing, kayaking and Nordic ski racing in the Czech Republic, from where she made a daring escape on foot from behind the Iron Curtain with her husband while she was two months pregnant. A keen rock climber, Martina has worked as a snowcat skiing guide, and she put her skills as a professional photographer to good use on their adventure.

Tania Halik uncoils the rope to tie into her daughter to cross a crevassed section of the Great Glacier on the Alaska–BC border. Photo Martina Halik/Raven Eye

In a real tour de force, the duo skied, hiked and bushwhacked through tangles of hemlock and baby alder, ate, slept and skied some more for five and half months. Filmmaker Grant Baldwin featured them and their journey, along with other Canadian mountain people, in his award-winning documentary *This Mountain Life*.

While they did not complete the entire route as they were forced to skip a couple of hundred kilometres to avoid impenetrable webs of Coast Mountains alder bushes, they did accomplish their gruelling journey without any serious mishaps requiring "more than a band-aid."

For the unavoidable forested sections they did carry bear spray and bear bangers. Up on the icefields bear sightings are rare, Martina said, as there's no food for them up there, although occasionally they travel across ice in search of their next meal.

Given their small body sizes, Martina and Tania opted to have their food dropped en route so they would only have to carry seven to ten days' meals at a time – a decidedly heavy load for two skiers who weigh less than 60 kilograms each. The weather had other ideas, and they ended up carrying 17 days' food along with glacier gear and an inflatable raft for river crossings when consecutive storms prevented their food drops from being delivered more frequently. They experienced the discomfort of bitter cold, the frustration of unfound food caches, persistent precipitation and relentless route changes.

They each carried a 30-metre rope to be used in case one of them fell into a crevasse, and employed the basic technique of poking deeply with their avalanche probes in suspect terrain, all the while scanning for telltale sags and concavities that might signal a slot. With the entrance plugged with windblown snow, it's often impossible to know if a hidden crevasse would be too small for a person to fall into, or wide and deep enough to swallow a school bus. While usually in mid-winter the snowpack has stuffed crevasses to their brim, early and late season conditions are not as reliable. Sometimes they felt the snow drop under their feet, and they would ski across those sections hoping the snow bridge would hold. Roped together, they kept moving, winding their way through the maze of crevasses. If that wasn't challenging enough, sometimes those places came during the middle of a whiteout too. At other times, they used their ropes to build pulley systems to lower their packs down steep forested slopes and over small cliffs. But, fortunately, they never did have to use them for any crevasse rescues.

Tania Halik crosses a boulder field with her skis and plastic sled attached to her backpack to travel from one glacier toe to the next above Taku Lake in northwestern BC. Photo Martina Halik/Raven Eye

More People Have Stood on the Moon

Up on the icefields, on some days Martina and Tania savoured fresh powder, painting elegant ski turns on an unblemished glacier canvas. But on many, many days they skied in whiteouts. It was during one of those stretches that they experienced the most terrifying moments of their trip when Martina was knocked over and swallowed in a size two avalanche – large enough to bury and kill her – while her mother watched in horror from a safe spot. While the avalanche ran for 200 metres, she was fortunate to not be buried deeply when the snow stopped moving.

"For my mom, it was the single worst moment of the trip," Martina stated. "We were in a whiteout, and I disappeared from view while she watched the slope just crack and shatter like a pane of glass. Then she had to wait, the longest seconds of her life, before she could safely ski down to find me."

Their adventure granted them the life-shaping challenges they expected, and more than once pushed them to their limits, experiences Martina shared in her blog.

"There were the unfound food caches, the alder-choked river valleys, the unrelenting, soul-crushing, gear-snapping cold," she wrote. "For a while, there was a constant wish to give up and go home. To go sit in a hot tub, eat non-stop and never, ever, venture onto another icefield."

Along with the intense discomfort and fright, however, they shared moments of profound wonder, of soul-warming beauty, the sort of ethereal experiences that entice skiers and climbers to return repeatedly to glaciers and icefields, experiences Martina described as "the most remarkable and beautiful moments imaginable; magical ice caves and full moons over remote icefields and dancing powder turns down 2000 m (6563 ft.) of vertical." Finally walking into Skagway after half a year of continuously demanding travel, she reflected on the abrupt return to the everyday world.

"In that strange northern twilight so near to the solstice, I tried to come to terms with the fact that I wouldn't be walking up another mountain the next day, or the day after that. Traversing had become our life."

Looking back two years later, Martina said she felt they had seized a perfect window of time to take on the journey. Tania was 60 and strong and fit enough – still is, as I write this. "My mom is the perfect partner for this kind of trip. She's got the right head space." Following the Coast traverse, Tania repacked and spent the next three months on a remote self-supported canoe trip with Martina's sister.

"We weren't the best people to do this trip, there's lots of other people stronger and faster," Martina said. "But we were the ones who decided to try."

One of the attractions was to experience a level of remoteness not possible in many places on Earth anymore. Other than seeing some snowmobilers twice as they skied through the Pemberton Ice Cap area, they didn't encounter other people.

"There were many places where we wondered, are we the first people to ever walk through here in winter? Are we the first people to camp in this spot, touch that tree? More people have stood on the moon. And it's one of those few places in the world you can do that, where the near-continuous icefields make it possible to ski from one place to the next. We crossed icefields bigger than I'd ever imagined. And we saw climate change first-hand, staring with disbelief at glaciers that had retreated over a kilometre in a single year."

Their maps and aerial photos turned out often to be nearly useless. Lena Rowat had generously shared her maps with them, but due to glacial recession the route the original team followed just 16 years earlier was no longer viable.

"It's not possible to do their trip anymore," Martina said. "Lena said they never bushwhacked for more than half a day. It's crazy how inaccurate the maps were. We'd be surrounded by alder, and the maps said we should be on a glacier, but it was more than two kilometres behind us.

"Even with more recent satellite imagery, kilometres of glaciers were missing."

The farther north they travelled, the less accurate their maps were, particularly in the Stewart and Juneau areas.

Tania Halik savours some hot tea in front of their cooking shelter, next to their sleeping tent on an unnamed icefield above the Iskut River in northern British Columbia. Photo Martina Halik/Raven Eye

"Google Earth looked like there was half a kilometre of glacier left, this photo is six years old," Martina said. "We got there and it was just ocean. I didn't know glaciers could melt that quickly. I don't think it's even possible – what we did – anymore."

And how does she feel about that?

"Definitely a bit of fear, sadness and amazement. A bit of hopelessness. And gratitude. My children won't be able to do that trip."

2–5 TERROR, LUCK AND TRAGEDY

The Pack Came Back

Good old-fashioned adventure was really all Robert Maiman had in mind when he and his buddy, Dave Stephens, began skinning up the Athabasca Glacier to launch a four-day ski mountaineering trip in May 2001. Deteriorating weather left visibility just adequate for the pair to thread the gauntlet below the massive cliff wall of Snow Dome on their right, from where house-sized chunks of serac ice regularly crash onto the glacier below, and the crevasse-riddled icefall to their left. Despite having the third member of their group cancel at the last minute the night before, and knowing the added risk of being just two on the rope, the pair, who had skied the route before, decided to go anyway. Carrying 30-kilogram packs, they broke trail in 30 centimetres of fresh snow and a howling wind.

Skiing in the lead, in a nanosecond Maiman's world turned dark.

"It was so abrupt; it was a complete loss of orientation, of all reality," Maiman recalled during an interview years later. "I was fully conscious, but everything was black. It all happened in a matter of seconds, and I was looking for clues. I started putting two and two together – I'm falling! Why am I falling? I saw the bottom of the crevasse rushing up to meet me and YANK! The rope stopped my fall and I slammed into the crevasse wall about five metres above a ledge."

Dangling in the frigid, confined dark space with his skis still attached to his feet, Maiman felt sharp pain as he hung in his waist harness with the heavy pack on his back. Spending the next few minutes trying to control his breathing, he gradually absorbed the horrible reality of his situation.

On the surface, Stephens had watched in stunned disbelief as Maiman simply vanished. As the rope connecting them zippered into the glacier's depths, he was all but certain he'd be yanked in after his partner, but thankfully, the rope stopped moving just three metres in front of him. Stephens quickly built an anchor in the ice to secure Maiman from falling any farther, but as he did some ice pieces hanging under the lip of the crevasse were knocked loose, causing orange-sized chunks to rain down on Maiman. One struck his left thumb, another his shoulder.

"To say I was freaked would be an understatement," Maiman stated. Collecting his thoughts, he drilled an ice screw into the translucent wall and carefully managed to remove his pack and hang it from the screw with a carabiner. Removing his skis proved a trickier, more laborious task. Once that was accomplished, he surveyed his surroundings. He figured he was 12 metres from the light above. The slot he'd

Robert Maiman holds his ski after it melted out from being trapped in a crevasse where it was mangled and crushed inside the moving and shifting glacier ice for 12 years. Photo Kathleen Maiman

fallen into was about 20 metres deep, 12 metres long and 2 metres wide. Wild ice sculptures above, and at either end, made him cringe. He realized the reason he had fallen so far was that they had unwittingly been skiing parallel to the crevasse.

From his place in the pit, he could hear Stephens on the surface yelling down to him but couldn't decipher a word. Shouting at the top of his lungs in reply, he later learned his companion never heard a sound. Maiman would also learn that Stephens hadn't felt capable of raising him from the crevasse on his own, so opted to get help. As Stephens retraced their track back to the parking lot, hoping he wouldn't fall into any slots, Maiman waited. Alone.

As he'd been wearing only light layers as he had laboured uphill, it didn't take long for the ice walls to siphon the heat from his body. Using the extra rope stored in his pack – a basic precaution of roped-up glacier travel – Maiman lowered himself to a platform about five metres below him, taking his pack with him. Once there, he quickly pulled every extra piece of clothing from his pack and put them on, topping his layers with his life-saving voluminous down jacket – not an easy task with his aching thumb and shoulder. The floor he stood on was just a metre wide, and he knew he was not at the bottom of the crevasse. His stomach sank when probing the snow in front of him revealed it was bottomless.

Focusing on keeping his mind from panicking, he removed his skis and dug his crampons from his pack and strapped them onto his boots. With a prussik (short length of cord) wrapped around the rope hanging from the glacier surface, he was able to climb a few steps up by stemming his feet into the opposing ice walls as he slid the prussik up the rope with his one good hand. His attempt at self-rescue failed after about five metres of upward progress when the walls spread outward and he could no longer stem across the space.

"I resigned myself to waiting and sat on my pack trying to keep warm," he said.

"I took out my sleeping foam and rolled it out over my head as a poor substitute for an icicle umbrella. I spent five hours sitting there, contemplating life and death and hoping a serac didn't choose that moment to enter my crevasse."

Skiing down the glacier safely, Stephens arrived at the staging area for the Athabasca Glacier snowcoach tour buses, from where he was able to call the park wardens for help. Despite unstable weather, a helicopter soon arrived and ferried rescue specialists to the scene. Thirty minutes later Maiman was free and he was shuttled to hospital in Jasper aboard an ambulance. He remained there for two hours of "extreme rehydrating" while his then-wife drove up from Calgary with his spare van keys, and after a night in a hotel they drove home the next day.

Although the Parks Canada rescue specialists tried to retrieve his pack and skis, the overhanging and lumpy angles of the chasm walls made it too time-consuming and dangerous a project to continue from their stance directly beneath the precariously perched seracs on Snow Dome. His gear stayed in the crevasse.

Fuel Bottle from Jaws

Afterward, Maiman counted his blessings; after four quarts of saline to balance his dehydrated state, his only injury was his sore thumb. After five hours inside the ice, he'd been rescued from the crevasse alive. He'd had the good fortune to fall into a slot large enough that he didn't become hopelessly wedged between its ice walls before the rope stopped his fall. He'd been very, very lucky.

Three weeks later he followed GPS coordinates back to the site hoping to retrieve his pack, but the crevasse had been violently plugged with serac debris crashing down from above. "*That* was sobering," he said. Then late in the summer of 2013, a full 12 years later, Maiman received an email.

"It was pretty bizarre, the email came out of the blue," he said. "At first I didn't know what she was talking about."

A glacier walking guide had found his name printed in permanent ink on a backcountry shovel she found while leading a tour group on the Athabasca. Through Facebook, she tracked him down. Photos she took helped Maiman realize his pack had indeed melted out. The following weekend, just a week before their wedding, Maiman and his (now) wife, Kathleen, trekked up to the site, which, since it was summer, was a lumpy field of sooty ice gravel and ethereal blue meltwater streams coursing along troughs melted into the ice. Strewn in a colourful three-metre-long debris trail among the surface stones and rubble like castaway party decorations were the contents of his pack that had been lost inside the glacier for 4,489 days. The debris was about half a kilometre downslope from where he had fallen in, where it had been

The contents of Robert Maiman's pack lay scattered on moraine rock after the pack melted out from the ice where it had been entombed in a crevasse 12 years earlier. Photo Robert Maiman

trapped in the slow-motion conveyor belt of the moving – and thinning – glacier before it eventually lay exposed on the surface. Astonished, Maiman inspected the items one by one.

"The smell was a bit rude," he said. "But it was all there."

Crushed by the shifting ice mass, his skis and bindings were destroyed. His sleeping mat was so smattered with holes it looked like it had been used for target practice. Outfitted with rubber gloves, he triaged the items he could still use from those he couldn't. A little worse for wear, his 80-litre backpack was still intact. Inside a plastic bag, a carrot appeared surprisingly unchanged. An energy bar was still inside its wrapper, but "the consistency was suspect." His winter-weight sleeping bag, just two weeks old when he'd stuffed it into his pack, was in good shape – except for the foul stench emanating from its down stuffing.

"My MSR stove looked like somebody had taken a sledgehammer to it," Maiman described. "The fuel bottles looked like they came from the movie *Jaws* and had been crushed in a shark's mouth."

Tempted to keep his mangled Nalgene water bottle as memorabilia, he changed his mind when he noticed green slime lining its inner walls. After separating the items into plastic garbage bags, he loaded the reeking trash into his old pack, then strapped it onto the outside of the one he'd worn up there.

While it took three years after his accident before he felt ready to ski onto the Columbia Icefield again, Maiman did return to fulfill his original dream with a solid team, making ski ascents of Twins Tower, the North Twin, Snow Dome and Mount Kitchener.

That trip, he said, felt like he'd come full-circle, and preparing for it had inspired him to improve his backcountry skills. That included adopting a more conservative stance on the ratio of risk over reward, such as choosing not to travel on glaciers he knows to be heavily crevassed with just a single partner. To his gear arsenal he added tibloc ascenders to make climbing up a rope easier. And he invested more research into his trips and improved his situational awareness, such as recognizing which way crevasses are oriented. He also doesn't hesitate now to probe into the ice if there's any doubt about whether crevasses lurk under a thin snow bridge.

"There were so many things [in 2001] that conspired to make that event really serious, but I escaped, for the most part, unscathed," Maiman said. "But it did make me a better mountaineer."

Ice Slots Swallow Snowshoers, Snowmobilers

Skiers aren't the only people exploring glaciers in winter, as modern lightweight snowshoes have become increasingly popular with people wanting to enjoy the mountain wilderness.

In April 2018, two snowshoers were walking on the Athabasca Glacier when one of them fell into a crevasse. Their original plan had been to attempt climbing Mountain Columbia – an ambitious objective on snowshoes, which are slower than skis and not nearly as efficient for travel across a long, flat icefield – but when the weather turned cloudy and snowy, as it so often is on glaciers and icefields, they decided to leave their glacier safety gear in their vehicle and just go for a walk. They made good progress following the road plowed on the Athabasca Glacier for the snowcoach tour buses, and once they reached the end of the road, they continued, since the weather had improved.

The duo, neither of whom had much mountain experience, used a GPS to follow a track they had downloaded from a travel website. Unlike hiking trails, tracks on glaciers are temporary, and it's necessary for travellers to reassess their routes every time they go out, as the ice shifts and crevasses open and close from one season to the next. Hiking along, they navigated around crevasse slots and walked under huge seracs teetering above them as they surmounted a first, and then the second bench of the icefall successfully. As they crested a third step in the icefall, one of the two fell into a crevasse. Since they had left their rope and harnesses back in their vehicle, his partner could do nothing to help him. Turning his avalanche transceiver to search mode, the man on the surface obtained a distance reading telling him his partner was 37 metres below him. He called out to his partner, but received no reply, so he turned around and walked back down the glacier to call for help. On this trip, he had to cross a pile of fresh avalanche debris covering their recent track.

While he was gone, the man in the crevasse regained consciousness after being out for some time. Calling for his partner but receiving no reply, he was fortunate enough to be in a place inside the crevasse where he could switch out of his snowshoes, retrieve his crampons from his pack and strap them onto his boots. He then climbed out of the crevasse on his own and headed down the glacier. Remarkably, he fell into another crevasse, but was lucky to only sink to his armpits and pulled himself out. Eventually he

While undoubtedly having a terrific time, this kite skier zipping across the Wapta Icefield was travelling solo, which is never recommended on a glacier. Photo Lynn Martel

encountered a snowplow operator working to keep the tourist area clear.

Both men were incredibly fortunate to have survived their mishaps. But with snowshoeing requiring virtually no instruction – unlike skiing, which takes time, effort and more money to learn – increasing numbers of people on snowshoes are venturing onto some of the more easily accessed glaciers. As backcountry skiing requires specialized skis and bindings that release at the heel for climbing up slopes, shops that sell that equipment employ personnel who are well versed in the safety considerations of travelling safely in avalanche terrain and on glaciers. Within the national and provincial parks, where most of the easily accessed glaciers are found, sharing awareness of the dangers of travelling on glaciers is an ongoing effort.

Outside of the parks, however, is where snowmobilers go to enjoy their sport. With powerful motors and highly specialized hill-climbing capabilities, modern snowmobiles can travel much farther and much faster in a few hours than anyone can walk or ski in a full day, or even several. And snowmobilers, too, are venturing onto glaciers, where, due in part to climate change–induced melt, crevasses are opening in new places all the time.

In March 2016, a group of nine snowmobilers were riding on the Appa Glacier, which descends from the Pemberton Icefield two hours' drive north of Vancouver, when they discovered one of their group had disappeared. Retracing their route, they noticed snowmobile tracks leading off the edge of a large hole in the ice. Those on the surface weren't able to establish any voice contact, so they initiated a call for search and rescue help. While they were waiting, they spotted a helicopter carrying a group of heli-skiers, so they set off a flare. As always, the heli-skiing group was accompanied by an experienced guide, so once they landed nearby the guide built an anchor and, with an assistant guide belaying him, rapelled into the crevasse. The snowmobiler had fallen some 30 metres – ten storeys – and had not survived. While some of the deceased man's friends attempted to lay blame on the volunteers running the local snowmobile club by suggesting the hazards should have somehow been marked, their cries were deemed unrealistic. Glaciers are ever-changing entities, and anyone travelling on one – either slowly and cautiously on skis or snowshoes, or screaming fast aboard a heavy snowmobile – must be prepared and constantly vigilant for an unknown and potentially large number of cracks and holes large enough to swallow them.

Several years earlier, a snowmobiler had fallen into a crevasse in the same area but was fortunately able to escape the hole. When they returned three days later to retrieve the snow machine that had been left behind, the hole had completely closed over.

"When you go into the backcountry you are responsible for your own safety and actions, and that is the standard under which we all operate," said Tyler Kraushar, Pemberton Valley Snowmobile Club vice president, in an interview with CBC. "There's hazards everywhere. [Marking] actually makes safety go down because now [snowmobilers] are going to expect all the hazards to be marked. Conditions are constantly changing in the backcountry. That's the reality of nature."

Closure in Ice

Backpacks are not the only things that melt out of glaciers after decades or centuries of being entombed in ice. Animal carcasses, birds and ancient plants are regularly discovered as glaciers melt away.

Sometimes, human bodies are found too.

In 2014, a body was found on the Athabasca Glacier by a guide leading a group of hikers on an ice walk. As such discoveries do, it launched an investigation by the Royal Canadian Mounted Police (RCMP) into missing persons' files. After the initial find, RCMP officers and Parks Canada visitor safety specialists flew by helicopter to the scene and determined the body had indeed melted out of the ice, and that it had been there for many years. Once it was recovered by helicopter, clothing, hair fibres and personal items found with the body were examined in the hopes of linking those clues with a long-cold missing person file.

The man turned out to have been a 28-year-old from New Brunswick who had been missing for 19 years. Once his identity was established, his body was sent to the Office of the Chief Medical Examiner in Edmonton to determine the cause of death, but foul play was not suspected. The family, the *Jasper Fitzhugh* weekly newspaper reported, was relieved to have closure after so many years.

Another body that melted out in 2010 revealed a more definitive story.

It was discovered by a pair of hikers exploring a lightly visited area of rubbly glacier moraines bordering the Dome Glacier, one valley north of the Athabasca Glacier. The man's body was found on the surface of a flat exposed area of glacial ice. The public safety specialists who recovered the body presumed the man could have fallen into a crevasse and became trapped. With four missing persons files to work with, the

A group of photographers hiking on snowshoes watch a serac avalanche fall from the summit edge of Snow Dome. Photo Lynn Martel

RCMP relied on dental records to help identify the remains. Through the process, a mystery was solved.

In 1989, a pair of US climbers from Maine hiked onto the Dome Glacier, where they encountered a pair of local Rockies climbers. They all had their sights on the difficult alpine ice climb called Slipstream, a serious, challenging route that is climbed only by the skilled and experienced. Beginning at a small, broken glacier in its lower reaches, they kicked crampons and swung their ice tools (specially curved axes for ascending vertical water ice) to climb up nearly a vertical kilometre of blue ice formed from meltwater flowing down from the glacier that caps Snow Dome. Nearing the top, they climbed up 50 metres of steep glacier ice to reach flat-ish ground on Snow Dome's summit.

Once there, the US duo untied from the rope that had safely connected them through the steep, tiring climb, then walked around on the summit glacier in search of their descent route. In stormy weather and whiteout conditions, one of the duo was probing into snow at the edge of the cliff they'd just climbed up when the cornice he was inadvertently standing on broke off, sending him tumbling 1000 metres to the glacier below. Since they had untied from the rope, his partner was helpless to stop his fall.

The Rockies climbers descended with the distraught American, and the following day a rescue team began searching for the missing man, even using a dog to sniff for him at the base of the climb. When they returned the next day, the site they'd been searching was covered in snow blocks and chunks of ice that had fallen from above. After a week, the search was officially called off, and the body remained there for the next two decades. Since his body was found a full kilometre away from where he fell, it's likely the man was encased in ice, perhaps inside a crevasse, and crept along with the glacier as it slowly advanced until it melted out.

Probe, Pulley and Deadman

In the Canadian Rockies, the Icefields Parkway grants ready access to dozens of glaciers, to the delight of sightseers and adventurers alike. While most mountaineers take glacier travel and crevasse rescue courses and make a point of travelling with more experienced partners as they develop their own skills, every so often some-one makes a fatal mistake. And, with casual tourists with no mountaineering skills or even basic awareness taking advantage of that easy access, sadly, accidents do happen.

As North America's most visited glacier, the Athabasca is a prime tourist attraction that welcomes more than two million visitors annually, the vast majority during the summer months. Its parking lot sits a kilometre from the glacier's toe. While climate change–caused melting lengthens the walk bit by bit every year, hundreds of families stroll the path lined with interpretive panels every day June through September. Some use makeshift bridges to span the outlet flow – a raging, silt-filled torrent on a hot day – to walk on the glacier, despite numerous signs warning them of the danger.

Tragically, more than once an adult or small child has fallen into a crevasse and succumbed to prolonged exposure while rescuers have tried frantically to save them. But it's not always casual tourists who fall deep into the ice. In September 2017, a pair of climbers lowered into a pool of water swirling in a millwell on the Athabasca Glacier. A professional glacier walking guide first led her group to a safe location, built an anchor in the ice using gear from her pack, and then enlisted help from by-standers to haul the climbers out with her rope. Both were cold and wet, and one of them, who was in the water for some time, was unconscious. He did not survive.

"My heart sinks a little bit every time we get a call, and someone is in a crevasse," admitted Lisa Paulson, an internationally certified ACMG mountain guide who works as a visitor safety specialist for Banff, Yoho and Kootenay national parks.

"Despite all the practice you do, you can never quite prepare for how compli-cated it can be. Crevasses have all these *odd* shapes, and they're always different. It's usually complicated, not straightforward. And commonly not a good outcome, al-though I am always hopeful. We always act as fast as possible to get to the scene as safely as possible."

In Collie's time, the group had one option – rescue Thompson, and fast. Today, speed remains a crucial fac-tor, but emergency satellite communi-cation devices make calling for help easy and potentially effective. In many areas of the Canadian Rockies, how-ever, as in British Columbia's interior ranges and Coast Mountains, as well as

A mountaineer uses a ladder to investi-gate the inside of a crevasse. Photo Mike Mokievsky-Zubok

vast expanses of wilderness in Canada's north, cellphone reception is unreliable at best. Helicopter rescue is never guaranteed in stormy conditions. For many adventurers, that sense of remoteness and unfettered wilderness is a big part of the appeal. Escaping the tether of electronic communication is one of the blessings of true wilderness trips. But exploring these remote places demands a high level of awareness and preparedness.

Paulson recalled a mission on the Gong Glacier, located up a trail-less side-valley branching off the Icefields Parkway not far north of the Columbia Icefield. To reach their peak, two adventurers had hiked and skied for several hours, navigating multiple unbridged creek crossings beginning with the heavily braided Sunwapta River, which, although at a low flow, continues to pulse with icy glacier melt right through the winter. Threading their way through subalpine forest, they skied uphill and followed a creek to a rocky moraine at the snout of Gong Glacier, which they followed to the summit. No doubt they were exhilarated to experience the profound isolation of unpeopled wilderness, with no sign or sound of motors, machines or electronics and a panorama of wild mountain peaks. But that remoteness had a downside.

"It was a party of two, they didn't have a rope on and one of them backed up to take a photo and fell into an open crevasse," Paulson explained. "This was before folks had access to satellite communication devices. They didn't have any means of calling for help, and his friend didn't remember how to do a crevasse rescue. He stayed with him until he lost consciousness, knowing it would be a long day's travel on his own to reach the road to get help. That's hard – when surviving partners have to ski or hike out through hazardous terrain by themselves." Sadly, when the rescuers flew in by helicopter to retrieve the body, they were able to pull him right out of the ice with ease.

While skiing the Spearhead Traverse, skiers built a rescue system to retrieve a skier from another group who had fallen into a crevasse. Photo Isabel Budke

Quite often, though, rescuing a person from a crevasse is not an easy exercise. First, the rescuers must judiciously survey and prepare a site before they can begin the work of extrication. Remnants of snow bridges broken by the force of the person falling into the pit are carefully cleared away from the rim, ideally without knocking more snow and ice on the victim – as happened to Maiman. When the accident area is surrounded by other open crevasses yawning like hungry alligator mouths awaiting a meal, the helicopter pilot might have to rely on all her skills to delicately sling the rescuer – clipped by carabiner to the bottom of a 35-metre, or longer, rope – to the very lip of the crevasse. On cloudy days that render a white glacier blank and featureless in flat light, this could be difficult. It might even be unsafe for the pilot and likely the rescuer too, and sometimes just impossible.

Calling in rescuers is just the beginning.

If the crevasse sits under a snow-loaded slope with the potential to avalanche, the rescue team will first evaluate the need to carry out avalanche control work by dropping explosives from a helicopter to cause an avalanche pre-emptively before anyone is placed near the site. Those rescuers working with Parks Canada use a variety of tools to help pull a person out, including a pneumatic chipper, a tripod, specialized shovels to dig in confined spaces, and a hand-cranked, human-powered winch. The winch can be especially helpful when the raising operation is confined to a small space, and in an area where other crevasses pose a threat to the rescuers on the surface. It also enables the rescuers to control the speed of raising the victim, the act of which often must be accomplished in small, measured amounts to protect the victim.

Paulson's team members also resort to restaurant-grade propylene glycol, an alcohol-based odourless, colourless liquid that's used as a solvent and wetting substance in some processed foods. When a warm body touches ice, ice melts. As the person cools, an ice film forms on the body, freezing it to the ice.

"We spray/douse the glycol where their body touches the sides and let it percolate down, and it melts the ice film, making it possible to pull them out," she explained. "Crevasse rescue can take hours. People get so stuck, in combination with ice chipping and glycol use it can take tremendous force to recover their bodies."

No Two Crevasses Alike

With no two crevasses alike, surprises are something rescuers count on. Standing on the surface peering down into a dark confined space, they can't know the shape of the walls until they are snug between them. To aid them, they wear headlamps and sometimes attach a second light to their boot to illuminate the hole below. Sometimes the angle of the walls or the location of the victim requires that the rescuer drill ice screws into the wall to provide directional anchors to position the rope as they manoeuvre toward the victim. A slender person who falls into a crevasse presents extra problems. When a person falls into a crevasse, the ice sucks heat from their body. Eventually they lose consciousness. The slimmer the person, the farther down they slide. This was but one problem Paulson and her team encountered during a rescue high on the upper slopes of Snow Dome, which are wrinkled with crevasses and menacing seracs.

In this case, the ice slot was so narrow and tight the rescuer who was lowered down by his colleagues had to turn his head sideways. For his hands to reach the victim, he also had to be lowered inside the constricted space upside down. If that wasn't enough, thick grey storm clouds shoved their way steadily across the low-hanging sky, heading straight for them. The trapped man lost consciousness; he was likely hypothermic from being wedged in the ice for more than two hours by the time rescuers were able to arrive on scene. Cognizant of the deteriorating weather, the team members had flown in with all the gear necessary for them to camp, knowing the storm was predicted to last overnight. It was a good call, as five of them did spend the night up there. Knowing speed was of the essence, though, they worked as fast as they could to free the man, so he could be flown out to safety before the weather closed in. But he was really wedged in, and after using glycol and the pneumatic chipper they felt they'd done all they could.

"But we gave it one more go," Paulson described, "and surprisingly, we managed to pop him out."

A brief window when the clouds lifted just high enough and just long enough granted them a few minutes to call the helicopter to pick up the victim. In challenging flying conditions, the pilot lifted off amidst swirling snow and dropping cloud. Pilots who work with the public safety rescue professionals are required to pass a rigorous exam with Parks Canada and a check pilot, mastering skills that make them among the best in the country. The difficult flying conditions, however, rendered it impossible for Paulson to perform any first aid, as she was obliged to strap on her seatbelt.

Matthew Breakey skis carefully past a large crevasse on the backside of Sugarloaf Mountain carrying a heavy pack during the nine-day, 130-kilometre Bugaboos to Rogers Pass ski traverse. Photo Phil Tomlinson

"I think the pilot did an amazing job of tracking the terrain and his instruments to safely lift us out," Paulson said. "I always feel I am in good hands with the pilots we use. We couldn't do what we do without them."

Two minutes later they landed safely in the parking lot where paramedics were waiting. The ambulance crew cared for him every way they could for the duration of the one-hour drive as they transported him to Jasper, and from there he was flown to hospital in Edmonton by STARS air ambulance.

Despite every effort, he didn't survive.

Of ten crevasse rescue events Paulson responded to in her career, in only a couple did the person survive. It's imperative, she advises, that adventurers seeking to travel on glaciers gain instruction from professionals such as those certified through the Association of Canadian Mountain Guides, ideally with the friends they plan to travel on glaciers with. While professional rescuers are often an hour or two away in the national parks or some provincial parks, in other areas the only rescuers available are volunteers, who, while highly trained and experienced, might not be as close by.

"Practice rescue techniques, a lot, and be ready to improvise and trouble shoot," Paulson suggested. "Learn how to avoid having an accident to begin with. We have talented rescue personnel in Parks Canada and rescue pilots who come together to help, but there's only so much they can do and they are usually at least an hour away – if the weather's good."

"At least with a rope on, the person should not fall too far in, and chances are the partners can arrest them," she added. "You might end up with a dislocated shoulder, but chances are you won't die. If you're not roped, it's serious. Crevasse calls – they're tragic for surviving party members. And for rescuers too."

A helicopter delivers two propane pigs to the site at the Rockies' Des Poilus Glacier during the construction of the Alpine Club of Canada's Louise and Richard Guy Hut. Photo Pat Morrow

3 COMMERCE FROM ICE

The value of rivers, streams and lakes are the highest of all ecosystem service values we calculate for nature, higher near urban centres. Intuitively you know that there would be no replacement value for glaciers once they are gone or melted away.

—Mark Anielski, economic strategist

3–1 ENCHANTED ICE CANYON

Clouds Thick as Dryer Lint

"Pack a big lunch and don't forget your headlamp."

It was Friday morning and I was industriously working my way through a lumberjack's breakfast of pancakes, sausage and hash browns cut from roasted potatoes left over from the previous night's dinner. Normally a fruit with a single slice of multigrain toast for breakfast kind of girl, I knew on this morning that I needed to pack in as much food as I could swallow.

I was one of a group of a dozen backcountry skiers who had been following our ACMG mountain guide, Larry Dolecki, up and down snowy mountain slopes day after day since a helicopter had delivered us to Icefall Lodge the previous Saturday.

The flight alone was eye-popping. Lifting off from the small railway/forestry/ski/mountain biking town of Golden, British Columbia, the machine flew north above the broad, flat Columbia River valley, then banked east straight toward shimmering snow-crowned rocky peaks. Threading through a narrow col, we cruised over deep forested valleys split by a broad, braided riverbed that dead-ended at a massive cliff wall decorated with frozen waterfalls hanging like giant holiday streamers. Then we banked a tight left and flew up a narrow valley thick with snow-laden cedar trees covering slopes that grew progressively steeper. Under the shadow of resplendent glaciated peaks and chiselled white ridges and cirques, the helicopter landed with precision on a tiny wooden platform amidst a cluster of log cabins nestled in the woods just below treeline. Once we, and all our gear and food for the week, were unloaded, and the previous week's skiers – all smiles and tired legs – had left to return to the real world, the helicopter flew away, not to return for a week. The enveloping quiet was glorious.

Our diverse group included two skiers and a snowboarder touring on her split-board (which separates for the climb up, then reattaches for the ride down), who were modelling for next winter's catalogue for a sportswear company. Two photographers – one a novice backcountry skier from Boston – plus two aspiring ski guides training under Dolecki's supervision completed our party. On our first day, Dolecki had instructed everyone in the group on the use of avalanche transceivers, probes and shovels, sharing key pointers on safe travel in avalanche and glacier terrain.

Every day we feasted on a big breakfast – thanks to the multi-talented apprentice guides who doubled as proficient backcountry cooks – and stuffed lunches into our backpacks alongside a thermos filled with hot tea, avalanche shovel, probe and extra clothing. Out the door and onto our skis by 9:00 a.m., we'd follow Dolecki, who broke trail, sometimes for two hours or more at a stretch, through knee-deep snow. Once we reached a col or high point on a forested slope, we'd strip off our skins and, hooting in delirium, float in fluffy, buoyant powder snow, gliding past giant cedars standing tall like forest sentinels. Then we'd skin up and do it again and again, saving barely enough energy to return to the hut – and the wood-burning sauna – and another scrumptious dinner before drifting off to dreamland under toasty down duvets. With no other humans for miles around – Icefall Lodge's tenure is ten times the size of Whistler Blackcomb's – the week was pure heaven.

A guest skiing at Icefall Lodge in the western Rockies watches as ACMG mountain guide Larry Dolecki prepares to ski through an unexplored canyon formed between 10-metre-high crevasse walls on the Tempest Glacier. Photo Lynn Martel

On this, our last day before the helicopter returned to retrieve us and deliver next week's eager guests, we knew we were in for something a little bigger.

With light snow falling, we skinned up toward Mount Kemmel, with Dolecki pushing a steadier pace than on the previous days. Feeling tired after a full week of ski touring, I half wished for a full-blown storm so I could retreat to the sauna. I never asked exactly where we were going; I resolutely pushed myself to fol-low. After two hours of climbing we stopped and peeled off our skins. Flat light pro-vided extra uncertainty for an untracked run down a glacier valley parallel to the one we'd climbed. Skiing in a monotone world, I was grateful for how the bright colours of the ski models' clothing stood out in vibrant presence against the white slope, helping to provide definition amidst an opaque landscape. At the bottom of the run on partially wind-stiffened snow, we regrouped for the next climb.

"If the light stays like this – which is just good enough," Dolecki said, pointing to silhouetted cliff bands looming above the milky snowfield, "we'll climb all the way up that glacier for about two and a half hours."

I purposefully ate and drank, summoning all my energy to embrace the pace of a long day out. Visibility was marginal, with a few closer mountains peeking through clouds thick as dryer lint. Massive rock faces rose up from the ice like dark brood-ing fortress walls. Then we rounded a corner on the moraine to face a giant jumble of blue-tinted glacier seracs. Instantly, anticipation evaporated all my tiredness like spindrift off the rocky peaks; we were climbing through an icefall!

Weaving a safe line through a maze of crevasses and broken serac towers, Dolecki led us past glacial formations that revealed tunnels and caves bored into the ice. Skiing slowly uphill in the snowy quiet, I felt like we were clandestinely investigat-ing an unknown planet. Then from a snowy bulge on the slope surrounded by silhou-etted jagged cliffs and glimmering blue ice blocks, we stripped off our skins for the long, long untracked 1500-metre run down.

But first, Dolecki skied a short distance down around a smooth, snow-capped knob and stopped at the mouth of a slot canyon cleaved right into the glacier.

"I think we can ski through here – follow me," he said with a wave.

Tingling with anticipation, we peered into a gorge in the ice that dropped five metres below the glacier's surface. Dolecki skied down into the chamber where two-storey-high walls of striated blue ice towered above him. Then, with appren-tice guide Corin Lohmann belaying him on a rope, Dolecki disappeared through the ice corridor. We collectively held our breath. Would the corridor allow him to pass through? After a distant shout from Dolecki, Lohmann pointed his skis and followed the voice through the chasm. Yippee, they'd made it through, the canyon was clear!

One at a time, we followed. With giant butterflies fluttering in my belly, I side-slipped down the launch ramp. Then with a deep breath I let my skis glide. For a few magical moments I whizzed through the blue-ice slot-canyon, at its narrowest less than three metres across, close enough for me to touch both sides of my many-thou-sand-year-old surroundings. Breathing in the crisp winter air, I felt fully immersed in a deep, mysterious pocket of the world. Like rings on a tree, the striated layers of the glacial walls revealed century upon century of natural history, preserved and concealed from any human interference. Since Dolecki had only been running Icefall Lodge a few seasons, and the location was too far to reach in winter except by helicopter, the chances of any other humans ever having skied through this ice canyon – which would quite possibly not even exist the following winter as the glacier shifted and moved – were nil.

Much sooner than I would have liked, I emerged on the far side of the frozen ravine to join those who'd skied through ahead of me where they had gathered on a small patch of flat snowy ground surrounded by gaping crevasses lurking on all sides. Bursting with excitement, we waited to savour the expressions of those yet to come through.

Jubilant, we skied 1400 more metres of untracked, and still falling, fresh powder down the glacier, over rolls and lower down through sparsely treed glades for 90 glorious minutes, periodically regrouping, hooting and laughing all the way to valley bottom.

While we would have to climb nearly a vertical kilometre on a gradually winding uphill track through thickly forested slopes to return to the lodge – two and half hours for the stronger skiers, yet an hour longer for a few of us, resulting in day that was ten and a half hours long – no one uttered the faintest word of complaint. We feasted on dinner and chatted excitedly over the last of our week's wine stash, reliving our day.

Guests at Icefall Lodge ski and snowboard through glacial seracs. Photo Lynn Martel

Through the course of that winter, Dolecki's Tempest Glacier tour was a big hit with subsequent guests, but our group was the first ever to ski through the enchanted ice canyon.

Tucked into our warm beds with the roaring wood stove keeping the lodge warm, that night we all dreamed of sweet powder turns. And for days, my mind's eye recalled the striated layers upon layers of glacier ice and wondered what stories those layers guarded about the centuries they'd seen without any human witnesses.

3-2 COMFORT IN THE CLOUDS

A Jewel Amidst Stones

Building small, self-contained cabins in high mountain locales is a cherished mountain tradition. The Swiss mountain guides employed by the Canadian Pacific Railway at its Lake Louise hotel through the first half of the twentieth century were well familiar with the custom and the benefits of climbers' huts, or refuges, as they are known in Europe's Alps. Rudolph Aemmer, Christian Hasler and the brothers Ed, Ernest and Walter Feuz had all emigrated from Switzerland in the first decade of the 1900s to work for the railway at its hotels under contracts that much favoured their employers in a time when hopping back across the Atlantic wasn't an option. Several of them settled permanently in Golden, British Columbia, where their wives and children lived in drafty, poorly constructed houses perched in full view of rail passengers atop a bench several long kilometres from the shockingly – from a more refined Swiss perspective – rural town. The guides lived there too, sporadically, during the off-season when they weren't out working on hunting trips or as labourers clearing snow from the hotels' roofs during the winters. Dapper in their wool knickers, felt hats and gripping sturdy wooden alpenstocks in their hands, the guides were very popular with the hotel guests. Women swooned.

For the well-heeled clients coming from sea-level homes in Toronto or Boston, just disembarking from the train at 1536 metres in the Lake Louise hamlet was – and still is – a breath stealer, and not just for the area's stunning beauty. From the luxurious Chateau Lake Louise on the banks of the postcard-perfect aquamarine lake, it's more than a vertical mile to the summit of Mount Victoria.

"By the time you got on top – if you ever made it that far – your tongue was hanging out, your heart pounding and your legs were dead," described Ed Feuz, who died in 1981 at the age of 96, in *The Guiding Spirit*, by Andrew J. Kauffman and William L. Putnam. "You had no taste for the view, nor, for that matter, for the cheese, the salami, the smoked salmon and the bottles of wine the hotel had carefully packed for our pleasure." Pre-dawn starts and long, long days were not easy for anyone. The project of building the Rockies' first climbers' hut, however, to make the Rockies "more civilized," would certainly not be easy on the guides.

The location was a logical choice. Abbot Pass is a narrow rock-strewn notch well into the cloud zone linking Mounts Victoria and Lefroy. Not quite flat for less than the width of a single-lane road, the pass drops steeply on the south side from where hikers choose a careful line to avoid tumbling boulders as they ascend a treadmill

Climbers strap on their crampons to climb Mount Huber, 1909. Photo Byron Harmon, Whyte Museum of the Canadian Rockies, Byron Harmon fonds (V263/I/A/i/a/na-168)

scree slope from Lake Oesa. Helmets are a must. The north side slithers down a narrow gorge pinched between steep rock walls via a long, slender glaciated arm that reaches down valley for about three kilometres. There it peters out into a wide field of moraine rubble below the Plain of Six Glaciers teahouse, which was built in 1924 by the railway as a rest stop for guests on their way up to Abbot Pass. From the glacier's toe, six kilometres of well-travelled trail leads back to the hotel.

Rudolph Aemmer and Ed Feuz drew up some plans, despite the fact the railway wasn't interested in their project. Eventually they found an ally in a Canadian Pacific construction superintendent named Basil Gardom, who convinced his employers a high alpine hut would be a sound investment. Construction on the shelter began in the summer of 1922. The logistics were stupendous. Two tons of cement, lime, timbers, windows and tools, plus a stove, beds, mattresses, bedding, cooking pots and pans, right down to the cutlery, had to be ferried up to the site. Food, too, to fuel the guides. It was all loaded onto a raft and paddled from the hotel to the southwest end of the lake. From there every piece was unloaded and carefully packed onto horses led by a wrangler who coaxed them onto the glacier – then extending some two kilometres lower than it does today – carefully guiding them around one crevasse and then the next. The steeds plodded upward on the bare summer ice until they reached a large gaping crevasse that stopped them in their tracks. From there the guides took over the Sisyphean job of man-hauling everything up the steep slope by rigging the jumbled icefall with a series of ladders and winches to facilitate carrying loads on a sled, each parcel weighing up to 35 kilograms.

Anything that couldn't be loaded onto the sled they carried on their backs as they continued up the Death Trap – as they named the steep upper reaches of the glacier in apt reference to the unpredictable blocks and chunks that crash down from the unstable ice cliffs above. Once they were at the pass, thankfully, all the stones they needed to build the walls of the hut were already strewn all over the ground. With the help of a skilled stonemason they'd hired, the guides just had to gather up enough of them in the right sizes and shapes. The structure was then fastened to the bedrock with cables. Naturally, their work efforts were interrupted from time to time by howling gales. Abbot Pass Hut opened its doors to guests early in the summer of 1923.

"The cabin had a big room for the kitchen and dining, a gentleman's dormitory, an attic with lots of mattresses," Feuz described. "There was even a sleeping room for ladies." For a time, there was even a pump organ for musical entertainment. As it was equipped with a pot-bellied stove, the guides carried firewood up to a spot below the hut where they kept it hidden, and then sold it by the bundle to hut users. No doubt they'd earned every cent, not an extra crumb of which was ever offered by the railway.

The Death Trap

On one trip to deliver firewood, Ed Feuz and Christian Hasler gained more than they bargained for as they hiked up with four young hotel workers who wanted to see the hut. "We'll be glad to have you," Feuz told them, "and you can carry some wood and maybe even make a little money."

Leaving the Plain of Six Glaciers teahouse –run by Feuz's wife, Martha – at 5:00 a.m., they moved up the glacier in two teams, each man with a load of wood on his back. "There's a lot of ice, big chunks like a house, that tumble off the mountains, mainly Victoria," Feuz described in The Guiding Spirit. "We called this place the Death Trap because it was so dangerous. We usually went through it as fast as we could. It was a spooky place, even for us guides."

At the time, however, the route granted the most direct access from the hotel to Abbot Pass and Mounts Victoria and Lefroy, peaks that were popular destinations for their paying guests. Nowadays most climbers and hardy hikers bound for the hut avoid the Death Trap by riding the bus up the Lake O'Hara road to walk well-built trails to Lake Oesa, then up a rough trail that switch-backs up the steep rubbly slope. In addition to the deadly falling ice, glacial recession has enlarged the crevasses and the bergschrund where Victoria Glacier separates from the mountainside not far below the hut, rendering the Death Trap mostly impassable.

On that day, though, with each guide leading two young workers, the two parties had spread out, as is normal practice, so that if they were hit by an avalanche, hopefully not everyone would be buried. Climbing slowly under their heavy loads,

Alpine Club of Canada members descend the Death Trap, 1907 or 1909. Photo Byron Harmon, Whyte Museum of the Canadian Rockies, Byron Harmon fonds (V263/I/A/i/a/na-37)

by 7:00 a.m. they reached the lower part of the Death Trap when the early morning quiet was pierced with a CRACK! Like thunder following a lightning bolt, a loud boom reverberated back and forth between the canyon walls. Leaving no time to react, an enormous white cloud of swirling snow poured straight toward Feuz. While the others scrambled to seek even the most optimistic shelter, Feuz was fully engulfed as hurricane-force winds lifted him and sent him tumbling into a washing machine of churning snow and ice. One moment he was on top of the turbulent flow, then in an instant he was submerged. As he felt himself being sucked under the rapidly settling snow and ice, he thrust one arm in the direction of the sky.

It was a move that would save his life.

"I couldn't even move a finger," Feuz described. "All that snow and stuff froze solid the second it stopped, solid as a rock. There was just a little pocket of air in front of my face, so I could breathe, but the air wouldn't last long." Fortunately, one of the young workers had eluded the avalanche and spotted Feuz's fingers sticking up through the snow. Without gloves, the young worker dug frantically, screaming in pain from the cold, abrasive granular snow. Alive but with a sprained ankle, Feuz and the boy searched for the missing hotel chef. Their packs, ice axes and other gear had all been stripped away and swallowed by crevasses. After half an hour and ready to give up, Feuz spotted the man's hat between two blocks of ice. Miraculously, his head was underneath it. Lying just under the snow surface, he lay immobilized with his hands folded on his chest, still breathing.

The other party didn't fare much better. The force of the wind had slammed Christian Hasler against the cliff. Long before the days of mountaineering helmets, one boy was bleeding from his head where he'd been hit by falling ice. Gathering what was left of their spirits and strength, the group limped back to the teahouse, where Martha and Ed's daughters, who also worked there, greeted them. Having heard the roar of the avalanche and seen the billowing snow cloud, Martha had prepared herself for the worst – that her husband might have been killed – and had stoically focused on the work of running the teahouse.

Such was the life of a mountain guide's family in the 1920s.

While the hut did make the guides' lives a bit easier, it didn't make them any richer. A guide's wage at the time was $4/day. Hazards including, but not limited to, avalanches, crevasses, rockfall and encounters with wildlife – Hasler was seriously mauled by a grizzly several years later – were part of the job. Workmen's compensation and life insurance for their families were not in the picture.

Treasure Under Threat

The presence of the hut at Abbot Pass, however, helped lure guests to Canadian Pacific's grand hotel at Lake Louise, and also to the Banff Springs Hotel. Huts were good for business.

To their credit, the Swiss guides knew what they were doing, not only as mountain guides – they made more than 400 first ascents, with not a single client ever dying on a climb – but also as hut builders. Nearly a century later, Abbot Pass Hut still stands; in 1992 it was designated as a National Historic Site of Canada.

While today it is cared for protectively by the Alpine Club of Canada, which has been charged with its maintenance and operation since 1985, it wasn't always the case. While the Swiss guides did their best to keep it in good order during the decades they used it regularly, by the mid-1950s interest in their services from the hotels had waned to the point that Canadian Pacific cancelled the program. Visitors to the Rockies were driving their own cars, not riding in trains, and they pretty much stopped hiring mountain guides. Consequently, the hut suffered from serious neglect, and was abused by rowdy partiers. Under the purview of Parks Canada in 1969 some suggested burning it, overlooking the fact it was constructed of stone.

Some local climbers, however, had better ideas. They took stock of its condition: it was filthy, a missing section of roof allowed snow and rain to pour inside, the entrance was broken, and the floor was cracked right through. They shared their concerns and expressed their willingness to carry out the work necessary to restore the building with Peter Fuhrmann, then alpine specialist for Banff National Park. As a rescue specialist and professional mountain guide originally from Germany, Fuhrmann was a keen climber and unabashed lover of mountain huts. He was also an effective manager and helped ensure an adequate budget was allotted, and a hardy team of volunteers tackled the massive job, which began with filling 30 garbage bags with refuse.

Today the hut is a favourite among the Alpine Club of Canada's two dozen backcountry huts and is booked throughout the summer months by recreational climbers, intrepid hikers and professional mountain guides leading clients up Mounts Lefroy and Victoria who each pay a fee to the Club for the privilege.

Abbot Pass Hut was built in 1922 with stones from the pass. At the time of publication, the foundation was undergoing remediation work as the warming climate had caused the foundation to deteriorate. Photo by Paul Zizka

As the hut is perched on the Continental Divide, not only does snow melting from its peaked roof flow to two different oceans, but the boundary separating Alberta and British Columbia runs right down the centre of the floor. Until the Club's Neil Colgan Hut was built in 1983 on a small col high above nearby Moraine Lake, Abbot Pass Hut was the highest permanent structure in Canada.

In recent years, though, Abbot Pass Hut has begun to suffer from a new kind of threat as the ground it was built upon begins to thaw as a result of Earth's warming climate. As of the summer of 2017, ice that has for millennia glued together the rocks and clay the hut is built on like cement has melted, causing the ground under the building to erode. The following summer, a sudden burst of erosion caused more terrain under the hut to crumble down the steep slope. Deemed unsafe, the hut was closed to visitors. A technical survey revealed that the ground under the building is mostly solid rock, so it was determined rock anchors could be drilled into that bedrock to shore up the foundation, and netting and other methods could be employed to counter the erosion.

As reported by the CBC, the Alpine Club of Canada was open and forthcoming about the cause of this new threat to the National Historic Site, explaining how the Swiss guides who built it never imagined the ground supporting the building would cease to be frozen.

"This is something that was not even on their radar in 1920, when the hut was [being] built," said Alpine Club of Canada spokesman Keith Haberl in an interview with the CBC. "It seemed like that ground would be frozen forever. It was frozen every summer. There didn't appear to be any risk of it melting at all. And now we're seeing consistently higher temperatures at that elevation."

Curiously, Parks Canada's official communication would only admit to climate change *possibly* being "a factor in the slope failure," adding that "without concrete evidence [we] cannot confirm it is a direct cause."

That statement left at least one long-time Parks employee shaking his head after reviewing a draft statement that was circulated (and which was amended after his response) that flat-out denied climate change could be responsible.

"I think we should acknowledge that this issue is directly related to climate change," wrote Glenn Kubian, a wilderness management specialist, in an internal memo obtained by CBC through the Freedom of Information Act.

"The slope is failing due to the melting of permafrost, which has been exposed for the first time in our known history. The slope is exposed due to the recession of glaciers in the area, an effect and correlation directly linked to climate change, which is well documented by glaciologists doing research in the mountain parks and Western Canada."

With that, Kubian reminded his colleagues that Parks Canada was a federal agency that falls under the responsibility of Canada's Minister of Environment and Climate Change.

"Given that this is a major platform for our minister we should take advantage of this important opportunity to educate the public on the direct effects of climate change," Kubian wrote.

Within the directors, management and staff of the Alpine Club of Canada, however, the cause is unquestionable.

"It's undeniable what climate change is doing to our mountains, and this is one example of it," Haberl said.

By the end of the 2019 summer work season, with the cost reported at $1.3 million, and climbing, the hut remained closed with hopes for the work to be completed by fall 2020.

Doorway to Glaciers

Following the heralded opening of then Canadian Pacific–owned Abbot Pass Hut in 1923, over the ensuing decades the Alpine Club of Canada orchestrated construction of several huts in the higher reaches of forested terrain to serve as bases for mountaineers heading up nearby peaks – many of them accessed by walking up glaciers. Their locations below treeline offered easy access for supplies to be delivered, and for the workers and the cooks feeding them to reach – not to mention ample firewood for cooking and heating the huts.

Fay Hut, the first built by the Club in 1927, was a dim, hobbit-like log cabin with small windows and a low ceiling planted on a bench in high-elevation timber above Prospectors Valley in Kootenay National Park. The location afforded gentle access from the south to several of the Ten Peaks towering above Moraine Lake, and the glaciers that filled the broad amphitheatres spread between their ridges. In winter, skiers based themselves from the hut to take advantage of long, cruisy glacier runs. Sadly, the charming cabin was incinerated in a wildfire in August 2003, but

Skiers prepare for a day of backcountry climbs and turns on the slopes around the Alpine Club of Canada's Stanley Mitchell Hut in the Rockies, as they have since the 1940s. Photo Lynn Martel

two summers later a bright, modern replacement was built by a small team of professionals assisted by a massive volunteer effort in time for the Club's centennial in 2006. Sigh. That hut also burned to the ground as the result of leaking hot exhaust fumes from the fireplace that ignited the roof. Thankfully, nobody was in the hut during either blaze. Today, the forest regrowth in the valley presents a spectacular fireworks of wildflowers nourished by meltwater from the steadily diminishing glaciers higher up. And since mountaineers today access Neil Colgan Hut to climb the area's peaks from the Moraine Lake side, no new hut will be built at that site.

Other Alpine Club of Canada huts are as popular as ever. In 1939, the Club built Stanley Mitchell Hut, a stately log cabin nestled beside a steep forested slope less than an hour's walk from the toe of The President Glacier. It's fully booked with summer hikers and climbers reaching it via two different well-graded ten-kilometre trails. In winter, it's a cherished retreat for strong skiers willing to endure the 26-kilometre approach, since the Yoho Valley Road remains unplowed and closed to vehicles for the season. Others reach it via the Wapta Icefield. Another valley-bottom cabin built by the Club in the Rockies in 1930, then later replaced in 1947 and again in 1967, is the Wates-Gibson Hut in Jasper National Park's Tonquin Valley within walking distance of a cluster of more than a dozen glaciers and remnant glaciers.

In Glacier National Park in the Selkirk Mountains, 1947 marked the opening of A.O. Wheeler Hut at valley bottom in Rogers Pass, tucked amidst a forest of giant cedars just a few hundred metres from the ruins of Glacier House. Named for the Alpine Club of Canada's co-founder, the log cabin has since been enlarged to sleep two dozen. While only partially booked during the summer, it is fully booked through the winters by backcountry skiers lapping up the area's famous steep and deep powder, and long, untracked runs on the Illecillewaet, Asulkan, Bonney, Tupper and other smaller glaciers.

It wasn't only in the Rockies or the Selkirks, however, that climbers of that era began building huts and cabins to access big glaciated climbing objectives. In 1940, members of the University of British Columbia's Varsity Outdoor Club constructed the Elfin Lakes cabin near the base of Diamond Head in Garibaldi Provincial Park. Throughout western Canada's mountain ranges, dozens of other locally and privately owned and operated huts and cabins and yurts and shelters are scattered just at or below treeline to provide skiers and climbers access to routes with glaciers leading up to high summits. While many are built, maintained and operated by volunteers and small local clubs, dozens of remote lodges are operated as private, for-profit businesses. The tradition of high alpine shelters is a long-established and lovingly appreciated one.

The Whirly Crane

The 1960s ushered in a whole new dimension of high alpine hut building with state-of-the-art helicopter technology. In the popular Moraine Lake area of Banff National Park, where the Valley of the Ten Peaks is walled by a jagged fence of summits, several of them wrapped with glacial ice like ermine shawls, something of an informal race played out as the Calgary Mountain Club and the Alpine Club of Canada jockeyed to be the first to build a prefabricated alpine hut far above treeline. The Calgary Mountain Club's chosen site was a small notch overlooking the lake at the top of a steep, narrow couloir cleaved between peaks three and four, Mounts Bowlen and Tonsa.

The other location was a rocky saddle resting above the (now) heavily crevassed Asulkan Glacier on the east, and the upper reaches of the Swanzy Glacier on the west in Rogers Pass in Glacier National Park. Called Sapphire Col for the glacial pool that forms there in summer, the site was championed by the Alpine Club of Canada not only for its attractiveness to climbers but also for backcountry skiers seeking long, untracked runs on the glaciers. By contrast, the site chosen by the Calgary Mountain Club was set smack dab amidst steep, rocky peaks, and was primarily a climber's destination.

For such huts, the design had to be simple and efficient, since the building would be flown up in pieces, then assembled on site. For this the expertise of Philippe Delesalle, a Calgary architect, but also an accomplished mountaineer and keen skier, was enlisted. Delesalle also happened to be a close friend and climbing partner of

Views of The President and Mount McArthur fill the windows of the Louise and Richard Guy Hut. Photo Lynn Martel

mountain guide Hans Gmoser, and the two were developing the idea for a chain of alpine huts in Glacier National Park where Gmoser could bring clients for skiing and climbing adventures.

With limited funds and Delesalle's blessing, the Calgary Mountain Club crew handed his designs to architectural technology students at the Southern Alberta Institute of Technology (SAIT). The exterior shell would be made of aluminum, with the heaviest piece weighing in at no more than 700 pounds. While small, the hut had to be insulated with two inches of fibreglass and be sufficiently sturdy to withstand the high winds that would pummel it on a regular basis. To keep the whole class busy, two huts were built, with a location for the second to be decided later. The costs for materials and helicopter would total $1000. Permission from Parks Canada was applied for and helicopter flights arranged.

In July 1964 the pieces of both the Alpine Club and Calgary Mountain Club huts were assembled in Calgary before being dismantled and then flown up to their respective sites. To deliver the sections to the Ten Peaks site, the pilot made a fly-by to locate a landing site that was large enough and level enough, which he found on the glacier just over the boundary into British Columbia's Kootenay National Park. The work crew members who flew in on the first flight stomped around in the snow to flatten the site for subsequent flights. It took six flights for all the materials and workers to arrive. By then, however, the weather had closed in and all that could be accomplished was to cover all the building supplies with a plastic tarp, which the crew members then crawled under for the night. It was not a pleasant night. The weather didn't improve the next day, so eventually they secured their precious load by placing heavy rocks all around the perimeter of the tarp and then hiked down to Moraine Lake and drove back to Calgary. Thirteen volunteers returned the following weekend and climbed up the 3-3 1/2 Couloir, which, once the sun hits it, becomes a deadly steep bowling alley of rocks and boulders.

"The snow slope became gradually steeper as the party gained height. Several times they had to stop and watch for falling rocks breaking off the west face of Peak Four. They varied in size from small pebbles to pieces as large as two fists together," Klaus Hahn described in Herb and Pat Kariel's book *Alpine Huts in the Rockies, Selkirks and Purcells.* While they reached the top of the col unscathed on the way up, sadly, Graham Cooper was fatally injured by falling rocks on his way down the very day construction was completed. The hut was named for him.

Unfortunately, Cooper was not the only person to die accessing that hut, and many others were injured by falling rock. In 1983, it was replaced by the Alpine Club's Neil Colgan Hut nestled between the low-angle slopes of Mounts Little and Bowlen. Two safer access routes are now used by mountaineers all summer long, one of which crosses Fay Glacier. With space for 18, it is well equipped with propane stoves, pots, utensils, sleeping pads and a terrific view from the outhouse. And at 2955 metres, it's the highest permanent structure in the entire country.

While a bit lower in elevation, the climb to reach Sapphire Col in Glacier National Park is considerably longer and more complicated. But it was a walk in the park for the team of 12 who hiked up to meet the helicopter in the summer of 1964. Other than having to use their ice axes to open the crate containing their crowbar, assembling the hut went without a hitch. Providing lofty views from its perch at 2590 metres, today Sapphire Col Hut, operated by the Alpine Club of Canada, continues to provide one of the most spectacular settings in all of Canada's mountains. It has space for six, or in a tight squeeze, eight sleeping bags, and visitors bring their own sleeping pad, cookstove and pots to this basic shelter. While otherwise unequipped, it does have an outhouse with an outstanding raven's eye view of the Asulkan, Bonney and Lily glaciers right out the door. As such, reaching it requires the skills and experience to travel safely through avalanche terrain and navigate heavily crevassed glaciers prone to whiteouts and, in summer, narrow exposed ridges.

In a bonanza of hut building, 1964 also saw the construction of Great Cairn Hut (re-named Ben Ferris Hut in 1996), again with helicopter support. For its construction, the team repurposed a large pile of stones from a seven-metre-high cairn that was built in 1953 by a group of impatient mountaineers from Harvard University who were sitting out a rainy day. Facing massive Mount Sir Sandford, the Selkirks' highest peak, which is draped with icefalls on its many glaciated faces, the small six-person hut is tucked near the toe of Sir Sandford and Silvertip glaciers. Construction was led by William "Bill" Putnam, who took his plans one step further the following summer with his friend and climbing partner, Ben Ferris. The next location of their desires was a few kilometres and a couple of ridges and glaciers to the north. There skiers and mountaineers would have immediate access to glaciers from the veranda of the deluxe (thanks to multiple renovations since) Fairy Meadow Hut, which was renamed in 2003 to honour Putnam's exceptional contributions to western Canadian mountaineering. The location remains unmatched. With access to numerous granite peaks and glaciers, plus a full kitchen complete with an oven for baking fresh cookies and a wood-burning sauna, it is so popular as a backcountry skiing destination that the Alpine Club of Canada awards ski weeks via a lottery system.

Canada's Haute Route

While Hans Gmoser's plans for a chain of huts in Rogers Pass took a back seat to other projects, it was another working mountain guide who spearheaded the development of several huts on the Wapta Icefields that helped kick the business of hut-based adventures amidst Canada's glaciers into a higher gear.

Mountaineers had been crossing glaciers to access the big summits in the Wapta Icefield area since 1910 when Conrad Kain led a party on the first ascent of Mont Des Poilus. Spurred by Hans Gmoser's article documenting his team's exploration of the area during their partial Great Divide traverse, in the following years skiers and mountaineers began launching adventures onto the Wapta and Waputik icefields. Among them, several mountain guides, some working for the Calgary Ski Club, regularly led clients onto the icefields and the dozen or so smaller glaciers descending from them.

On one such trip in 1963, Peter Fuhrmann was guiding his clients, Lucio and Vicki Mondolfo from Chicago. While they were in the vicinity of Balfour Pass, two days' ski from Bow Lake, stormy weather trapped them in a snow shelter for three solid days of howling winds and swirling snow. Cold, damp and cramped, the Mondolfos, who were accustomed to Europe's hospitable hut system, were not amused. They were downright miserable. By the time they descended to the warm fireplace at Num-Ti-Jah Lodge on the shore of Bow Lake, they'd convinced Fuhrmann that skiers exploring the Rockies' glaciers were in desperate need of some civilized shelters.

Never one to shy away from a challenge, Fuhrmann took charge. He turned to architect Philippe Delesalle, fast becoming the go-to guy for backcountry hut designs, who decided the structure should be a modular, fibreglass igloo. The Mondolfos generously agreed to pay for its construction.

Finally, after the structure sat in Fuhrmann's backyard for two years awaiting permission from Parks Canada, the paperwork came through and the $350 dome was transported in pieces to Bow Lake. Art Patterson, a Calgary geologist, organized the helicopter at no cost. His work in Canada's far north was facilitated by helicopters shuttling him from one remote job site to the next all summer long, and he had some valuable connections. In October 1965, Fuhrmann, Patterson and his son, Harry, with Bruno Engler and Jimmy Gibson, built a platform at Balfour Pass, a flatish rocky area separating the snouts of the Vulture and Balfour glaciers. There, the 12-person shelter was erected. It was turned over to Crown ownership and open to the public free of charge.

The following winter, Fuhrmann stayed at the hut for several nights, during which he endured two storms. Survival without the shelter, he attested, would have been uncertain. But then, when he returned in the summer with a Parks Canada mountain rescue school group intent on learning safe glacier travel practices, he encountered a different surprise.

"We found that the igloo was on an ice-core moraine which had melted all around, leaving a cone underneath that had pushed the floor right up to the roof," Fuhrmann described in *Alpine Huts in the Rockies, Selkirks and Purcells.*

With rain in the forecast and long hours of hiking between them and their vehicles, let alone a warm, soft bed, they had their sights set on sleeping in the igloo. So the crew reverted to using the only tools they had with them – Swiss army knives – to dismantle the entire hut, screw by screw. They moved the panels seven metres over to a flat spot and reconstructed the orb, pounding the floor flat with piton (rock-climbing hardware) hammers. Realizing the location was not sound in the long term, Fuhrmann later arranged for a helicopter to move it over to a more dependable patch of ground near Mount Olive. The move wasn't entirely without excitement, though, as the G47 helicopter lacked the power to lift the structure and crashed it into the moraine. A bigger, stronger helicopter was enlisted to complete the job.

Fuhrmann, Patterson and several others, including Fuhrmann's wife, Bini, were responsible for the Wapta's second hut too. Identical to the Balfour igloo, it was built in February 1967 on a rocky knoll just above where Peyto Glacier begins its tumble down from the Wapta Icefield. It was named for prominent Banffite Peter Whyte, who died in 1966, and whose wife, Catharine, funded its construction. It was later renamed the Peter and Catharine Whyte Hut (read more about the Whytes in section 5).

Ski mountaineers relax in the spring sun outside the Alpine Club of Canada's Rob Ritchie (Balfour) Hut in the Canadian Rockies. Photo Lynn Martel

While skiers appreciated the shelters, unfortunately so did wandering wolverines that had no trouble breaking into them when they were unattended, making themselves messily at home. Both saw second- and third-generation designs, and in the case of Balfour, now named Rob Ritchie Hut, a couple of different sites before their current versions were built. Its present location at the base of the Vulture Glacier has served skiers well since 1989. Overseen by Alpine Club of

Canada volunteers and with funding for the hut at the Peyto site coming again from the Whyte family, today's versions both sleep 16 comfortably in winter, and although they have no heat source, they warm up quickly once users start cooking on the propane stoves – comforts well worth the small fee.

The third hut built on the Wapta Icefield was Bow Hut. The most easily accessed, the original was planted on a rocky patch near Bow Glacier in 1968. Funded again by the Whyte family, spearheaded by Fuhrmann and designed by Delesalle, the project featured a construction team including members of the Alpine Club, Calgary Mountain Club, Calgary Mountain Rescue Group, Calgary Ski Club and the Association of Canadian Mountain Guides, of which Fuhrmann was founding president. Located midway between the Peyto hut at the Wapta Icefield's northern end, and Balfour at the south, Bow Hut linked the two and facilitated Canada's first hut-to-hut glacier ski traverse. The downside to its easy access – less than ten kilometres, or a three-hour ski from Bow Lake – made it a victim of its own success. Some estimates claim as many as 7,000 users overcrowded the building annually, leaving behind destruction and refuse from partying as well as contaminating the surrounding snow and ice for a couple of hundred metres. It wasn't good.

This time the Alpine Club's huts committee chair, and later president, Mike Mortimer, led the project. Ushering in a new era of alpine huts with a price tag of $98,000, which was raised primarily by members of the Club's Calgary and Edmonton sections, the new modern Bow Hut was built at a new site 500 metres away in 1989. Renovated several times since, the hut is the Club's flagship, featuring two separate buildings – one that sleeps 30 comfortably linked by a breezeway to the other boasting a spacious kitchen and common room complete with propane cookstoves and a wood stove for heat and drying wet clothes. It even has a custodian's room, and with a combination lock on the door it is well managed and regularly maintained. It also sets a high standard for waste, water and energy management for alpine huts in North America. Although originally run by Parks Canada, Balfour, Peyto and Bow huts have all been run by the Alpine Club of Canada since 1989.

With an aim to complete the vision of Canada's Haute Route glacier ski tour, the Alpine Club built the 12-person Scott Duncan Hut in 1988, tucked high on a rocky shelf at the south end of the Waputik Icefield. Its construction was funded largely by Calgary's Duncan family in memory of their son, an accomplished long-distance ski mountaineer who, sadly, died at the age of 25 from rabies resulting from a chance encounter with a bat.

Symbiotic Business

The Wapta Icefields huts story doesn't end there, though. For decades skiers setting out from Bow Hut on the Bow-Yoho traverse had two choices: wait for ideal conditions and be fit enough to ski the 20-kilometre distance carrying multi-day packs over two high cols in a single day to reach Stanley Mitchell Hut in the Little Yoho Valley; or pitch a tent or build a snow shelter on the Collie or Des Poilus glaciers to complete the distance over two days, as our group did. Constructed over the summer of 2015, the state-of-the-art Louise and Richard Guy Hut sleeps 18 upstairs with a bright spacious kitchen and common area downstairs. Running on a combination of solar, wind and propane, it features walls and ceilings constructed of structurally insulated panels that are designed to provide excellent insulation while reducing interior condensation – a long-endured problem at many alpine huts. The electrical systems can be remotely monitored from the Alpine Club of Canada's main office in Canmore, 90 kilometres away as the raven flies. Its location, on a rocky shoulder above the Des Poilus Glacier, grants a stunning panorama of peaks and glaciers. Relying on donations, as with all its huts, the Club received a substantial boost toward reaching the $500,000 price tag of this one with the generous contribution of long-time member Richard Guy, a mathematician who was then 99, and still going to work at his University of Calgary office five days a week. The hut is co-named for his wife, Louise, a well-loved Club member who died in 2010 at the age of 92; Richard died in 2020, at 103. Richard Guy was flown up for the dedication ceremony. A winter-only hut, it is closed in summer to protect the grizzly bears that make their home in that area of Yoho National Park.

The sun sets behind the state-of-the-art Louise and Richard Guy Hut in Yoho National Park. Photo Lynn Martel

Despite five Wapta huts now offering comfortable shelter and regularly serviced outhouses, in recent years a small cadre of über-fit skiers have travelled the entire 45-kilometre distance from Peyto Lake parking lot on the Icefields Parkway to Sherbrooke Lake on the Trans-Canada Highway in a single day. The current record is 6 hours, 34 minutes.

Most, however, happily choose to pay for at least one night at a hut.

While the Alpine Club of Canada is a

not-for-profit organization that represents and advocates for the country's climbing and mountaineering community, it does provide jobs for 35 full- and part-time employees at its national headquarters in Canmore. Among them are several hut-maintenance staff (often assisted by volunteers) to service cookstoves and light fixtures, repair broken windows and wood stove glass doors, paint walls and clean sleeping mattresses, among a long list of never-ending tasks. The crew works with skilled helicopter pilots to remove full outhouse barrels and deliver fresh empty ones and firewood to those huts with wood stoves. Propane pigs are also delivered to supply fuel to run the cooking stoves and lanterns, with helicopters being hired at $2000 per hour to get those jobs done. Most of the huts are serviced just once a year, but the busiest ones twice. Hut maintenance accounts for 30 per cent of the Club's operating budget, with about 25 per cent of that figure being allocated for its 14 high-alpine huts. Aside from the nationally operated huts, the Club's Vancouver and Whistler sections also operate a couple of huts on the doorsteps of glaciers. All but four of the Alpine Club of Canada's 26 nationally operated and half-dozen regionally operated backcountry huts are accessed only by hiking, skiing or mountaineering.

Beyond maintaining its huts system, the Club hires professional ACMG guides for mountaineering camps and backcountry skiing adventures, as well as camp cooks and managers. Through the Alpine Club, hut users can hire porters to help ferry their gear and supplies to those sites – a welcome source of income for (usually, but not always) young mountaineers looking to stay fit while earning a day's wage. As they have since 1922, professional guides use the huts regularly as bases from which to launch climbing and skiing adventures with their clients in a symbiotic and profitable business-mixed-with-pleasure relationship. For a century now, alpine huts nestled by frigid glaciers have been well appreciated for their comforts, and for contributing to the livelihood of mountain guides, backcountry cooks and helicopter pilots across western Canada.

The Spearhead Huts Super Project

In the summer of 2017, Coast Mountains skiers hoisted the first beams of the highly anticipated Spearhead Huts project. More than 50 years had passed since members of the British Columbia Mountaineering Club first submitted a proposal to build a series of huts along the Spearhead and Fitzsimmons ranges in Garibaldi Provincial Park, long before any chairlifts provided access to the alpine in that region.

While they weren't the first to attempt the traverse, it was Karl Ricker, Bert Port, Chris Gardner and Alistair MacDonald who succeeded in navigating the horseshoe-shaped loop in 1964. After completing their spring exams, the four members of the University of British Columbia's Varsity Outdoor Club boarded a train from North Vancouver to Whistler. They set up their first night's camp on Blackcomb Mountain near the current site of the Rendezvous Lodge. In the morning they launched their nine-day backcountry adventure, skiing southeast in a clockwise direction over cols and across some 14 glaciers, passing many peaks that hadn't even been named yet.

Since then, hundreds, likely thousands have skied the 40-kilometre route that links a dozen glaciers bearing names that include Trorey, Tremor, Ripsaw, Macbeth, Iago, Diavolo, Benvolio and Overlord. It's an exceptional high alpine adventure. While most who have skied the traverse have carried all their avalanche and glacier safety equipment on their backs along with food and winter camping gear, in 1984 Brian Finnie, Brian Sheffield and Graham Underhill were the first to ski the entire traverse in a single day, albeit a shortcut version of the original. Considered visionary at the time, with the advantage of ski lifts taking them high on Whistler or Blackcomb ski hills, one-day traverses have since become common. The current record, set by Eric Carter and Nick Elson, is a staggering three hours, ten minutes.

Not contending with any speed records, in 2014, Ricker, still spry at 78, and Port, fit and trim at 81, embarked on a 50th anniversary trip of their pioneering traverse. Not only an accomplished backcountry skier and climber with more than 500 summits under his boots, for more than 40 years Ricker, a retired geologist, diligently recorded ice volumes on the Wedgemont and Overlord glaciers of Garibaldi Provincial Park.

For this trip, they were in the capable company of Port's son, Andrew, Ricker's daughter, Maëlle –who became the first Canadian woman to win an Olympic gold medal (in snowboard cross) on home soil at the Vancouver games in 2010 – and several others. Taking advantage of the motorized facilities, they rode lifts to their start point on Blackcomb Mountain, and again at the end of their tour to descend to the Whistler ski hill base after they ran out of snow at the top of the Fitzsimmons Express lift. On their last night, the group made themselves comfortable inside the aging Himmelsbach Hut while it drizzled outside.

Backcountry skiers paint smooth turns in fresh snow on Trorey Glacier on the Coast Mountains' Spearhead Traverse. Photo Isabel Budke

It was that hut, built on the shores of Russet Lake in 1968, that was first to be replaced as part of the three-hut project. The second and third huts are to be located at Mount Macbeth and Mount Pattison. Planned to service what is arguably the most popular ski traverse in the country, the huts are being built with summer hikers and mountaineers in mind as well as backcountry skiers. Years in the planning, the Spearhead Huts Committee is made up of several volunteer-run groups and private funds, including the Vancouver and Whistler sections of the Alpine Club of Canada, the British Columbia Mountaineering Club, the Brett Carlson Memorial Foundation and the Kees and Claire Memorial Hut Society. The latter was created in honour of Kees Brenninkmeyer and Claire Dixon, two energetic, accomplished young ski mountaineers who died in a collapsed snow cave they'd dug for shelter while skiing across the Wapta Icefield in 2007, likely as a result of being asphyxiated by gas fumes from their cookstove. In addition, the Lílʼwat First Nation provided their support for the project.

While commercially guided trips are expected to use the huts, they will be open to all manner of self-propelled users who will pay a fee to enjoy the comfort of the shelters, which will accommodate about 38 people each. Expectations are for as many as 7,000 overnight guests per year, but with the area already being popular, containing people inside the shelters as well as their waste is expected to lighten the environmental degradation that widespread tenting and uncontrolled human waste have proliferated. Late in 2017, the project benefited from a substantial $1.5 million donation from two Vancouver philanthropists – Brian Hill, CEO and founder of Vancouver-based retail clothing chain Aritzia, and Andrea Thomas Hill, chair of the Cause We Care Foundation – sufficient to fund construction of the entire second hut.

The state-of-the-art, energy-efficient Kees and Claire Hut was opened in September 2019. Photo Paul Geddes

The state-of-the-art Kees and Claire Hut opened in fall 2019, with sleeping space divided into six areas, indoor composting toilets and energy-efficient heat and electricity. The big opening party doubled as a fundraising effort to fill the $300,000 gap between the budget and the little more than $2 million it cost to build – not counting the huge number of volunteer labour hours. As user numbers increase, so do the huts' degrees of sophistication, and correspondingly, their price tags since the Mondolfos' initial $350 donation.

3–3 BIRTH OF AN INDUSTRY

Canadian Mountain Holidays

While Hans Gmoser was one of the guides taking clients on Wapta Icefields adventures accessed from Bow Lake in the 1960s, his real business was nurtured on the west side of the icefield in the Little Yoho Valley.

When he and his lifelong friend, Leo Grillmair, arrived in Canada from Austria in late 1951, they had dreams. Postwar Austria was a grim place, and the young men focused their sights on the new country as the land of opportunity. Boarding ships to cross the Atlantic buoyed by optimism, Gmoser and Grillmair made their way to the Canadian Rockies. That year alone, some 3,500 Austrians, many of them tradesmen like Gmoser, an electrician, and Grillmair, a plumber, arrived in Canada.

Both men were already skilled climbers and capable skiers. Over the following years they connected with members of the local climbing community, and on their days off from various jobs they explored existing rock climbs and industriously established a series of progressively difficult new routes.

Gmoser's first introduction to the Little Yoho Valley came in the autumn of 1952, as part of a hiking trip with Alpine Club of Canada members from Calgary. His attraction to the sheltered alpine valley nestled between the hulking twins, The President and Vice President, to the south, and the giant rocky hedge comprising Mount McArthur, Isolated Peak and Whaleback Mountain to the north, was immediate. Better yet, it was October and snow had already begun to accumulate.

"The snow brought an irresistible magic for us," Gmoser wrote in his journal (published in his biography, *Deep Powder and Steep Rock*, by Chic Scott). "Every fibre in our legs itched and twitched and asked for the enchantment of the down-hill ski run." By Christmas of that year they and several friends started out one morning at 4:00 a.m. to ski the arduous 26 kilometres from the parking lot near Field, British Columbia. After marking the day with good food and drink, candles adorning a freshly cut Christmas tree and singing songs of their homeland, they spent the next few days exploring the area under bluebird skies. Minus 25–degree temperatures granted them excellent snow for skiing.

Thanks to some fortunate connections over the ensuing years, and not without a lot of hard work, Gmoser moved to Banff and focused on earning his living as a mountain guide. When a client, Fred Pessl from Detroit, whom he met guiding at Assiniboine Lodge and who would become a long-standing and beneficial friend, suggested he organize a spring ski tour in 1956, Gmoser knew exactly the spot for a ten-day camp – Stanley Mitchell Hut.

While the log cabin served as a comfortable, well-equipped base, he solved the problem of the long approach by skiing halfway and spending the first night with his clients at the Takakkaw Falls warden cabin before continuing to the hut the next day. That spring camp was just the first of many he would run in that valley, as they gained a popular reputation. He would enlist the help of Grillmair and others to help ferry food and supplies to the hut. He hired cooks for $50 a week to prepare tasty meals. At the first camp, two young women from Germany, Renate Hick and Sigrid Wirte, shared the duties so they could each spend days skiing. Gmoser rose before dawn to light the fires for cooking and to warm up the hut, and to mount skins on his clients' skis. Day after day – some camps lasted six weeks, as fresh guests replaced tired ones – he led his clients on the prized tours of the area in sunny weather and stormy, up The President Glacier to President Pass, sometimes to the summit, and up and down the neighbouring peaks. That first year Pessl filmed them painting ski turns on the snowy canvas amidst glorious surroundings, providing Gmoser with what would become valuable marketing material.

With a short season in which to earn as much as possible, Gmoser wasn't done yet, as he followed that camp with one based out of Wheeler Hut in Rogers Pass. With the Swiss guides program no longer operating from the Canadian Pacific hotels – and the original Swiss guides all retired – Gmoser was then the only mountain guide operating full-time in all of Canada. Year after year, he guided backcountry ski trips and summer mountaineering and climbing adventures on the area's glaciers and rocky peaks. Then he'd launch gruelling expeditions with his friends – including their partial Great Divide traverse. With Leo Grillmair, Philippe Delesalle and others, he led expeditions to climb daunting new routes on giant peaks in Alaska and Yukon. On one such adventure, he and Delesalle were joined by four others, including Karl Ricker, Don Lyon, Ron Smylie and Willy Pfisterer, who would

CMH self-published anniversary books celebrating the business and gave them to their guests.

become Jasper National Park's first alpine rescue specialist, to be the first all-Canadian team to climb Mount Logan, by the east ridge. With their food resupplied by aircraft, and with 40-kilogram packs on their backs, the team walked and skied the entire 137-kilometre approach, gaining the Kaskawulsh Glacier on the second day.

"As we gained altitude on the smooth, hard ice, we soon realized the immense size of the Kaskawulsh. The glacier was four to six miles wide and had at least a half dozen medial moraines on its surface," Ricker wrote in the 1960 *Canadian Alpine Journal*. ("The All Canadian Mt. Logan Expedition," at p. 15.)

"The next day our troubles began; at the junction of the North and South Arms of the Kaskawulsh the laws of elasticity gave way, for ahead of us were many huge ice waves, seracs and crevasses. The snow bridges were rotten and we wore ourselves out negotiating the 'salad of ice cubes.'"

Finally reaching the base of the mountain after more than a week of arduous skiing, they managed to make just the second ascent of the ridge in a speedy seven days. Their exit route was no easier than their approach, albeit quicker as they skied for three long days up the Hubbard Glacier then down the Donjek Glacier before launching their raft to float – not without capsizes – down the Donjek River. The term *epic* accurately describes their accomplishment.

Schussing Onto the Silver Screen

It was during these years that Gmoser married a second profession with guiding – that of filmmaker. While other ski filmmakers focused on lift-serviced ski areas, he took his camera into the backcountry. Films of people enjoying the snowy glacier slopes and climbing opportunities in the vast, undeveloped Canadian mountain wilderness proved enormously popular with his audiences. Between 1957 and 1968, he produced ten feature-length films bearing titles such as *High Road to Skiing* and *To The Forbidden Snowfields*. Every year he'd embark on a road tour in his Volkswagen Beetle, sleeping in the back seat to avoid pricey hotel costs. From Denver to Nelson, British Columbia, to Boston to Vancouver to Berkeley, California, he would give 50 presentations from October to January. One screening in Detroit drew 2,500 people. Hearing him narrate the action in his lilting Austrian accent, audiences appropriately attired in Norwegian sweaters and sealskin après ski boots were mesmerized. They lapped him up. By becoming a filmmaker and casting the Rockies' and Selkirk glaciers in starring roles, Gmoser made himself into a one-man national marketing campaign. And he became a steadily employed mountain guide.

In spring of 1962, he led a ski trip to the abundantly glaciated Cariboo Mountains in British Columbia, west of Jasper. To gain the Canoe Glacier at the base of Mount

Sir Wilfrid Laurier, he hired Banff airplane pilot Jim Davies to ferry him and his guests, landing them right onto the glacier. No ordinary guests, they included Jim McConkey, one of Canada's first "extreme" skiers, and three members of Canada's national women's ski team – Nancy Holland and the sisters Elizabeth and Nancy Greene – the latter of whom would win silver and gold medals at the Grenoble Winter Olympics a few years later. With talent like this, Gmoser's next film was sure to be a hit. Nancy Greene wowed audiences racing past gaping crevasses, and McConkey upped the ante by building a kicker out of snow and launching himself into the air to soar over the aircraft parked on the glacier. The film was a hit.

"With his winning smile and personality," Chic Scott wrote in *Deep Powder and Steep Rock*, "he had become the mountain idol of the early '60s."

The following February, Art Patterson approached Gmoser with an idea. As a geologist who was transported by helicopter to remote jobsites in Canada's far north, Patterson was keenly aware those same helicopters sat idle through the winter months. He was also an avid skier. How about, he suggested, using a helicopter to deliver skiers to the top of a run.

Hans Gmoser's sideline as a filmmaker served as a huge boon to his guiding business. Photo Calgary Mountain Club Collection

Gmoser agreed to give it a try, and the two organized a day in the Spray Lakes area of Alberta's Kananaskis Country. The windy conditions were less than ideal, but about 20 clients paid up to try the "next thing." A couple of months later, Gmoser tried helicopter skiing again, this time returning to the Canoe Glacier in the Cariboos with an all-star cast of talented ski racers and a photographer on assignment for *SKI Magazine*. After sitting out a two-day storm in a snow cave, Jim Davies – by then flying helicopters – landed the crew on the airy 3516-metre summit of Mount Sir Wilfrid Laurier, from where they skied an outstanding 1200-metre run down to their campsite.

The footage is still spectacular.

Hans Gmoser film collection

It's an image worth remembering.

Hans Gmoser dressed in his favourite Austrian sweater, standing on stage, speaking into a microphone. Behind him, displayed in all their glory on the big screen, were the powder-covered slopes, sculpted peaks and expansive glaciers and icefields of his favourite Canadian mountains – the Purcells, the Selkirks, the Rockies.

Between 1957 and 1968, Gmoser produced ten films showcasing the spectacular beauty and skiing and climbing opportunities of his adopted home, all set to melodious classical music. Year after year he toured tirelessly across North America from one venue to the next, drumming up clients for his Canadian Mountain Holidays guiding business and sharing his unabashed love for western Canada's mountains.

"Many of us have wonderful memories of those presentations," said Chic Scott. "For many of us, those evenings were the beginning of our long love affairs with the mountains."

For Scott, the life-long affair hasn't only been with the mountains, but also with Gmoser's films. In an effort to preserve and re-release them, in 2013 he partnered with climber Marg Saul and the Whyte Museum of the Canadian Rockies. Professional filmmaker Willi Schmidt was enlisted to provide the technical expertise necessary to digitize and reassemble the films to match their original glory.

The High Road to Skiing was just one of ten ski films Hans Gmoser shot and produced to help sell his backcountry and glacier skiing adventures.

When Gmoser presented his films, the footage rolled on the screen and a soundtrack of classical music played independently while he narrated the story, live on stage. All three elements, Scott said, came together in a remarkably seamless and beautiful production.

The films captured gorgeous scenes from the Rockies and Selkirks, and the sublime wilderness expanse of Yukon and Alaska on expeditions Gmoser led to climb Mount Logan and Denali. They showed rock climbing adventures in the Bow Valley on Mounts Yamnuska and Louis, and Castle Mountain. They also capture a historic treasure trove of images showing Gmoser employing the first helicopters to provide his guests access to the untouched powder slopes of the Bugaboos in 1965 and '66 – the activity that launched western Canada's heli-skiing industry.

All ten films, as well as seven of the original scripts, are stored at the Whyte Museum of the Canadian Rockies in Banff. In order to be properly preserved they were transferred to a digital format. Then, to fill in for Gmoser, who died in 2006, his nephew, Michael Hintringer, volunteered to provide narration following the scripts. Now living in Canada but born and raised in the same Austrian town where Gmoser grew up, Hintringer speaks in an accent nearly identical to his uncle's. For the films to which an original script didn't exist, Scott narrated a commentary to explain the action.

The complex project required many hours in a sound recording studio. Music was integrated into the films, and since much of the music Gmoser used – which exists on tapes at the Whyte – is under copyright and the original performers difficult to identify, rights to suitable music had to be secured. Scott also interviewed 14 men and women who starred in the films to create additional chapters along with archival photos and narration to explain the stories behind each film. Scott had to raise $106,000 to see the project completed.

"I did this project because the films were so important in their day and are still relevant today," Scott said. "These films helped to put Canadian mountain adventure on the map and inspired thousands of young people across North America to climb and ski. And on top of that they are just very good and should be seen again."

Containing 20 hours of priceless viewing, the full DVD set is a bargain at $100.

Business Takes Off

The client-guide relationship is, by nature, a symbiotic one. While showing the footage from that day at Boston's Massachusetts Institute of Technology on his next film tour, Gmoser was approached by US Olympic ski champion Brooks Dodge about doing some ski touring in western Canada. Oh, and could they use a helicopter for a day or two? It was, as they say, the beginning of a beautiful, lucrative friendship.

The ski trip didn't happen that year. But Gmoser knew the ideal place for such an adventure – Rogers Pass. Parks Canada, to its credit, was not enthusiastic about helicopter-assisted skiing in Glacier National Park. That spring, however, after multiple weeks of ski touring with clients at Assiniboine Lodge, the Freshfield and Columbia icefields, Yoho and Rogers Pass, Gmoser led a group on a ski adventure in British Columbia's Bugaboos – hands-down the most eye-popping mountain landscape in the southeastern corner of the province, featuring 3000-metre granite spires that jut straight upward from massive glaciers coiled around their bases. While the rugged drive up a muddy logging road left a lot to be desired, Gmoser knew he'd found the place for helicopter skiing.

For his 1965 spring ski season, Gmoser listed two weeks of helicopter skiing in the Bugaboos. One week would be reserved for Brooks Dodge and his friends. Gmoser hoped to attract enough clients to support a second week. "For the first time we are organizing ski touring weeks where we use helicopters for the uphill transportation in Canada's most spectacular ski country," his brochure announced. Depending on the group size, each skier would enjoy seven to twelve trips on the machine over the course of the week. Each lift would grant ski runs five to eight kilometres long. On days when the weather prevented flying, "regular ski tours" would be offered. The cost, for a party of 15, including accommodation, guiding and a cook, would be $203 each.

The first commercial helicopter skiing week launched April 4, 1965. Six of Gmoser's long-time clients, including one woman, Inga Thompson, settled into an out-of-use lumber camp. They slept on iron bedsteads in their own sleeping bags. Emily Flender, from Cambridge, Massachusetts, cooked their meals. Jim Davies flew the CF-BHC helicopter, ferrying them high among the spires, from where they skied deliriously long, long runs down the Vowell and Bugaboo glaciers.

While historic, the enterprise was not yet the glamorous adventure it was to become. For members of Brooks Dodge's group, the drive on the 45-kilometre logging road took a miserable nine hours as they repeatedly extricated their vehicle from mud bogs. It didn't take long for one of the guests to suggest to Gmoser that he charge an additional $30 and fly them in and out from the handful of houses that make up Brisco, where the paved road ends. While the skiers ate their breakfast Davies warmed up the helicopter, then began flying the guests to the top of the run two at a time. Although it featured state-of-the-art technology, it was only marginally faster than skinning up.

Safety concerns were sobering too. Midway through the second week, the brand-new business of helicopter skiing experienced its first helicopter crash. While Davies was landing on a flat mountaintop, the landing gear sank in the deep snow, causing the machine to tip over. The main rotor sliced at the ground, and at the machine itself. Miraculously, Davies and his two passengers escaped unharmed. The helicopter didn't fare so well, leaving Davies to ski, walk and drive to the nearest town, Golden (75 kilometres from Brisco), to acquire a new helicopter so the guests could enjoy the rest of their ski week.

Pilot Jim Davies, sitting on a 1965-era Bell 1 machine, helped pioneer the helicopter part of the heli-skiing business. Photo Jim Davies Collection

No doubt everyone's nerves were a little frayed, but the world's first heli-skiing clients were a hardy bunch and they were unanimous in declaring the two weeks a roaring success.

Industry Explosion

Gmoser began planning for the next year. The new business of heli-skiing quite literally took off in a big way. For the 1966 spring season, he offered six weeks of heli-skiing, with 70 clients paying $240 each per week. Flying a turbocharged Bell 47G-3 B1 helicopter specially designed for higher elevations, and equipped with a single bench to fit the pilot and two passengers, it took Davies 75 minutes to ferry ten guests to the top of a run. Guests were over-the-moon to ski two or three runs in untracked powder per day. A favourite run began at the top of Bugaboo Glacier and ended a thigh-burning five kilometres and 1200 vertical metres down the valley. Whenever the skies were clear enough, they skied high on the Vowell Glacier and down a 1500-metre run on the Conrad Glacier on unfettered natural ski slopes with smooth, consistent surfaces. The following year Gmoser's company, Canadian Mountain Holidays, offered ten weeks of heli-skiing to 150 guests who paid $270 each for a week. In addition to hiring a cook, Gmoser enlisted the services of a young skier and climber from Germany named Bob Geber to assist with the guiding. A young mountaineer from New Zealand, Lloyd "Kiwi" Gallagher, who, over the course of several trial-by-fire winters would learn how to ski well enough to guide his own groups, was hired as general handyman and lodge helper.

With the rustic charms of the abandoned sawmill buildings having already worn off, Gmoser negotiated with the British Columbia government to lease the land in the Bugaboos, where he replaced the decrepit camp with a lodge in time for the 1968 season. Philippe Delesalle was enlisted as architect, and to finance its construction, Gmoser turned to his friend, Jack McKenzie, with whom he'd shared several skiing and climbing adventures. The Calgary resident was an oil industry businessman with financial know-how who had repeatedly suggested to Gmoser that when he was ready to build a lodge, he'd contribute. McKenzie ponied up $25,000 in equity, while Gmoser and Grillmair put up $15,000. To raise the balance required to meet the $100,000 building price, Gmoser offered "skier's loans" to his clients. The loans were sold for $5,000 apiece and paid 6 per cent interest. In return, the investing skier would enjoy a "free" week of heli-skiing every year until the loan was repaid. As a bonus, these bond holders were granted priority booking over which weeks they preferred to ski. It didn't take long for Gmoser to sell the 15 skier loans, and construction was soon underway. A favourite story about one of the biggest construction challenges centres on the rigorous debate about whether the lodge should offer indoor plumbing.

"I didn't think an outhouse was any hardship. It worked perfectly well," Gmoser said in *Deep Powder and Steep Rock*. Plus, he added, it made construction simpler without all that pesky plumbing in the walls. Gmoser lost the argument, and the guests were thankful to use indoor facilities, which were one floor downstairs from the six-bed dorm rooms. Today's guests at Canadian Mountain Holidays – commonly known as CMH – lodges sleep in two-person rooms complete with full bathrooms and in-slab heating in the floors.

The responsibility of handling such a large sum of money was not lost on Gmoser. But he was a self-made man. He'd taught himself to ski and climb and speak and write in English, and to be a businessman. On the latter point, he often turned to his successful and knowledgeable clientele for advice. And he would need it.

The modern helicopter technology that made it possible to ferry two passengers at a time to a mountaintop, then three, then four, steadily improved over the next few decades. The company opened an office in Banff and hired two women to answer the phones. With the success of Bugaboo Lodge, Gmoser and Grillmair – who would run the lodge for 22 years – discussed how to expand the business. Increasing the capacity in the Bugaboos, they concluded, would diminish the quality of the skiing experience. Construction on CMH Cariboos Lodge was completed in December 1974, offering more skiers the opportunity to paint fresh tracks on the massive glaciers that draped the mountain landscape. By 1976 the company was running heli-skiing at five areas and planning the next.

Choosing the sites was a basic formula – existing accommodation to house the guests until a lodge could be built, mature forest suitable for tree skiing on stormy days when the helicopter's range would be limited, and large expanses of untouched glaciers for skiers to lap up on the bluebird days. Oh, and outside of the national and provincial parks where motorized activities are prohibited. Gmoser and his lodge managers reached the conclusion that the ideal configuration comprised 44 guests per lodge, divided into four groups of 11 skiers with one guide per group, each group perfectly accommodated by the

Following their guide, heli-skiers make their turns in soft fresh snow on a glacier at Canadian Mountain Holidays' Adamants Lodge. Photo Scott Rowed

Bell 212 helicopter. Over the years, options were expanded to offer private and exclusive groups using smaller helicopters, and a couple of smaller lodges were built to accommodate those groups.

From the Bugaboos in the south to the Cariboos in the north, through the 1980s and '90s skiers from around the world lusted for their chance to try the greatest thing since step-in bindings. Daryl Hannah, King Juan Carlos of Spain and Prime Minster Pierre Elliott Trudeau, whom Gmoser guided on a climb of Bugaboo Spire – royalty, politicians and Hollywood stars all wanted to fly in helicopters to experience skiing and climbing amidst Canada's glaciers. Iconic photos captured by some of the top photographers of the day showcased the hippest ski fashion and schussing style of the era against a backdrop of striated seracs and glowing blue glacier ice.

With demand routinely outstripping capacity, for many years one business expense CMH didn't worry much about was advertising. Financing the lodges, however, was something of a seat-of-their pants affair, and there were years where the company teetered on the edge of bankruptcy. But then, the guests did their part to keep the company solvent. Remarkably, some returned several times a season, at times bringing their entire families. The loyalty to Gmoser's company, and its unique product, was strong, and many of those early guests continued to ski with the company over the decades until long after their knees wore out.

Three Million Acres

While the skiing was adventurous, oftentimes just transporting the guests to and from the lodges was an enterprise unto itself, and sometimes still is. At peak season, the company transports some 900 guests every Saturday – 450 arriving, and as many departing – to and from airports in Calgary, Kewlona or Kamloops. The guests are then ferried by bus, passenger van or private vehicle to and from the lodges, some of the drives seven hours, one-way. The Banff office on a Saturday resembles mission control and, on a stormy weekend with road closures, mission control during Apollo 13. The logistics involved remain beyond impressive.

So do the numbers.

With three million acres of ski terrain divided among 12 lodges on the doorstep of the massive glaciers of the Selkirk, Purcell, Cariboo and Monashee mountains, the season runs five months. More than once during the 12 winters that I worked as a CMH bus "escort" – as we were then called – I watched savvy guests while away their time on the bus calculating the company's annual earnings.

As CMH Heli-Skiing & Summer Adventures – as it is now officially called – grew, so did costs. The spectacularly deluxe Monashee Lodge took a reported $10 million to

Guests at CMH's Bobbie Burns Lodge explore the area's via feratta with a spectacular glacier backdrop. Photo Carl Trescher CMH Heli-Skiing & Summer Adventures

build. The 2019 renovations of Bobbie Burns Lodge, including a modernization of existing rooms and the addition of a new wing, were budgeted at $8.4 million. When CMH renovates, it doesn't mess around. Construction is just one expense; another is staffing. Currently the Banff office and warehouse employ 70 staff, while at the height of the winter season, another 400 are employed as guides, plus chefs, bakers, housekeepers, massage therapists, ski technicians, lodge maintenance experts, helicopter pilots and engineers for each lodge, along with the crucial food truck drivers.

The remote lodges boast rooftop hot tubs, steam rooms, saunas, indoor climbing walls, games rooms and, for non-heli-skiers, groomed cross-country ski trails, snowshoeing and fat bikes. Of course, there is complimentary wi-fi. Fully included meals are plentiful and the cooking divine, the wine list top-notch (not included, and with prices to match), and avalanche transceivers and specially designed skis are part of the deal too. The cost for a premier week running mid-February to late March can run as high as $15,000 – not including bar tab, massages or purchases at the lodge ski shop.

And the company's offerings don't end with skiing. Since 1977, at the suggestion of respected US tour operator Arthur Tauck, CMH opened up its spectacular glaciated terrain to heli-hiking in summer. The program continues to operate from a select couple of lodges where the alpine wildflowers bloom in a dazzling kaleidoscope, and glacier ice glints sapphire blue. A few valleys north of the Bugaboos, the Bobbie Burns hosts a sphincter-puckering via ferrata with tiny rope bridges stretched across icefalls crinkled with crevasses and seracs. Glaciers have always figured in CMH's marketing and its appeal. Many of the lodges have glacier views out the windows. Interestingly, though, the company does not track what percentage of its leasehold consists of glaciated terrain.

While Gmoser would, in his later years, express conflicted views about the industry he so enthusiastically developed as he witnessed so many of his guests' insatiability for more runs of a more perfect pitch and snow consistency, he did maintain a strong ethic of care and respect for the mountain wilderness throughout the decades he ran his company. Lodge sizes were capped so that the guests would spend their time experiencing a large wilderness area over the course of the week without bumping into any other skiers – or their tracks. Each lodge was managed by an internationally certified mountain guide. In his quest to find qualified guides to lead his skiers, Gmoser repeatedly lured young men (yes, they were men, until Jos Lang and Sharon Wood were hired in the mid-1980s) from Switzerland, Germany and Austria, the cradle of the guiding profession.

Having co-founded the Association of Canadian Mountain Guides in 1963, Gmoser maintained a strong connection to Canada's professional guiding organization. It was with extra pride for Gmoser and colleagues that the ACMG became the first non-European member admitted to the International Federation of Mountain Guides Associations (IFMGA) in 1974. And as the demand for skilled heli-skiing guides increased with CMH's growth – as well as the other smaller heli-ski companies that sprang up – the entire mountain guide training program was restructured to suit western Canada's unique needs. While European guides followed a path that culminated in becoming a mountain guide or nothing, the ACMG offers options for candidates to pursue alpine climbing- or ski guiding-only careers. Those who complete both paths are certified as internationally qualified mountain guides. And ACMG-certified guides are *the* professionals qualified to guide clients on glaciated terrain in Canada.

Accessed only by helicopter, Battle Abbey was founded by Hans Gmoser and Bill Putnam. The lodge opened for ski touring only in 1979 and was run by CMH until 2004, when operations were transferred to Roger Laurilla and Robson Gmoser, Hans's son. Putnam, who oversaw several renovations of the famously eclectic lodge, died in 2014. Robson, who helped build it as a teenager while dreaming of becoming a guide – he did – died in an avalanche in 2015. Laurilla continues to run the 19-bed (including staff) lodge nestled amidst the Selkirk Mountains' Pequod, Typee and Ommo glaciers. Photo Roger Laurilla

In May 1995, Gmoser sold his company to Alpine Helicopters, the smallish company that had for many years constituted the helicopter side of the business, for a reported $15 million. The mountain guide who had slept in his Volkswagen to avoid hotel costs enjoyed an adventurous retirement bicycle touring around Japan, South Africa and Europe with his wife, Margaret, and Philippe and Mireille Delesalle, and with his and Margaret's sons, Conrad and Robson. He'd been invested into the Order of Canada. Come wintertime, he and Margaret spent many peaceful weeks skiing up and down the gentle glades and meadows beneath the towering pyramid of Mount Assiniboine, where he was first employed as a guide in Canada, the lodge by then managed by his brother-in-law, Swiss-born mountain guide Sepp Renner. No doubt he appreciated using the outhouse. In July 2006, as the result of a fall from his bike, Gmoser died, and his ashes were spread near Sunburst Lake below Mount Assiniboine and its glimmering remnant glaciers.

Recreation on Ice

In creating and growing his helicopter skiing business, Gmoser didn't just launch a company, he ignited an entire industry. Currently, a total of 41 heli-ski and catskiing companies operate on and amidst glaciated terrain in the mountains of British Columbia, as far north as Atlin and right up to the Yukon boundary, and west into the Coast Mountains. Snowcats offer wilderness skiing at relatively affordable prices compared to heli-skiing, transporting skiers up into the alpine in heated cabins to access long, untracked powder runs. While slower moving, snowcats have the advantage of being able to operate in pea-soup cloudy conditions that sometimes cause helicopters to be grounded.

Together, according to a 2019 report, those operations employ 2,846 full-time and part-time staff, and contribute a GDP of $164 million annually for the province. Some operate from backcountry lodges, others from nearby towns where guests stay at local accommodations. A handful of backcountry ski lodges operate in Alberta's Rockies too, but the big snow, and business, is in British Columbia.

That's where the backcountry touring lodges are, too. From the Canadian Rockies to the Selkirks, north to Burnie Glacier near Smithers, west to Bella Coola in the Coast Mountains, ski touring lodges offer a smorgasbord of wilderness ski slopes to skiers willing to skin uphill. Icefall Lodge, which borders Banff National Park's western boundary adjacent to the Lyells, a cluster of five of the Canadian Rockies' peaks higher than 3353 metres (11,000 feet), is the largest of the touring operations, with a tenure of 200 square kilometres. British Columbia hosts more than 30 backcountry skiing lodges tucked high

Ski mountaineers kick steps up a steep glaciated slope at a camp run by ACMG ski guide Sam McKoy in the Coast Mountains' Waddington area. Photo Sam McKoy

in remote terrain where reliably heavy snowfall delivers the product – slope after slope of untracked snow. Nineteen of them host glaciated terrain. Apart from steeper sections where the jumbled sculpture-like blocks and pinnacles of icefalls and seracs pose potential hazards to skiers, lower-angled glacier terrain provides a relatively uniform base layer that allows for skiing early in the season, as well as winter-quality light, fluffy powder late into spring when the snow in the lower elevation forests has deteriorated into a consistency akin to bottomless oatmeal. This works for heli and cat operations too.

Interestingly, while all the heli, cat and touring lodges with glaciers and icefields within their tenure feature the unique experience of skiing on glaciers as part of their marketing, neither HeliCat Canada nor the Backcountry Lodges of British Columbia industry associations keep any actual numbers as to what area or percentage of those operations' terrain is glaciated. The guides who work at those areas, though, especially those who return to the same areas season after season, are aware the ice is melting, and frequently record their observations through the Mountain Conditions Report, a service provided for the public by the Association of Canadian Mountain Guides.

If you ask a lodge owner, or their guides, they will tell you how many glaciers or remnants thereof their area has. They know exactly where each glacier is, not only on a map, but in their mind's eye. They can describe their individual characteristics – where the crevasses are, where the seracs hang and threaten a potential ski route, where there's a sagging bergschrund here, a steep toe there. They know them by their names. And they notice, from one season to the next, when things

One of four privately owned and operated huts in the Icefall/Lyell area, the Mons Hut sleeps 12 and offers easy access to the Mons Glacier on its doorstep, and a bit farther away, one of the Rockies' highest peaks, Mount Forbes. Photo Lynn Martel

change. They notice as they thin, shrink or shrivel, and when they are fat and full and gleaming in winter – but not as full and robust as they were 10, 20, 30 years ago. They see them in late summer looking rough and scruffy and worn and haggard. Scrawny and malnourished. Naked, exposed. Like a moulting elk, like a coyote with mange, except there's no new coat growing back. This cancer can't be cured.

Within Icefall's massive tenure are 37 glaciers of varying sizes, the largest of them blanketing 20 square

ACMG ski guide and photographer Sam McKoy organizes and leads week-long camps for adventurous skiers in the wild and heavily glaciated Mount Waddington area of the Coast Mountains. Photo Sam McKoy

kilometres. To access several of the area's seven peaks above 3353 metres, Larry Dolecki has built three satellite huts, two near the toes of the Lyell and Mons glaciers, each sleeping 12. The main Icefall Lodge can accommodate 18 guests, with the wood-burning sauna and shower building a short walk away.

While some of these lodges can be accessed by vehicle, usually on bone-jarring forestry roads, helicopters serve as the taxi to the door of touring lodges. Then they fly away, not to return for a week. The silence that ensues is nirvana to those who spend between $1000 and $2500 per week – depending on whether they are guided and fed by professionals or self-guided and cooking their own meals. They gleefully apply skins to their bases and climb up every metre they ski down. Although this is labelled by some the "poor man's heli-skiing," aficionados prefer to call their self-propelled, old-school method "earning your turns."

Having experienced heli and snowcat lifts, I can say that ski touring is by far my favourite. Even though two-, three- or even four-hour climbs can be tiring, I find the ascents infinitely more interesting up-close, on the ground weaving a track up a smooth glacier slope or through an icefall with its jagged pinnacles glistening in sunlight, than from an enclosed, fast-moving, noisy helicopter. Such climbs make the downhill turns, though fewer in number, much, much more precious in value. Some would say priceless.

3–4 ROAD TO ICE

The Wonder Trail

Hands down, the most accessible glaciers in western Canada are those along the aptly named Icefields Parkway, or, in French, the far more romantic Promenade des Glaciers. Despite the shimmering blue icefalls that cling high to north-facing cirques, and which are photographed by millions of tourists annually, the route followed by the two-lane strip of pavement today was not favoured by the earliest travellers heading north from Lake Louise. The First Nations peoples and the early European explorers preferred to travel the broad, open and comparatively cruisy Pipestone River valley in the Rockies' front ranges.

It wasn't until James Hector, travelling with the Palliser Expedition in 1858, that a non-Indigenous party followed the Bow River north and crossed over Bow Summit into the drainage of the North Saskatchewan – and with good reason, as the ground oozed with swampy areas and recurring forest fires had choked the narrow valley floor with piles of deadfall like giant tangles of pickup-sticks. Travelling in thick timber much of the way, it's a wonder any of the small number of determined explorers who chose that route saw many glaciers at all. But it was the giant glaciated peaks of the Continental Divide that drew mountaineers to follow it.

In 1896, American explorer Walter Wilcox and his companion R.L. Barrett, led by Rockies outfitter Tom Wilson, a packer and a cook, headed north from Laggan with five saddle horses, ten pack horses and food for 60 days. When they reached the confluence of the North Saskatchewan and Alexandra rivers, they climbed to a high point to decide which valley to follow. The Alexandra valley appeared to be blocked by a glacier (long since melted) so they continued straight north and eventually crossed Sunwapta Pass, but soon found that beyond there the valley was blocked by the Athabasca Glacier. Turning up a side-valley to the east, they crossed what we now call Wilcox Pass.

In 1904, outfitter Jim Brewster, whose descendants continue to own and operate several Brewster family businesses in the Rockies, led the first complete horse train from Banff all the way to Jasper via that route. After A.P. Coleman followed the same route in 1907, he dubbed it "The Wonder Trail," and, along with surveyor A.O. Wheeler, he was among the most ardent supporters of developing it into a proper road. By the 1920s Jack Brewster was running his annual packhorse trips on the "Trail of the Glaciers," each trip from Banff to Jasper taking a full three weeks – one way.

The first version of the Parkway was a federally funded work project to provide employment for hungry men during the Great Depression, the largest project of its sort in the country. Construction began in 1931 with work crews starting from Jasper and Lake Louise and labouring toward each other. At the height of the operation, 625 men felled trees, swung pickaxes and shovelled gravel. Other than a single motorized tractor assigned to each camp, very little in the way of machinery was available to aid their efforts as they toiled in cold rain and snow through tangled forests and over several steep and long hills to forge the 230-kilometre single-lane gravel track. At night the labourers were sheltered in relief camps housing 50 men each, spaced 24 kilometres apart. The pay was 20 cents a day.

Finally, in 1939, the north and southbound crews met at the Big Bend near the toe of the Saskatchewan Glacier to complete the project. Their remarkable creation was 6.5 metres wide, and, impressively, with a grade never steeper than 8 per cent. In 1940, the first automobile travelled the route, no doubt stopping at the Columbia Icefield Chalet, which had been recently constructed by the well-established Banff-based Brewster Transport company just a short walk from the toe of the Athabasca Glacier. Business was open.

Tourism expanded rapidly; between 1939 and 1940 the number of visitors to Banff National Park tripled. In keeping with the times, and the traffic, the Icefields Parkway was upgraded in 1961 to the two-lane paved road it is today. Impressively, most of the original grading was maintained, testimony to the top-notch job carried out by its original designers and workers. Today, the Parkway is a busy road that sees at least a million vehicles annually, the vast majority in July and August. Several adventure travel companies offer supported cycling tours on the Parkway lasting five to seven days, while independent cyclists might ride the route in two or three days, camping or staying at one of the handful of rustic hostels or small hotels along the way.

Travelling the route by bike certainly delivers a much fuller and richer experience than by car, as the hills last longer – both up and down – and the glaciers feel much bigger and closer, the sounds of rushing water and songbirds as frequent companions.

Every summer morning, northbound traffic between Lake Louise and the Athabasca Glacier is often bumper to bumper, with licence plates from as far away as Texas and Florida and Colorado and Quebec affixed to every size and style of camper van, motor home and fifth wheel ever designed. With a couple of hundred distinct glaciers and remnant glaciers of varying sizes visible from the pavement, and with many viewpoints and pullouts to facilitate such sightings, it is consistently rated – with very good reason – among the most scenic drives in the world.

Every summer, a few hundred people choose to travel the Icefields Parkway by bicycle, some as part of organized tours. While the climbs are long, so are the descents, and the views are jaw dropping and a lot more powerful than from inside a vehicle. Photo Lynn Martel

Come winter, the Icefields Parkway is an entirely different world. On a busy Saturday, fewer than 100 cars might be found parked in clusters of a dozen or two at various known backcountry skiing or ice climbing locations. By sundown it is all but deserted. There is no cell reception, and road closures due to severe snowstorms and avalanche control efforts happen regularly. Filling your trunk with a sleeping bag, shovel, gravel and other winter essentials, especially good winter tires, is highly recommended. And most who venture into the Rockies' wilderness during those months like it just fine that way.

Profit From Ice

Construction of the Icefields Parkway ushered in an entirely new form of glacier tourism. Prior to its existence, only hardy adventurers enthusiastic about spending the better part of the summer sleeping in canvas tents and eating campfire grub ventured into the wild landscape between Lake Louise and Jasper. Now the route was suddenly open, with the turn of an ignition key, to an increasingly mobile public.

Jimmy Simpson left England for Canada in 1896, and it didn't take long for him to begin earning his place among the legendary guides and outfitters of the Banff area. Bow Lake was his favourite place, and by 1900 he had established a camp there. In 1920 he was granted a lease, and three years later he completed building his first cabin at that site as a permanent base for his outfitting tours. As work began on the

In the 1950s the Athabasca Glacier was twice as big, and the Columbia Icefield Centre building less than half the size it is today. Photo Harry Rowed

Icefields Parkway, Simpson seized the opportunity to expand his business, and the iconic round lodge opened in 1937, just as the road reached Bow Lake. He named his lodge Num-Ti-Jah, a Stoney word for the small, cute yet unruly furry critter, the pine marten. In 1940 the lodge boasted six rooms, and by 1950 it housed 16 rooms. Simpson died in 1972, and his son, Jimmy Jr., carried on running the lodge – and like his father, telling stories – until 1996. Still in operation, the place oozes history and the floors creak; it hasn't changed much since 1950. A true Rockies treasure, it has persisted: while the views of Crowfoot and Bow glaciers have changed some, the beauty and appeal of its setting haven't.

Simpson wasn't the only one to listen when opportunity knocked with the construction of the Parkway, particularly at the toe of the Athabasca Glacier, which, at that time, descended close to the road.

In 1939, Alex Watt from Banff began offering tours on the ice aboard a Model A Ford rigged with metal tire treads. His efforts were sufficiently successful that the National Parks Service decided it should grant a concession licence to a suitable candidate. To Watt's dismay, the lucky bidder was Jasper local Bill Ruddy, who, in 1952, began providing motorized travel on the Athabasca Glacier, or, as it would become known, the Columbia Icefield tourist attraction.

A keen entrepreneur, Ruddy brought in a six-passenger snowmobile manufactured by Quebec creator of the Ski-Doo, Bombardier. At first passengers would park on the gravel at the glacier's terminus and board the snowmobile for a scenic ride on the gently inclined glacier slope. Before long, however, the melting glacier left behind a snout that was too steep for the snowmobile to access. By the mid-1950s, the Canadian government acquiesced to building a gravel road on the lateral moraine that flanks the south side of the ice. The road served as access route to the glacier for many years, and by 1968 Ruddy was running 20 snowmobiles on the ice with a staff of more than 100.

Thanks to the doubling and paving of the Parkway in 1961, the tourists eager to take their ride on the glacier kept lining up. In 1969, Ruddy sold his Snowmobile Tours Limited to Brewster Transport Co. (by then no longer owned by the Brewster family, having been sold to Greyhound Canada in 1965). Brewster Travel recognized their need to replace the aging, noisy and rough-riding Bombardier machines. Enter the era of passenger bus bodies fitted with track mechanisms that were originally developed for arctic exploration. Although the non-airconditioned, non-shock-absorbing snowcoaches were better capable of accommodating the ever-growing tourist numbers, the vehicle soon earned its unflattering nickname, "Shake and Bake." On top of that, it also became increasingly apparent that the metal tracks caused considerable damage to the ice surface.

One of the earliest snowmobiles ferries passengers up onto the Athabasca Glacier, circa 1940s. Photo Byron Harmon, Whyte Museum of the Canadian Rockies, Byron Harmon Fonds (V263/I/A/i/a/na 5735)

To solve this problem, Brewster partnered with Foremost, a Calgary-based manufacturer of industrial vehicles, to develop the modern Terra Bus, or as

Brewster called it, Snocoach, equipped with giant low-pressure rubber tires. Now called Ice Explorers, these 20-ton coaches carry 56 passengers at a time who sit back in comfort for their tour onto the steadily diminishing glacier. Running on diesel fuel, the vehicle has a top speed of just 40 kilometres per hour, but for the tour the average speed is just 20. With 6 x 6 all-wheel drive, its suspension enables it to handle a 30 per cent grade sidehill, and it can crawl straight up a 60-degree slope. While the über-fat tires don't cause too much damage to the glacier, what the brochures don't mention is that highway-sized graders and snowblowers plow a large cul-de-sac right on the glacier ice from April to October to maintain a safe area for passengers to disembark on the ice and room for the giant machines to turn around. Or that when you're skiing on the glacier in the months the machines aren't operating, you can still smell the diesel fuel they run on.

Just 24 of these machines exist in the world. Two are on duty at McMurdo base in Antarctica, while the others are all at the Athabasca Glacier, running tours every 15 minutes in rain, snow, sleet or sunshine, all of which could happen in the same afternoon. With a $1.3 million price tag for each machine, the investment has paid off; some half a million people annually pay $114 per adult and $57 per child to experience the ride. The Athabasca is North America's most visited glacier.

More than just the boarding gate for the Ice Explorers, however, the Columbia Icefield Discovery Centre, now operated by Pursuit (as Brewster Travel was rebranded in 2017), includes a gift shop, restaurant, public washrooms numerous enough to serve an Olympic-sized sports arena, cafeterias and the Glacier View Inn. It's a solid performer for Pursuit, whose head office is located in Arizona, one of two arms of Viad Corp, an international "experiential services company." It's not the only foreign-owned company profiting from Canada's national parks; among others, the iconic Banff Springs and Chateau Lake Louise are part of the international Fairmont luxury hotel chain.

Ice Attraction

The experience is certainly unique. At the time of writing, passengers ride a shuttle bus over to the staging area ten minutes from the main centre, then board the Explorer to roll slowly down a road bulldozed onto a moraine whose ice core is covered with a thick layer of rocks and rubble. Naturally, the road requires constant maintenance, as the covered ice gradually melts through the season. The vehicle rumbles and gently sways down the steep slope and onto the glacier, driving through a large pool of meltwater in an effort to rinse any undesirable dirt from the tires before rolling on to the ice. The exercise puzzles me, since the meltwater drains to the

Sun, wind, snow or rain, every day all summer long hundreds of tourists from around the world ride the Ice Explorer onto the Athabasca Glacier, making it the most visited glacier in North America. Photo Lynn Martel

glacier's toe like all the meltwater does. After it pulls up beside other Explorers in the clearing whose perimeter is flagged to mark the safe area, everyone disembarks to spend 30 minutes snapping photos and sipping from cupped handfuls of freshly melted glacier ice.

On my 2019 visit, our vehicle was piloted by a 24-year-old woman from a small Alberta town who was taking a gap year from her studies. Along with some 200 other young adults from towns and cities across Canada and a few from other countries on work visas, she was living at the centre's staff accommodation for the duration of the season. She joked about how the "Ice Palace," as it's been dubbed, has lousy Internet and no cell service.

Like her cohorts, she'd been extensively trained and while expertly driving the vehicle was capable of reciting impressive reams of facts and information about glaciers in general and the Athabasca in particular. Moraine types and mountain building and the depth of the Athabasca and how it is currently melting at a rate of five metres annually, and how scientists estimate it will have completely receded by 2100 as a result of Earth's rising temperatures. How the vehicle's tires cost $6000 apiece. How Mount Athabasca has 13 different climbing routes. How Collie and Woolley climbed Athabasca and Wilcox discovered the pass that bears his name. Not a word, though, about the First Nations people who travelled this landscape as their home for centuries before them.

Throughout the tour, the message was consistent. "Glaciers have always been moving, advancing and retreating, carving this landscape." And this was the reply she recited when a passenger asked her if climate change was contributing to the melting of the glacier we were standing on. While she did state that scientists were learning that Earth was warming faster than it ever had before, it's natural, she assured him, and humans are having only a small impact. With the staggering amount of knowledge about glaciers she had been trained to share, how could she miss that key detail? The current warming phase being experienced on Earth is not natural. Since 1990 the thousands of scientists contributing to the IPCC (Intergovernmental Panel on Climate Change) reports have repeatedly arrived at the same conclusion – this change is happening

Gail Crowe-swords and Dominic Fredette, carrying packs laden with five days' food and gear en route to the Columbia Icefield, stop for a moment on the Athabasca Glacier where a snowblower clears the track for the glacier tour buses. Photo Lynn Martel

on a global scale, and is not regional as past warming phases have been. And it's happening as a consequence of humans burning fossil fuels and living energy-intensive lifestyles. Everything in our modern, affluent lifestyles relies on fossil fuels, not only driving cars and flying in airplanes, tourist traffic included, but everything we manufacture and package and transport, from toothpaste tubes to running shoes to fridges and bicycles to home construction to cruise ships. And $6000 tires.

From the staging area, the shuttle transported us five kilometres north along the Parkway to the Glacier Skywalk. With its primary product steadily diminishing, Brewster Travel (since rebranded Pursuit, as noted above) applied to Parks Canada to build an "attraction" on the site of a scenic pullout ten minutes' drive north of the Athabasca. Despite petitions signed by 200,000 people, vocal opposition and countless letters to the editor in the pages of the local Banff, Jasper, Canmore and even Calgary and Edmonton newspapers from those who viewed the proposal as inappropriate within the boundaries of a national park, where the spectacular scenery and natural splendours ought to be attraction enough, Parks approved the project in 2012. The exercise left plenty of locals wondering, if our national parks aren't places we can go to escape motors and machines and wi-fi and elaborately constructed "attractions," then where will those places be?

In the spring of 2014, the $21 million platform opened. The giant horseshoe-shaped cantilevered walkway is embedded into the bedrock and fitted with a glass floor that extends 30 metres from its base to hang 280 metres above the rubbly Sunwapta valley bottom. An approach walkway connecting the shuttle drop-off and the platform completely blocks any views of the riverbed and lovely waterfalls below from anyone driving the Parkway. This view, which used to be available to anyone who paid the Parks entry fee to drive the Icefields Parkway, is now exclusively available to those who pay Pursuit an additional $34.

Within the attraction, the boardwalk is lined with entertaining and informative panels and stations manned by enthusiastic interpreters sharing knowledge on local wildlife – including animal prints embedded in the floor – 500-million-year-old

The year the author first arrived in the Canadian Rockies, the Athabasca Glacier reached all the way down to this marker. Photo Lynn Martel

Burgess Shale fossils and Snow Dome's role as a hydrological apex. Scrolling through the options on an audio phone, I asked a staff member if there was any information on climate change.

"I find it really annoying that we don't have anything about climate change here," replied one young man at an interpretive booth.

Yup, I did too. Throughout my tour, the message was repeated, again and again. Climate change is natural, and glaciers have melted and returned many times in Earth's history. Facts about the melting glaciers were plentiful, but skinny on the how and why. When I asked a staff member manning the Parks Canada booth inside the main centre if he had any info on climate change, he said he didn't know enough to tell me anything, and that I should visit the exhibit downstairs.

In addition to a spectacularly large two-dimensional map of the Columbia Icefield, I found interpretive panels sharing some history of the Parkway and the Icefield Centre – but with no mention of First Nations – lots of information and facts about the current melting, and some about science conducted on local glaciers and predictions of potential water shortages for regions downstream of the Icefield. The new exhibit is much improved from the previous one and showcases panels suggesting that people carpool, compost, take road trips, ride bikes, grow a garden and unplug from their screens as examples of what individuals could do about climate change and to help reduce CO_2 emissions. But the only place I could find the simple phrase "Human fossil fuel use contributes significantly to climate change" was outside on a kiosk. Comparative photos of the Athabasca in 1918 and 2011 – showing a staggering difference – were displayed on the back wall, on the side least likely to be seen by anyone walking up the stairs into the building. Front and centre it was not.

On the boardwalk, I listened to the audio messages until the very end. The final message came from Brewster Canada president Dave McKenna speaking of how Canadians share concerns about their melting glaciers. He spoke of how people are all connected by water on a molecular level, whether from Europe or Asia or North America, "anywhere on a coastline," forgetting how the hydrological cycle ensures water is delivered to inland dwellers too. He encouraged his listeners to learn more about how climate change is affecting them in their areas. Then he finished by saying, "fresh drinking water is a very precious commodity." Water, of course, like air, is a vital substance all humans – and every other creature and organism on Earth – require fair and equal access to.

Riding the shuttle back to the main building, everyone disembarked – right through the gift shop doors, on the way to the cafeteria's prominently displayed plastic water bottles for sale. Clearly, last chance tourism – travelling to see something on the verge of disappearing – is good for business at the Athabasca. I couldn't help feeling like I was visiting Canada's sacrificial glacier.

Sadly, in July 2020 an Ice Explorer featuring side and ceiling windows and carrying 26 passengers and a driver rolled repeatedly down the rubble slope. Three people died, 14 more were seriously injured. The investigation into the cause was ongoing at the time of publication.

Not Hard to Tell Anymore

Riding inside a vehicle, however, is not the only safe and informative way for tourists to experience the Athabasca Glacier. And as with most people with long-term connections to the Columbia Icefield area, changing perspectives run deep and strong for Peter Lemieux.

Since 1985 Lemieux has guided the hundreds, now thousands, every summer who seek a more up-close and personal experience through two- or five-hour walking tours. When he first began his Athabasca Ice Walk tours, Lemieux simply thought his workplace was among the coolest on the planet. Over those decades, however, his perspective has morphed.

"It's been an evolution," he said. "At first you think, wow, this is one of the coolest places on Earth. But over time you see it as not isolated, you see how connected it is, globally. You realize stuff that happens here affects people all over the continent – particularly with water."

On a typically sunny, cloudy, bluebird, snowy July day – fondly referred to by locals as a four-season day – I tagged along as Lemieux and assistant guide Mike Mariash led 11 guests on the glacier. Stopping intermittently as we walked with spiky cleats attached to our boots, we listened as Lemieux shared his prodigious knowledge about the Athabasca and its parent Columbia Icefield. Facts about the size, depth and age of the icefield, about how water from its apex flows to three oceans, about how glaciers serve as Mother Nature's water storage systems by releasing flow during warm summer months when rivers are at their lowest flow, all while watching meltwater course and meander along the troughs that water carves into ice surface.

Approximately six kilometres long today, the Athabasca advances about 15 metres every year – the ice mass moving slowly downslope under its own weight is a qualifying factor for any glacier. Since 1898, however, this glacier has shrunk back at least two kilometres. Not only the length, Lemieux explained to his group, but its mass and depth have diminished substantially too.

"See that big boulder?" Lemieux said, pointing to a refrigerator-sized rock sitting amidst a field of stones. "It used to be beside the edge of the glacier. The glacier has moved it 30 metres since last year. People used to ask, is it hard to tell the glacier is melting? It's not hard to tell anymore."

Lemieux began guiding tours on the Athabasca as a Parks Canada interpreter. When Parks cancelled its interpretive hiking program in favour of privatization in the mid-1980s, Lemieux, having recently earned his ACMG assistant ski guide certification (he guided heli-skiers for 27 winters), recognized an opportunity.

"I had a sense it would be a viable business," Lemieux said. "Parks was only providing crampons. I thought if we could get people the right footwear, provide them with rain gear, sunscreen, it would fly."

Slowly, it did. Now, he employs nine full- and part-time guides, all ACMG certified. The Ice Walk tour season typically begins in late May and runs through early October. A second company, Rockaboo Mountain Adventures, run by Jasper-based ACMG mountain guide Max Darrah, has also been taking guests on guided walks on the Athabasca Glacier in the past couple of summers. On the day of our tour, 40 people participated in Lemieux's half- and full-day walks. Like all his guides, Lemieux shares the story of the Athabasca Glacier. He points out how the ice surface becomes dirty as rock dust falls from the giant peaks rising on both sides of the strip of ice; how cryoconite and stones melt out pockmarks and pools of various sizes, some of them expanding to millwells; how the glacier constantly changes as cracks, gullies and icy creeks form.

IceWalk founder and guide Peter Lemieux leads a group to the edge of the heavily crevassed icefall on the Athabasca Glacier. Photo Lynn Martel

Spotting a piece of paper, I stoop to pick it up. It's a ticket for the semi-final match between the Leicester Tigers versus Racing 92 taking place at the City Ground in Nottingham, UK. Barely a week old, it's testimony to the diversity of visitors from around the world who come to visit this glacier, to experience the ancient, many-thousand-year-old ice first-hand.

Our full-day walking tour granted us time to cover the four kilometres to the broken, jumbled, extraordinary landscape of the lower icefall. Having been there several times on adventures with friends while skiing farther up onto the icefield, I studied the familiar routes that climbers and ski mountaineers navigate around the icefall via its smoother – and narrow – north and south shoulders; direct passage is blocked by ice shelves, arches and towering unstable wedges. As we walked, Lemieux described how icefalls such as this are created when a glacier drops over steep bedrock, as gravity causes tension and the ice cracks and splits. The features reveal striations created by successive snow layers reminiscent of how rings in the trunk reveal the age of a tree.

It's a fascinatingly beautiful, astonishing and spectacularly humbling work of nature.

Interpreting Ice

Of the more than half-million annual visitors to the Athabasca glacier, most don't see the icefall up close since the snowcoach tours turn around halfway to that point. For those not capable of hiking for two hours, the snowcoach provides an excellent option, and certainly it was how I first experienced the Athabasca some 30 years ago. My first glacier experience. Although I was aware then that it had melted back some distance since the first photographs were taken in the early 20th century, there was no sense of alarm yet about how quickly that was happening. Or why.

A guest on an IceWalk tour gets a steadying hand to safely look down into a gushing mill-well. Photo Lynn Martel

Lemieux, however, embraces the opportunity to share information related to how Earth's warming temperatures are affecting glaciers globally, and more specifically, the one that has been his workplace for three decades.

"My clientele tends to be extremely intelligent, well-educated, curious and physically fit," he said. "What keeps me going is the variety of people I get to meet on the glacier. And they get jazzed."

Skirting the lower reaches of the icefall, we returned to the glacier's toe by walking along its north bank, which is noticeably thicker than the south side. Soon we reached a millwell, a circular shaft created by the force of water pouring into it.

Lemieux shared some unhappy stories. In 1998, a young girl from Israel fell into a crevasse near the toe. He and one of his guides went to help.

"She was small, and she went in a couple of metres," Lemieux recalled. "She was stuck where the crevasse got narrower, but it opened wider underneath her and she was close to slipping through. We got our guests in a safe spot and then we lowered a couple of prussic cords with drop loops on them. She was able to grab two of those loops and we yanked her out like pulling a cork out of a bottle."

Not all of Lemieux's memories are so positive. He recalled a German doctor who wandered onto the glacier on his own a decade ago who was not pulled out alive. In 2001 a nine-year-old Japanese boy fell through a thin snow bridge and became wedged in a crevasse. Rescuers spent hours trying to extricate him. They eventually pulled him out, but it was too late. He had frozen to death. For some years the interpretive signs that line the well-travelled gravel trail that loops onto the moraine and back to the parking lot warned, with vivid illustrations, of the dangers of venturing onto the ice unguided, sadly with the young boy's story serving as an example.

No one on a guided tour has ever fallen in. While it's still unwise for anyone inexperienced in glacier travel to venture onto the ice unguided, Lemieux does mention how significant melting has now made the lower tongue too thin for deep crevasses. And how that thinness causes the melting rate to accelerate. Acknowledging that his observations are anecdotal – but in agreement with scientists studying the Athabasca and other glaciers, with whom he shares what he sees – Lemieux has no doubt that climate change is happening, and that science has proven that human activity has accelerated the effects, including glacial melting. At the start of the season he brings books up to share with his guides bearing titles such as *Nonsense on Stilts: How to Tell Science from Bunk*. And while most of his clientele are already realistic and well informed about climate change and the contributing human factors, he admits it pisses him off when he encounters climate deniers.

"I let the land speak for itself," Lemieux said. "But I have started to say, you can make a case that it's not caused by human activities, but if you do, you're studiously ignoring enormous masses of evidence that prove it is."

With that, he's noticed how the accelerated melting in recent years has forced him to lead his guests over more than a kilometre of rubble to reach the glacier, an endeavour that becomes more difficult each summer. Apart from the nuisance of the increasingly rough approach, watching his workplace of more than three decades shrink and shrivel takes an emotional toll too.

"It's quite traumatic, and a little depressing," he said. "I realize now, I have been here for half the years of my life. There's value in being in one place for an extended period of time. You do see the changes. It's a bit like watching a friend die." And watching those changes provides another interesting element that he thinks will keep him guiding his walks for some years to come.

"It's still enjoyable. It's a great place to be, the glacier is really cool and you're out in the fresh air. I've worked with film crews, scientific researchers and curious public. The best compliment I ever got was from a guy who said, 'you make people who don't think, think.'"

"If I can do that, that's pretty damn good."

Steadily Changing Workplace

Slender streams of moonlight slice through flannel-grey clouds floating in an inky black sky. Inside the campground cook shelter a cluster of headlamps illuminates a hissing gas stove coaxing a pot of water to boil. Hushed voices are tinged with anticipation as hot water is poured into thermoses, the quiet interrupted by gurgles.

Eight novice mountaineers are experiencing their first alpine start.

His warm breath rising in the frosty June air, ACMG mountain guide Mark Klassen runs the group through a last-minute gear check: helmets, crampons, ice axe, toque, gloves, sunscreen, warm layers, lunch, drinks. A ten-minute drive later, at 3:38 a.m., the group begins hiking up the spine of a rubbly moraine, following a small trail flattened over decades by thousands of boot steps. Below them, a half-dozen Ice Explorer tour coaches are parked side by side. With sunrise this station will percolate to life as mechanics and drivers begin their work shifts ferrying tourists in the buses to experience their own Athabasca Glacier tour.

ACMG mountain guide Mark Klassen (centre) measures out rope lengths for his clients to tie in before walking onto the north-face glacier to climb Mount Athabasca. Photo Lynn Martel

Leading the procession of headlamps upward into a cold world of snow, rock and ice, Klassen, too, is embarking on a routine workday. Since he first climbed the iconic peak in 1985, he has guided clients up Mount Athabasca more than three dozen times. Over those decades he's climbed seven different routes on Athabasca, as well as several other nearby peaks, many more around the world. An hour into the ascent, Klassen stops at a baseball diamond–sized snowfield where he and assistant guide Todd Anthony-Malone help their clients into their harnesses and crampons to rope up to cross the peak's north glacier.

"It's a pretty straightforward day at work up here – usually," Klassen said. "The north glacier of Athabasca has changed a lot over the years. It's thinned and receded on the toe and we have to access it higher than we used to. The ramp is tilted more and is therefore steeper and is harder to guide now; there is a higher risk of avalanche and falling ice than there used to be."

Well into his career, Klassen doesn't believe the changing glacier will significantly affect his livelihood. He does, however, believe the melting will affect guides whose careers are beginning today.

"Mountain guiding, as I've known it, is a dead profession," Klassen said. "A hundred years from now it will be a completely different game."

With 11 of the Canadian Rockies' highest peaks in the immediate vicinity, plus several more just beyond the icefield's reach, the Columbia Icefield area has lured climbers since Collie and Woolley first stood on Athabasca's summit in 1898. While the cold, wind-raked landscape attracts only devoted ice climbers and ski mountaineers in the winter, every summer dozens of climbers set off to climb Athabasca and its neighbouring peaks equipped with their own experience, skills and decision-making ability. Hundreds more sign up for professionally guided adventures.

"The Columbia Icefield area is one of our premier guiding areas," said Dave Stark, director of operations for Yamnuska Mountain Adventures, an alpine adventure company based in Canmore, Alberta. "Probably not a week goes by in the summer that we don't have a group up there. There's Athabasca, Andromeda, Boundary Peak, and occasionally we guide Columbia. Easy access means you can climb an 11,000-foot peak in eight to twelve hours. We can have someone who has never done anything on snow and ice before and on day three they're summitting Athabasca."

Like Klassen and other guides who have lived and worked in the Rockies for decades, Stark can't help but notice how much the Rockies' glaciers have melted and shrunk during his career. Season after season, the guides are watching their workplace change drastically, and so far they've been able to adjust their work practices accordingly. On Athabasca guides are intimately aware of places where rockfall has increased, where slopes have steepened and sections that melt to bare ice earlier in the season than in past years make kicking steps more difficult.

"The recession is significant, and it's created some additional hazards to deal with. But Athabasca is still a good mountaineering objective and can be well managed with experienced guides," Stark said. "It seems for a long time you didn't really notice the recession, but now when I'm up there I think, holy smokes, the glacier is so far back now. And thinner. It's a fascinating place."

He's not alone with that thought. Glaciers grow, they move, they support life, they perform invaluable functions in nature. Each is unique, scarred and imprinted with streams and millwells and crevasses and seracs. They glow blue, glint cold silver. For those who spend a lot of time around glaciers they are living entities that inspire personal connection.

For Yamnuska Mountain Adventures guide Barry Blanchard, glaciers are more than a workplace. Their value reaches beyond aesthetics. Climbing glaciated terrain, he said, is key to his identity as an alpinist.

"I've just always loved being up in the alpine," Blanchard explained. "My big attraction has always been technical mountain climbing, which by my definition has to involve rock, ice, snow and glaciation. I've seen huge changes. Places we used to go in the 1980s that were fantastic places to teach vertical ice climbing – they're gone now. That area used to be hundreds and hundreds of metres of ice; it's just gone. Not there anymore. Some great pictures taken of us in crevasses in 1993 – now it's bedrock."

For Klassen, the changing landscape provides a teachable moment for his clients.

"The Athabasca Glacier itself has receded and thinned significantly. I often point these changes out to clients. Climate change is often hard for us to notice in our everyday lives and this is a good example of how things change due to it."

Mountain Conditions Reports

Mountain Conditions Reports, known as MCRs, are compiled on a volunteer basis by professional ACMG guides climbing, skiing and hiking in mountains across Canada as part of their commitment to the ACMG's mandate of protecting the public interest. The reports consist of field observations and are shared with the public to assist recreational outdoorspeople in making reasonable, informed decisions when out on their adventures.

With glaciers being their workplace on a daily basis, all year round, mountain guides are the front line for informed glacier observations. Their reports share real-time conditions.

Stanley Peak – no freeze, poor snow

Posted on Mon, 06/17/2019 – 14:30 by Parks Canada
by Grant Statham and Jonas Hoke

We had hoped for a freeze overnight and a fast ascent of the N Face of Stanley Peak early on Monday morning. Despite the clear night, there was no freeze this morning at 0400 and we bailed at 2400 m near the toe of the glacier due to iso-thermal snow. Thigh deep postholing. The snow on the N face itself is melting fast. There are lots of melt runnels and a patch of bare ice that soon will span the whole face. Quite surprising for mid-June. Of note was the significant recession of the west toe of this glacier. I had not been that way for over 20 years and was surprised to find a complexity of rock ledges and snow patches to gain access to the glacier. The usual crevasse band at the top of this section looked particularly menacing today in the soft snow. Snow climbing is out until we get a solid freeze in this area.

Bugaboos conditions

Posted on Thu, 09/05/2019 – 11:15
by Eric Ostopkevich

ACMG AAGE candidates were climbing in the Bugaboos from August 26 to 29. We experienced generally good weather although at times it rapidly deteriorated. There was a strong overnight freeze on the 26th and 27th; however, warm over-night conditions on the morning of the 28th led to rapid melting. The Bugaboo Glacier conditions were rapidly changing and the descent from the Pigeon/ Snowpatch rappels are becoming more complex. While travelling below Son of Snowpatch on the Bugaboo Glacier we noted high rockfall hazard which can be avoided by travelling in more complex glacier terrain to the skier's right. The B/S col is melting out rapidly and on nights with no overnight freeze high rockfall haz-ards exist even in the mornings. We chose to travel through the B/S col on ap-proaches but avoided it after any daytime warming occurred. While climbing Ears Between a large scale rockfall event was noted on the talus slope below the Crescent Spires. This moraine is supported by glacial ice which is rapidly melting out. We consider this zone to be highly unstable.

**ACMG Mountain Conditions Summary for the Coast Mountains —
September 5th, 2019**

Posted on Thu, 09/05/2019 – 23:00
by Andrew Councell

As I just wrote a conditions report for the Joffre and Tantalus areas a few days ago, I don't have much to add for the coming weekend. That said there are a few things to keep in mind going into the weekend. We had a lower-than-average snowfall last winter and despite (or maybe because of?) a fairly rainy summer there have been a number of reports of rockfall events. Water helps to loosen rocky slopes and also erodes rocks that have melted into the glacier ice. We are entering into the leanest time of year for glaciers: crevasses continue to widen, moats are becoming massive and problematic, and areas of the mountains that haven't melted out for some years (or ever) are becoming exposed now. Keep an eye on overhead terrain that may produce rockfall: hanging glaciers, brown-smeared snow/ice faces, steeper ice slopes strewn with rocks and boulders that may melt out. The weather outlook at the moment is a bit of a mixed bag. Friday marks the end of this stretch of summer weather we've enjoyed this week. Saturday looks to be partly cloudy but without any major precipitation and overall a good day to be out. On Sunday, however, forecasts show rain beginning. And then, of course, we've always gotta remember "global weirding" where even the experts can't forecast what's on the horizon. Last night, for example, there was a powerful thunderstorm raging deep in the Park over Garibaldi and Mamquam mountains. Even farther out it looks like maybe even some flurries above ~2500m on Monday? Have a great safe weekend and let's keep our fingers crossed for more sunny and dry weather well into the Fall!

The Cost of Falling Ice

It happened, most serendipitously, in the wee hours of the morning.

Sometime after midnight on August 10, 2012, a massive block of glacier ice estimated at about 125,000 cubic metres – enough to fill 50 Olympic-sized swimming pools – sheared away from high on the east-facing cliffs of Mount Edith Cavell in Jasper National Park. The massive ice chunks crashed into Cavell Tarn, a jade-tinted glacial pool at the base of steep rock walls, where, normally, a scattering of ice blocks float placidly in the silty water.

This avalanche was anything but placid. And, if that mass of ice and the rock detritus carried with it wasn't enough to blow beyond the banks of the tarn, the ensuing air blast and debris wave demolished a large section of the parking lot, picnic area, outhouses and plenty of trees and left a significant segment of the access road littered with massive boulders. According to a report compiled by Jasper National Park visitor safety specialist Rupert Wedgwood, the largest of these moved by the water was measured and estimated to weigh more than 1200 kilograms. The speed at which the initial wall of water travelled was estimated at between 16 and 27 kilometres per hour. The explosive overflow also destroyed a stretch of the gently graded interpretive "Glacier Trail" path that led from the parking lot to the bank of the meltwater lake where visitors had excitedly snapped photos and dipped their fingers into the icy water every day, summer after summer, for decades.

The destruction was first discovered by a pair of climbers around 4:00 a.m. on their way to ascend Edith Cavell's coveted east ridge. Driving in pre-dawn darkness, they were stopped by a gushing torrent of water with volleyball-sized chunks of ice and rocks being pushed along in the current. Realizing their VW Golf would not be able to drive through the torrent, they parked a distance back from the flow and then bushwhacked around the area to reach the climbers' access trail to carry on with their climb. It wasn't until a German tourist encountered the same debris flow more than four hours later that authorities were notified. By 9:22 a.m. the road was closed at its junction with Highway 93A and would not reopen for ten months. Ghost Glacier had literally fallen off the mountainside it had adhered to for millennia.

Just a 40-minute drive from the Jasper townsite, Edith Cavell is accessed via a narrow, twisting road, with hairpin turns and bordered by spruce forest, that was built in the 1930s and would make a spectacular setting for a Jason Bourne car chase if it wasn't inside a national park. It's named for a British nurse who was celebrated for saving the lives of soldiers from both sides during the First World War, but who was later executed for helping Allied soldiers escape from German-occupied Belgium. The towering pyramid is among the Rockies' highest peaks and dominates the view for miles around. The site draws some 200,000 tourists between June and October, with those numbers peaking in August. When the monstrous icefall happened, the glacial lake was at its highest water level, a factor that contributed to the severity of the damage.

Tourists view hanging Angel Glacier and the Cavell tarn from the safety of the newly rebuilt (2019) viewing area. Photo Lynn Martel

According to Wedgwood's report, the early weeks of the 2012 summer were wet, with rain adding to already high runoff after an exceptionally snowy winter, which resulted in flooding in many areas of the park. Just three days before the Ghost Glacier collapse, ten landslides rendered the road skirting the shores of Medicine Lake – barely 30 kilometres away as the raven flies – impassable. Whether the severe convective storm that generated those landslides could have caused the glacier collapse, the report concluded, was unknown.

The Cavell road reopened in late June 2013 with a repaired parking area and outhouses, and with brand-new signage urging visitors not to walk down to the edge of the pool, and describing how the area was under threats of falling ice, avalanche and flash flooding. Parks Canada commissioned an $85,000 geotechnical assessment to guide plans to repair, rebuild and monitor the area in the future.

There were a lot of questions. How did 70 per cent of the Ghost Glacier just fall from the mountain it had clung to for thousands of years? Could the same fate befall its much larger companion, Angel Glacier, which drops down like a giant pendant from a basin above the same small lake? Are tourists who visit one of the park's most popular sights at risk?

Hanging glaciers are just that – bodies of ice that adhere to the bedrock high on a mountain face, often in a cirque or shallow valley that ends abruptly at a cliff. Testimony to the impressive tensile strength of ice, their forms often curl over the edge of the cliff, stretched and cracked with crevasses. Eventually, gravity wins, and hunks of ice break off to land lower down the mountainside or, as it did at Edith Cavell, in glacier-melt lakes at the mountain's base.

Safety signs advise tourists not to walk down to the shore of the pond at the base of Angel Glacier at Mount Edith Cavell. In 2012 a massive collapse of the Ghost Glacier caused the pond to overflow its banks, destroying parts of the parking lot and access road and trails. Photo Lynn Martel

According to glaciologist Martin Sharp, a professor at the University of Alberta, the Edith Cavell ice avalanche was the result of one of two things. One is that the mass of ice reached its tipping point as gravity caused it to creep downslope under its own weight to the point where a steepening of the slope caused sufficient stress that the whole thing slid right off. Option B is that as the glacier melts – as they do in summertime – water seeps down through the ice and around the sides and collects between the glacier and the bedrock supporting it. This, of course, acts as a lubricant allowing the glacier to slide downhill more easily.

"When that happens," Sharp explained to the *Jasper Fitzhugh*, "the ice is moved faster toward the bottom end of the glacier and that makes it more likely to fail."

In this case, the speed of the glacier's movement will accelerate over the weeks leading to the failure. Some places in Europe's Alps have installed monitors to keep an eye out for such events, which are becoming more frequent as Earth's temperatures rise, so that people and property might be protected. Meanwhile, at Edith Cavell, several hikers snapped photos of an ice avalanche falling from Ghost Glacier less than 12 hours before its collapse, which they posted to various social media pages, some mentioning that about a hundred people were hiking along the lakeshore at the time.

Then, two years almost to the day after the original glacier collapse, Cavell Tarn overflowed again, sweeping away a section of road even farther below the parking lot and causing the site to be closed beyond the Edith Cavell Hostel and the Tonquin Valley trailhead popular with backpackers and horse outfitters. This time the over-flow was attributed to a combination of factors, including hot, dry weather, high water levels and heavy rainfall the night before. Thankfully, that flood didn't damage any of the new facilities built after the 2012 event, and again no one was hurt.

The entire Edith Cavell Road was closed again through the summer of 2018 as con-struction was carried out to reroute the road's entry point into a rebuilt and ex-panded parking lot higher above the outlet creek. Overall, $2.6 million was spent to reconstruct the day use area, parking lot, viewpoints, trails and interpretation pan-els. The expenses weren't limited to physical destruction, though, as the entire event cost Parks fees for overtime for search and rescue operations, helicopter flights and the expense of contracting a risk assessment report. Beyond that, local tour operators lost revenue due to the area's inaccessibility for the remainder of the season.

The investment is worth it, said a Parks Canada spokesperson, since the Mount Cavell area is one of Jasper's most popular day use areas, providing visitors the oppor-tunity to hike up to a subalpine/alpine area with relative ease on a well-graded and well-travelled trail. And while there, they can read the interpretive signs describing the collapse of the Ghost Glacier, a real-time example of how Earth's warming tem-peratures are affecting Canada's glaciers.

3-5 ICE DOLLARS

Lift Off to Ice

From James Bond movies to Red Bull videos, images of skiers schussing on spectacularly large and dramatically crevassed glaciers have been a hallmark of European skiing for decades. But while western Canada is home to thousands of glaciers, mechanical lifts installed at ski resorts to deliver skiers and boarders to glacier runs are essentially limited to one area – Whistler Blackcomb. In Canada, almost exclusively, skiers seeking to make turns on glaciers do so deep in backcountry wilderness using either a helicopter, snowcat, snowmobiles or their own human power to access those slopes.

At Whistler Blackcomb, though, Blackcomb and Horstman, which are small remnant glaciers, continue to exist within the ski area boundaries. In winter, Horstman Glacier is accessed by a T-bar and advised for advanced and expert skiers and riders only. In summer, ski and snowboard skills camps are hosted on Horstman, and viewing of nearby and distant glaciers outside the hill's boundaries is one of numerous activity options on the hill, alongside mountain biking, zip lines, bear viewing, hiking through alpine flower meadows and photography tours. Hikers are instructed to stay off glaciated areas for safety reasons.

Unlike much of the glaciated terrain in the Canadian Rockies, the glaciers in the Whistler region are not protected within national park boundaries. This distinction opens the door for local helicopter companies to offer a range of glacier-related experiences from sightseeing to weddings to professionally guided glacier walks to exploring ice caves and azure glacier-fed tarns. They'll supply mountaineering boots, rain jackets and pants, ice axe, harness, helmets, gloves and daypacks, plus a picnic lunch.

Helicopters are used to transport people and supplies into glacier areas, as well as provide sightseeing adventures throughout the mountains of British Columbia, Yukon and a few places in Alberta. This one is ferrying participants of the 2018 Alpine Club of Canada General Mountaineering Camp at Hallam Glacier. Photo Lynn Martel

In the Rockies, helicopter tours are popular businesses outside of the national park boundaries, offering, as one company advertises, the chance to see the Columbia Icefield "the way it was intended." In the eastern slope foothills, helicopter tours cruise up close to the "Matterhorn of the Rockies," and the small remnant glacier that rings the upper slopes of Mount Assiniboine. Canmore-based Alpine Helicopters runs daily glacier viewing tours year round. From its launch site at the Stoney Nakoda First Nation resort and casino in Kananaskis country, the two-person Great Divide Tour – the *othnikta* tour in the Stoney Nakoda language – includes the same up-close views of Assiniboine, plus a 15-minute stop near a lake just outside the Banff park boundary.

Toward the north end of the Rockies, at Mount Robson Provincial Park, for those lacking in time or fitness to hike 23 spectacular kilometres through multiple eco-zones from the parking lot to aquamarine Berg Lake, helicopters are permitted to land near Robson Pass. A leisurely hike from there brings you to Berg Lake, or to the spot a few kilometres away where Robson Glacier dunks its toe into a silty turquoise outlet lake. Thankfully, for those who venture into the wilderness to escape the noise of motors and machines, the landings are permitted only two days a week.

The pinnacle of aircraft-assisted glacier-viewing tours, however, happens in Kluane National Park, where the gargantuan Yukon glaciers stretch on for dozens of kilometres. Climbers and skiers charter flights to deliver them as near as possible to the bases of their intended routes, as do some backpackers intent on traversing the region's ice masses during the brief summer season. Those who do always pack extra food, as the same storms rolling in from the Pacific that so generously feed those glaciers frequently shut down all flying for days at a time.

Stormy weather aside, glacier viewing from helicopters and airplanes contributes to local and regional economies. The paradox, of course, is that whatever the purpose – sightseeing, as an air taxi delivering skiers, climbers or scientists to a lodge or a research camp for a week or a month, or for a heli-skiing operation where pilots routinely clock 100 landings and take-offs daily – the burning of jet fuel comes at an environmental cost. Jet fuel is a fossil fuel.

With this in mind, Blackcomb Helicopters boasts carbon neutral flights. They've done this by measuring the greenhouse gases emitted during each hour of flight from all their helicopters operating in all varieties of work they do, including utility installation and maintenance, tourism, wildfire suppression, film projects and rescue operations.

"We have mitigated these emissions from our flights by purchasing the equivalent amount of carbon offsets, where the money will go to fund green projects," their website states.

To accomplish this, they have enlisted the services of Offsetters, a Canadian carbon offset company.

A carbon footprint is an inventory calculating all the greenhouse gas emissions emitted by a person or business over a specific time period. A carbon offset represents a one-ton reduction in greenhouse gas emissions. To be carbon neutral, you need to purchase offsets equivalent to the amount of greenhouse gas emissions you produce. Offsetters work by having those emissions validated and verified by third parties to ensure that the emission reductions are real, additional and permanent. Each offset is listed on a registry with an associated serial number.

Blackcomb Helicopters elected to support the Quadra Island Forestland Conservation Project, which the company describes as "a local project that sequesters the equivalent amount of greenhouse gases that we emit – thus neutralizing the climate impact of our flights." This project ensures that 418 hectares of forestland along the Quadra Island coastline that was previously designated to be logged or converted to vacation homes now remains protected parkland. Joining two existing parks, the area protects rare second-growth hemlock trees and harbours ten Aboriginal heritage sites and an historical Aboriginal portage route. According to Blackcomb Helicopters, the British Columbia government had been trying to protect the area for nearly two decades, and the promise of funding from carbon offsets, along with contributions from a diverse group of donors and a land trade, was what made it possible for the government to purchase the site.

The company first purchased offsets for its discretionary business, tourism flights, in 2018. Within a year they could afford to make all their flights carbon neutral. They chose to protect an already standing forest because while planting new trees is also an important action, trees take a long time to grow. Protecting an already established forest provides an immediate and larger beneficial impact.

"We're trying to be great stewards of the areas we work and live in," explains Blackcomb Helicopters director Jason McLean. "If we want to be one of the great mountain access companies of the world, it's important that we address our carbon profile and be proactive about it."

The trick, of course, is to resist the temptation to fly more just because offsets are available, and recognizing that not all carbon offsets are equal in value and effectiveness. According to *Purchasing Carbon Offsets: A Guide for Canadian Consumers, Businesses, and Organizations,* the most effective carbon offsets are those supporting sustainable development and renewable energy projects, as they address the issue of fossil fuel reliance while improving peoples' lives. While forest-focused offsets sound good, a wildfire could wipe away their purpose in an instant. The Pembina Institute, David Suzuki Foundation and more than 60 non-governmental organizations around the world support the Gold Standard offsets.

Development Dreams

It was an odd phone call.

Around 2001 I was working as a reporter for the weekly *Canmore Leader* newspaper when the receptionist patched through a phone call.

"This is Oberto Oberti. Why do you say the glaciers are melting?"

I was startled. "Because they are?"

I really didn't know how else to answer the man with the thick Italian accent. I had recently begun to interview glaciologists who assured me that what many of us living in the mountains had already noticed – our local glaciers were shrinking at a perceptible rate – was indeed happening. It took me a moment to connect who the caller was, and why he might be phoning long-distance from Vancouver to query a small-town newspaper reporter. Then I remembered I'd recently written an article about an adventurer who had completed a multi-day backpack in British Columbia's Purcell Mountains, traversing a route that crossed the Jumbo and Commander glaciers. The adventurer, Dave Quinn, a wildlife biologist and outdoor educator, was scheduled to give a presentation in Canmore about his trip, and I had quoted him saying that glacial melting had presented some difficulty for him and his companions as they navigated hiking on and off steep snouts. Oberti, I learned, was a Vancouver architect who wanted to build a massive ski resort that would incorporate Jumbo, Farnham and Commander glaciers.

His was a big dream. Estimated to take 20 years and cost $750 million (which later rose to $1 billion), the Jumbo Glacier Project would consist of a hotel with 6,250 beds (including 750 staff accommodation beds), vacation homes and condos, shops and amenities. There would be 23 ski lifts, some of them installed right on glacial ice, capable of transporting an average of 2,700 skiers daily. Overall, the development would cover 60 square kilometres. Gondolas strung across the landscape would carry visitors into the heart of the high alpine amidst a wonderland of snow-capped peaks and sprawling glaciers. Skiing would mainly take place on the southwest rim of Glacier Dome, whose inaccessible east flanks drop in sheer cliffs down to the Lake of the Hanging Glacier.

From a ridge above Jumbo Pass, backcountry skier Monte Paynter savours the view of Horseshoe Glacier and Truce and Cauldron peaks at the head of Glacier Creek in British Columbia's Purcell Mountains. Photo Pat Morrow

Winter or summer, the views would indeed be splendid. The Jumbo Glacier master plan compared the potential of its vision to the highly developed alpine regions of Europe's Alps. They expected large numbers of visitors would enthusiastically spend money to see such a grand development in British Columbia's mountains.

But first they would have to get there. The closest town to Jumbo Glacier is Invermere. With a full-time population of about 3,400, it's at minimum a full hour's drive, and only the first 18 kilometres are paved. Beyond the Panorama Mountain Village ski resort, the road is a gravel road, part of which is maintained by British Columbia Highways. The remaining 15.5 kilometres is Forest Service Road that is not plowed in winter, leaving it accessible only to snowmobilers, backcountry skiers and snowshoers.

The Columbia Valley Hut Society operates a rustic (wood stove for heat, BYO white gas for cooking, plus outhouse) eight-person hut at Jumbo Pass a few kilometres from the proposed village site. Access to the hut is by hiking in summer or backcountry skiing in winter. Many locals view the area as their wilderness backyard playground. Their quiet, undeveloped playground.

For years, the proposal generated intense debate in the local community between those who believed the developers' argument that their project would bring economic development to the rural southeastern corner of the province, a ten-hour drive (when the roads are good) from Vancouver, and those, including members of the Columbia Valley Hut Society, Wildsight and the Jumbo Creek Conservation Society, who wanted to see Jumbo and its neighbouring valleys and peaks and glaciers remain undeveloped. Although the Jumbo area was once home to a small portable sawmill, the only remaining evidence is an overgrown clearing and regenerating logged cutblocks on the slope above that are used for heli-skiing.

The provincial government (which supported the plan) granted approval in March 2004, under the condition that substantial work be started in five years, a timeline that was later extended to ten. As the deadline loomed, all that the developers had to show for their efforts were the beginnings of a road bulldozed by Caterpillar right onto the lower moraine of the Farnham Glacier in 2008. At the very last minute, literally, the partial foundation for a day lodge was, inexplicably, erected at the base of what had been identified by professional consultants as an active avalanche path. The developer had failed to meet the terms of the province's Environmental Assessment Certificate prior to its expiration date, and the province ordered a halt to its construction.

"It's about building the economy. It's about creating jobs," the project's senior vice-president Grant Costello had said in support of the project. "That results from investment and that's what strengthens the economy."

Location, Location

Many locals, however, weren't buying it, a sentiment echoed by the abundance of "Keep Jumbo Wild" bumper stickers on mud-splattered pickups and SUVs throughout southern British Columbia and even in Alberta. Those opposed were diverse in their backgrounds and passions. And they were organized. When potential investors were given a tour by helicopter, they were greeted by a very large JUMBO WILD message painted with blue food colouring in the snow.

Wildlife biologists attested that the viability of the local – and legally designated as threatened – grizzly bear population would be irreversibly put at risk by such large-scale development in the middle of a critical migration route running right through the Jumbo area. First Nations spoke out as well, claiming that for the Ktunaxa people Jumbo – or Qat'muk in the Ktunaxa language – represents the home of the grizzly bear spirit. In November 2017, the Supreme Court ruled in favour of allowing the resort to be built on the Jumbo land, effectively showing that Canada's Charter of Rights and Freedoms protects the freedom to worship but not the focal point of worship, such as a mountain, a forest or a glacier.

Others questioned the financial viability of building a resort so far from anywhere. Invermere already has a dozen ski resorts within less than three hours' drive, which, _ely, if ever, run to capacity. From the em-_reas in western Canada are famously staffed _ustralia, New Zealand, the UK and eastern _visas – the only people willing to work the _p the bulk of positions available at ski hills. _onal airport is a four-hour drive away in _pass four other ski hills en route, including _een Invermere and Jumbo, making the journey an impressive commitment with impatient children in the back seat. The unpaved road beyond Panorama is threatened by no fewer than 22 avalanche paths. According to BC's Ministry of Transportation and Infrastructure, the developers would be responsible for the costs of paving the road to a provincially approved standard, after which BC taxpayers would carry the costs of

Fresh cougar or lynx tracks mark the snow on the unmaintained forestry road leading to Jumbo Glacier in British Columbia's Purcell Mountains. Photo Lynn Martel

protecting and maintaining it. In summertime – after the snow and avalanche debris melts out – anyone is welcome to drive the narrow, twisting roads paralleling the rushing Toby, Jumbo or Horsethief creeks to see the area's glaciers. For free, 4 x 4 recommended.

Then there's the local heli-skiing business, RK Heliski, based at Panorama, which has been taking its clients skiing in the Jumbo area since the early 1970s.

"I've skied in the Jumbo area more than anyone in the world – I know that for a fact," said Rod Gibbons, an ACMG mountain guide who was RK's operations manager for a quarter-century, who made no secret of being steadfastly opposed to the Jumbo plan and whom I interviewed for a feature story on Jumbo in the Whistler *Pique Newsmagazine* in 2013. "It would be devastating to our business. Where the village is being proposed, that's our bad weather skiing. The terrain they are potentially taking away represents where we ski sixty-five per cent of the time. There's not a business in the world that can expect to survive that – not in any way that's recognizable."

Like all glaciated areas, Jumbo does get its share of sunny, bluebird, skier-friendly days. But, like all glaciated areas, Jumbo is visited by storms – the same forces that created and replenished the glacier for thousands of years. In addition to whiteout conditions that make helicopter flying – and any glacier travel – unsafe, broad flat glaciers such as Jumbo generate powerful katabatic winds that propel high-density air from a higher elevation downslope under the force of gravity. Heli-ski operations choose different runs every day, not only to ski fresh snow, but because crevasse, avalanche and weather conditions are constantly changing, thus dictating safety considerations. By necessity, heli-skiing on glaciers is balanced with a calculated amount of lower-elevation forest or glade skiing. Despite the marketing claims, very little of the terrain from the summit of Glacier Dome is actually glaciated. Or skiable. While Commander Glacier appears to offer a desirable pitch for sweet turns, it is riddled with crevasses. And, of course, those glaciers are smaller and more broken today than when the Duncan Lake 82K/7 topographic map was printed in 1979.

"Commander has ski terrain, it's a nice pitch, but it's unbelievably wild with crevasses and serac fields," Gibbons explained. "It's not normal commercial heli-ski terrain."

Gibbons also responded to suggestions about how snowcats might be used to fill in crevasses, noting that machinery had historically been used in the Jumbo area to fill in crevasses on Farnham Glacier. During the 2007, '08 and '09 summers, RK Heliski provided the safety contract for the Calgary Olympic Development Association as Canada's alpine ski team trained in preparation for the 2010 Winter Olympics in Vancouver and Whistler. The team has not returned to the site since.

"I can tell you from experience, Farnham is as benign as it is because of all the excavator work CODA did there," Gibbons said. "The excavator ran countless hours. What I learned from that is if you want to tame a glacier, you use an excavator. That's what they do in Europe."

Glacier Zoning

The entire proposal became highly politicized. In 2009, the Regional District of East Kootenay voted eight to seven to ask the Province to legislate the proposed Jumbo Resort site as a Mountain Resort Municipality – a request that would skip over the rezoning and public consultation processes for local residents. Despite demands for a new vote on charges that the public review process had been inadequate and previous directors' votes undemocratic, there was no second vote. In November 2010, the Ktunaxa presented their Qat'muk Declaration to the Province at the legislature declaring the area sacred to the grizzly bear and their culture.

Then in March 2012, after making specific changes to Bill 41 to facilitate creation of a "mountain resort community," British Columbia's then Liberal government approved the project. In February 2013, a mayor and two councillors were appointed by the Province to oversee a municipality with a human population of zero, with $260,000 of taxpayers' money to get started. The decision was roundly slammed by the Union of BC Municipalities and resulted in the West Kootenay EcoSociety launching a lawsuit, arguing the appointment of municipal councillors without any electors violates the constitution and various provincial statutes. By the end of 2018 the municipality had received $782,824 through government grants, with $255,000 annually expected through 2023.

With the Environmental Assessment Certificate due to expire in October 2014, locals opposed to the project monitored developments closely. The developer failed to meet the terms by the deadline, and the certificate expired.

Hikers explore the wilderness of the Farnham Glacier area in summer. Photo Lynn Martel

Ice Guardians

The diligence of those opposed was impressive and unfailing. In addition to countless letters to the editor to newspapers across the province, a symphony orchestra played a Requiem for a Glacier within stone's throw of Farnham Glacier. In 2008, when the developers, armed only with permission to ski on Farnham Glacier but none for installing a lift or road construction, began bulldozing their way to the west Farnham Glacier, volunteers managed to get the heavy equipment removed and manned a blockade for eight weeks to ensure they didn't try to sneak back in. The destruction created by the bulldozer remains visible.

Clearly, Jumbo and its neighbouring glaciers were worth fighting for. From both sides. And while some see money in glaciers, others see something they believe to be of greater value.

Hikers, mountaineers, backcountry skiers, trappers, outfitters, snowmobilers and First Nations have been enjoying the wild solitude of this undeveloped area for generations, dating back to legendary mountain guide Conrad Kain, who made the first winter ascent of Jumbo Peak on snowshoes in 1919. The Ktunaxa for much, much longer.

In his lifetime, Pat Morrow has photographed and filmed mountain ranges and the people and cultures inhabiting them all over the world. In October 1982, he became the second Canadian to stand on the highest point on Earth two days after his teammate, Laurie Skreslet, planted Canada's flag on Mount Everest's summit. Four years later Morrow made his own unique mark on history as the first person to climb the Seven Summits – the highest point on each continent.

A Columbia Valley native and resident of Wilmer – a tiny sidewalk-free hamlet just

Protestors manned a camp for eight weeks to ensure unauthorized road construction did not resume on Farnham Glacier. Photo Dave Quinn

outside Invermere – who has explored countless peaks and valleys and glaciers in his backyard Purcell Mountains, Morrow credits the Jumbo area for providing him an experience in his youth that inspired a deeper love of high alpine wilderness.

"One of my early memories is of a wonderful multi-peak enchainment I did around 1976 with my friend Willi Schmidt," Morrow recalled. "The trip took us into the heart of the Jumbo area.

Protestors march on the downtown streets of Cranbrook, British Columbia, to voice their opposition to development of a resort near Jumbo Glacier. Photo Dave Quinn

The prospect of having that whole skyline compromised by a gondola line stretching across this magnificent landscape just makes my heart sink."

In that sentiment, Morrow has plenty of company throughout the East Kootenays. Garnering attention beyond the immediate region, Patagonia, the environmentally active US-based outdoor clothing and gear company, helped sponsor production of a film about the threatened glacier called *Jumbo Wild*. They, like Morrow, asked, "Why develop Jumbo at all?" From an environmental perspective, constructing anything on a glacier is downright foolish – glaciers are the ultimate birthplace of freshwater. And as, inch by inch, wilderness areas around the world are developed, does it not make better sense for British Columbia to protect the unpopulated and undeveloped corners of its backyard?

"If chair lifts and gondolas are what people want to see, they can go to Europe or any of a number of other ski areas in this region, if what they want to do is get up high effortlessly," said Morrow, now in his sixties and still skiing and climbing to local summits. "In the Alps you just don't have that kind of pristine terrain experience. It devalues the experience as soon as you put gondolas and buildings there.

"Apart from a purely aesthetic appreciation for the glaciers in the Jumbo area, though, at a more fundamental level, I'm concerned about the consequences of their drying up as they form the basis for the headwaters of the king Columbia River. As human population and development soars in the Rocky Mountain Trench, the water table and river flows drop...."

Glacier Gamble

With the Jumbo dream in limbo, Oberti's son, Tomasso, turned his attention to plans for a big glacier skiing resort near Valemount, west of Jasper. A 3½-hour drive from Kamloops, and 5½ hours from Edmonton – when the roads are not snow-covered – the destination is, again, out of the way. Described in promotional material as "one of the rare available sites for new mountain resort developments in North America," it is adjacent to Canadian Mountain Holidays' Cariboos and Valemount ski tenures, which have been operating since the 1970s, as has nearby Mike Wiegele Helicopter Skiing. The glaciers in the area are considerably large, large enough that they might still be worth seeing while the Athabasca – less than three hours' drive to the south – diminishes into economic oblivion. Designed with a 20-year buildout, it promises a "unique and magical location, with large, majestic mountains and glaciers." The project aims to provide a lift system spanning from one peak to the next over Twilight and McLennan glaciers that operates year round, for skiers and sightseers alike. Regional support for the $175 million project exceeded opposition, but the initial completion date of December 2018 has been pushed to 2020. As of late 2019, no work had yet begun.

Meanwhile, in August 2019, the British Columbia Court of Appeal ruled that the decision made in 2015 by the Provincial Minister of Environment – that the Jumbo Glacier project's environmental assessment certificate was expired because the project had not been "substantially started" – should be reinstated after being previously overturned by a lower court.

"With the resort dead in the water, Jumbo is going to stay wild," said John Bergenske, Wildsight's Conservation Director. "Now, it's time for Qat'muk to be legally recognized, and beyond Qat'muk, wildlife need long-term protection in the broader central Purcell Mountains, all the way from the Purcell Wilderness Conservancy to Glacier National Park."

I am among those who cheered the decision. I've never understood the logic behind wanting to build a resort – a significant part of whose investment strategy includes dozens of vacation properties – in the heart of forest fire country. In recent years, forest fires have begun earlier in the summer season and lasted later, smothering western Canada's mountain ranges in thick, unpleasant smoke and a substantial coating of dread. And as Earth's climate continues to warm, as all predictions and evidence indicate it will, those conditions are expected to persist. It's unknown how this might impact western Canada's tourism industry, especially for a resort built at the end of a dead-end valley, with absolutely minimal firefighting resources. The location would turn into a death trap with lightning speed if a fire started at the bottom end of the valley and worked its way uphill, as fires often do. But, with

This bulldozer was used to clear a track on the Commander Glacier by Winsport in preparation for CODA – Canada Olympic Development Association – summer training. Salt was also used to melt ice. Photo Pat Morrow

human-caused climate change predicted by all measures to result in warmer winter temperatures with more rain and changes in snowfall amounts and consistency for alpine ski resorts across western Canada, how detrimental these changes will be to the ski industry is yet to be determined.

Then, in January 2020 the announcement finally came. The Ktunaxa Nation and the Province of British Columbia would create an Indigenous Protected and Conserved Area in Qat'muk. Encompassing 700 square kilometres, the protected area would connect with the vast Purcell Wilderness Conservancy to the south to provide critical protected habitat for grizzly bears extending to the Canada–US border, not to mention the birds, the creeks, the forests and the glaciers of Jumbo Valley.

Industrial Ice

Long before the first ski town blossomed in western Canada, miners lured by dollar signs bullied their way up valleys clogged with devils' club and convoluted webs of willow and alder bushes. Gold, copper, zinc – decades before skiers' eyes lit up at the sight of fresh powder sparkling like diamonds, prospectors' eyes lit up at the smallest suggestion of real diamonds.

Every so often, prospectors outdo themselves in terms of imagination and tenacity. In the case of the Granduc copper mine, positioned on a rock ridge with a cliff on one side and a glacier on the other, it's a wonder that the deposits were ever sniffed out in a location so remote and inaccessible.

Deep in the Coast Mountains a thousand kilometres north of Vancouver, as early as 1899 a base camp was staked on the Unuk River, which flows from heavily glaciated peaks of the Cambria Icefields to empty into Alaska's Behm Canal. There's no evidence those prospectors followed the Unuk Glacier to its source at what is now known as Granduc Mountain, and it's probable at that time that the mineral treasures of the lower Granduc were concealed under glacial ice.

Prospectors did, however, keep searching through the 1920s, and in 1931 a claim stake was recorded near Granduc Mountain. It lapsed, but by the early 1950s glacial melting combined with advancing industrial

The regularly maintained road cuts a swath on the Knipple Glacier to provide access to the Brucejack Mine near Stewart in British Columbia's Coast Mountains.

technology nudged open the door for what would become history-making accomplishments in mining engineering. After two well-known prospectors staked claims for what showed promise of a significant copper deposit in 1951, two big players in the mining industry, American Smelting and Refining Company and Newmont Mining Corporation, pooled financial and technical resources to create Granduc Operating Company. A camp was established with necessary exploratory equipment flown into the site. Five years later their findings were confirmed – Granduc Mine would yield bountiful, high-quality copper ore.

The fact that the deep ore body was partially covered by a glacier was regarded as inconvenient but not insurmountable. Rendering the site workable meant drilling a 17-kilometre-long tunnel from the Leduc mine site on Granduc Mountain's west flank to the planned site of concentrator facilities at the glaciated area of Tide Lake in the Bowser Valley. In addition, they'd have to build a 52-kilometre road from Tide Lake to Stewart, Canada's most northerly ice-free port, where facilities would be built to accommodate deep-sea vessels at the head of the 145-kilometre-long, narrow Portland Canal that forms the Canada–US border.

The challenges of the rugged mountain terrain were never far from mind in the area, where summers are short and soggy, and winter snowfalls average more than 20 metres; in 1965 an avalanche took the lives of 26 men and destroyed much of the camp and the portal to the partially constructed tunnel. To overcome the extra costs brought on by that tragedy – including the hiring of a professional avalanche consultant – and associated redesigns, some organizational and financial restructuring was undertaken to enable continued development of the mine. At this point the infrastructure included crushing and concentrating facilities, pump house, power plant, residences, shops and sewage treatment facilities. A substantial flow of groundwater provided ample supply for both human and industrial needs. The well-drilling activities were carried out in what was the site of Tide Lake, which has since emptied and vanished.

A blasting truck transports workers on an ice road plowed onto the Knipple Glacier to maintain access to the Brucejack Mine.

The rail tunnel, completed in 1968, is still spoken of enthusiastically among mine engineers and historians. Workers were transported in specially designed cars, and ore in side-dump cars, through the $4^{1}/_{2}$-metre-diameter tunnel at speeds of up to 60 kilometres per hour on an efficient modern system that passed under no fewer than three mountain ranges and three glaciers. Safe and comfortable passage was facilitated during the 27-minute (one-way) ride by seven underground compressors that supplied high-pressure air for all the mine's underground operations and the world's longest mining operation tunnel. The operators spent $115 million to make the mine operational, and the first shipment of concentrate left for Japan in January 1971. Production at that time was 5,000 tons per day, a rate that increased in later years to 9,000 tons per day, making Granduc a key player in Canadian mining until it shut down in 1983. In 2010, Castle Resources Inc. acquired a 100 per cent interest in the Granduc property, and some mining and tunnel rehabilitation was carried out on site over the next few years.

While Granduc no longer operates, other mines in the area continued to; mining operations in the area date back to 1910. At one point some 150 properties were being worked on both sides of the Canada–US border. Just north of the Granduc site, Brucejack Gold Mine poured its first gold bar in 2017. Reaching that milestone required more than a decade of preparatory work that included winterizing the camp, stringing a 57-kilometre transmission line to connect the site to grid power, and ongoing maintenance on a ten-kilometre road. Threatened by avalanches from the steep mountain slopes bordering it, the road is carved right into glacial ice, and demands 24/7 maintenance work carried out by highway-size graders and snowcats. With avalanches threatening the camp site too, professional mountain guides and avalanche technicians are contracted to control the avalanche hazard using explosives tossed from helicopters.

Glacier in a Glass

It's astounding how often the word *glacier* is used to market a product. For ages clever entrepreneurs have attached the word glacier to the names of myriad products and services, ranging from toilet paper to craft beers to chewing gum and plastic bags filled with factory-manufactured ice cubes made of ordinary water. More than one businessperson has packaged and sold actual frozen chunks of glacier ice for profit too – refrigeration not included.

In advertising, the word glacier is used to denote clear, pristine, cool, clean and pure, although it's often associated with items that bear no connection to glaciers of any kind.

Then there's Park Distillery.

The Banff-based business includes a restaurant, a bar and a distillery that crafts

Meltwater from five Rockies glaciers is used in the production of Park Distillery's vodka, gin and rye.

vodka, gin and rye. Distilling in the "purest place on the planet," Park uses water to distill its spirits that is drawn from the Bow River watershed, which is fed by six Canadian Rockies glaciers – the Wapta Icefield via the Bow and Crowfoot glaciers, the Waputik Icefield via the Balfour and Bath glaciers, Victoria Glacier and Fay Glacier – in addition to many smaller pocket and remnant glaciers adding to the mix along the way.

Cheers!

Nature's Dollar

While glaciers contribute to the tourism economy of British Columbia, Alberta, Yukon, Nunavut and even a wee corner of the Northwest Territories, Canada's ancient ice earn its keep, every single day, simply by existing.

One man who has calculated this, as best he is able, is Mark Anielski, an economic strategist living in Edmonton, Alberta, who specializes in measuring the well-being and happiness of nations, communities and businesses. With a master's degree in forest economics, for a decade he taught corporate social responsibility and social entrepreneurship at the University of Alberta's School of Business. As a consultant, he lectures around the world on the economics of happiness and well-being. After all, isn't that what we all hope to achieve?

Meltwater from western Canada's glaciers feeds creeks and rivers that provide fresh water to millions of Canadians in British Columbia, Alberta, Saskatchewan, Manitoba, Yukon and even the Northwest Territories, as well as millions of Americans in Washington, Oregon and five other US states. Photo Lynn Martel

"My work is attempting to value nature in terms of the many non-market ecosystem services or functions nature provides our economy for free," he explained to me. "Glaciers are perhaps the most important of all strategic 'water' assets whose replacement value can never be expressed in terms of money, unless you were able to engineer the equivalent of what glaciers do in terms of providing water regulatory/supply services."

Glaciers provide services that are critical to our water security, annual flow rates and clean drinking water. While he hasn't yet found any studies to have actually done the math, Anielski has determined some steps that would need to be followed to attach a dollar figure to those services.

First, the annual discharge, or flow rate, measured in terms of cubic metres of water that flow through each watershed running from both the Alberta and British Columbia sides of the Continental Divide would have to be determined so that a value of the water flow could be calculated. The replacement value of water could be calculated using treated waters as a proxy, but any numbers arrived at would be inadequate as a proxy value since the quality of glacier water cannot be matched by human endeavours. Usually, the ecological value of rivers and streams is measured by the area of land they occupy, and then by multiplying an estimated annual economic-ecological service value.

One challenge facing that approach, however, is that ecosystem service values vary depending on the proximity of rivers and streams to human populations. That means urban rivers and streams have higher values per hectare of area simply because of their importance to human populations. As a result, putting monetary values on such services is ultimately tied to human population, since grizzly bears and spruce trees don't care about monetization.

To arrive at a value for each glacier and river, and their relative importance to any given human population, city or town, you'd have to derive a scale of human economic values to these populations. One means of accomplishing this could involve determining the total volume of water – drinking, household and other uses – used per capita and in total by all the communities that benefit from a glacier and its watershed. In conjunction with that, you'd also have to figure out a way to determine what percentage of that annual flow comes from the glacier versus rain, snowfall, groundwater or other sources.

"That relative volume of glacier water can then be valued, say, at the purchase price of bottled water or the cost of treated water per cubic metre," Anielski suggested. "The challenge, though, is that even glacier water would likely require some form of filtration or treatment to be potable."

From a geopolitical perspective, the

A popular tourist spot, Takakkaw Falls – the name means magnificent – is nourished by snow and glacier melt in Yoho National Park. As the glaciers feeding it diminish, will it continue to be so? Photo Lynn Martel

process of determining which communities benefit from a particular glacier and its watershed is simpler, since provincial boundaries – and the international Canada–US border – are defined by precise lines drawn on a map. Formal agreements concerning the sharing of water resources between nations and provinces are nothing new. Add to that the fact that no country could afford to build the number of dams it would take to provide the upstream water storage glaciers and icefields provide - not to mention the ecosystem damage such barriers would inflict.

"Establishing provincial budgets that reflect the relative importance, value and state of regions or watersheds from a budgetary perspective could be done, but rarely, if ever, are," Anielski said. "There is the long-standing challenge of being able to match different socio-economic and other data boundaries with varying geographic boundaries used by different government agencies. These will remain long-standing challenges."

Replacement Ice?

While a number of methods to apply dollar values to ecosystem services have been outlined in literature, such as a study Anielski completed for Ducks Unlimited in 2015, many of those values employed come from research and don't necessarily represent real economic values in the sense that often there are no markets for services such as pollination, biodiversity or even climate regulation. We have, it appears, a long way to go before human populations can arrive at dollar values for the countless services we count on nature to provide with nary a thought. That said, the emergence of carbon values and associated markets, such as taxes, are a step in that direction.

"My favoured way of measuring the value of healthy watersheds and their ecosystem services is to compare a healthy watershed that currently provides clean and filtered drinking water – for example the Catskill Mountains that provide clean water for the large city of New York – to the full amortized cost of a water treatment facility that would otherwise be built to perform similar services that the watershed and its forests did for free."

This approach, called replacement cost valuation, is preferable to academic research, since it uses a reverse calculation of what would need to be paid for the ecosystem services if they did not otherwise exist in healthy ecosystems.

At the very start, for any province in Canada to arrive at a monetary value for ecosystem services, there would first have to be a complete inventory conducted – of wetlands, cropland, forest land (of all cover types), rivers, streams, lakes, alpine terrain and more. Then, estimates would have to be calculated on the current ecological health or condition of those landscape sectors per hectare or acre of land using data from previous studies to then derive total annual ecosystem service value estimates. While Anielski has made these calculations for several watersheds in western and northern Canada, including the Mackenzie, the North Saskatchewan and the Bow, no province has yet committed to preparing natural capital accounts. And, he added, such a tally has never been done – in Canada, nor anywhere else he is aware of.

"Typically, ecological services per area of land – hectares – can be two to ten times more valuable than the market or economic value of land used for economic purposes," he said. "But then again, this doesn't really help us make the necessary trade-off decisions between conserving ecological value or integrity and optimizing economic well-being conditions."

The value of glaciers, however, extends far beyond the tangible.

"The benefits of seeing a glacier or walking next to one like the Iceline trail in Yoho have no real replacement value, though we might otherwise hike in other places where we did experience glaciers if the Iceline no longer did," Anielski said.

"These values can be calculated but they will be nowhere near the value of glaciers as sources of water. The value of rivers, streams and lakes are the highest of all ecosystem service values we calculate for nature, higher near urban centres. Intuitively you know that there would be no replacement value for glaciers once they are gone or melted away." When you think about it, human habits defy all logic. We factor the use of water into so many of our everyday actions – making coffee, or beer, taking showers, maintaining lawns – a questionable use of water and stealer of leisure time if ever there was one – and in virtually all manufacturing processes from cars to food products to plastic pink flamingos. We affix a dollar value to all of these, but all without calculating the dollar value of that water. And with glaciers – which store water for human use at no cost – dwindling, not one municipality or province in Canada has a plan for how to replace that service.

Ancient ice: there is no substitute.

Professor Glyn Williams-Jones and Dr. Alex Wilson approach a fumarole ice cave on Mount Meager, one of a group of volcanic peaks northwest of Whistler in the Pacific Ranges of the Coast Mountains, to take gas composition and temperature measurements. Photo Simon Fraser University

4 STUDY OF ICE

*Of all the phenomena that attract the nature lover in the high
mountains, possibly none is more interesting or appeals more
strongly to the imagination than the glaciers.*

—William Vaux, 1907 *Canadian Alpine Journal*

4–1 INTO THE SCIENCE ZONE

Just Another Walk to Work

Having squeezed my Mazda into a three-quarter-wide parking spot sandwiched
amidst a hodgepodge of rental cars, camper vans and duplex-sized motor homes,
I hoisted my backpack. I was headed to the Peyto Glacier glaciology research site, a
place I had previously passed while skiing to and from overnight trips to the Alpine
Club of Canada's hut on the Wapta Icefields. As skiers, we had viewed the research
station with curiosity. But I had never hiked the route in summer, so I was excited to
be invited to spend a couple of days observing the scientists studying the glacier for
a newspaper article.

Threading my way through a traffic jam of tourists walking the short trail to and
from the postcard-perfect viewpoint overlooking cerulean Peyto Lake, their feet
clad in a variety of flimsy sandals and spiky heels that tottered on the uneven gravel,
just before the final crush of cameras
I deked left onto a narrow dirt trail.
Hiking steadily downhill through a forest of brawny old-growth spruce and
fir trees rising like stately columns, in
just a few breaths I crossed from heavily populated tourist attraction into se-
cluded, quiet wilderness. Thirty minutes later, I emerged from the aromatic
forest onto the breezy expanse of gravel
beds braided with aqua ribbons of glacial melt, all flowing to fill the lake.

Scientists plan their day in the early morning light at the Peyto Glacier research station, built in the 1960s, and still well used today. Photo Lynn Martel

Before setting out I had learned that the long-established trail that skirted the south side of the surging outflow creek would lead to a dead end a few kilometres upstream from the flats, since the bridge spanning the rowdy flow just below an impassable cliff had been washed away by the previous summer's floodwaters. Hiking solo, my safest option was to walk directly across the succession of narrow, shallow outflow streams feeding the lake rather than the concentrated, turbulent and much deeper current upstream at the old bridge site. Once across the streams, I could follow a makeshift trail hewn by hikers' boots on the north bank of the creek and regain the main trail at the old bridge site. From my vantage point a few hundred metres from where the glacier's snout had reached just a century ago, I understood firsthand how the melting glacier, now four kilometres and 450 vertical metres farther up valley, is in a constant state of flux, shoving rocks and water downstream, altering the paths we humans so optimistically build to suit our purposes.

Skipping and hopping across the gently flowing rivulets, I came to a larger channel pulsing toward the lake. It was considerably wider and deeper than any of the others and was the final torrent between me and the north-side trail. Walking back and forth along the water's edge, I studied the current to choose the broadest, shallowest flow.

Slipping off my backpack, I sat on a bleached deadwood tree trunk and unlaced my boots and secured them to the outside of my pack up near the top. Then I unzipped the lower leg section from my hiking pants. Strapping into the lightweight sandals I'd carried for just this purpose, I stepped into the ankle-deep stream. Instantly, the icy water engulfed my warm, tender skin. "WHOO!!!" Exhaling helped relieve the smarting. Bracing myself with a hiking pole gripped tightly in each hand, I willed my bare legs into the forceful current that shoved against my shins, eager to send me hurtling downstream. Step after step the water grew deeper as my feet sought out the flattest stones that didn't wobble underfoot and the cold water rose, surging at my knees. I was immersed in the flow, the life-blood gushing from the glacier and its parent icefield to fill the lake that forms the headwaters of the Mistaya River, which pours into the North Saskatchewan River downstream. The chilly water swirling above my knees would ultimately flow through Edmonton to central Saskatchewan and finally pour into Hudson Bay, where polar bears hunt for seals on its winter-frozen surface, and walrus, dolphins and orca swim and feed.

Just as I feared being knocked over and flushed into the lake and beyond, I took one more step. Phew, the flow wasn't quite as deep. A few breaths and curses later I reached the dry rocky beach, and warm summer air. Boots back on and invigorated head-to-toe, I quickly found the start of the rough and ragged north-bank trail.

Hiking along the skinny track, and two thankfully smaller creek crossings later, I eventually made the final ascent up a long, steep hogsback moraine ridge until the glaciology buildings emerged into view, all the while cognizant that for the researchers who had hiked the same route a few days ahead of me, this was just another walk to work.

Canada's First Family of Glaciology

It was a grand family vacation. George Vaux VIII and his three children, Mary, William and George IX, journeyed from their homes in Philadelphia across the United States to the Pacific coast. They turned north and crossed the border to Vancouver, then boarded the new Canadian Pacific Railway to travel all the way back east to Montreal. Along the way they stopped at Glacier House, the quaint yet elegant hotel nestled in the lush forest at Rogers Pass.

The year was 1887, and the three siblings, ranging in age from 27 (Mary) to 15 (William), had been raised in a liberal Quaker tradition that encouraged formal education and especially study in the natural sciences. They were also keen participants in the growing art of photography. Walking for half an hour on a rough path fitted with bare logs spanning rushing creeks that wound along beneath imposing old-growth cedar trees with stubborn devil's club hugging their trunks, they arrived at a mound of ice that towered over their heads. The Great Glacier, nowadays known by its proper name, the Illecillewaet (Shuswap for "swift water"), at that time pushed right down to the forest floor. Much higher up the valley the glacier stretched half a kilometre across, but at its terminus where they stood it tapered to an arrowhead, plump and creased and wrinkled with crevasses around its perimeter like the cracked skin of chapped lips. Today, reaching the glacier's toe involves a good two hours farther of rugged off-trail scrambling up colourful lichen-dotted moraine rocks streaked with ribbons of meltwater.

While they couldn't see the massive Illecillewaet Icefield from which the glacier descended, the Vauxes were sufficiently impressed by their surroundings that Mary, George IX and William enthusiastically returned seven years later. On their second visit, though, they couldn't help but notice how the glacier's snout had melted back up the valley a significant distance.

Formally trained as an engineer and architect, William got to work. He devised several methods by which the glacier could be scientifically studied, including setting up a prismatic compass near the terminus and installing a series of plates on the ice to record measurements that would enable him to estimate how fast the glacier was moving. With one of the siblings returning annually, they also took photographs

One of the Vaux brothers takes a bearing at the forefoot (toe) of the Illecillewaet Glacier during the family's visit to Rogers Pass in 1898 (8/17/98). Photo Whyte Museum of the Canadian Rockies, Vaux Family Fonds (V653-ng-315)

from the same location year after year, a spot that came to be known as Photographer's Rock, lugging an unwieldy large-format field camera fitted with a hefty Bausch & Lomb lens to the site on every visit. The photos didn't just back up their measurements; they continue to provide valuable information for researchers today.

Presenting their findings to the Philadelphia Academy of Natural Sciences in 1898, they identified, correctly, the source of the Illecillewaet and other glacial attributes. "The source of the glacier is in the great snow field of névé which covers the comparatively level portions of the higher mountain ranges. By the action of the Sun and pressure, this snow is very much compressed, till the crystals are frozen together and form clear ice. It is at this point that the glacier proper begins."

Employing the relatively new technique of dendrochronology – counting tree rings to gauge a tree's age and the atmospheric conditions during that period – they studied other clues. They deduced that some mature alders growing near the toe had been there three decades, suggesting the glacier had not crept beyond that point during that time. Accompanied by intricately detailed sketches, their meticulously recorded measurements revealed a significant rate of melting, some ten metres per year between 1898 and 1906. With some mathematical adjustments they calculated that between 1890 and 1898 the glacier had retreated an astonishing average of 17 metres annually. They learned that the melting rate fluctuated from year to year due to different snowfall amounts, warmer or colder temperatures and other factors, but that the overall rate remained relatively stable. They also discovered a series of boulders that had been branded in tar by the Reverend William Spotswood Green when he had explored those trails the year after the Vauxes' initial visit.

"These boulders, together with Mr. Green's photographs taken that year, showed that but little recession occurred during the preceding twelve months. At the time of our visit in 1887, the ice rose above this moraine as an almost perpendicular wall many feet in height, thus indicating that a period of advance had been going on for some time previously. The marked recession which had occurred since then has naturally given the whole vicinity of the forefoot a very different aspect."

Although technically amateur glaciologists, the Vaux siblings accomplished some terrific baseline science. Their observations and conclusions align with modern scientific understanding that was gained decades later which shows that the apex of the last glacial advance, known as the Little Ice Age, occurred during this period. How fortuitous that they were there and chose to study the glacier when they did.

Today, the invaluable collection of photos, sketches, charts and tables is kept at the Whyte Museum of the Canadian Rockies in Banff. While William died in 1908, and George IX's corporate and real estate law practice, and his growing family, prevented him from returning after 1912, Mary continued to visit the area nearly every year until her death in 1940. A prize-winning Guernsey breeder, during a visit to the Rockies in 1912 she met Dr. Charles Doolittle Walcott, a Smithsonian Institution administrator and an esteemed paleontologist who had discovered the Burgess Shale Cambrian fossils near Field, British Columbia, three years earlier. Despite her father's objections, they married in 1914 and during many subsequent trips to the Rockies she assisted Walcott in his work. She also left an impressive legacy of her own photographs, and 400 of her illustrations of the region's wildflowers were published by the Smithsonian in 1925 in her five-volume *North American Wildflowers*. She was elected president of the Society of Women Geographers in 1933. And she carried on the family work studying the Illecillewaet Glacier until her death at 80.

Generations on Ice

The Vaux family work continued through the efforts of the next generation, George IX's two sons, George X and Henry. From the late 1920s through the 1930s, they continued to record measurements and take photographs not only at the Illecillewaet Glacier but also the Asulkan, which descends from the Illecillewaet Icefield one valley farther west. They ventured into the Rockies and recorded images and measurements of the Yoho, Victoria and Wenkchemna glaciers. They collaborated with Arthur Oliver Wheeler, who, in 1906, had begun measuring the Yoho Glacier regularly, a practice he continued for 13 years until the ice melted back so far that accessing it with scientific equipment became onerous.

Overall, their work showed that glacial recession was not limited to the Rogers Pass area, but was a more regional, perhaps universal phenomenon. "There is often a melting away of the forefoot of the glacier more rapidly than the fresh ice from above comes down to take its place. At the present time this gradual recession seems to be common to nearly all observed glaciers in temperate climates," stated William, who published several reports on glaciers with his brother and presented lectures for scientific and related organizations.

While the Vauxes had already been taking repeat photographs of the Illecillewaet from Photographer's Rock year after year, George X carried on the practice, with encouragement from Wheeler. Like his father and father's siblings, George X was educated and skilled, trained as a physicist and a keen shutterbug. One significantly revealing set of photos shows the Yoho Glacier to be so far receded by 1930 that it is almost unrecognizable compared to photos taken in 1906. While his brother, Henry, a forester who served as dean of the School of Forestry at the University of California at Berkeley, was more causal in his photographic pursuits, he too recorded images during his visits to the Rockies in the 1920s and '30s, and later, in 1957 and 1984. Images he captured in 1957 of Biddle and Bow glaciers have since become valuable evidence of the extent of the glacial recession in that era.

The story doesn't end there. A third generation of Vauxes has continued to document glacial recession in the Rockies and Selkirk mountains: two of George X's children, Trina and Molly, and two of Henry Sr.'s children, Henry Jr. and Missy. Most notable among their accomplishments is Henry Vaux Jr.'s splendid coffee-table book of repeat photography titled *Legacy in Time: Three Generations of Mountain Photography in the Canadian West.*

Henry Jr. initiated the project in 1997, following a dinner conversation with his father. What, they speculated, would the landscapes in the original photographs look like if taken today? In an effort to do the project justice, Henry Jr. enrolled in courses to hone up his black and white photography skills, and then embarked on a whole lot of hiking between then and 2003. Several family members, including some from the fourth generation, joined him at the opening of an exhibit at the Whyte Museum in Banff in 2003 featuring his and his family's historic photographs.

Mary Vaux stands at the toe of the Illecillewaet Glacier in 1898, where she and her brothers would record the first glacier measurements in North America. (No. 30) 8/28/98. Photo Whyte Museum of the Canadian Rockies, Vaux family fonds (V653-ng-453)

"The work of this first generation of Vauxes, then, transcended their impressive photography," Henry Jr. wrote. "They were among the first to document scientifically the fact that glaciers on the North American continent were shrinking. The scientific evidence which these Vauxes gathered and interpreted is solid and incontrovertible."

Henry Jr., it should be noted, has more than kept up the family interest in science. A world-respected expert in the field of economics of water resources, he is professor emeritus of resource economics at the University of California, Riverside, former chair of the Rosenberg International Forum on Water Policy, and a national associate of the US National Academy of Sciences, among other positions. Glaciers, it could be said, are in his blood.

The glacier measurements meticulously recorded by Mary, George and William are respectfully admired and appreciated today as the genesis of glaciology, the scientific study of glaciers, in western Canada's mountains. The level of detail in the Vauxes' maps, diagrams and tables, and the clarity of their photographs, is spectacular. Their recording of glacial history in western Canada's mountains is invaluable. Their observations of tourist habits at the time are insightful too. With the railroad stopping just a few hundred metres from the glacier's terminus, the Illecillewaet was arguably the most accessible glacier in all of North America at that time, and they were the right people in the right place at the right time, a circumstance for which history is fortunate.

"In the heart of the Selkirks, amid surroundings which attract the lover of nature and the mountaineer, the globe-trotter and the health-seeker, its proximity to one of the most desirable of all the transcontinental railways makes it easily accessible during the whole summer season," the Vauxes wrote in the 1907 *Canadian Alpine Journal.*

Today, with the glacier having dwindled to a stunted remnant of itself, the railroad having long ago been rerouted inside tunnels to protect it from the massive and numerous avalanche paths of Rogers Pass, and even with the Trans-Canada Highway passing a short walk from the few moss-caked ruins of Glacier House, outside of the activities of backcountry skiers during the winter months the Illecillewaet Glacier has been long replaced by the Rockies' Athabasca in accessibility and popularity.

Illecillewaet Reinvigorated

For the first site Jocelyn Hirose chose to set up her camp and a weather station on the Illecillewaet Glacier, it was April and the snowpack was so deep she didn't realize she and her colleagues were camped right on top of a crevasse. "Luckily, we probed each time we were up there and realized this before the snowpack became too thin," she said. "I moved the camp to a safe spot on the glacier ice."

From 2009 to 2011, Hirose studied the Illecillewaet Glacier and the icefield of the same name it flows down from, and then continued examining the data until 2013. That first year she spent six months living in Rogers Pass from April through October, during which time she made weekly visits up onto the glacier accompanied by a variety of field assistants, staying on the ice for periods ranging from one night to two weeks. Accessing her site meant hiking up – wearing crampons on the ice – or, earlier in the season when there was sufficient snow, skiing up.

"That meant leaving my skis on the glacier to where I last had snow," she said. "Luckily I didn't lose them in a crevasse!"

To ferry all the equipment she needed to set up several research sites at different elevations on the glacier and the icefield higher up, and to retrieve it all six months later, she did appreciate being able to partner with Glacier National Park to fly it there by helicopter.

For her field sites, she chose locations in the middle of the glacier and high on the icefield where there were fewest crevasses, with her lowest site at valley bottom and the highest at about 2600 metres on the Illecillewaet Névé.

The focus of her research was to gain a better understanding of the relationship between the meteorological parameters – wind, precipitation, temperature changes – and glacier-melt in an effort to develop a local melt-model that she could use to determine the contributions of the glacier to streamflow to the upper Illecillewaet River. She then extrapolated her model to other glacierized zones of the upper Illecillewaet River basin to determine how much the upper basin was being fed by glacier melt based on the weather variability. Through this, she examined the sensitivity of the glacier to changes in climate – particularly increases in precipitation and warmer temperatures.

"This showed that mass balance is strongly influenced by summer temperature with one-degree Celsius increase and that the snowpack would have to increase approximately 30 per cent to offset these warmer temperatures," she said. "Unfortunately, we are not seeing that increase of winter precipitation, so we are seeing the Illecillewaet Glacier out of balance, retreating and thinning."

With this project, Hirose launched a long-term monitoring mass balance program on the Illecillewaet Glacier, research that is important in the effort to know more about how glaciers in the Columbia Mountains are responding to Earth's

Jocelyn Hirose, who holds a master's in glaciology, works at one of her research sites on the Illecillewaet Glacier in the Selkirk Mountains. Photo Jocelyn Hirose Collection

warming climate. The Rockies' Peyto Glacier is often used to represent the regional climatic changes of all glaciers in western Canada.

"It was my hope to be able to compare Illecillewaet changes over time to Peyto's changes," she said. "The Columbia Mountains have a much different hydrologic regime than the eastern slopes of the Canadian Rockies, so measuring the changes of a glacier in the Columbia Mountains seemed appropriate. In fact, Illecillewaet Glacier is located above an interior rainforest."

Having initiated a long-term mass balance monitoring program in Glacier National Park that now has a decade's data, which has shown cumulative mass balance declines, is among her proudest achievements, she said, along with the honour of reinvigorating studies on the glacier where such studies first began in North America.

"It was an absolute pleasure and honour to reinvigorate the studies on the Illecillewaet Glacier, though I felt like it was a lot of responsibility to represent it accurately and appropriately," Hirose said. "It was very important that the research was useful and relevant for the issues of our time such as water availability for downstream purposes and to inform water management.

"The Illecillewaet Glacier was forgotten for many years post–Vaux period, likely due to limited funding for glaciology and more interest in studying other glaciers in Canada such as Peyto Glacier and climate-sensitive glaciers in the high Arctic. I am glad I put Illecillewaet back on the glacier-map!"

Hotbed of Ice

Peyto (pronounced pee-tow) Glacier is named for outfitter, explorer and Canada's first national park warden, Bill Peyto. It lies 30 minutes' drive north of Lake Louise along the Icefields Parkway. The first documented photograph of it was snapped in July 1896 by American explorer Walter Wilcox, who stopped at a clearing overlooking the shimmering turquoise basin, very near the spot that is now an essential tick on the list for tourists from around the world during the bustling summer months. Before being christened with Peyto's name, the lake had been known as Doghead Lake, an appropriate moniker given that's exactly what it looks like from any high point near its south end looking north. Showing the glacier's tongue extending down below treeline, Wilcox's photo, first published in *National Geographic Magazine* in 1899, continues to prove its worth as a valuable reference point.

Peyto Glacier was photographed again in 1902 from approximately the same position by the Vauxes, and then in 1923 by another American, J. Monroe Thorington, an ophthalmologist, mountaineer and mountain historian who remains among the Rockies' most revered early explorers. Beginning in 1922, he studied the Lyell

Surveyor A.O. Wheeler took this photograph of Peyto Glacier in 1903. Photo courtesy Mountain Legacy Project

and Freshfield glaciers for 22 years. Thorington also explored and mapped British Columbia's Purcell Mountains, home of the Bugaboos granite spires. During those years he penned some 300 publications on mountain history, mountaineering activities and the Canadian Rockies.

In 1933, with an assistant, Thorington set up three separate camera stations overlooking Peyto Glacier that he marked with a circle, a line or the numbers 1933 with white paint on an obvious rock at each site. Others continued to photograph the glacier from those sites in the years following. That same summer, Thorington made the first measurements recording the position of Peyto Glacier's ice front, activity that marked the first scientific studies on that glacier. He reported in that year's *Canadian Alpine Journal* that, based on his and Wilcox's earlier photographs, the ice had melted a quarter-kilometre since 1896. Following this activity, Peyto was among several of the Rockies glaciers regularly surveyed from 1945 to 1960 as part of a program run by the Canadian government's Dominion Water and Power Bureau, which later became the Water Survey of Canada.

Then, the early 1960s launched a heyday period of glacial studies in Canada, with Peyto cast in a starring role. With its toe easily accessed by two hours' hike from the viewpoint parking lot, it was a natural choice. Having records dating back more than half a century was another highly desirable attribute.

Things got rolling when Canada's National Research Council submitted a report to the International Commission on Snow and Ice recommending that certain annual measurements be recorded on as many glaciers as possible in each country. The hope behind the suggestion was that simultaneous measurements recorded on glaciers around the world would create a reliable representation of the state of glacier-covered regions around the planet. It was also hoped that the data collected would provide a solid sense of the trend of glaciation, given that glaciers are sensitive to climatic changes. The report led to a meeting in Ottawa of some of the most brilliant glacier experts of the day, who were beginning what would be long and distinguished international careers. They compiled an extensive list of essential studies to be undertaken, including photography, general observations, snout position surveys, measurements of surface heights and observations of the transient snow line

A photocopy of the first photograph taken of Peyto Glacier by Walter Wilcox in 1896 is pinned to the wall of that glacier's research station. Photo Lynn Martel

(or equilibrium line), plus mapping and mass balance studies. Mass balance of a glacier is the net change in a glacier's mass over a fixed period, usually a year. When accumulation is greater than ablation (melting) for that year, then the mass balance is positive. If the amount of melting is greater than new snow accumulation, the mass balance for that year is negative. The equilibrium line, or snow line, separates a glacier's ablation zone from the higher elevation accumulation zone.

Next, a list of glaciers was compiled. It included glaciers in the Canadian Arctic, eight glaciers in the Canadian Rockies, some in the Columbia Mountains and nine in the Coast Mountains. The study, its proponents decided, would constitute a Canadian contribution to UNESCO's International Hydrological Decade, which would run from 1965 to 1974. Mass balance studies would be conducted on select glaciers on Baffin Island and in the Rockies. To that end, Dr. Gunnar Østrem, head of the glaciology section of the Norwegian Water Resources and Electricity Board, was appointed to run the project.

Not Too Steep, Not Too Crevassed

With a budget of any researcher's dreams, Østrem got to work. First, he tackled the inadequacies of Canada's 1:50 000 topographic maps, which at the time did not cover all the mountainous areas of the West. The solution was to narrow down his search for suitable glaciers to those located in areas for which those maps were available, since the 1:250 000 maps showed insufficient detail to be at all useful. For weeks he studied those maps for ideally representative glaciers, which, he wrote in *Peyto Glacier: One Century of Science*, "should be not too large, not too crevassed, and with a well-defined drainage basin, covering the height interval of most other glaciers in the vicinity." Other important factors to consider included accessibility and any existing information from previous studies.

With the help of his colleague Dr. Stig Jonsson, who travelled to Ottawa from the University of Stockholm to embrace the tedious job, an inventory of possible glaciers was created. Jonsson sketched each glacier on a cardboard filing card with notes on the glacier's size, height, accessibility, earlier observations, possible literature and other data. Establishing a transect that spanned from Alberta's foothills clear to Vancouver Island, he created 300 individual cards. Making use of the national aerial photography library, they were able to systematically weed out glaciers for defects such as too many crevasses, ill-suited catchment areas or unsatisfactory meltwater streams. That trimmed the list down to 30.

There the fun began. Making full use of their generous financing, Østrem and Jonsson booked helicopters to visit each of those 30 glaciers. "Stig Jonsson and I immediately went into the field and ordered the helicopter to land in the upper part of each glacier so we could ski down the glacier – one on each side – and be picked up again at the terminus." After schussing to a stop, they discussed the merits of each glacier in terms of their research requirements. Methodically they reached the conclusion that five glaciers would yield sufficient information for the mass balance studies. The finalists were Ram River Glacier in the eastern Rockies, Peyto Glacier in the western Rockies, Woolsey Glacier in the Selkirk Mountains, Place Glacier in the eastern Coast Mountains and Sentinel Glacier in the western Coast range. When funding was curtailed in later years, Ram and Woolsey glaciers had to be abandoned, since they could not be easily reached without expensive helicopter flights. Place Glacier continues to be monitored and is one of the index glaciers for Canada in the World Glacier Monitoring Service.

For its part, Peyto had it all: good accessibility, manageable size, well-defined basin, not too many crevasses, one single meltwater channel, and, the bonus card – although at times intermittent – more than six decades of previously recorded observations.

When the Peyto Glacier research station was built the glacier reached close to the door and was much thicker and wider than it is today. Photo Lynn Martel

Next came the accommodation phase. For that, another University of Stockholm professor was recruited to help kick off the field work. During the spring and summer of 1965, Wibjörn Karlén built A-frame huts at Ram River, Peyto and Place glaciers – including the very hut that still stands at Peyto today. Soon the first Canadian, Dr. Alan Stanley, newly graduated from the University of British Columbia, joined the staff. Each summer temporary field assistants were hired, usually two per glacier. The application process included questions regarding levels of physical fit-ness and skiing ability. From time to time the most suitable candidates were those who professed water-skiing skills. They worked out fine. Sometimes snowmobiles were used to tow the researchers up the glaciers. Long before the era of satellite phones, for those times when students needed answers to inevitable questions, they turned to hefty reference books that provided detailed guidance in all manner of field work duties and expectations.

Rounding up suitable equipment presented some challenges too. The only type of ice drills available in Canada at the time were ice fishermen's drills, which, while serving well for drilling into a frozen lake, proved ineffective for drilling into glacier ice. And while it was possible to order stainless steel tubes for snow sampling from a local metal workshop in Ottawa, the cumbersome and time-consuming process of filling out forms for bids, price quotes, ordering, quality control and other bureau-cratic considerations led the team to import all the requisite specialized glaciological equipment directly from Norway.

Among the various studies conducted, a most ambitious – and expensive – one took place in August 1966 when all the glaciers along the east-west transect were photographed from the air during a three-day period of clear sunny weather. With the last of the previous winter's snow all melted at the end of the summer, the im-ages identified the height of the transient snow lines on all the glaciers – elevations of which vary across the western ranges. The special photos served numerous purposes, including enabling the production of large-scale glacier maps to be used for field work. Wheeler had created the earliest known map of the Peyto Glacier in 1903/04; his 1:50 000 scale map showed 100-metre contours, but only on land and not on the glacier ice itself. While later maps provided more detail, the 1966 aerial photographs were crucial to the creation of maps that were practical and useful for field research – and to grateful adventurers too. As a sign of the times, one year prior to the air photo blitz, the map of British Columbia's Place Glacier was the first in Canada to be com-piled from air photographs using the metric system, which Canada would adopt in 1970.

Students benefited too from the intensive glacier studies during this period. With glaciology traditionally being taught as a subject within the physical geography or hydrology departments, Carleton University in Ottawa began designing programs for graduate studies that included field training courses on Peyto Glacier. During the summers of 1972, 1974 and 1978, groups of five to ten graduate students lived up at Peyto Glacier for two-week sessions during which they were trained in vari-ous aspects of glaciology and glacier hydrology. It wasn't just Canadian students who

From the late 1960s thru the late 1980s, Oleg Mokievsky-Zubok maintained long-term mass-balance studies on a dozen glaciers in the Coast Mountains, from Garibaldi Park to the Alaska Panhandle. In this image he and his son, Mike, assemble ablation stakes used to measure changes in glacier ice on the Tiedemann Glacier, in the Mount Waddington area. A memorial bench in his name overlooks Sphinx Glacier in Garibaldi Provincial Park, where his work spanned 22 years. Photo Mike Mokievsky-Zubok Collection

profited, as some of the participants were foreign students who returned to their countries to become leaders in the field of glaciology.

Overall, the decision to include Peyto Glacier as a link in the glaciological mass balance program for the International Hydrological Decade proved to be a wise choice, Østrem wrote. "The many photographs taken during 100 years, the numerous observations of the front and *in situ* studies since 1933, put Peyto in a special position among the glaciers in the area. Finally, the more than 30 years of annual detailed mass-balance measurements, forming the longest series of its kind in western Canada, have made Peyto Glacier a key location for glaciological studies in this part of the world."

In 1996, the Peyto Glacier 100th Anniversary Workshop took place in conjunction with the Canadian Geophysical Union's Hydrology Section annual meeting in the town of Banff. It was a party that's still spoken of by some of the participants. And through the efforts of dedicated and persistent scientists, many of whom partnered with colleagues from other countries during years when funding from Canada's federal government ran dry, glacier studies have been ongoing at Peyto continuously since the International Hydrological Decade of the 1960s and '70s.

Morphing and Shifting Underfoot

Bending at the waist, I gripped the U-shaped handle attached to a plastic skid that extended a metre to either side of a cracker box–sized radar receiver, my eyes searching the rock-strewn ground for solid footing. Reaching a steep section of bare black ice shimmering like polished obsidian, Mark Ednie stepped carefully a metre ahead of me, manoeuvring a nearly identical rig supporting the radar transmitter. Working in tandem, I did my best to keep the string measuring the distance between the two assemblies taut as we moved up and down the undulating rubbly moraines bordering the glacier's north flank. Following a transect line that Ednie had marked with neon orange flagging tape wrapped around rocks at carefully measured distances, we stopped at two-step intervals. Setting the radar assemblies on the ground, we pressed the button to take a reading. Another two steps, another reading. Repeat.

On that calm, cool August morning, with cotton puff clouds floating lazily by, glaciologist Mike Demuth led the procession carrying a monitor hung from a shoulder harness that was attached to both radar assemblies by two umbilical-like strands of fibre optic cables encased in nylon webbing. The work was repetitive and somewhat tedious, as the radar signal was sent down into the ice under the rubble and monitored as it bounced back. Sounds of water surrounded us, gurgling, trickling, splashing. The ice-core moraine we were standing on was morphing, shifting, changing; the mountain landscape was slowly melting right under our feet.

As head of the glaciology program with Ottawa-based Natural Resources Canada's Geological Survey of Canada, Demuth had teamed up with Ednie, an NRCan colleague whose speciality was in permafrost studies in Canada's north. They were conducting the summer session of NRCan's annual maintenance program of the mass balance network, which included ongoing studies on Peyto and, resurrected from decades earlier, Ram Glacier. Assisting them was Christophe Kinnard, a Canadian glaciologist visiting Peyto on a break from his position with CEAZA institute in Chile, where he was studying several glaciers similar in characteristics to Peyto. Part of an exchange program that had seen Demuth visit Chile the previous January, their collaboration served as a prime example of how scientists continually compare and learn from each other's projects and methods.

Liberally splattered with rocks and boulders, at first glance the moraines appeared to be nothing more than piles of rock crashed to the ground from the Rockies' notoriously crumbly limestone cliffs looming above. Only recently, glaciologists had come to realize the lateral moraines – formed as the glacier pushes piles of rocks and debris to either side and which run parallel to the ice tongue as it plows its way down valley – may not be composed of rock but could harbour cores of solid ice. While the carpet of pebbles and stones, which could be dozens or even hundreds of metres deep, serves to protect the ice from the heat of the sun, the melting ice does contribute to

Glaciologist Mike Demuth, front, works with researchers Mark Ednie and Christophe Kinnard using ground-penetrating radar to study the ice core moraine in an effort to determine how much water may be stored as ice under the rubble. Photo Lynn Martel

the total volume of freshwater stored in the glacier. They wanted to know, how much?

Back at NRCan labs in Ottawa, the data gathered from the radar surveys would be used in conjunction with LiDAR – Light Detection and Ranging, a remote sensing method that uses light from a pulsed laser to precisely measure distances – to be analyzed to help determine just how much freshwater may be stored in the ice-core moraines. And with the approximately 700 glaciers in this segment of the Canadian Rockies forming the headwaters of the region's major river systems – the Athabasca, the South and North Saskatchewan and the Columbia – melting steadily, gathering that information is a vital pursuit.

To accomplish their task, Demuth, Ednie, Kinnard and several others had moved into the Peyto Glacier research station, a trio of small, weathered cabins installed on a rock-cluttered knoll overlooking the glacier's frontline. The mid-1960s-vintage A-frame cabin, storage shed, outhouse and kitchen trailer with a peaked roof tacked on bore evidence of the obviously harsh, windy glacial environment that had ravaged them season after season since 1965. Inside the kitchen cabin, a sheet of office paper photocopied with a black and white image stuck to the fake wood panel wall with tape under its crumpled corners caught my eye. Smudged with fingerprints, the photocopy showed a much larger, fuller and longer glacier reaching the valley floor almost to Peyto Lake. Printed in sharpie in the bottom right corner was "Wilcox 1896." Two more sheets, also torn and dog-eared, showed images taken from different vantage points, and were labelled "Dickson + Vanderberg 1933" and "Harmon 1923." Outside, a collection of small colourful backpacking tents occupied flat spaces around the site, providing private sleeping accommodations for the researchers, some of whom would stay a full week. While their equipment and supplies were flown up to the site by helicopter, most of them, like me, had made the trip on foot.

Diligence, Technology and Time

Early studies conducted on Peyto and other glaciers focused primarily on measuring glacier mass balance, surface energy balance and glacier water discharge. To do this, they relied on cumbersome sensors that connected to mechanically driven recorders that didn't always work in cold, harsh alpine environments. Despite those shortcomings, consistently diligent monitoring did produce good baseline information. Today's technology allows scientists to take their studies several degrees deeper and further. Satellite Internet connections make it possible for remote sites to be monitored from glaciologists' offices thousands of kilometres away for months at a time. And with many of the basic glacier functions better understood, scientists augment time-proven mass balance measurement techniques with remote sensing – primarily RADARSAT and aircraft-borne LiDAR technology. Modern efforts include computer modelling to predict the future of glaciers and icefields, as well as studying the evolution of debris-covered ice and peri-glacial landforms that will exert an influence on the region's water availability.

"Before the satellite era, researchers tended to concentrate on the behaviour of the glacier in the summer, when on site," Demuth explained. "Now we can recognize important processes that occur during winter, when the glacier is being nourished."

On the ice, Demuth worked with technician Steve Bertollo. On a previous assignment a decade earlier – one of many they collaborated on – the two spent five months meticulously measuring Yukon's Mount Logan. Suffice to say their happy places are cold and windy ones. Glaciologists are not the only scientists who study glaciers, though. At the Peyto site they were joined by Scott Munro, a professor of geography with the University of Toronto's Mississauga campus who was there to maintain his own long-term glacier energy mass balance studies. For Munro, time spent on the Peyto was personal; his history with the site began in 1971 while working on his PhD.

This time around, Bertollo was assisting Munro with dismantling and reassembling weather stations and ensuring that two dozen stakes drilled into the ice to measure its thickness and snowfall amounts through the winter and through summer melts had not fallen over, or were not about to – as commonly happens on a moving, melting glacier. Situated in the ablation zone at 2183 metres elevation, that station had been moved up the glacier repeatedly since it was first installed in 1995. With no solar panels to power instruments available in those days, the research team had hooked up the data logger to the biggest car battery they could carry up to the site. It was about 60 amps.

"We took a chance, and that was enough to get it through the winter," Munro said. "We buried it in a big Rubbermaid container. Threw a couple of rocks on top to hold the lid on and hoped no snow or water would get in."

Modern stations are fitted with state-of-the-art instruments that accurately measure temperature, relative humidity, precipitation, wind speed and direction, and solar panels to keep the data logger juiced up. One instrument records the distance between it and the snow surface as it rises through the winter, and the ice melt as it drops during summer. Installing the station involves drilling, by hand, a trio of five-metre-long tripod legs into the ice to establish a fixed, solid base. After sitting on the ice as the previous winter's snow accumulated under it, this station now appeared to be resting on stilts, as the snowpack had since melted out.

The team also tended to two higher sites that used to be considered the equilibrium line and accumulation areas – both of which have melted back much higher since. If the weather remained hot and sunny over the next few weeks, Munro said, the lower station could drop a metre and a half. On the other hand, a sudden cold spell bringing early autumn snowfall – as routinely happens at higher elevations in the Canadian Rockies in September – and the costly instruments could be suddenly buried and stop working.

"This lower one is the easiest to maintain," Munro explained. "The highest one in the accumulation zone is the toughest one to keep going; it's high on the glacier so it's exposed to lots of high wind and rough weather. The lower ones fall over, the top one gets buried. But, Peyto is one of the best instrumented sites anywhere. People have cared enough over the years to keep it going."

Munro has been one of them. Science takes time, and like anything that takes time it demands faith, support, money, perseverance, patience and passion. It also demands adaptability. That night as we huddled together around the tiny kitchen table over Melmac plates piled with pasta and curry, and sipped single malt from a hodge-podge of cups and glasses, Munro described his hike up to the site the previous summer. As the first scientist to visit that season, he had parked at the Peyto Lake lookout and began walking down the familiar trail through the old-growth spruce forest to the gravel flats. Hopping easily over a couple of shallow meltwater braids, he passed dozens more dry grooves that creased the sandy, rock-strewn ground, evidence of the great amounts of water that have flowed for decades from the glacier as it melted back.

Hiking along the well-worn trail ascending the creek's south bank, he expected to cross the turbulent outflow creek farther upstream via the old familiar footbridge. On that day, however, he noticed the watercourse wasn't flowing the way he remembered. A massive chunk of the lateral moraine had very recently collapsed, sending tons of rock down into the creek bed. The rock avalanche had destroyed the wooden bridge and altered the course of the flow.

From left, researchers May Guan, Scott Munro and Steve Bertollo install a monitoring station on Peyto Glacier in Banff National Park. Photo Lynn Martel

"The big boulder that was always a landmark was gone," Munro recalled. "There was dirt where there had been water. The landscape was completely changed. Something had happened and scraped off the side of the moraine."

"Every hundred years or so," he said with a shrug, "these big events happen."

Later, cocooned in my sleeping bag in the crisp night air, the jet-black sky twinkling with stars much older than the Rockies' glaciers, I listed to the plink, plink, trickle and dripping of glacier ice until it lulled me to sleep amidst a landscape of ancient ice, modern science and perpetual mysteries.

Longevity Matters

When it comes to studying glaciers to determine, as accurately as possible, how much water will be released as the previous winter's snowfall melts, having records that span decades is extremely valuable.

Draining to the north and forming the headwaters of the North Saskatchewan River, Peyto shares very similar characteristics with its sibling one valley to the south, the Bow Glacier, which drains south, although both descend from the Wapta Icefield. As the headwaters of the Bow River, that glacier contributes to the freshwater supply of the most populated region of Alberta, flowing past Banff and through Calgary all the way to where it joins the Oldman River in the southeast of the province to form the South Saskatchewan River. Midway through their namesake province, the North and South Saskatchewan rivers merge to course into Lake Winnipeg, and ultimately drain into Hudson Bay via the Nelson River. Water draining from the Wapta Icefield nourishes no fewer than three provinces.

As one of the longest-running glaciology sites in North America, the Peyto station represents not just a key component of Canada's network of studied glaciers and their associated freshwater resources but also a cog in a global network. Information gathered there is shared with the UN Framework Convention on Climate Change, as well as industries including mining, hydro power, irrigation, tourism, ecosystem services, and with Alberta Environment and Parks to make water management and allocation decisions. The monitoring work is funded through partnerships between NRCan, Parks Canada and several academic networks and individual researchers. With several of the glaciers being studied as part of NRCan's

The hike from Peyto Lake up to the glacier research station covers four kilometres of moraine hills composed of rubble and rocks where trees and bushes have begun to establish their presence. When Wheeler took his photo in 1903, the glacier descended almost to the lake. Photo Lynn Martel

observing network situated on federal lands in western Canada's mountain parks, Parks Canada uses the information for its mandated requirement to produce regular state of the park reports. While for some, the mountain parks represent playgrounds for Canadians and international visitors to explore for the price of an entry pass, the wilderness protected by law within the parks' boundaries encompasses headwaters and ecosystem services that are not only essential but irreplaceable and invaluable.

For Dr. Gordon Young, the Peyto Glacier research site was one of significant discoveries. For five months in 1969 and '70, Young conducted research there toward his PhD in physical geography with a specialization in glaciology. He returned to the glacier for a few weeks every summer until 1981, and then sporadically through the late 1980s and most of the 1990s. Overall, Young figures he spent a total of 18 months living at Peyto Glacier over 30 years. Since completing his PhD in 1974, he's enjoyed a respectable career as a research scientist with Canada's Department of Environment, followed by a distinguished tenure as professor of geography at Wilfrid Laurier University in Waterloo, Ontario. He founded that university's Cold Regions Research Centre, from which he conducted high mountain hydrology research in Canada, Europe's Alps, the Himalayas and Pakistan's Karakoram mountains. He's served as chair of the Intergovernmental Council of the UNESCO International Hydrological Programme, as vice president of the International Commission on Snow and Ice, and as secretary general of the International Association of Scientific Hydrology. And that's just the short list.

I spoke with Young when he visited the Rockies as a keynote speaker at a conference in Canmore that focused on the monitoring and prediction of western water and weather. With participants including representatives of industry, utility providers and the provincial governments of British Columbia and Yukon, the conference was one of numerous such events since 2000 that have helped establish Alberta's Bow Valley as a key hub in Canada for glacier and water-related sciences.

"Glaciers have been a big love all my life," Young admitted. "The practical reason is that as glaciers melt, and as snow melts, they send water running downstream, and lots of people use the water. On Peyto, and on many other glaciers, I have always been interested in determining how much water is supplied to the rivers from melting snow, and melting ice, such as glacier ice melting out of permanent storage. And rainfall."

He finished his thought with a noticeable twinkle in his eye.

A Glacier's Numbered Days

In addition to studying Peyto Glacier, Young remapped the Columbia Icefield and studied glaciers in British Columbia's Selkirk Mountains, in Norway and on Axel Heiberg Island in the Canadian Arctic. Long-term records, he explained, are extremely important as they enable researchers to witness and gain understanding of patterns and trends. As it turned out, at the height of his PhD research, 1970 was an eye-opening year, as Young's work led to the understanding of how, in low snowfall years, the ice melts much more during the hot, dry late-summer weeks. This allows the glaciers to discharge more water into rivers when they need it most, an action by which glaciers serve as a buffer that regulates nature's flow. They are nature's savings account for freshwater. But as glaciers disappear, he said, that service society has learned to count on will become diminished, or eventually, altogether unavailable.

"Glaciers are most important in times of drought," Young explained. "As the glaciers gradually melt away, they will have less and less effect on providing water in times of low flow – this is likely to be very important in future years – especially as the demand for water from growing cities, agriculture, industry and energy continues to increase."

Dr. John Pomeroy (centre reaching toward instrument station), demonstrates data collecting methods with visiting delegates at the Athabasca Glacier. As director of Global Water Futures, Pomeroy oversees the largest university-led water research program in the world, a massive collaborative effort involving hundreds of researchers around the world, focusing on solutions to water-related problems brought about by the effects of Earth's warming climate. Photo Lynn Martel

Like glaciers the world over, Bow and Peyto are shrinking, not only in length, but also width, depth and, by consequence, volume. As the ice surface diminishes, the rate of melting increases.

In the interest of continuity, Mike Demuth, who was then approaching retirement, had worked with Dr. John Pomeroy, who heads the University of Saskatchewan Centre for Hydrology, and his team to carry on studying Peyto. Pomeroy's data reveals a steady pattern: Peyto and Athabasca glaciers are receding, firn lines are migrating to higher elevations and exposing more bare ice, air temperatures have increased, annual and seasonal precipitation patterns have changed, and rainfall ratios have increased. Peak stream-flow for Peyto has advanced by a month from August to July. Streamflow volumes from the glacierized basins are increasing; streamflow components are rainfall-run-off (15–24 per cent), snowmelt (52–64 per cent), firnmelt (intermediate stage between snow and glacial ice, 8–11 per cent), and icemelt (32–35 per cent). That increased streamflow is due to climate change (10–31 per cent) and is attenuated by glacier retreat (4–5 per cent). Streamflow from both glaciers is still in the increasing phase (4–19 per cent) as the climate warms.

Given these and other facts, Demuth estimated Peyto's snout would retreat uphill to the point where the top of the icefall sat in 2011 by about 2060. That's just 50 years, a nanosecond in glacier terms. The lake that has formed at its current toe will continue to expand, gradually submerging moraine stones that I walked on during my visit. The valley floor is a big concave area where 3,500 years ago a large lake existed, a fact that scientists were able to determine by studying trees that were left behind like beached driftwood as the glacier melted back. As it has in the past,

During the hot and smoky summer of 2017, the muddy glacial till just beyond the toe of Peyto Glacier showed the effects of the dry season. Photo Nick Fitzhardinge

the Rockies landscape that elicits oohs and aahs from visitors and residents today will, in the future, look very different again.

And with Peyto shrinking daily, the ice core moraines that border it are opening up a new field of study, from which scientists plan to learn as much as they can.

"A lot of the big signal reference sites around the world are disappearing," Demuth said as we stood outside the Peyto station's kitchen cabin watching the last of the evening sun's rays turn the surrounding mountaintops honey gold. "The utility of Peyto Glacier as a glacier climate monitoring site is not long for this world. As this place disappears it's an excellent place to study what's being left behind, though. In this valley, more and more ice is being covered by debris. In time it will shift and there will be less and less exposed ice, and ice-core moraines will characterize this place more and more."

While the debris acts as an insulator, slowing the rate of melting, the researchers were excited to study how much ice is preserved under all that rubble. "The whole eastern range of the Rockies is composed of lots of ice-covered moraines," Demuth said. "We're trying to learn more about that process and phenomenon. Whether it's a significant contributor to our water supply – that's another question. But Canada has a lot of cryosphere – the frozen part of the earth system. When the frozen stuff changes temperature or phase, those are indicators of changes in the earth's energy balance. Canada has a unique role in the world to be the canary."

4-2 FROZEN APEX

Bathtubs and Coffee Machines

For Mike Demuth, Peyto Glacier was just one piece of the puzzle.

Earlier that summer, I had accompanied him on a research mission to another glacier about an hour's drive north along the Icefield Parkway.

Walking across the water-polished rocks of a glacial moraine carrying a laptop-sized padded case in one hand and a blue plastic box resembling a textbook in the other, the scientist looked very much like a man heading off to work. Which was exactly what Demuth was doing that June morning, when a helicopter dropped him (and me) near a small lake below the toe of Castleguard Glacier, a location that would have taken two days to access by foot.

Stopping at what he called a "ground control point" previously identified from aerial photos, Demuth connected a saucer-shaped antenna to a GPS receiver and programmed it to triangulate its position. Later, the data – accurate to within ten centimetres – would be used in conjunction with satellite imagery and historical photos to create 3D digital terrain models. Employing a technique called photogrammetry, the study would yield a representation of the Columbia Icefield – from which the Castleguard and a dozen smaller and six major glaciers descend – for each decade from the 1940s onward.

The work was being conducted as part of the Geological Survey of Canada's efforts, with support from the Canadian Space Agency and Parks Canada, to use the latest technology to conduct a complete analysis of the volume of ice contained in the Columbia Icefield.

Covering about 220 square kilometres today – twice the size of Vancouver's city limits – the Columbia Icefield is the largest icefield in North America to straddle the

Glaciologist Mike Demuth, then head of the Geological Survey of Canada's glaciology section, assembles a GPS receiver and its antenna as part of a research project to map and measure the volume of water contained in the Columbia Icefield. Photo Lynn Martel

Continental Divide. Meltwater from the summit of Snow Dome – its hydrological apex – dribbles and trickles, then rushes and pulses from six outlet glaciers – Athabasca, Saskatchewan, Dome, Stutfield, Castleguard and Columbia – to three oceans. As such, the Columbia Icefield is a valuable reservoir that feeds freshwater to Canada's three major river systems.

One is the North Saskatchewan River system, which originates from the Saskatchewan, Peyto and other smaller glaciers, whose waters ultimately pour into the Atlantic Ocean via Hudson Bay.

The Columbia River is nourished by glaciers whose meltwater creeks tumble down the icefield's steep, thickly forested west slope to spill into Kinbasket Lake. Its flow is restrained by the massive Mica Dam, where the Columbia, until then flowing north, hairpins south to eventually flow across the US border into Washington State, where the river forms the boundary with Oregon all the way to the Pacific.

The third is the Mackenzie River system. From the expansive icefield, the namesake Columbia Glacier crawls down the northwest shoulder in successive low-angled tiers to where its arm, wrinkled and creased with crevasses, breaks off at the wrist into a blunt terminus that sheds ice chunks into a long, narrow turquoise drainage lake. Rushing out of the Rockies heading northeast, the Athabasca River pushes across foothills and prairie to spill into northern Alberta, then emerges into the Northwest Territories, where it feeds Great Slave Lake. Draining from the giant lake's western spout, it surges north to the Arctic Ocean. At 4241 kilometres, it's Canada's longest river system, North America's second-largest drainage basin, after the Mississippi, and the largest river in North America that flows into the Arctic. It's a colossal watershed that drains about 20 per cent of Canada.

For its 1.8 million square kilometres, though, the Mackenzie basin sustains just 400,000 people, roughly 1 per cent of Canada's population (37.6 million, July 2019). More than half of the basin lies north of Great Slave Lake, a cold, austere landscape that is sparsely inhabited by Dene, Inuvialut and Gwich'in First Nations. Its boreal forest and wetlands make up one of the most intact ecosystems in North America, sustaining some 215 avian species, including a wide variety of migrating birds, and water mammals such as beavers and muskrats. Despite its remoteness, however, human activities, including oil extraction operations on the Athabasca River that deposit toxins in waterways, as well as the warming climate, continue to have detrimental effects on the region's ecosystems.

While considerably smaller in size, by comparison the Columbia and North Saskatchewan river basins provide sustenance to much larger human populations. And the accelerated melting of the Saskatchewan Glacier, a long slender branch of ice that snakes gradually down from the Columbia Icefield on its east flank, combined with that of the Peyto and Bow glaciers, will affect nearly 10 per cent of Canada's population.

With some three million people living in the combined North and South Saskatchewan river basins, glacial melting has consequences. Added to that, the South Saskatchewan basin is fully allocated. If everyone holding a licence decided to withdraw their full allotment, the river would not have enough flow left to sustain its own existence. Humans. We have so much to learn.

Through his research, Demuth determined the annual average of the estimated ice volume wastage for these two basins combined (as of 2011) was equivalent to the amount of water use of approximately 1.5 million people.

That's a lot of bathtubs, coffee machines and micro breweries.

Canadian Ice Core Lab

On the surface, Edmonton – a four-hour drive from the nearest Rocky Mountains in Jasper – may seem an unlikely place to host one of the world's most highly valued collections of ancient ice.

Housed in a high-tech freezer at the University of Alberta campus, however, is the Canadian Ice Core Collection. With more than 10,000 years of evidence of changes to Earth's climate stored in 1.4 kilometres of ice core samples, the collection represents invaluable potential for researchers around the world to answer critical climate change questions.

The more than 1,300 samples were drilled from ice caps in Canada's high Arctic, including the Devon and Prince of Wales ice caps, and from non-polar mountain regions across Canada's provinces and territories. The oldest sample dates back some 79,000 years.

Consisting of three rooms, the facility keeps the ice cores frozen at minus 40 degrees Celsius in the archive room. The working freezer, where researchers cut and examine samples from the cores, is kept at minus 25 degrees Celsius. Inside that room are bandsaws, chop saws, a horizontal saw and two ice core scanning systems, including an Intermediate Layer Core Scanner and a Large Area Scan Macroscope, both of which are designed specifically for the digital scanning of ice. The analytical lab is a comfortable room temperature and is equipped with various instruments and systems for measuring the chemical and isotopic composition of liquid ice core samples. Common analyses performed at the lab include measurements of oxygen isotopes, which enable researchers to reconstruct past temperature, and major ions, which allow researchers to investigate historical changes in sea ice cover and oceanic conditions. Other tests are contracted out to Environment Canada, including those for contaminants stored in the ice, which may be increasingly released as Earth's climate warms, and for the presence of black carbon from major forest fires in western Canada. Cores retrieved from Devon Island are being investigated by Environment Canada scientists for potential living organisms, while those from Ellesmere Island have been studied for pollutants such as mercury deposition.

Collecting the cores is a complicated and downright frigid endeavour.

Is summer 2017, glaciologist Alison Criscitiello, technical director and lead investigator for the lab – and an accomplished climber and professional alpine guide – led an expedition to Ellesmere Island to drill glacial ice cores with two colleagues. Camping and conducting scientific research at 82 degrees north latitude for two weeks was one of several such trips for Criscitiello.

Working as Criscitiello's research assistant, Jocelyn Hirose (see page 187), whose work with Parks Canada in Banff included firearms training, was tasked with keeping a shotgun next to her ice core processing spot in case a polar bear might visit. Just 800 kilometres from the North Pole, Quttinirpaaq National Park boasts rugged peaks, ice caps,

glaciers and tundra sparsely inhabited by Arctic hare, foxes, wolves, muskoxen, Peary caribou and polar bears.

Using a single-barrel Kovacs drill, they drilled the ice in one-metre segments, adding one-metre sections of pipe to the drill to retrieve the next segment. The process is repeated until the 20-metre-long drill cuts the twentieth core.

Glaciologist Alison Criscitiello, director of the Canadian Ice Core Lab, weighs a glacial ice core near the site where it was drilled on Ellesmere Island in 2017. Photo Alison Criscitiello Collection

"It's very physical work to operate," Criscitiello said. "There's no winch, that's why we hit a max depth with this drill. It also becomes prone to getting stuck if you attempt to drill deeper with a Kovacs, in part because the whole system has a bit of wiggle to it due to the way that the one-metre pipe sections attach to one another."

Drilling one 20-metre core took one full day – in Ellesmere's 24-hour sunlight. Each metre section was packaged in long tubes of thick, flexible plastic sealed at both ends, with nine segments packaged into large insulated boxes for shipping. Criscitiello flew with the ice cores on a "cold deck" Twin Otter – an entire plane that's kept frozen – to Resolute. The boxes then flew by commercial plane to Edmonton to be stored at the Canadian Ice Core Lab.

Natural Resources Canada, the Natural Sciences and Engineering Research Council of Canada and the W. Garfield Weston Foundation have funded much of Criscitiello's arctic projects; for the remainder she's collaborated with scientists from Environment Canada's Northern Contaminants Program, which looks at environmental contaminants in the remote Canadian high Arctic. Criscitiello studies paleoclimate records to reconstruct the climate of past time periods, analyzing the chemistry of each core to see what that location tells her. The cores taken from Ellesmere in 2017 provide a record back to about 1960.

Dr. Alison Criscitiello retrieves one of the 1.4 kilometres' worth of ice core samples stored at the Canadian Ice Core Lab at the University of Alberta in Edmonton, Alberta. Photo Alison Criscitiello Collection

"With respect to how much time any one ice core represents, it depends on where you are, and what the accumulation rate is at that location," she explained. "On some of Ellesmere Island's ice caps the accumulation rate can be relatively low, meaning that every year is a thin slice within the core; therefore, a twenty-metre core goes back relatively far in time – 40 or 50 years."

With the high Arctic being especially impacted by Earth's warming climate, she pointed out, collecting cores from that region is an urgent endeavour.

Ice Laboratory

While relatively easy access has generated a useful amount of knowledge about the Saskatchewan and Athabasca glaciers – the Saskatchewan can be reached on foot via a few hours' hike or ski, the latter via the parking lot 20 minutes' walk from its toe – little was historically known about the main ice body that feeds those and four other major glacial limbs.

That information gap motivated Demuth throughout his career. In addition to his work session at Peyto Glacier, every spring from 2010 thru 2015, he and several colleagues spent three to five weeks living in a spartan camp dug into the snow surface at 2920 metres' elevation right on the Columbia Icefield. While their scientific equipment, tents, two-burner cookstove and a propane tank to run it, plus voluminous sleeping bags, food and a few treats would be delivered to the site by helicopter, Demuth and his colleagues would ski into the camp for a commute that, on a quick day, took 11 hours. If visibility was good. They skied carrying a small tent, sleeping bags, stove fuel and food for a couple of days in case stormy weather moved in unexpectedly – as commonly happens on an icefield – to strand them and also shut down any helicopter flights. One trip took two and a half days due to a newcomer's blisters. When any of the researchers left the icefield for a few days' break, they skied out and then back in too.

A helicopter delivering supplies comes in for a landing at a researchers' camp high on the Columbia Icefield. Under the direction of Natural Resources Canada glaciologist Mike Demuth (now retired), small teams of four or five scientists set up the camp and lived there for several weeks each spring through sun and snow and sleet and howling wind to conduct studies on the massive icefield. Photo Lynn Martel

The camp, like other mass balance study sites on glaciers across western Canada's mountains, was always planned at the end of winter when the snowpack is at its maximum, before beginning the summer melt. It was situated in the same general area each year in a large flat expanse where crevasse hazards are few, and not far from where a broad ramp of snow rises gradually to form Snow Dome's summit mound. Ideally in the first day or two of the camp, the helicopter would arrive, and once unloaded it flew away. On rare windless days, when the engine roar was finally out of earshot, silence settled onto the icefield, wrapping around the tiny camp

A snowshoe hare leaves telltale tracks stretching across the Rockies' Campbell Icefield. In addition to numerous birds – in particular ravens, which are exceptionally talented at opening zippers on tents or backpacks, or tearing into food caches – other wildlife, including grizzlies and wolverines, or their tracks, are occasionally seen on glaciers. Photo Lynn Martel

like a peaceful, comforting blanket. Stillness. The smooth, white icefield unfolded for kilometres in every direction, ringed by a perimeter on the horizon of peaks chiselled from black rock and diamond-bright ice glinting in the sun. A few kilometres west of camp the southeast slope of Alberta's highest point and the Rockies' second-highest peak, Mount Columbia, thrust into the sky like a gargantuan toboggan ramp, its 3747-metre summit dropping to sheer vertical cliffs on its other sides. During multi-day stretches of sunny, robin's egg blue-sky days, small parties of mountaineers routinely skied past the camp en route to their prize.

Before pitching the tents, the researchers speared three-metre-long avalanche probes into the glacier's wind-sketched surface to ensure there were no crevasses underfoot within the camp's perimeter. They marked out tent pads by stomping the surface with their skis to create a firm platform, then pitched small one-person sleeping tents several metres apart, staking down the corners with sturdy snow pickets so the tents would withstand the fierce winds that were more likely to visit them than not. The larger kitchen tent was erected, the propane stove assembled, and a makeshift table and seats arranged using storage trunks and equipment cases. Snow walls were built to encircle all the tents, and knee- to hip-deep pathways were shovelled to connect the tents and the communal outhouse, also concealed behind a wall of snow blocks, and the contents of which would be flown out when they left. The paths would need to be re-dug multiple times during their stay, as would the flat helicopter landing pad that had to be maintained in case of emergency.

While spring flowers began sprouting in the valley bottoms, the camp's inhabitants would see no green - no bushes, no trees - for the duration of their stay. Ravens were faithful visitors, and since they'll quickly probe their beaks right through a tent wall, one team member always stayed back to guard the camp's precious supplies. Some mornings – definitely not all – the researchers rose to spectacular views, gathering for breakfast and steaming mugs of coffee in the cook tent kept warm by a small propane heater. Then they pulled on thick puffy down jackets and set out to work. Their mission: taking measurements to accurately determine the depth of the icefield.

Using a "Finnish snow fork," researcher John Sekerka assists with data logger entry while Selena Cordeau inserts a dielectric probe into the glacial ice in two-centimetre increments to measure density and moisture content. Photo Mike Demuth Collection

Answers Beget Questions

Taking advantage of an empty co-pilot's seat on a resupply flight during their 2013 spring field session, I visited Demuth's site for a few hours. The team included Sasha Chichagov, a remote sensing specialist with NRCan whose work involved converting National Topographic System (NTS) maps from the 1980s to a format compatible with modern, extremely accurate LiDAR-created ones. To accomplish this, data was collected by flying an aircraft over an area with LiDAR equipment that sent laser beams down to the glacier's surface. Using aerial photos from both eras, Chichagov created highly accurate 3D digital elevation models for successive decades. Subtracting one digital model from another revealed the difference in the height of the glacier by showing where it had become thicker or thinner over the past four decades. While early aerial photography photogrammetry always showed certain slopes in shadow, LiDAR captures it all equally.

With John Sekerka, an NRCan technician who doubled as popular camp cook, research technician Steve Bertollo and two student volunteers rounding out the group, that year's session marked the second year of a five-year project to make a complete analysis of the volume of ice contained in the iconic icefield. Continuing from the previous year, they measured glacier thickness and conducted GPS surveys of the elevation of the icefield surface.

Dragging ground-penetrating radar equipment on sleds, the crew recorded radio waves that were transmitted from the surface through the glacier and reflected back from internal layers and the glacier bed. Assessing the amount of water stored in the glaciers is challenging because measuring their mass, not just area, is difficult, since the configuration of the ground bed upon which the glacier sits is unknown, and not uniform. Photogrammetry has provided some answers.

"Knowing something about the thickness of the ice and the information we gain from photogrammetry will help us model what the icefield's fate will be in the future," Demuth explained. "But how will that impact river flows, public safety, ecosystem integrity, even visitor experience, including the snow coach glacier tours?" Science is about questions as much as answers, and one answer quickly begets the next question.

During their research expedition, Demuth and his team recorded a range of evidence signifying ongoing changes, including some unexpected ones. When stormy weather kept them tent-bound for much of their third week that season, work was paused as they were forced to dig out their tents every six hours. Winds rattled and shook their tents, at times pelting the nylon walls with snow and ice bits that sounded like violently flung buckshot. They maintained a series of wands planted in the snow to use as guidelines to make sure everyone could always find their way back to the main tent. In the middle of the storm, to escape boredom and some festering cabin fever, they seized the opportunity during a lull to ski up Snow Dome in a whiteout. Drilling a shallow ice core to examine melt layers, they found a surprise.

Researchers Warren Helgason and Bruce Johnson fly a kite on the Athabasca Glacier as a means of – effectively – measuring wind speed, temperature, humidity and pressure at different elevations at different times of the day so they can learn how wind affects the melting rates of the glacier. Run under the University of Saskatchewan's Centre for Hydrology in 2015, the project was part of an ongoing study of changing cold regions in western and northern Canada through which scientists are working to quantify the impact of climate warming on water supply, ecosystems, weather extremes of drought and flood, and changing snow and ice. Photo Lynn Martel

"Interestingly, there was lots of melting in the middle of the previous winter at 11,000 feet," Demuth said. "We're not talking just a little glaze crust sun layer, but massive ice layer development, really strong melting – which is unusual at that elevation in the middle of winter."

From his office in Ottawa, Demuth had been aware of successive weeks of above-freezing sunny weather in the Rockies through much of February and March that spring.

"So, we asked, is that mid-winter melting we saw unusual?" Demuth said. "Are mid-winter melt events becoming more frequent?"

Sadly, his seniors in Ottawa did not

share his enthusiasm for this and other research initiatives. Once a glaciologist, how-ever, always a glaciologist, and even though he's since retired Demuth continues to mentor junior scientists, and happily contributes his expertise as a senior fellow to the University of Saskatchewan's Centre for Hydrology. Combined with a position as adjunct professor with the University of Victoria's High Country and Northern Weather Impacts Laboratory, he's been able to complete some work from his high Arctic projects. He also teaches river ice and glacier hydrology modules, doing his part to inspire the next generation.

Glacier Math

Funding for glacier science – as with so many Earth sciences – tends to ebb and flow like a river through the seasons depending on the leanings, sometimes whims, sometimes convictions of the current government, not only in Canada but around the globe. While NRCan did not replace Demuth with another research glaciologist, other scientists have been able to continue some of the work he initiated. To be a pro-ductive research scientist, it turns out, it helps to be a talented and enthusiastic net-worker adept at partnering and collab-orating not only with universities across provincial boundaries but across inter-national borders, even oceans. Having witnessed such efforts for more than a decade, I've always found their capacity for collaborating to stretch their re-search dollars as far as possible quite im-pressive. And we're all the luckier for it.

As part of the University of Saskatchewan's Centre for Hydrology's ongoing studies on how the Athabasca and Saskatchewan river basins will be affected in response to Earth's warming climate, Dr. Jonathan Conway col-lects data from an instrument site near the toe of the Athabasca Glacier in Jasper National Park. "The Athabasca is as good as it gets for a glacier – easy access by road, easy to walk onto," Conway said. "But even one hundred metres from the parking lot this site is still harder to maintain than any in the prai-ries. Monitoring glaciers is significantly harder. Glaciers are always moving, always changing." Photo Lynn Martel

In 2015, glaciologist Garry Clarke, pro-fessor emeritus with the University of British Columbia's Department of Earth, Ocean and Atmospheric Sciences, pub-lished a research paper in the premier magazine *Science*, written with several colleagues. In it they shared results of their studies conducted by using a com-bination of LiDAR and ground-pene-trating radar that revealed the first truly accurate measurements of the form and thickness of the Columbia Icefield and how much ice it contains. From that, the water equivalent of the ice was derived, and from those calculations they were able to estimate with considerable accuracy how long individual glaciers, and even the Columbia Icefield, might last under a number of projected climate change scenarios.

The findings were sobering.

Past estimates that the icefield was 350 metres thick appeared to be optimistic, as their research suggests the thickness currently varies between 150 and 300 metres. The area of the icefield was calculated at 223 square kilometres. And shrinking.

Through the work of the Western Canadian Cryospheric Network, a research project that ran from 2006 to 2010 and involved the contributions of scientists, grad students and post-doc fellows from six Canadian and two US universities with Dr. Brian Menounos, a professor in the geography department at the University of Northern British Columbia in Prince George as lead investigator, more staggering realities were revealed.

In 1985, there were 1,155 glaciers in the mountain national parks of Alberta and British Columbia. By 2005, there were 1,006. That means 149 glaciers disappeared in just 20 years. Jasper National Park lost 135 of its 554 glaciers; Banff National Park lost 29 of its 365, and its total glaciated area shrank by 20 per cent. That's 1 per cent every year. During those same two decades, British Columbia lost 10 per cent of its glacial cover.

Here begins the Sunwapta River, carrying water newly melted from many-thousand-year-old glacier ice on Mounts Athabasca and Andromeda and Athabasca Glacier. This water flows to join the Athabasca River, and more than 1200 kilometres to the north, the Mackenzie River, pulsing all the way to the Arctic Ocean. Every year the glaciers become smaller, but hopefully snowmelt will continue to keep these brilliant river beauties blooming. Photo Lynn Martel

Estimates based on current conditions and trends are that western Canada's mountains will lose 70 per cent of their glacial ice by 2100. The greatest effects of this melting will be experienced in the Rocky and interior ranges. The Coast Mountains are looking at 60 to 85 per cent loss of glacier ice.

From my perspective, having visited the Athabasca Glacier nearly every year for the past decade, I can't imagine there will be much glacier left there at all in another 50 years. Probably not even 30. Research reveals the Athabasca is currently melting back an average of 5.5 metres every year. I doubt the tourist buses will run for even 20 more years.

I try and imagine what our mountain

landscapes will look like by the time my niece is my age – about 40 years from now. I picture a whole lot more rock, especially in the summertime. In the winter, when we have snow – and that's not a guarantee on a warming planet – it's not always easy to tell where the glaciers end and moraines begin if they are all covered by a thick white cloak. But once summer comes the stark truth is revealed. In the Rockies, and the Selkirks too, a glacier in September is a sorry sight, naked of snow, exposed and withered and bedraggled after months of summer sun and nights and winters too warm for them to grow. I imagine very little glacier ice left to be seen in those months the way those of us who live and play and work in these mountains today have learned to admire and celebrate those patches of vibrant blue amidst all that dull grey and brown. I imagine it will feel like watching wildflowers go extinct. Then, of course, some wildflowers that thrive downstream of glaciers, watered by summer runoff, could do just that.

4–3 INTERIOR ICE

Time Recorded in Rocks

At the southern end of Canada's Rockies, Waterton Lakes National Park no longer has any glaciers, only a few dwindling patches of old, deteriorating snow. Across the international boundary, the US's Glacier National Park currently retains about 26 active glaciers, each of which is small and rapidly shrinking. Few are expected to last beyond 2050. In British Columbia's Coast Mountains, where the higher elevations receive more snow than the Rockies – which are at the far end of the food chain for storms generated by the Pacific – thousands of glaciers persist, from the Yukon border to nearly as far south as the city of Vancouver. While the ice cover in British Columbia is known to be dynamic, only a handful of the 7,400 or so glaciers located in the south and central coastal regions of British Columbia, and those in Alberta, are regularly studied. Determining how much water is locked in these snow and ice reservoirs is being done by a variety of methods, including observations made by satellites and airplanes to investigate large-scale questions. Newer methods incorporate data obtained using drones and archival photos to help determine historic and present rates of ice loss, and gain knowledge as to how this will likely influence the rest of the hydrological cycle. As the local, regional and global average temperatures on Earth rise, scientists are continually learning how individual species as well as the larger ecosystem are being affected. In the Coast Mountains, researchers are working to learn more about how the region's glaciers and icefields play a role in supporting the numerous temperate rainforest valleys. In particular, growing concern is spurring studies to learn how the salmon rivers of the Pacific coastline are being affected as climate change impacts the snow and glaciers. One thing scientists are learning is that warmer stream and river water are not beneficial to salmon populations. Salmon like it cool.

In the interior ranges, the southernmost glacier larger than one square kilometre is the Kokanee Glacier, while the farthest south in British Columbia is the Dibble Glacier, tucked behind a ridge connected to Mount Fisher. Across the provincial boundary – which doubles as the continental divide – Alberta's southernmost glacier is 105 kilometres farther north: Mangin Glacier in the Rockies' Peter Lougheed Provincial Park. A few hundred kilometres in latitude, your distance from an ocean or which side of the divide you're on make a difference when you're a glacier.

For now, there are more glaciers in the mountains of Alberta and British Columbia – not to mention Yukon and the Canadian Arctic – for scientists to study than there are funds or personpower available to study them. Thankfully, research projects are ongoing, and glaciologists and hydrologists and other scientists are continually learning new things about these wondrous ancient bodies of ice.

One such surprise discovery happened during a study at Castle Creek Glacier, tucked in the Cariboo Mountains not far from the hamlet of McBride in eastern British Columbia. As part of a comprehensive project endeavouring to determine the number and total area of glaciers in Alberta and British Columbia, Matt Beedle, then a post-doctoral student at the University of Northern British Columbia, made 15 trips to the Castle Glacier between 2007 and 2015 to measure changes in its volume.

The five-year program was led by UNBC's Brian Menounos, in partnership with colleagues from universities in Alberta, British Columbia and even Washington State – which retains some 450 square kilometres of perennial snow and ice features in the Olympics, North Cascades and other smaller mountain areas – as well as scientists from Canada's federal government. Their aim was to document recent glacier melting and the current health of glaciers in numerous locations so they would be able to better predict what their state would be looking forward, up to the year 2150.

PhD student Matt Beedle (left) and professor Brian Menounos measure changes in glacier thickness using GPS. Photo University of Northern British Columbia

The team focused efforts on several

glaciers and icefields in British Columbia. In addition to Castle Creek, they studied the Lloyd George Icefield in Kwadacha Wilderness Provincial Park, a remote, roadless area in the northern Rocky Mountains. Others included the massive Klinaklini and Tiedemann glaciers in the Coast Mountains, and glaciers in the province's southern interior that drain into the Columbia River Basin. There are currently about 2,200 glaciers draining into that basin.

At each site, researchers set up instruments to measure and record air temperature, wind speed, precipitation and humidity to gather information about how the glaciers are nourished, and how they melt. They recorded changes in thickness, extent, volume and movement, not only of these glaciers but of glaciers throughout the mountain ranges of western Canada, work that involved analyzing thousands of aerial photos, some of which were more than 70 years old.

On some visits Beedle flew to the site by helicopter from Valemount or McBride, but on many others he hiked up the Avalanche Valley trail with a colleague, often carrying an ice auger and aluminium poles for drilling ablation stakes, plus shovel, probe, snow samplers and scales for measuring accumulation. Add to that a GPS receiver, antennae, base station and real-time radios. A deep-cycle marine battery had to be flown in.

Access, Beedle said, is always a big challenge when studying glaciers. Helicopters are expensive, so one of the attributes that made Castle Creek Glacier a good candidate for their study was its access trail. Even so, the hike in was arduous.

"It is still a super difficult hike, particularly with all the science gear, camping gear and glacier travel safety equipment," Beedle said. "It wasn't uncommon to have to carry 70-pound packs to access the glacier. The hike out was particularly bad as it came at the end of three to five days of difficult field work hiking all around the glacier every day. I remember getting to McBride and feeling like I couldn't walk, my knees hurt so bad. We often drove straight to Prince George for a big meal and a hot tub at the aquatic centre. It took days to recover physically from these efforts."

PhD candidate Matt Beedle and professor Brian Menounos examine the moraine left behind by the Castle Creek Glacier in 2007. Photo University of Northern British Columbia

Their vehicles, too, suffered, as marmots would eat the rubber tubing under them when they were parked at the trailhead for several days. On two occasions their vehicle had to be towed to Prince George for repairs.

"Luckily – even without brakes, as all the brake fluid had drained out after the marmots ate the rubber tubing – we were able to drive back down to McBride keeping the vehicle in first gear and having the emergency brake as a backup," he recalled. "We first thought the issue was porcupines. We got better at putting chicken wire up around the vehicles while parked for a few days after the marmots tore it down the first time."

National Treasure

Another feature that made Castle appealing as a study site was its configuration. Steep glaciers are often heavily crevassed and too dangerous to work on. Castle Creek Glacier fell into the "relatively easy/safe to work on" category. Its large elevation range enabled them to better study snow accumulation and ice melt at different elevation bands.

During the month of August 2015 the ablation stake, an eight-metre pole he'd inserted into the ice with just a few millimetres showing at the top, had melted out to the point that the equivalent of his own height was exposed. Using highly accurate GPS equipment, Beedle was able to confirm that the glacier had lost a full metre and a half in thickness in only one month.

But it didn't end there.

He also discovered that as the glacier melted back, the rock and rubble and earth of the moraines that were left behind were arranged in a series of rows that precisely indicated the amount the glacier retreated each year. In a manner similar to how tree rings can be counted to determine the age of a tree, the rows extending from the edge of the glacier down into the valley for 750 metres mirrored the geological record of the glacier's retreat for the past 50 years.

The moraines left behind by Castle Creek Glacier were arranged in a series of rows that precisely indicated the amount the glacier retreated each year. Image University of Northern British Columbia

The discovery, Beedle said, was an entirely new one in Canada. Only a few locations in Norway and Iceland have revealed similar phenomena. "These moraines allow us to see even subtle annual variations in glacial retreat," Beedle said. "This was an exciting, fortuitous discovery. For me it combined a bit of exploration and discovery with science. It was a fun mapping puzzle to use the historic aerial photos to date the moraines."

While glaciers form annual push moraines regularly, to have an intact series mapping decades of glacier recession is rare, and valuable.

"Glacier monitoring is an incredibly important, often thankless task – arduous work, year after year to put one more data point in a long time series," Beedle said. "The decades-long records from around the globe represent thousands of person-hours, hundreds of thousands of dollars and heaps of personal dedication. To be able to reconstruct that data from a series of moraines bypasses decades of toil, significant investment, and adds significantly to our understanding of glacier change. What a global treasure!"

For Beedle, who has since successfully defended his PhD, the study of glaciers is a constant source of awe and wonder.

"I love their dynamism," he said. "'Glacial pace' is often used to convey a lack of speed, but I'm always amazed at how much they move, change, from year to year. When you visit a glacier year after year you really see this dynamism; new land is exposed – land likely not exposed for thousands of years. The shape and nature of the margin changes dramatically, you're continually shocked by how much the ice melts. They are these monumental features of our environment that are otherworldly in many ways, but with direct linkages to environmental systems that have a profound bearing on our lives."

Mountain Legacy Project

Boasting the world's largest collection of systematically taken historic mountain images, Canada is truly fortunate.

This treasure trove came to be thanks to the efforts of Édouard-Gaston Deville, surveyor general of Canada in the late 19th century. Facing the challenge of mapping the extensive mountain landscapes of the young and very large country, in 1886 he introduced a mapping method called phototopography to his surveyors, a made-in-Canada technique that required a specially designed camera to be packed up to summits or other high points where a series of panoramic images were captured. Altitude measurements at the photo station – along with angles back to other stations, peaks and/or fixed points – were also recorded.

The images were captured on 6 x 4–inch glass plates. They were paired with field measurements and used to create topographic maps. For this technique to work, it was essential that the features to be mapped could be seen in at least two images taken

This photo taken by surveyor A.O. Wheeler in 1901 shows Mount Sir Donald (right of centre) and the Illecillewaet Glacier descending toward the valley floor in British Columbia's Selkirk Mountains. Photo Mountain Legacy Project
This 2011 photo shows the extent of the Illecillewaet Glacier's retreat (upper right), the glacier now a fraction of its former self. Photo Mountain Legacy Project

from stations some distance apart. This method proved very successful and was used for much of Canadian mapping in mountainous terrain from 1887 until 1958.

The mountain ranges of Alberta, British Columbia and Yukon were extensively photographed, the earliest dating back to 1861. Of the 120,000 images known to exist, the vast majority were created through topographic mapping efforts. Most of these images are housed at the Library and Archives Canada/Bibliothèque et Archives Canada in Ottawa, the BC Archives in Victoria, the Whyte Museum of the Canadian Rockies in Banff and the Glenbow Museum in Calgary.

In 1887, surveyor James McArthur was one of the earliest to use phototopography while mapping mountains around Banff. McArthur was but one of many surveyors whose names are synonymous with the early days of Canadian mountaineering, along with Alpine Club of Canada co-founder Arthur Wheeler and his son, Edward Oliver Wheeler, who went on to become surveyor general of India. The maps they produced, combined with their field notes, early survey reports and thousands of highly detailed historic photographic plates, are now providing not only spectacular views but also deep insights into the mountains of western Canada.

In 1996, Dr. Eric Higgs with the University of Alberta (now at the University of Victoria) and Dr. Jeanine Rhemtulla (then a grad student at the University of Alberta, now faculty at the University of British Columbia) were researching mountain landscape change in the Athabasca Valley around Jasper when they discovered Morrison Bridgland's 1915 Jasper Park survey images of the area. That led them to retake the same images and compare their modern photos with the 1915 ones. To do so effectively, they determined exactly where Bridgland stood and made their way to the same spot. In order to arrive at results close to the same resolution afforded by the glass plates, they used professional medium format camera equipment to capture the modern images.

Since then the Mountain Legacy Project has grown, as has its team, who have repeated more than 7,000 historic photographs. Over the years, the project researchers have developed and improved techniques for shooting the modern retakes, and for curating and analyzing the image pairs, and publishing the results. The images are available for use by scholars, students, government agencies, NGOs, schools, even the general public (see http://mountainlegacy.ca/).

Home, Sweet Glacier, Home

Tucked into a glacial cul-de-sac at the end of the valley from which Ventego Creek drains into Kinbasket Lake upstream from Golden, British Columbia, Sorcerer Lodge is one of some three dozen backcountry lodges in British Columbia accessible only (by any reasonable standard) by helicopter. In winter or summer, guests are ferried up to the lodge a half-dozen per flight – Sorcerer sleeps 18 – then left in idyllic solitude until the airborne taxi returns a week later. There's minimal, solar-powered electricity, no running water, outhouses only and a delightful wood-burning sauna, and the nearest human neighbours are several pathless valleys away in any direction.

Glaciers descended almost to the shore of Lake Magog at the base of iconic Mountain Assiniboine in 1913. Photo Mountain Legacy Project
The diminishing of the glaciers around Mount Assiniboine is extensive, as seen in this 2017 photo. Photo Mountain Legacy Project

From the back deck of the lodge, perched atop a cliff overlooking the tranquil waters of tiny Wizard Lake, White Russian and Nordic glaciers form a dazzling vista. The lower reaches of the larger of them, Nordic, fan downward like short, stout arms of a giant starfish draped over the undulating bedrock. A third glacier, Escargo, descends like a graceful tongue curled around the base of Nordic Mountain's steep northern walls, the two glaciers separated by a giant rock hump and tower that together resemble a snail of mythical proportions.

Tannis Dakin calls Nordic *her* glacier.

As owner and operator of Sorcerer Lodge for three decades, she has

Tannis Dakin, who began operating Sorcerer Lodge in 1989, has watched Nordic Glacier, reflected in the lodge's living room window, grow smaller and smaller every year since. Photo Lynn Martel

watched Nordic, and its companion glaciers, from the living room window of her lodge week after week, season following season. As she watched her two sons grow and strengthen and mature, she watched her glaciers become plump with generous cloaks of winter snow, and then shrink and diminish under the penetrating summer sun. She has skinned up their broad, glistening flanks in the dead of winter to stand at White Russian or Black Russian cols, or the summits of Nordic and Perfect peaks. She has skied down (on a museum's worth of progressing styles, materials and vintages over the years), gliding in flowing arcs on the glaciers' surfaces, some days smooth like velvet, other days scoured by sastrugi ripples and creases so rigid that her fillings rattled in her teeth. In summertime she has walked on moraine crests created hundreds of years ago, in some places sharp as a shark's fin. She has hiked across fields of ancient ice that roll gently in ripples and waves and curls and drop into deep, dark, sinister clefts.

For a blissful Internet/cellphone-free week during the 2015 summer – Sorcerer under Dakin (since retired) proudly and adamantly remained an "unconnected" lodge – I explored her world. I stripped down to swim in a cool alpine tarn and walked alone for an afternoon across a low-angled rocky mountain flank to the halcyon shore of Ventego Lake, the alpine quiet interrupted by shrill marmots' calls. I wandered to where the toe of Escargo Glacier gently tapered like a ballerina's satin point shoe to where it kissed the rock bed. Downstream, the accumulation of dozens of delicate rivulets flowing atop the glacial ice merged into forceful streams gushing from the underbelly of the ice in fat, brown, turbulent creeks, slapping and slamming over boulders, pushing and shoving ice and rock and silt into Nordic Lake. Wildflowers – arnica, river beauties, Indian paintbrush – sprang up from the stream banks like yellow and fuchsia and crimson fireworks.

I listened as seracs spit off ice chunks from high on Nordic's glaciers, straining and crashing below. Avalanches and serac falls scarred the glaciers like wounds revealing raw blue ice beneath. Strands of meltwater trickled down Nordic's rubbly lower slopes like dainty liquid ribbons streaking the gravel beds.

These moraines, these rubble fields, Dakin explained, were still covered with glacial

Nordic Glacier, in British Columbia's Selkirk Mountains, extended down to its outlet lake in 1991. Photo Tannis Dakin

ice when she first signed the licence of occupation with the British Columbia government to her 54-square-kilometre tenure in the Selkirk Mountains in 1989.

Watching the glaciers melt and dwindle has been part of her life for more than half her own years. She remembers vividly how, in the mid-1990s, she and her guides were forced to alter their approach onto Nordic Glacier when the ice terminus formed a vertical wall. The changes have been continuous.

"We notice the changes in crevasse formation," she said. "The size of the rock features sticking up out of the ice. The fluctuations in icefall activity are glaring – and a bit problematic. Avalanches run in different places and at different times, and more frequently since the firn snow has melted on some of the steeper mountainsides."

Overall, she added, the glaciers are smaller. And thinner. Guests who return from one season to the next notice the change in size right away.

"Folks always notice the total area covered by the ice, but they don't notice the change in depth so much," Dakin explained. "We are seeing this dramatically. In some places, easy walks up onto the ice have become icefalls or are now rock. In other places icefalls are now laid-back, easy slopes. Every summer we go up to the edge of the ice and get to walk on new land that we've never seen before."

Ice Partnership

Her own fascination with the ongoing changes happening before her eyes prompted Dakin, whose family settled the Columbia Valley five generations ago, to seek a way to help fund some glacier research. Her search brought her to the Columbia Basin Trust, which funds projects that benefit residents of the region and had recently partnered with the Canadian Columbia Basin Glacier and Snow Research Network. The network involves research being conducted by the University of Northern British Columbia and the University of British Columbia, with support from BC Hydro.

Between 2014 and 2018, Sorcerer Lodge provided researchers from the two universities free use of the lodge, help with meals, grunt work of carrying measuring equipment up onto the glaciers and assistance with the expense of helicopter flights to and from the lodge. Sorcerer also helps publicize the researchers' work through its website and extensive client base.

By 2019, Nordic Glacier had melted and thinned considerably since Sorcerer Lodge owner Tannis Dakin first began running her business. Photo Tannis Dakin

Nordic was one of six chosen for a five-year study as a representative example of glaciers in the Columbia River Basin, spanning the length of the basin from Kokanee Glacier, near Nelson in the south, to Zillmer, near Valemount, in the north. The purpose of the research was to study the current state of the glaciers. The researchers' methods included both field measurements and aerial surveys taken at the end of winter to measure snowfall, and the end of summer to measure ice melt. This work would allow them to determine how much runoff the glaciers were contributing to streamflow, their current rate of change and, most importantly, said Ben Pelto, a PhD candidate with the University of Northern British Columbia's geography program, the balance gradient.

"The balance gradient is the relationship of elevation to mass change and is critical for predicting how glaciers will fare moving forward," Pelto explained.

To gather their information, Pelto and colleagues visited Sorcerer nine times, in early May and late August each year, shovelling out deep snow pits to record snowfall depth, and in the fall measuring any snow depth and density that might have been retained. Taking core samples yielded the value of the snow's density. They drilled eight-metre-long ablation stakes into the glacier to measure ice loss and tracked their location as they moved along with the glacier to determine the velocity of the ice mass.

On Nordic they set up a weather station over three summers, and mapped surface elevation heights and measured ice thickness. Airborne surveys using altimetry or LiDAR produced a detailed 3D map of the glacier during their two seasonal visits. By comparing the spring and late-summer maps they could estimate changes in height.

A time-lapse camera focused on Nordic Glacier – purchased with the help of funds donated by the Alpine Club of Canada's Toronto Section – provides images that will be valuable in several capacities as seasonal changes occur.

Dakin had hoped her 30 years' worth of snowfall and weather records might be of use, but it wasn't as helpful as she'd imagined. Helicopter, snowcat and ski touring lodges operating in the province's backcountry all record snowfall measurements daily throughout the winter, year after year, which is collected and shared within the industry-only system called InfoEx. The InfoEx data was shared on a one-time basis with the cryosphere researchers for the Columbia Basin Trust report, but its value was limited since the primary concern for the ski operations is snowpack depth and stability relating to avalanche hazard. For Pelto and others studying glacier accumulation, melt rates and the equivalent water volume contained in glacial ice are most important. To know that, the density of the snowfalls must be recorded, something that is not done for InfoEx reports. (For its part, the Province collects virtually no snow data above treeline – 2000 metres.)

Their study determined that while melting snow from the previous winter contributed to much of the runoff from May through July, come August and, to a lesser extent September, the contribution of glacier wastage runoff becomes critical, and depending on the catchment, rises to between 10 and 35 per cent of total streamflow.

Overall, their detailed study of six glaciers located across a mountain range was the largest of its type to date that the team was aware of. The data set will be of great value in understanding the current state of the glaciers and high elevation snow in the Canadian Columbia River Basin and also for modelling studies attempting to project regional glacier response to ongoing climate change. Having Dakin's support and co-operation, Pelto added, was invaluable.

For his part, Pelto comes by his interest in glaciers honestly – his father is a glaciologist who has conducted studies in Washington's North Cascade Mountains for decades, and projected slide shows of his summer field trips on the wall for his family once he returned home. When he was 15, Ben accompanied his dad for his first field season.

"These field seasons are quite arduous, covering around a hundred miles and 30,000 feet over two and a half weeks while visiting nine glaciers per year each August,"

Tannis Dakin (right) knows the glaciers, the moraines, peaks, ridges and meadows of Sorcerer intimately. She calls Nordic *her* glacier. Photo Lynn Martel

Pelto recalled. "For eleven years from 2005 to 2015 I came along for the field season as an assistant. I loved the mountains and particularly the glaciers."

His academic path took him from geology and environmental studies, where he was drawn to water and climate and studied lakes and rivers, to paleoceanography, studying sediment cores from the Bering and Chukchi Seas between Russia and Alaska to examine the oceanographic history in that region over the period 25,000–5,000 years before present. After graduating with a master's in science in 2014, he decided his real passion was present-day climate, particularly as it relates to water resources. Harbouring a love for mountains, snow and glaciers since his field days with his father, he also decided he wanted a job where he would spend at least some of his time in those environments. When he met UNBC's Dr. Brian Menounos at the American Geophysical Union fall gathering in San Francisco – the world's largest gathering of geoscience professionals – they hit it off. Pelto knew he'd found his match: an opportunity to conduct a large-scale project across the Columbia River basin in British Columbia with lots of field work and cutting-edge airborne laser surveying. All amidst glaciers.

"I find glaciers to be glorious," Pelto admitted. "They are so unique and add so much character – and life – to a landscape. They seem almost sentient, moving inexorably downhill, responding to changes in climate, sculpting landscapes, and providing water that feeds mountain ecosystems. They change so much, year to year, season to season. Glaciers give mountains a certain character, and their power and mystery add a level of awe and respect for nature that is hard to match."

While she's appreciated the presence and contributions of Pelto and his colleagues, Dakin has learned over her many years at her lodge to never underestimate the expertise of her guests, either. One such visitor, a retired geologist from Toronto and long-time Alpine Club of Canada member, Roger Wallis, discovered a new fault line while hiking in Perfect Valley. It had been covered by ice in the early 1960s when J.O. Wheeler (grandson of A.O. Wheeler) conducted geological surveys while passing through the area with fellow mountaineers. And Sorcerer also shares information from the wilderness surrounding the lodge with researchers studying wolverines, mountain goats and endangered whitebark pine trees.

Ben Pelto (centre), a PhD candidate with the University of Northern British Columbia's geography department, holds a snow corer, a device used to take snow or ice cores. Working with Pelto on Kokanee Glacier in British Columbia's Kootenay Mountains in 2016 are Tom Hammond of the University of Washington and Micah May of UNBC. All snow and glacier science reports snow and ice in metres of water equivalent, so researchers can determine how much water the snow holds. Photo Jill Pelto

Glacial recession, though, Dakin admits, is a constant topic of conversation at the lodge, and she's continually surprised and delighted at how many of her guests are knowledgeable in many fields that relate to melting glaciers and Earth's changing climate. The changes happening to *her* glaciers provide a constant source of discovery.

"I have reached a point of acceptance," Dakin said. "This doesn't mean that I don't find the rate at which it's melting alarming and discouraging, but I can't go through life being sad. We work with the changes. We constantly change where we ski, and when. We dodge new icefalls, skirt new crevasses, and ski and hike in places where there is no longer any glacier at all. We find ice caves that are gone in a month, and then we discover new ones. Plants are changing too; trees grow where they didn't. New small tarns and lakes show up and then dry up. Really – it's very beautiful in a way. And fascinating."

Ash on Ice

Fire and ice: opposites, mortal foes.

In western Canada, forest fires shrouded the landscape in thick smoke for weeks during the 2017 and 2018 summers. While they caused misery and a foreboding sense of gloom across mountain and foothills communities in British Columbia and Alberta, the fires, which are projected to grow more frequent and more intense as global temperatures rise, didn't do the glaciers much good either.

With sufficient data since 1880, scientists have calculated that the global average temperature on Earth has continuously risen since the 1980s; 18 of the 19 warmest years ever recorded have happened since 2001. As reported by NASA and the National Oceanic and Atmospheric Administration, who conducted independent analyses, Earth's average global surface temperature in 2019 was the second warmest since modern record-keeping began. July 2019 was the warmest month ever recorded on Earth. With greenhouse gases and, as a result of warming temperatures, water vapour levels in the atmosphere increasing, more energy from the sun is trapped within Earth's atmosphere, which in turn acts like a blanket trapping more of the sun's radiation in the system.

And every summer, as the sun grows warmer, its heat penetrates the glaciers' surfaces. Layer upon layer of snow melts away until the hard ice surface is exposed. Then the ice begins to melt, forming creeks that flow on the glacier's own skin to become outlet lakes and fill rivers. As the ice melts away, another layer is stripped away to expose the next layer down. The ice surface is less reflective than the snow cover that protected it, so it absorbs more of the sun's penetrating rays. The melting is self-perpetuating.

With that, scientists are learning how increasing numbers and intensity of forest fires might literally be fuelling the fire when it comes to glacial melting. The summer of 2018, it turns out, was a bonanza, and not the good kind for glaciers.

As fires burned across western Canada through the summer months, soot and ash and debris landed everywhere – on roads, on lawns, on rooftops and on peoples' cars. And on the glaciers. Because soot and ash are dark in colour, they have the opposite effect that a snowpack does – they attract heat and absorb it. The more soot and ash that accumulates on a glacier, the darker the surface becomes, and the more the glacier beneath it melts.

On a few days, the smoke was so thick it actually blocked some of the sun's warmth, and thus held the melting in check, but that situation – thankfully from the perspective of people living and breathing in the region, but not from the glaciers' – didn't persist.

Researchers conducting studies on a number of glaciers from British Columbia's Purcell Mountains to the Rockies witnessed and recorded elevated melting levels in response to significant ash and soot layers covering the ice. Ben Pelto was one of them. Their consensus is that wildfires should be factored into calculations about how much longer the glaciers will continue to exist in these mountain ranges.

"It would be interesting to further study the effects of ash on melt rate," Pelto said. "But it certainly only constitutes an extra kick to total melt, not a major component. That said, it may be a big player in bad fire years. But temperature takes the trophy for causing most of the melt."

Fire under Ice

While forest fire ash and soot can affect a glacier's melting from above, melting glacier ice, in turn, can have potentially destructive effects on the mountains underneath that ice.

Once such place is Mount Meager, one of a group of volcanic peaks northwest of Whistler in the Pacific Ranges of the Coast Mountains.

Approaching a fumarole ice cave is a delicate business, since the gases being released are toxic. Photo Simon Fraser University

One summer day in 2016, a helicopter pilot was flying in the area to deliver a biologist working on a mountain goat population survey. As the machine flew past the Job Glacier on Mount Meager, the pilot, Hannibal Preto – who happens to have a background in geology – noticed something unusual. There were three holes in the glacier, each of which was spewing gas. Remembering the smell of rotten eggs he'd detected earlier, he recognized the venting holes as fumaroles – openings in or near a volcano through which hot steam and sulphurous gases emerge. News of his discovery made its way to the Earth sciences department at Simon Fraser University. Scientists had suspected the existence of fumaroles on Mount Meager, since for years people had reported a sulphur-like stench in areas of the mountain. Hot springs are found there too. But now, with the glaciers melting and their cover of snow and ice washed away, the fumaroles were exposed.

Before long word of the discovery reached Dr. Kelly Russell, a University of British Columbia professor who has been studying Meager for three decades, and who visited the site with Simon Fraser University professor Glyn Williams-Jones to measure the gas rising from the fumaroles. They found H_2S (hydrogen sulphide), which is extremely toxic, and CO_2, both at very high levels. But while the gas is a potential hazard to anyone visiting the immediate area, another larger and potentially more devastating hazard lurked in the forefront in their minds.

Meager is among the farthest north in a chain of volcanoes known as the Garibaldi Volcanic Belt, the Canadian volcanic arc north of the notorious Cascade volcanoes, which include Mounts Baker, St. Helens and Rainier south of the US border. And Meager, like all volcanoes, is an unstable mountain. Volcanic rock is not as strong as other types of rock because it forms quickly as the volcano erupts. Meager last erupted 2,400 years ago – the youngest eruption of the Garibaldi Volcanic Belt. Moreover, Meager is a glaciated volcano, and glaciers that form on volcanoes can act as a protective layer that holds the mountain together. When that ice melts, the mountain underneath the ice can literally crumble.

Enter Gioachino Roberti, then a PhD student (he's since successfully defended his thesis) with Simon Fraser's Department of Earth Sciences. He became interested in studying Meager during his first visit to Canada from his home country of Italy in 2012, when he learned about the largest landslide in recorded Canadian history. It happened on August 6, 2010, when about 50 million cubic metres of mud, rocks and melted ice flushed down from Meager's slopes for 13 kilometres downstream. His research led him to divert his studies to glaciated volcanoes – glaciovolcanology is an emerging science – and how melting glaciers are impacting the stability of mountains such as Meager. A multidisciplinary science, volcanology requires different expertise to better understand the natural system. For this reason, the study of Mount Meager is a collaborative effort wherein Simon Fraser University, the University of British Columbia and private partners are working together. The group is led by the Canadian Centre for Natural Hazards Research at SFU, which has done extensive

Simon Fraser University professor Glyn Williams-Jones and Dr. Alex Wilson set up instruments to measure gas composition at the first fumarole ice cave high on Mount Meager. Photo Simon Fraser University

work for remapping and monitoring Mount Meager volcano.

With the town of Pemberton located about 60 kilometres directly downstream from Meager, the potential for devastation as a result of melting glaciers is worthy of considerable concern.

"You can imagine the ice as some sort of protective layer," Roberti describes in his "three-minute thesis competition" video posted on YouTube. "When the ice melts, the mountain is free to collapse. If your mountain is a volcano, you have another problem because a volcano is a pressurized system, and if you remove pressure by ice melting and landslide, you might have an eruption."

To study Mount Meager, Roberti made repeated visits to the site. On some trips he flew by helicopter, but on other occasions he chose to approach on foot.

"When you fly in, you lose some of the connection to the rock, to the geomorphology," he explained to me in his lyrical Italian accent during a phone interview. "Too quickly you arrive there. There's too much going on to understand it well."

I understood fully. While I do appreciate making use of a helicopter as an airborne taxi to reach a remote, inaccessible mountain locale where I will spend a whole week exploring on foot before the helicopter returns, I always much prefer self-propelled activities in any natural landscape. Like paddling a canoe or kayak on a river or ocean, like cycling a road rather than driving it, hiking or ski touring necessitate moving slowly through the landscape, methodically climbing up slopes. Relying on a mechanized lift leaves me missing so much of the natural environment by whizzing by or over it, rather than slowing down to travel through it and more fully experiencing the place with my ears, my eyes, my nose and the snow under my skis. It's so much more interesting, and by extension, that single run, or handful of downhill runs, is so much more tangible.

Glue Holding the Mountain Together

Roberti began his own self-propelled research trips by driving beyond Pemberton for about 70 kilometres on the bumpy and dusty Upper Lillooet Forest Service Road. From there he paddled across the Lillooet River either by kayak or canoe, as there is no bridge. Then he shouldered his backpack and began hiking – and bushwhacking, as there are no trails – up to gain the glacier.

"It's very beautiful, and very wild," he said.

He usually spent most of the first day hiking up to the site where he'd set up his tent to camp for two nights. The next day and the third morning would be spent collecting data before it was time to pack up and hike back down.

While on Mount Meager, he and his colleagues were careful to stay away from depressions in the landscape where CO_2 could accumulate, since it is heavier than air but has no odour to warn of its presence.

"You really need to be careful," Roberti said. "You need to keep away from the fumaroles. CO_2 – you don't feel it, you'd fall asleep. You would just die. Sulphur smells like rotten eggs, too much makes your eyes cry, and you get a headache. When you get dizzy, it's time to get out!"

On his hike up, though, he would study the evidence of past landslides that flowed down from the glacier to the valley floor. He was particularly interested in the many extremely large landslides that happened approximately every 2,000 years, since the melting trend that began about 12,000 years ago at the end of the last glaciation had left no ice in the valley bottom. While the glaciers were still thick and fat at the higher elevations, volcanic gases heated and bubbled up causing the rock to fail, and combined with the glacial ice that was melted by those actions and also by warming temperatures, many huge landslides, larger than the 2010 event, sent massive debris floods down the valley – the very deposits upon which people are now developing infrastructure.

In 2016, professor Glyn Williams-Jones and Dr. Alex Wilson began investigating three fumarole ice caves on the Job Glacier on Mount Meager, a volcanic peak about 200 kilometres north of Vancouver. Photo Simon Fraser University

"These catastrophic events happened in the recent – by geological standard – past and can happen today again," Roberti said. "The increases in mean and extreme temperatures are changing weather patterns: the alpine environment is very fragile and even small changes can have devastating effects there."

Through his studies, Roberti aimed to gain a better understanding of the erosion processes that occur on glaciated volcanoes – how the processes of volcanic activity, which produce hot gases and molten rock and cause the mountain to move, interact with glacial ice. To accomplish this, he needed to understand both the volcanic systems *and* the glacial systems.

Using historic aerial photographs and digital elevation models, he was able to measure the changes in the glacier. Using InSAR, a satellite radar signal with millimetric precision, he studied large areas of the mountain's formation. Another PhD student, Swetha Venugopal, measured the gas composition to gain understanding of how the volcano works by identifying what type of magma it contained, since each volcano has a different soup of gases. Inside the magma chamber is a concoction of molten rock and gases, and when the liquid pushes to the surface, bubbles of gas become trapped inside the rock as it solidifies. Being able to configure the composition of that gas is useful since the eruption style depends on the gas content and rock fluid composition.

All this sub-surface activity will affect a glacier lying on the surface, but it works the other way around too.

When Canada was buried under a thousand metres of the Laurentide and Cordilleran ice sheets, volcanoes erupted far below the ice surface. The weight and mass of all that ice definitively affected how those volcanoes erupted.

"A volcano is a source of heat under the glacier," Roberti explained. "It changes how the glacier flows. The volcano influences the shape of the glacier; the volcano controls what's happening with the glacier. But the ice sheet would have affected the type of volcanism that happened underneath it. The glacier dictates the shape of the volcano."

Through their studies, Roberti and his colleagues were able to document the occurrence of melting ice and slope deformation prior to the 2010 landslide.

"The glacier at the base of the slope retreated and during the hottest part of the summer, the slope failed, catastrophically," Roberti said.

The more fluid the landslide – as when it contains a high content of melted ice – the farther it will flow downstream. The entire slope began moving at high velocity down the valley, damming the river and demolishing bridges, roads and equipment. The event happened when the ice melt was at its peak, as it sent water dripping and funnelling into the mountain through cracks and fissures, which contributed to the rock fracturing. Roberti found definitive evidence of a correlation between high temperatures, melting ice and landslides.

That melting ice created openings for fumaroles, allowing gases to escape, which in turn lowered the pressure. Hot gases steaming from the volcano also caused more ice to melt. And, as the ice cover thinned, more hot gases escaped. Lessening of the pressure could also reach down and create a magmatic eruption. All this led to the unstable rock of the volcano shifting, moving.

In May 2019, two catastrophic landslides that happened three days apart caused a massive section of the north face of Joffre Peak in the southern Coast Mountains to collapse (yellowish rock scar). Several climbing routes were obliterated by the landslide. Joffre being a prominent tourist attraction easily viewed from a scenic pullout on BC Highway 99 that links Pemberton and Lillooet, those slides and other precursor events that occurred over the six months prior were recorded and shared via social media, providing the geoscience community with quick ability to collect data. A report published in the respected journal *Springer Nature* in 2020 concluded that although other factors, including unfavourable structure, rock mass weakening by chemical weathering, and alpine glacier erosion and retreat contributed to the collapse, the trigger was likely rapid snowmelt. "The May 2019 Joffre Peak landslides may be one more of a growing list of events responding to human-induced climate change factors (glacier retreat, permafrost degradation, extreme weather), and indicates that we should expect more large landslides to occur throughout the Coast Mountains in this century," said the report. Photo Pierre Friele

"The equilibrium of the mountain is changing. In this valley, we see that changing pressure of the magmatic system following ice melting and landslide may trigger an eruption," he said. "Climate change is decompressing volcanoes, just like uncorking a bottle of champagne. Today's increasing temperatures will cause other large landslides. The slope is moving now. If the same thing happens, it could be a big problem."

Through Roberti's and others' studies, scientists determined the volcano had lost nearly 1.5 cubic kilometres of glacier cover in just three decades since 1987. Mount Meager harbours 27 large, potentially unstable sites, 17 of which only recently became exposed after glacier ice had melted away. Of them, 15 of the slopes are sufficiently large that, were they to fail, the infrastructure of the mountain in that area would certainly be affected. While relatively remote, the nearby area is also home to two hydro power plants and multiple forestry operations.

Given that the 2010 landslide was the

largest ever recorded in Canada, Roberti and the other researchers are, understandably, concerned that the next landslide – and they are confident there will be a next time – could be even more devastating to downstream communities.

And it's not just Meager; other slopes and peaks in the area are showing signs of deformation.

Roberti is now working as the geo-hazard section head with Minerva Intelligence, using artificial intelligence to create hazard mapping.

Meanwhile, a local ACMG mountain guide, Eric Dumerac, who owns and operates Mountain Skills Academy and Adventure, has tenure in the Mount Meager area. From time to time he takes clients on guided tours to see the fumaroles. With safety as his top concern, he also views the opportunity as one that is too fascinating not to share. On the job he's also guided scientists interested in studying the fumaroles and how the melting glaciers are affecting them. And he's offered to provide the scientists more frequent reports.

"To me, this is one of those places that, when I go there, every time my jaw drops," Dumerac said. "It's a really, really cool thing."

Permafrost Ice

It's not just glaciers gluing volcanoes together. In Canada's far north, and in arctic regions around the top of the globe, warming temperatures are causing permafrost to thaw. In Alaska, Yukon, Northwest Territories and Nunavut, with Earth's rising temperatures, land forms are collapsing, roads are cracking and heaving, and the buildings people constructed in places they expected to remain frozen long beyond their own lifespans are breaking apart. Scientists are only beginning to learn how much our modern society has relied on cold to keep our world, our infrastructure, our communities and our way of life stable.

As if that wasn't enough, the active layer of soil that forms the top 2 to 13 feet of permafrost thaws in the summer, allowing plant life to sprout and thrive. The roots of these plants respire out CO_2, which, along with microbes in the soil, release carbon from that soil layer. Some of those microbes break down the organic matter into CO_2, while others produce methane instead when conditions are such that they have no water or oxygen available. Methane is at least 20 per cent more potent than CO_2 at exacerbating Earth's rising temperatures. The speedy rate at which these changes are happening has never before been experienced by humans.

That's the thing about climate change, about our planet's current warming trend. Yes, Earth's glaciers have melted before. And returned. But the rapid rate of melting happening today is not following previous natural patterns. In August 2019 the

Greenland ice sheet broke all records by losing 12.5 billion tons of ice – the most ice to have ever melted in one day since records began in the early 1950s. Daily ice losses of this magnitude were not projected to occur until around 2070. Around the world, high mountain ranges are now warming as fast as the Arctic. In 2018 alone, Switzerland lost 2 per cent of its glacial mass; it lost 10 per cent in just five years before 2018. Since glacial loss lags behind CO_2 rise, glaciers would continue to melt indefinitely even if all the world's CO_2 emissions were halted next week. These changes are happening 50 to 70 years sooner than scientists predicted. Some countries have fully grasped the urgency. In September 2019 Switzerland joined 16 other countries that have pledged to end *all* CO_2 emissions by 2050. Canada has not yet joined them.

Earth is 4.54 billion years old. The Burgess Shale fossils found in the Canadian Rockies at sites in Yoho and Kootenay national parks are about 505 million years old, formed during the Mid-Cambrian Period. Dinosaurs walked where their bones are found today along what is now the Red Deer River in Alberta's Badlands 75 million years ago, in the Late Cretaceous Period. Our human ancestors date back six million years, but the modern form of humans we are familiar with evolved only 200,000 years ago. The Industrial Revolution happened in Europe and the United States between 1760 and 1840. While it took more than 200,000 years for Earth's human population to reach 1 billion, it only took 200 years to increase to 7 billion.

In less than a blink of an eye in geologic terms, humans have managed astounding accomplishments – we built the Pyramids, created a polio vaccine and put a few of us on the Moon. For many of us living in the Western World, we've created downright cushy lives, living in large houses kept warm or cool depending on our immediate needs – so comfortable that instead of avoiding glaciers, as some of our ancestors did, we enthusiastically explore them. And our activities, particularly in the past two centuries, have altered, or at least marred, every single species and system in nature. The bellies of whales – those that manage to survive dodging freighters and cruise ships – have been found full of plastic, which was only invented in 1907, and didn't become popular until after the Second World War. We're rapidly and insanely cutting down old-growth forests quicker than we can learn exactly how vital they are to our own survival. Lake Winnipeg, the tenth largest freshwater lake in the world by surface area, and sixth largest lake in Canada, is threatened by eutrophication, an ecological imbalance caused by too many nutrients – primarily phosphorus and nitrogen from agricultural fertilizers and sewage entering the watershed. The high, and rising, levels of CO_2 in our atmosphere – caused at least in part by human over-use of fossil fuels – have actually altered the jet stream.

Since 2006, husband and wife research team Janet Fischer and Mark Olson from Franklin & Marshall College in Pennsylvania have systematically studied the ecology of mountain lakes in the Canadian Rockies, carefully documenting the effects of catchment characteristics such as glacial and vegetation cover on water transparency, a key lake feature that is linked to colour. Among their discoveries is that as small pocket glaciers disappear, the lakes that they feed become less turbid and their colour shifts from brilliant turquoise to deeper blue. Photo Fischer/ Olson Collection

Humans have caused changes in just about every natural process on the planet. Billions among populations of animals have been lost in recent decades, a situation becoming known as the Sixth Great Extinction. The epoch we are now living in is being called by many (but not yet officially recognized as such) the Anthropocene – a time where humans have made significant impact on Earth's geology and ecosystems, including, but not limited to, anthropogenic climate change.

Those mysterious and momentous forms we know as glaciers are but one piece of the puzzle of Earth, and our activities are causing the arms of those puzzle pieces to break off so that they no longer fit together, so that they can no longer support each other to keep all of Earth's systems working in the ways our lives depend on.

The study of glaciers, and their role in our ecological cycle, is a relatively young study, one that is revealing new discoveries all the time. We've just begun to scratch the ice surface.

How many more fascinating and critical things about glaciers do we have still to learn? Are there ways we depend on them, or other natural systems, that we aren't even aware of yet?

4–4 LIFE IN ICE

Glacier Chemistry

Standing in a fast-flowing creek winding along a broad rock-strewn basin fenced between sky-scraping cliffs, Andrea Gordon appeared patient and focused, despite frosty graupel pellets bouncing off her rain jacket. With icy glacial meltwater lapping over her boots, she methodically recited readings from an instrument measuring the velocity of the water current, gripping the rod tightly to hold it upright in the stream.

Equally tolerant of the mid-July alpine squall, Melissa Lafrenière diligently recorded multiple sets of numbers in a weather-resistant notebook.

Lafrenière, assistant professor with the Department of Geography at Queen's University in Kingston, Ontario, and Gordon, who was heading into her fourth year at Queen's, were studying the stream flow generated by the meltwater of Robertson Glacier in Alberta's Kananaskis Country. While the length, depth, mass, even weight and, importantly, rate of melting of glaciers have been studied in western Canada's mountains for more than a century, glacier science does not end with those numbers. Lafrenière and Gordon were seeking to learn what elements that meltwater was composed of.

To reach their study site, I'd hiked with them for three hours along a gravel trail that was at first double-track wide and smoothed by decades of steady foot traffic, but then

Researchers camped at Robertson Glacier in Alberta's Kananaskis Country during the summer of 2008 conducted studies to learn about the elements contained in the glacier meltwater. Photo Lynn Martel

diminished to a faint path zigzagging around the boulders and stones of glacial moraine. Carrying backpacks stuffed with hydrological instruments and sampling equipment, the scientists dropped their packs and set up water gauges in the creek that splashed and gushed from the melting glacier higher up the valley. To prevent any microbes on their clothing from contaminating their samples, they donned extra-large plastic over-gloves before scooping shovels full of snow into a dozen large zip-lock bags.

The previous day, Lafrenière and Gordon had made the same trip with four researchers from Montana State University in Bozeman, each of them hauling a plethora of stream sampling equipment, including pH meter, electrical conductivity meter, filtration units, sample bottles and even picnic coolers to store their samples.

In what was her third consecutive summer studying the Robertson Glacier, Lafrenière said she chose the Robertson site for several reasons: first, because she knew previous studies had been conducted there in the mid-1990s; second, because other glacial and climatological research was being conducted in the Rockies; and lastly, because the Barrier Lake Field Station run by University of Saskatchewan's Centre for Hydrology, located about an hour's drive from the Robertson trailhead, provided valuable storage facilities – not to mention hot showers.

While working on her PhD at the University of Alberta in Edmonton several years earlier, Lafrenière had focused on trying to understand how the hydrology of glacial systems contributed to pesticide contamination in glacial lakes. Now, her research on the Robertson Glacier concentrated on trying to understand the rate of nutrient deposition in glacial systems, and the human and climate change impacts on how those nutrients behave in glacial and alpine systems.

"I'm trying to understand how much nutrient gets deposited by snow and rain, and to determine how much is natural and how much is anthropogenic," Lafrenière said. Snowfall carries very little nitrogen or organic carbon, while rainfall carries much more. These glacial streams appeared to be carrying more nutrients than they were receiving from the atmosphere, prompting her to wonder if those nutrients were coming from the rocks through mineral weathering. Or was there a biological component?

Researcher Andrea Gordon and Dr. Melissa Lafrenière take readings to determine the meltwater volume of a stream flowing from Robertson Glacier in Kananaskis Country. Photo Lynn Martel

"I'm trying," she explained, "to understand the system's water chemistry."

To gather stream-flow data, she used a temperature sensor, a pressure sensor and an electrical conductivity sensor. The pressure sensor yielded information about changes in the water levels, while the conductivity sensor recorded the amounts of dissolved solids in water. She discovered a cocktail of minerals – including calcium, magnesium, sulphate and nitrate – that have a charge that increases the capacity of water to conduct electricity. Measuring the conductivity acts as a surrogate for determining the amount of dissolved material. Using a string marked off at 25-centimetre intervals that they pulled taut across the width of the stream, Gordon and Lafrenière recorded water depth and velocity readings at each interval. This technique would enable them to determine how much water flows through the channel.

Nutrients in Ice

On that day, a few minutes' walk downstream from their research site, Lafrenière and Gordon had company. Montana State biogeochemist Andy Mitchell was studying how microbes interact with rocks and minerals, and how that leads to rock dissolution and the release of metals and nutrients in water.

"The bigger picture is to learn how climate change leads to glacier response changes in water, snow melt and changes in nutrients downstream," Mitchell explained. His colleague, Montana State Earth sciences professor Mark Skidmore, was working on his own project, examining the microbiology of organisms in environments that are permanently cold, between zero and 1 degree Celsius.

Assisted by two students, Skidmore was collecting samples to learn what kinds of micro-organisms live in the sediment beneath the glacier. He was also studying materials flushed by the streamwaters coming from beneath the glacier using sterilized filtration apparatus. Back in the lab, the researchers would extract DNA from the filter to find out what kind of organisms might be present. To do that, they put some of the sediment samples into different types of growth media at temperatures close to those of the natural environment. Then they watched for results.

"I think it's really interesting studying the chemistry of waters that come from glaciers," Skidmore said. "This glacier has two stream flows and the waters of each have different chemistries. This suggests different biogeochemical reactions going on in different parts of the sub-glacial environment."

These studies, and others, reveal how much microbial life exists not only in glacial meltwater but in the very soil that supports the glacier. While from a distance, glaciers appear as static masses of ice – buried by snow in winter; exposed, rotting from the surface and draining meltwater during the summer – these studies reveal them to be much more. They also raise the question, how much more is there that we have no idea about?

Skidmore first conducted studies on the Robertson a decade earlier, while working on his master's and PhD at the University of Alberta. After a decade's hiatus, he returned with a renewed perspective on glacial systems.

Researchers Dr. Melissa Lafrenière, associate professor at Queen's University, and researcher Andrea Gordon collect samples from the Rockies' Robertson Glacier to be analyzed later for their chemical composition. Photo Lynn Martel

"Roll the clock back ten years, nobody would have considered there were microbial communities in these sub-glacial habitats," Skidmore said. "But when you start digging into sediments and looking under a microscope, you find bacteria. Wherever we look, there are microbes in these sub-glacial environments. To the naked eye, they appear cold and barren, but when you look through geochemical and microbiological investigative tools at the waters and sediments from beneath glaciers, it's interesting to discover the active microbial world beneath the ice."

With his own familiarity with glaciers stemming back to his time as an undergrad conducting research in Switzerland, Skidmore said introducing young students to field work is essential and valuable.

"From my perspective as a professor, if I don't encourage them and introduce them to field work, they're less likely to go on to a career in science."

For her part, Lafrenière planned to return the following summer with a student researching how much anthropogenic pollution is coming down from the high mountains in the form of snow by examining the sulphate and nitrate composition at high altitude.

"How much effect is human activity having on these environments?" she asked. "To understand these environments, you need a critical mass of people. There are the challenges presented by the environment, and the time and effort it takes to get up here with all our sampling equipment and do the work. With six of us looking at a glacier system through six different lenses, hopefully we'll put it all together for a clearer picture."

That clearer picture, she added, should extend beyond scientific circles, as the knowledge gained from research can be valuable for helping direct policy and planning strategies, with baseline data representing a key step.

"Baseline data of water quality and quantity, and what's changing in weather and climate, is essential to understanding what we're doing to the environment," Lafrenière said. "I think it's very valuable to government in terms of understanding our impact on what we think of as pristine environments."

Led by ACMG mountain guide Cecelia Mortenson (orange jacket, second from right) and ACMG assistant hiking guide Rachel Reimer (far right, blue jacket), teen participants of the 2019 Girls on Ice express their enthusiasm for the project in British Columbia's Glacier National Park with the Asulkan Glacier behind them. Photo Lynn Martel

ACMG mountain guide Merrie-Beth Board helps a Girls on Ice participant fasten her crampons in preparation for ascending the Asulkan Glacier. Photo Lynn Martel

"The more research I do, the more I realize nothing is pristine anymore, not in the high alpine, not in the high Arctic. What goes up must come down."

Girls on Ice

It's all in the name of new experiences, scientific study, glacier adventures and introducing the younger generation to the potential of pursuing careers in science.

Ten girls from across Canada are chosen from a pile of applications to participate in the Girls on Ice Canada program. The girls, aged 16 or 17, gather in the mountains, having come from as far as Yukon, Saskatchewan, Ontario or Nova Scotia.

Over the course of 12 days the girls camp – some sleeping in a tent for the first time – at the Illecillewaet campground in Glacier National Park and then spend several nights higher up at the Alpine Club of Canada's Asulkan Hut.

They hike onto glaciers, where they learn how to travel safely and become comfortable using their equipment in a new environment. They learn about the ice and snow and the ecosystem that depends on them. And all the while they develop observational skills as they begin the process of immersing themselves in science. As they gain those essential skills, they develop confidence in their abilities. And if the weather co-operates, they climb a mountain.

Led by a team of all-female mountain guides, glaciologists, ecologists and artists, the program is the Canadian branch, launched in 2018, of one that's been running in the United States since 1999. One key component of the program – which relies on donations – is that it is tuition free, so that girls from all backgrounds can afford to participate.

Girls on Ice Canada was co-founded by glaciologist Alison Criscitiello (see page 206), ACMG mountain guide Cecelia Mortenson, Eleanor Bash, a PhD candidate in glaciology at the University of Calgary, and Jocelyn Hirose (see page 187). After providing valuable support for the inaugural Canadian Girls on Ice in 2018, the Alpine Club of Canada stepped up and took over running the program as a Club adventure beginning in 2019, with support from the Girls on Ice Society, US program initiator Inspiring Girls Expeditions, the University of Alberta and the Open Mountains Project Society. More than 40 volunteers assist with planning, promotions, applicant reviews and as "gear fairies," helping to ferry gear and food up to the hut.

As part of the expedition the girls conduct scientific field studies and create art pieces that reflect their interactions with glaciers and their perceptions of mountain environments. During their wrap-up presentations the girls share the questions, hypotheses and conclusions of their scientific experiments on various glacier-related topics such as glacier dynamics, glacial organisms, geomorphology and the flora and fauna of a glacial environment.

"I see the excitement the program brings; the passion it unlocks," said Bash. "It teaches the girls they are so much more capable than they realized and that they can take on more challenges."

Treasure in the Depths

Jonathan Boutin (blue jacket) of the National Science and Technology Museum and University of Alberta glaciologist Martin Sharpe examine deposits deep inside the Athabasca Glacier. Photo John Price

Sometimes scientific discoveries begin as simple curiosity.

That's exactly what happened when, after decades of travelling around the world climbing frozen waterfalls and exploring cool, damp caves deep underground, Will Gadd decided to combine the two passions right in his own backyard. And, quite by accident, what started out as fun for the Canmore-based professional adventurer – whose previous projects include climbing frozen Niagara Falls – turned into an exciting and entirely new discovery for science.

In December 2016, Gadd led a team of adventurers and scientists to explore a giant ice cave deep inside the Athabasca Glacier. The idea was sparked by a friend who scouted out an appropriate millwell, which he then marked with his GPS. Gadd assembled a team that included Martin Sharp, a University of Alberta glaciologist (now retired) who for years has studied how water moves along and underneath glaciers through self-generated drainage systems, mainly in Canada's Arctic. In recent years Gadd has employed his ice-climbing skills and professional guide training to assist scientists in reaching inaccessible places, and it was in that capacity that he would help Sharp in his pursuit of understanding how water moves under glaciers so that scientists can better model glacial recession as Earth's climate warms.

On that day, though, the team endured minus 37 Celsius temperatures on the glacier's surface as they located the millwell without much difficulty. But there, the work began, as windblown snow had plugged the entrance.

"It took a massive amount of digging and tunnelling, it was not easy to find," Gadd said. "It was the human-ground-squirrel-show for the better part of a day to get in there."

Eventually they'd shovelled enough snow to uncover the entrance. They built solid anchors by drilling ice-climbing screws into the glacier, then attached climbing ropes to lower themselves into the vertical shaft. As they dropped deeper inside the cavern, they encountered warm air rising from the depths – a stark contrast to the frigid temperatures outside on the surface, which resembled a barren, frozen desert. Inside, their thermometers registered the air temperature at a comfortable minus 1 Celsius. All around them smooth ice walls were curved and bowed, testimony to the natural sculpting power of the glacial meltwater that plunged and swirled down the sluice during the summer months. Once they'd descended 100 vertical metres, Gadd and his teammates stood tall and walked along horizontal passages that had been bored by a forceful flow.

"We went from this incredibly harsh world on the surface to this amazing place down there," Gadd described. "It was amazing blue light for about the first 30 metres, then it got dark. At 50 metres a headlamp was essential. This was real exploration – there's no map, no idea what's down there."

And what they found down there, about 50 metres down, surprised them all. Two distinct colonies of biofilms were living on the ice walls, one red algae and one green. A biofilm is a group of micro-organisms that stick to each other and together adhere to a surface – like the plaque on our teeth, which is a biofilm. They didn't expect to see insects flying around inside the glacier either, but they did. Equally fascinating were the pools of water they discovered deep under the ice in the dead of winter.

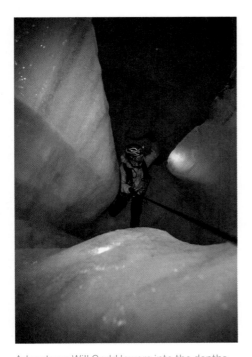

Adventurer Will Gadd lowers into the depths of the Rockies' Athabasca Glacier as part of an expedition to learn more about ice formations and composition dozens of metres below the surface. Photo John Price

For Martin Sharp, the discovery of the biofilms was a terrific bonus.

"They were colonizing things like cracks in the ice where there was water seeping out of the crack," Sharp described. "Also, where there was a water pocket that was partially open on the tunnel wall, there would be films on the surface, in the water."

The biofilms were discovered about 50 metres below the surface, a depth where some – not much, but some – light does penetrate. Sharp suggested the biofilms could be converting light energy into chemical energy through the process of photosynthesis. Even though the glacier surface was swathed in a metre of new winter snow, sufficient light penetrated to allow the biofilms to exist, likely by extracting nutrients out of the water as well as by photosynthesis.

What was especially exciting for the adventurers and the scientists alike was that no one had ever found living organisms so deep below a glacier's surface. Scientists had previously searched for microbes inside ice, and some had discovered living organisms within ice cores retrieved from deep inside icefields and glaciers, but until this discovery on the Athabasca, researchers had only looked in the micro-channel, between individual crystals, where very small amounts of water are present. The macro channel, where a lot more space, air and, likely, light, are present, had never been studied for micro-organisms.

Following their adventure, which included participants from the Canada Science and Technology Museum and a Discovery Canada film crew, Sharp investigated to see if there was any existing information about the organisms they'd discovered. He couldn't find a single record.

"When you think about it, it's not terribly surprising. Microbes have a propensity of finding ways of living pretty much anywhere," Sharp said. "But as far as we know, this is the first time anybody's seen this."

Questions in Ice

On a return visit to the ice cave a few weeks later, one of Sharp's students, with permission from Parks Canada, retrieved some samples of the biofilms. They were sent to the University of Bristol in Britain to be analyzed under the direction of Ashley Dubnick, a PhD candidate and a recognized expert on the biology of glaciers, in the hopes of identifying the organisms. Once some preliminary information was understood, the scientists could develop experiments to answer specific questions. And they had a list.

Are the biofilms capable of surviving the entire winter? That's at least seven months for the Athabasca Glacier. Or, are they in a sort of transition stage between when cooler temperatures in autumn stop the glacier from melting and the creeks on the surface dry up and no longer pour water down the millwells? Does the winter snowpack provide sufficient insulation to trap heat in the tunnels and caverns deep inside the glacier? Do the deep vertical ice chutes retain enough warm air in their lower reaches that cold air from above doesn't penetrate?

Then there's the question of temperatures. With the inside of the glacier holding steady at minus 1 Celsius, the ice walls of the millwell and all the other glacier features are preserved. But, as Earth's temperatures rise, the temperatures inside the glaciers will rise too. It only takes 1 degree of warmth to melt glacial ice that is preserved at minus 1, on the surface or deep inside, causing significant, drastic changes. That certainty begets its own list of questions about what will happen inside glaciers as they melt. And this isn't something that's *going* to happen. It already *is* happening.

Discovery of the biofilms opened a large, and potentially dark, Pandora's box of questions. And the preliminary findings did shed some light on the nature of the biofilms.

University of Alberta glaciologist Martin Sharp explains ice formations in a passage deep inside the Athabasca Glacier. Photo John Price

"The microbes found in the snow on top of the glacier are totally different from those found in the biofilms and in glacier ice in the walls of the channel system," Sharp said. "The communities from within the glacier are all very similar to each other regardless of depth in the glacier and light level – suggesting that they are by and large not phototrophs – while those in the snow might be."

Sharp and Gadd did return to the Athabasca early in the 2018/19 winter

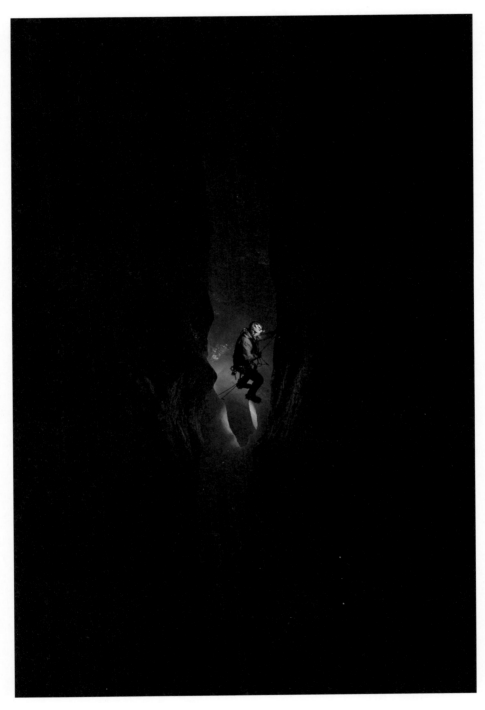

Will Gadd descends through a small opening in a winter-frozen millwell to explore 100 metres down into the Athabasca Glacier. Photo John Price

in the hopes of retrieving new samples to do some single-cell analysis to help understand how the biofilms got their energy, but due to a significant September snowfall, which was mixed with freezing rain, the upper part of the millwell was completely plugged and impossible to excavate through. They plan to try again.

In addition to the members and professional adventure photographer John Price taking plenty of photos, the crew recorded video and sounds from inside the glacier, some of which Gadd found unsettling. At 100 metres below the surface, they began to see extraordinary cracks in the ice walls. Another ten metres deeper, the tension of the environment crossed into the realm of disconcerting.

"At 100 metres, I felt the pressure of the unknown unknowns, the kind of stuff that is often fatal in new high-risk environments," Gadd explained.

While the team had hoped to penetrate all the way to the bed surface – the interface where the ice connects with the ground that supports it – they stopped and headed back up. The ice walls were creaking and groaning under the intense pressure of their own weight, and that force was causing them to crack. Later the team determined they were between 20 and 60 metres from bedrock, knowledge that will help glaciologists to calculate the loss of depth, which results in much greater loss of ice volume than the easily viewed and measured horizontal recession.

Having lived much of his life in the Canadian Rockies, with his first visits to the Athabasca Glacier happening when he was a young boy more than 40 years ago, Gadd said he is continually amazed by the rapid pace at which the Athabasca is melting due to climate change. And now, having explored deep inside the ice, his perspective has expanded.

"Whenever I'm travelling on glaciers to climb or ski, I've always looked down into millwells and wondered what's going on down there," Gadd said. "Now when I drive by the Athabasca Glacier, I don't see just this chunk of ice. There's this whole world going on down there."

And that's the thing.

Like all Earth sciences, from biology to forest ecology to oceanography to atmospheric studies and beyond, glacier science is dynamic. There is always more to be learned. Science has taught us that glaciers are much more than ice masses grinding and sliding slowly on a landscape. Glaciers are much more than melting masses of ice filling creeks and rivers and lakes. They are more than convenient and intriguing surfaces on which to schuss on a pair of skis.

Moving, mysterious, mesmerizing. And, yes, melting.

Glaciers are nature's bellwethers, nature's teachers, nature's water-storage system. And they are so much more, again, that we have not yet learned. Like many who explore the mountains to ski and climb, Gadd has now added the pursuit of scientific knowledge to his list of intentional activities.

And those questions about what other mysteries glaciers might harbour really hit home when he showed pictures from his Athabasca adventure to his preteen daughters.

"The shapes and colours entranced them," he said. "But then, as I looked at the mesmerizing pictures with my kids, it hit me that I wasn't helping them prepare for just a warmer world, but a world that will change in ways far, far more radical and unpredictable than we can imagine."

"This isn't just about less ice. It's also about a world where my life as a climber and guide is left unknown. And, frankly speaking, this terrifies me."

Banff-based photographer Paul Zizka has gained international attention and success for his stunning and highly creative style, resulting in images such as these ice climbers ascending a Canadian Rockies glacial cave under a halo of Northern Lights. Photo Paul Zizka

5 INSPIRATION IN ICE

Throughout human history, wilderness has provided a place of solace and comfort, a place of spiritual renewal. Its timelessness and scale provide a perspective that restores a sense of balance and completeness to us as we live our busy lives. Lying on the mossy floor of the forest, swimming in alpine pools and climbing high onto icefields, we have come to feel part of the wilderness.

—John Baldwin, *Soul of Wilderness*

5-1 ICE THROUGH THE LENS

The Thrill of Scouting

CRACKKKK!!

Boooommmm. Rumbbbblleee......

"Wow, that's cool!"

"Sure is!"

"Glad we're not under it!"

The avalanche of snow and ice chunks tumbled down the sheer rock face, the resulting snow-dust cloud billowing up and outward to obscure the entire cliff. The early morning sun had been kissing the glacier-capped summit of Snow Dome for barely an hour, but the rosy peach glow had warmed the layer of ancient ice just enough to weaken the serac towers and cause giant sections to cleave off. Although decidedly front and centre, from our vantage point some two and half kilometres away in an open valley, we were totally safe to enjoy the show.

For the seven of us on this exploratory trip, witnessing the serac avalanche was indeed a bonus.

None of us was there to climb the test-piece route up the adjacent cliff, nor were we there to ski across any icefields. Rather, the dead-end valley, fenced by a horseshoe of vertical walls twice the height of Toronto's CN Tower, was our destination.

Our outing had been organized, informally, by Banff-based photographer Paul Zizka. After several weeks of message threads and two cancelled dates - when the biggest snowstorm of the winter (always a good thing for the glaciers) closed the Icefields Parkway for nearly a week so Parks Canada public safety technicians could trigger avalanches on snow-laden slopes lurking above the road, and then clear up the resulting piles, and during which time temperatures had dropped to minus 35 Celsius – finally, Zizka had rounded up a crew of several photographer friends to explore potential shooting locations.

To reach the site by first light, I had risen at 3:40 a.m., driven for 20 minutes to Banff to pick up Zizka and then continued up the Icefields Parkway. A virtual conga line of motor homes, tour buses and cars all through the summer months, the scenic drive in winter is all but deserted. Especially before dawn on a Tuesday. For two hours we encountered not a single car driving in either direction. A few were parked at the usual ice climbing locations and the Peyto Lake skiers' pullout providing access to the Wapta Icefields. Two vans parked at the Saskatchewan Glacier pullout, I would later learn, belonged to a group of Edmonton-based Canadian Army servicemen training for cold weather mountain living. They'd hit the jackpot, as overnight temperatures had sunk below minus 20 Celsius, and it would be a few hours before the sun rose high enough to warm up any valley bottoms. A handful of vehicles parked at the Athabasca Glacier parking lot belonged to more military personnel who had camped in tents far up that glacier.

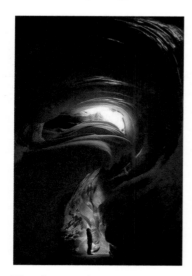

"The photographer in me sees beauty in impermanence. The earthling in me feels responsibility for how fast these changes are happening." Photo Paul Zizka

As we drove, the sky lightened ever so slowly, black fading to deep purple, then mauve, to reveal ridgelines and snow-sculpted peaks, the light to the north becoming a glowing hue of lavender/periwinkle/lilac. Winter light, never seen by summer tourists. With the only gas pumps for more than 100 kilometres in either direction closed and wrapped in blankets, and the Columbia Icefield Centre sitting deserted like the Overlook Hotel in *The Shining*, just being there exuded an aura of mystery and excitement.

For Zizka, who had returned home from a trip to Easter Island just days earlier, and who would leave again two days later to teach a photography workshop in Antarctica, this morning's visit to his home glaciers was a coveted treat. Zizka had been a highly sought-after professional photographer for the past decade, and it was his images combining elements of star-splattered night skies with aurora rainbows and ice climbers ascending giant glacier caves that initially launched his success. Throughout his career, Zizka's jaw-dropping images of night skies, celestial bodies, Northern Lights and off-the-popular-trail locations have presented the well-photographed Rockies in an entirely new light. And for him, scouting for new locations is part of the thrill. While the majority of Rockies visitors witness the glaciers in summer, the frozen glaciers of winter are Zizka's domain, his muse. Several months earlier, he and fellow photographer Kahli April Hindmarsh had hiked up a rarely visited valley to explore a small glacier. Rounding curved ice hills and soft-edged valleys carved by water running during summer months, they found treasure – a massive cave formed in the ice, larger than several rooms, with plenty of space for the two of them to walk around admiring sculpted walls and ceiling, giant boulder-sized blocks littering the floor. It was a truly magical place, and the photos they posted on social media were astonishing.

Kid in a Candy Shoppe

It was darned cold when we set off from our vehicles parked by the side of the pavement, travelling on snowshoes and skis. A frosty wind nipped at my cheeks, and I pulled a light hood under my toque to give my face some protection. On my legs I wore three pairs of long underwear beneath my outer pants, on my torso five layers beneath my biggest, warmest down jacket, hood up. I'd come prepared, toe warmer pads in my boots, extra thick down/Gore-Tex mitts on my hands, with a smaller pair of gloves underneath. The snow surface was wind blasted and uneven – a four-inch-thick crust supporting our weight in some places, breaking apart into dinner-plate slabs in others.

Surveying the neighbourhood – which he had explored only once before a decade earlier, and new to the rest of us – Zizka noticed a broad, flat-topped sub-peak connected to the moraine.

"We should come back in the summer, spend a few hours up there doing astral photography," he suggested.

"Great idea!"

As a sought-after workshop leader, Zizka is continually seeking fresh locations. Several of our group met him while taking one of his courses.

Carrying backpacks filled with cameras, lenses and tripods, we were a keen team accompanying Zizka on a scouting mission. With thousands of social media followers, Zizka has made glacier photography cool.

"The cool thing about glaciers is that they are always changing," he said. "If we see something today, it could be gone next month, even next week. Hopefully we'll

Paul Zizka shows his delight in discovering a new glacial ice cave to photograph. Photo Pam Jenks

find something today. Regardless, it's always memorable. Sometimes you get great photos, sometimes not. That's why I think it's important to put the experience ahead of anything else."

And with that experience, he added, comes awareness too, as the Athabasca Glacier he's been photographing for more than a decade changes, drastically, right in his viewfinder.

"It is, for me, a place that holds unlimited photographic potential, and so it never ceases to inspire," he said. "I find the scale and the surreal feel of the features there fascinating. And you can't beat the access. But my feelings are mixed. The photographer in me sees beauty in impermanence. The earthling in me feels responsibility for how fast these changes are happening. Regardless, though, it remains something to document, and that is what I try to focus on."

While from the road, the landscape toward the end of the cul-de-sac valley appeared smooth with only subtle features, rather like rounded foothills, before long we left the moraine behind and entered the land of ice, a translucent blue slope rising steeply on one side, a gently winding frozen creek bed leading us into a shallow valley to the left. I could imagine glacial meltwater coursing along this meandering trail on a warm sunny day. But today, all was firmly frozen in place and time. Layers of rocks and pebbles coated mounds of ice and appeared suspended in ice a metre above the deck. Clambering up a steeper pitch, we rounded a snow-covered ice hill corner to find a bulging wall intersecting with another forming a deep corner. Spotting rime ice crystals in the notch, Zizka cleared away some of the frost and snow. His hunch was right: warm air emerging from a small cave had caused the frost to form. The small cave gave him hope and he crawled inside to investigate like a kid in a candy shoppe. Emerging a few minutes later, he reattached his snowshoes and hoisted his camera bag on his back.

"Exploring," he said, "That's the fun part!" Motioning to the rounded slope above and farther up the glacier, his face beamed with enthusiasm. "I'm excited to go up there, there are all these dips and curves, it's convoluted. I can't wait to see what's there!"

Worth a Thousand Words

Prior to the first photographic image being developed in 1827, visual documentation of landscapes and people travelling through them was accomplished by artists who were invited along for the journey. Of course, men – and let's hope women too – have been drawing on rock walls for millennia, often as they moved from one region to another, hunting and gathering food. Pictographs found at Grassi Lakes and Grotto Canyon near Canmore in the Canadian Rockies date back many centuries. Usually showing hunting scenes or prey animals, the Grotto Canyon drawings depict the Hopi figure Kokopelli, providing hard evidence of the legend of a clan that travelled from the US southwest desert landscape north to a land of snow and ice. No drawings depicting glaciers spilling down from steep rocky cirques or, thousands of years earlier, choking the main valleys like generously applied foam insulation, however, have yet been discovered in western Canada.

This, like so much of life in the mountains of Alberta and British Columbia, would change with the construction of the Canadian Pacific Railway. Before the track was completed, in 1871 and 1884 two photographic parties were sent to the Rockies by a Montreal firm. Their images were used to create black and white engravings to illustrate a dazzling pamphlet titled The New Highway to the East, published in 1888. Tourists, too, were as keen to capture images from their travel destinations then as everyone with a cellphone is today. Doing so in the late 19th century, though, was a little less convenient.

William Spotswood Green and Reverend Henry Swanzy brought two cameras, one for quarter-plates and one for half-plates, plus another half-plate instrument and

Images created from woodcut engravings that were printed in Reverend Spotswood Green's 1890 book, *Among the Selkirk Glaciers*, helped lure early tourists to western Canada's magnificent glaciated peaks. Lynn Martel Collection

a small Stirn's detective camera. They also packed along sketchbooks and watercolours, plus surveying instruments, including a prismatic compass, two aneroids, a set of thermometers and a hypsometer, a plane table, legs and alidade, which packed up neatly into a knapsack and weighed a mere 12 kilograms. Going one step further, as they ventured onto the glaciers several hours' walk above the valley-bottom train tracks and climbed along knife-edge ridges, they sometimes attached their camera by a screw onto the head of an ice-axe stuck firmly in the snow. Selfie sticks are not that new.

Treasure Trove

Over the following decades more visitors made images of the magnificent glaciers of Rogers Pass and the Rockies' Banff and Yoho parks, including Walter Wilcox's now invaluable image of Peyto Glacier taken in 1896. Although likely better known for her painting and photographs of wildflowers, like her friend and mountain travel companion, Mary Vaux – who eventually devoted her talents to wildflower illustrations – Mary Schäffer Warren also created images of the Rockies' glaciated landscape during her extensive backcountry travels, including the first images of Jasper's Maligne Lake in 1908. Back home in Philadelphia, Schäffer – who later married her outfitter Billy Warren and lived out her days in Banff – would show her hand-painted lantern slides to people to encourage them to visit western Canada's spectacular mountains.

As technology improved, black and white photography equipment became less expensive to use, and cameras less prohibitive to transport. From its inaugural 1907 volume, the pages of the *Canadian Alpine Journal* showcased an impressive array of adventure and mountain photography. From the snow-capped Goodsirs – as they were then, and not the largely bare rock piles they are now – to Mount Assiniboine to the Wapta Icefields, Alpine Club of Canada members recorded their ascents, many of them firsts, both in finely written accounts and in black and white images.

In a section of the 1907 volume titled Glacier Observations – renamed the Scientific Section in subsequent volumes – reports by George and William Vaux and by A.O. Wheeler are accompanied by terrific glacier images. They were often shot with a person in the frame to illustrate a sense of scale, and it's impossible to imagine the participants weren't thoroughly awestruck by the sheer size and magnificence of the ice forms. Although fuzzy by today's standards, the photos guard a treasure trove of glacier information from the era from the Rockies to the Purcells, the Selkirks and the Coast Mountains and Vancouver Island.

While many photographs, however, then and now, show glaciers as part of the scenery, A.O. Wheeler, and especially the Vaux siblings, deliberately focused their pictures on the glaciers, up-close, personal. Carrying their cumbersome large-format field cameras fitted with hefty lenses, they captured photos in an effort to record the advance or retreat of individual glaciers.

They also adeptly captured the essence of being among glaciers. On a warm summer day, the hypnotic sounds of water would have been everywhere, surrounding

At an Alpine Club of Canada camp circa 1914, Byron Harmon made this captivating image of mountaineers taking in a birds-eye view of Yoho Glacier. Yoho Glacier was among the earliest of Canada's glaciers to be studied. Today it has melted so far back that it is rarely visited. Photo Byron Harmon, Whyte Museum of the Canadian Rockies, Byron Harmon fonds (V263/I/A/i/a/na-153)

them with the energy of life and motion. Splashing, gurgling, trickling, rushing, and downstream where the Illecillewaet's outlet creek crew fatter with meltwater pouring down from the Vaux Glacier, the music would have risen to a crescendo, a full and mighty roar. Standing close to the wall of ice, compressed and formed of layers of snow thousands of years old, streaked with residue from volcanic eruptions and soot from wildfires, by photographing the glaciers with tiny humans standing close enough to reach out and touch the ice gingerly as if they were approaching a great beast, they allowed us not just to see the ice but to feel it.

Master of His Craft

Byron Hill Harmon, too, knew how to draw his viewers into an image to connect with the mountain environment he photographed. Arriving in Banff in 1903 as a young travelling photographer originally from Tacoma, Washington, he was a bold and ultimately successful entrepreneur who opened Banff's first photography studio in 1909. He would ultimately run a movie theatre, a curio shop, a drug store, a fountain lunch and tea shop, a bookstore and lending library, a woollen shop and even a beauty parlour. He also designed and built much of the darkroom equipment he used to develop his images, as well as the screen in his theatre.

But it was his photography that set him on a path of adventure and created a legacy that endures today.

Famous for his boundless energy and physical stamina, he was hired as the Alpine Club's official photographer, a position he held from 1906 to 1913 and a plum job that provided him a tent, meals, and hiking and climbing adventures at the annual mountaineering camp, which was located in a different area of the Rockies or Selkirk Mountains each summer. Harmon appreciated the opportunity to continually explore and photograph new locations. His position also granted him passage on several VIP exploratory expeditions to remote areas led by A.O. Wheeler, sometimes with the added assignment of photographing distinguished visiting climbers, such

With a man – and a dog – standing on the ice, this image portrays the scale of the glacier ice shelf at Lake of the Hanging Glacier in the Purcell Mountains. Photo Byron Harmon, 1920, E-38, Whyte Museum of the Canadian Rockies, Byron Harmon Fonds (V263/I/A/i/a/na-283)

as Britain's Dr. T.G. Longstaff, a revered Himalayan climber and Arctic explorer.

One three-week journey in 1910 into the Purcell Mountains on the west side of the Columbia Valley would result in some exceptional images. While one of the purposes of the trip was to provide Longstaff an opportunity to hunt some of the region's then-abundant game – the postcard Harmon produced from an image of the three grizzlies Longstaff shot in a single afternoon would be a bestseller for years to come – the other purpose was to explore. Setting off from Golden aboard a paddlewheeler, they travelled south on the Columbia River. One particularly rewarding day, while travelling ahead of the main party with the packers, Harmon discovered a massive glacier that he described around the campfire that evening as having "a collection of the most striking aiguilles ... [which] shot up from behind the glacier like arctic nunataks out of an ice cap: quite sheer, without a speck of snow." While for a time it was known as Harmon's Glacier, that spectacular place is now known around the world among both rock climbers and heli-skiers as the Bugaboos.

His companions wrote about how he was inseparable from his camera, and how he impressed them with his vitality as he routinely helped the packers cut trail, and how on one day he hiked 36 miles of rugged mountain terrain carrying his pack of heavy and awkward camera equipment, consisting of 4" x 5" and 5" x 7" view cameras (plus, after 1910, a movie camera), wooden tripods, changing bag, extra film packs and glass plates. His photos tell the story of a man who immersed himself fully and deeply in the wonders of the landscape he was privileged to explore.

This sentiment is evident in one photograph taken in 1922 where a man – with his dog – appears so tiny standing atop a shelf of glacier ice floating in the Lake of the Hanging Glacier that he's little more than a stick figure atop the three-storey-high wall of ice creased with dark lines and cracks like unpolished marble. The main subject having long since diminished, the image is as jaw-dropping as any taken with modern cameras today. And it leaves me wondering, could the man feel any movement in the ice underfoot? Did it shift, rise and fall with the lake water? Did any half-severed chunks of ice break off the cliff face to land with a splash in the lake, causing Harmon's model to jump in surprise?

Nearing the age of 50, in 1924 Harmon embarked on an ambitious project, a ten-week pack trip following the Continental Divide from Lake Louise to Jasper and Maligne Lake. En route the party ascended the Saskatchewan Glacier onto the Columbia Icefield itself, with their horses, and by the time they returned to Banff they were travelling in early autumn snows.

One thing that clearly stands out about Harmon's images is how he saw the glaciers, and how he portrayed them not as massive expanses of ice lying dormant on the landscape but as exquisite forms sculpted by water and wind reminiscent of the most delicate desert rock arches or finest stone cliffs.

The details of his images are planned to perfection, none more evident than in one image captured at Bow Glacier in which two men stand inside a rather erotically shaped ice cave entrance. Their pose is so perfectly balanced we can almost hear Harmon instructing them, "now stretch your right leg outward, and you, lean in toward the ice wall just a bit...."

On a Columbia Icefield trip in 1924, Byron Harmon photographed his party's horses crossing the Saskatchewan Glacier. Byron Harmon photo, Whyte Museum of the Canadian Rockies, Byron Harmon Fonds (V263/I/A/i/a/na-2289)

Harmon left for us some 6,500 glass plates, nitrate negatives, negative copies and prints, which are housed at the Whyte Museum of the Canadian Rockies in Banff. As well, a website created and maintained by his granddaughter, Carole Harmon, offers prints for sale of his timeless and masterful photographic works.

Mountain Romantic

While Harmon's images portrayed so beautifully the mystery, the sense of awe and power of the glaciated mountain West, Bruno Engler's celebrated the pure joy of spending time amidst high glaciated peaks.

Engler grew up in Switzerland, the son of a talented amateur actress and a professional photographer. To escape terrible arguments between his parents centred around his father's affair with the family maid, as a boy Engler ran off into the mountains. Through his teens he developed his climbing skills, and like any Swiss mountaineer worth his alpenstock, he took up skiing too. These passions would serve him well, along with a three-year apprenticeship to become a professional photographer, which he completed in 1936 just before his 21st birthday. While he loved the craft of photography, he didn't much enjoy the requisite long hours spent in the darkroom, so after a brief stint as a journalist, he decided to become a mountain guide.

Along the way, and not unlike his father, Engler also nurtured a fine appreciation for women. His romance with a woman of independent means two years his senior opened his eyes to the impending war Europe would soon be mired in, so in 1939 on her recommendation he dropped everything and immigrated to Banff. The romance wouldn't last, but before long he was working as a ski instructor at Sunshine Village in winter, and in summer as an assistant mountain guide at Lake Louise under the direction of the hotel's senior Swiss guides.

When the war halted Rockies tourism, he taught skiing in Quebec's Laurentian Mountains, which led to him enlisting in the Canadian army to teach training in mountain warfare. During a four-month exercise named Operation Polar Bear, Engler helped lead hundreds of troops from Terrace, British Columbia, across rugged and glaciated mountain terrain to the Pacific coast. During one training exercise he carried out a rescue of a couple of soldiers who fell into a crevasse on a glacier on Hudson Bay Mountain near Smithers. Lying in pain at the bottom of a ten-metre-deep slot, one of the men had become injured when another man landed on his chest wearing ten-point steel crampons. The arduous rescue took ten hours.

In the 1950s, Bruno Engler helped organize recreational ski races on Mount Victoria's lower glacier. This Mount Victoria ski race happened in August 1956. Photo Bruno Engler, Whyte Museum of the Canadian Rockies, Bruno Engler fonds (V190/I/A/i/a/4/na-5)

While Engler would spend a number of years raising several of his ten children – he married four times – in the Crowsnest region of southern Alberta, Engler's home in Canada was the Rocky

Mountains. His gregarious personality, his love of a good laugh and his enthusiasm for having a "parrrrrrty!" gifted him a colourful and story-filled life – stories he loved to entertain his guests with. He guided politicians, including Alberta Premier Peter Lougheed, Governor General Roland Michener and Prime Minister Pierre Elliott Trudeau. As a cinematographer and location scout, he worked on Hollywood productions with Paul Newman, Jimmy Stewart, Richard Gere and Dustin Hoffman. Wherever he went, his over-the-top bon vivant personality endeared him to many. Rockies author R.W. (Bob) Sandford edited an entertaining collection of Engler's tales in a charming book titled *A Mountain Life: The Stories and Photographs of Bruno Engler*.

As an avid downhill skier, Engler was especially adept at capturing motion in his photographs. For this, he also benefited from ever-improving technology that made cameras small and easily portable, and film that could clearly capture fast-moving subjects. His talent for capturing movement is most evident in his images of cascading waterfalls, sometimes revealed as a thin plume gliding off a cliff next to an imposing wall of glacier ice. In another image of a skier schussing down Bow Glacier with crevasses splitting the ice in the foreground and the rocky point of Saint Nicholas Peak behind him, the smooth motion of the skier delicately accentuates the vastness of the landscape.

His fourth wife, Vera Matrasova-Engler, an astute Czech film archivist, film historian and former Olympic shot putter, expressed her deep love for him by editing a stunning coffee-table book of some of his finest images, titled *Bruno Engler Photography*. They met while both serving as jury members for the Banff Mountain Film Festival in 1994. They were married in 1996 at Mount Engadine Lodge, a charming retreat in Kananaskis Country, and the two were inseparable until his final day.

Bruno Engler. Photo Bob Sandford

While a businessman might have reaped a tidy fortune from sales of his sublime black and white photographs, Engler preferred to be out in the mountains creating images of bears and goats, forests and wind-whipped peaks, and sharing adventures with people rather than tending to business chores. His generosity and accessibility were legendary. Until the day he died at 85, Engler's heart was in the high alpine amidst the peaks and glaciers.

High-Mountain Journalist

Trained as a journalist, Harry Rowed knew intuitively how to use his camera to tell a story, of people and place. He also understood the value of good light on his subjects, especially the unpredictable light of mountains and glaciers.

Growing up a Saskatchewan farm boy, he loved spending time outdoors. By his early twenties, his interest in writing and cartooning led him to work as a reporter for the *Prince Albert Herald*. His editor, however, decided that his reporters should carry a camera, learn how to use it and, on top of that, pay for their own camera. By the time Rowed had been promoted to sports editor he had purchased his first Leica. Naturally, his skills included processing his negatives and making his own prints.

Work took him to Winnipeg, where he rose to the position of chief photographer at the *Winnipeg Tribune*. Over the course of his career, he covered stories from the Mackenzie River north of the Arctic Circle to the 1936 Berlin Olympics to Fiji and Tonga and Samoa. As an editorial photographer he captured moments in history including the rise of Nazi power in Germany and the early days of the oil industry in Alberta. During the Second World War he applied his skills with the Wartime Information Services, and during this time made his first visit to Jasper and the Rockies. This job led him to become chief of photo services of the National Film Board, but rather than

Rockies-based photographer Harry Rowed knew how to capture the immensity of the Athabasca Glacier, circa early 1940s, against the tiny people in the forefront. Today the glacier is about one-quarter the size and no longer visible from the parking lot, which is at least four times larger (not counting the one at the icefield centre building, which holds a couple of hundred more vehicles). Photo Harry Rowed

be "promoted" to a supervisory position – which promised plenty of desk time – he decided to gamble on the life of a freelancer and moved to Jasper. The move paid off, as he became one of the most sought-after photographers in the country. And certainly, in the Rockies.

In Jasper, Rowed founded a photography shop and teamed up with a partner, Ray O'Neil. O'Neil managed the day-to-day people assignments, enabling Rowed to spend much of his time outdoors shooting the spectacular landscape. That paid off too, as their popular postcard series drew plenty of tourists to the area. Rowed also shot on assignment for magazines and commercial clients. A feature photo essay of a ski trip with friends to Mount Assiniboine titled High-Mountain Holiday ran in *Weekend Picture Magazine.*

Two members of the Lovat Scouts, a high-calibre British Army unit that trained in snow travel and winter survival skills during the Second World War on and around glaciers in the Canadian Rockies, practise building a sled using their skis and packs. Photo Harry Rowed

In 1939, Harry Rowed published a magazine article titled "The girl who climbed Athabaska," as it was then spelled. In this image, Swiss mountain guide Ernie Niederer assists Margaret in lacing up her crampons for their ascent. From Toronto, 19-year-old Margaret worked her summers through university at the Jasper Park Lodge en route to becoming a biologist. Photo Harry Rowed

Rowed's work shows a finely tuned appreciation for glaciers, as evident in one photo taken at Mount Robson showing Berg Glacier as a magnificent jumble of ice blocks and lumps tumbling into Berg Lake, spitting small icebergs to float in the water. In the Rockies, many of his lasting images are those captured at the Athabasca Glacier area in the 1940s and '50s. Rowed often enlisted his wife, Genevieve, and their kids Daphne and Scott to serve as models, lending terrific scale and perspective. Photos of the Athabasca taken from the same viewpoint today would show a very different glacier, a thin, dirty, benign strip of ice lying on the valley floor like castaway ticker tape. It's unlikely Rowed could ever have imagined the Athabasca, and the other Rockies' glaciers, diminishing as much as they have in his children's lifetime.

His day-in-the-life photos of the Lovat Scouts, a high-calibre British Army unit that trained in snow travel and winter survival skills during the Second World War in Jasper, and especially on the Saskatchewan and Athabasca glaciers, have endured as touchstones of the period. In addition to appearing in several books on the region, some are on display at the Columbia Icefield Centre, albeit cropped and, unfortunately, often with little or no context.

Rowed's son, Scott, became a heli-skiing guide, and followed in his father's footsteps as a successful Rockies commercial photographer, as well as a recognized ski photographer, with his images appearing on the pages – including a few covers – of magazines including *National Geographic*, *Powder* and *Skiing*. He now manages his father's archive of some 30,000 negatives and transparencies.

In 2017, Scott Rowed set out on a unique project with his daughter, Kylie. Seventy years earlier, Harry (who died in 1987) had photographed Scott's mother, Gen, reclining on a boulder in the middle of the moraine, with the Athabasca Glacier in the background and the Dome Glacier slithering down the next valley behind it. After hiking around in the rubble for a few hours, Scott and Kylie located the exact boulder by lining up the moraines, the trees and the peaks. There, Scott guided Kylie to strike the same pose her grandmother had in the original image. While the similarities between the two women generations apart are remarkable, and endearing, the landscape tells its own story. The Athabasca, which formed a significant band of ice across the landscape in the original, has completely vanished from that vantage point, leaving a lake in its place. The Dome Glacier has disappeared far from view too.

Darcy Monchak

It's the simplicity, said Darcy Monchak, that lures him to photograph glaciated terrain.

Now retired from his career as a professional forester working with the British Columbia provincial government, the Golden resident has been exploring and photographing the backcountry of the Canadian Rockies and neighbouring mountain ranges since 1980. Having pursued this passion for so many years means he learned to transition from Kodachrome film to digital. One thing that hasn't changed is that he carries a tripod, which he uses extensively, while still travelling as light as possible in rugged mountain terrain.

Through those years, he's captured many of his photos while travelling solo, camping in remote, difficult-to-access locations, but over the past decade more often on half- and full-day hikes.

In the high country, the landscape is his muse. Especially talented at spotting wildlife such as mountain goats in their

Sunlight illuminates layers of multi-coloured rock exposed as The President Glacier melted back over recent decades, with the twin peaks perfectly reflected in a puddle. Photo Darcy Monchak

Icebergs float in the meltwater lake that has formed at the toe of the Des Poilus Glacier, which has become one of the largest water bodies in Yoho National Park over the past couple of decades. Photo Darcy Monchak

native habitat, he's always been drawn to glaciers and recently glaciated places.

"It's the simplicity and raw elementary feeling of these areas that is so appealing – the lines, textures, patterns," he said. "As well, if you are in these areas it often means that you are high up in an isolated area – there is a feeling of excitement I still get every time when there."

Having spent more than three decades returning to some of his favourite places repeatedly, it's been impossible, he said, not to notice big changes.

"I have years of comparison witnessing the change to such areas as the Reef Icefield in Jasper, and the Des Poilus Glacier areas of Yoho," he said. "The meltwater pond below the Des Poilus Glacier has become one of the largest water bodies in Yoho Park over the last couple of decades."

"While photographing these places, I love to see the newly exposed bedrock areas and ice caves. But mainly I think about how the water supply will be dwindling for downstream users and wildlife, and how generations to come will not see these glaciers."

Mystery Ice

The Icefields Parkway opened spectacular views of several hundred glaciers and pocket and remnant glaciers to travellers admiring – and snapping photos of – the ancient ice from the comfort of their vehicles. A few valleys west, hundreds more glaciers exist, but they are mostly hidden from view to anyone restricted to travelling on the roads that wind along the valley bottoms. Following the closing of Glacier House in Rogers Pass in 1925 and the rerouting of the train tracks into tunnels safely out of the path of destructive, deadly avalanches, the peaks and ice of Glacier National Park were rarely photographed again until the Trans-Canada Highway was opened through there in 1962.

While the railway and the Icefields Parkway did make the glaciers accessible to photographers of the day, few of the mountaineers who explored deeper into the Monashee, Cariboo and Selkirk ranges devoted more than a minimum of time to photographing the glaciers they encountered. They were focused on being the first to stand on remote and difficult-to-reach summits. And with few roads penetrating the deep valleys that concealed them, the massive glaciers of British Columbia's

Mount Garibaldi, a stratovolcano located in the Sea to Sky Corridor that links Vancouver and Whistler, was a popular playground for Phyl and Don Munday. Photo Isabel Budke

Coast Mountains did not then, and still do not, easily give up their secrets – to casual or even serious photographers.

Nonetheless, intrepid Vancouver residents did snap more than a few images along the way to their mountaineering objectives. The 1912 *Canadian Alpine Journal* features a summary of an outing by B.S. Darling and cohorts who explored into the Mamquam Mountains at the head of Howe Sound. Following a previously blazed trail to the foot of Mount Garibaldi, they set out mainly to bag summits – which they did. But they also captured photos showing glacier-cloaked mountains. One, taken by Darling, shows five men in climbing attire walking across one of the Garibaldi glaciers. On another outing the party climbed Mount Tantalus, a peak that's visible not far north of the city. "The expedition is of importance, for it shows that within twenty-four hours of Vancouver, the devotee of the noble sport of mountaineering can reach an almost unknown region of towering peaks, wide snow-fields and magnificent glaciers, with rolling alplands and cliff-encircled meadows at their base." Those images retain their value as testimony to the size of Garibaldi, Alpha, Serratus and Tyee glaciers a century ago.

Munday Ice

While their primary motive in exploring some stupendously large and intricately featured glaciers in the Coast Mountains was their unquenchable desire to climb them, Don and Phyllis Munday made some terrific photographs of glaciers and icefields in a region that few, if any, humans had ever seen.

They met on a mountaineering adventure, and for three years lived in a tent, then eventually a small cabin, on Grouse Mountain, where Don worked cutting a trail to the summit and Phyllis served tea and snacks to hikers, all the while looking after their baby daughter, Edith. They often brought Edith along on their climbs, and once she could walk she had her own boots fitted with tricouni nails for glacier travel.

For 12 summers they embarked on multi-week trips (leaving Edith with family members or friends for five weeks at a time), intent on reaching their mystery mountain, which they'd spied in 1925 and which held promise of being the highest in the province. They'd leave Vancouver by steamer, or some years piloting their own sailboat, to reach Knight Inlet. Then they'd travel by small motorboat to the mouths of the Homathko or Franklin rivers. That's where the real work began, slashing trails through devil's club five metres tall to force paths up steep-walled river valleys, making multiple trips carrying heavy backpacks to reach the glaciers that cascaded down into the lush coastal rainforest.

The photos they captured during their arduous journeys were not only revealing but downright stunning. In the 1926/27 *Canadian Alpine Journal*, Don Munday exhibits a fine sense of balance, with bushes in the immediate foreground, a person's reflection standing in still pond water in the centre, and distant peaks and glaciers reflected in the water. It's flawless, the scene sublime.

Another image looking down on the long flowing arms of Scimitar Glacier taken by Phyllis captures an astounding scene of a massive tongue of glacial ice striped with debris piles created by landslides, and the formations of medial moraines. Her companion vertical compositions of Mount Combatant and Waddington's northwest face powerfully portray the vertical relief of 1500 and 1900 metres, respectively, with steeply tumbling icefalls funnelled by knife-edged rock walls, photos that capture well the power and brute force of the rugged, sometimes impenetrable Coast Mountain terrain.

By the 1930 *Canadian Alpine Journal* they had concluded skis "were logical equipment to overcome the obstacles imposed by the immense snowfields." And throughout their travels, they included observations and descriptions of significant glacial recession, as Don wrote in that volume.

"Remarkable changes had taken place on the glacier since 1927. The wide white corridor between the two medial moraines was now a gorge from 100 to 200 feet in depth. Areas of formerly clear ice were now littered with moraine. Some of the surface streams flowed in canyons 50 feet below the general level."

For all their arduous visits to the majestic glaciers of the area, they never did capture their prize. Reaching the northwest summit of the mountain that would be named Waddington in 1928, they decided the main summit was too risky. The imposing spear-headed peak was ultimately climbed by Fritz Wiessner and Bill House in 1936. The Mundays, however, continued to bring back beautiful images of the region, and successfully financed their trips through his exceptional writing and her exquisite photographs. And with the *Vancouver Province* newspaper sponsoring their expeditions in exchange for exclusive dispatches – a common means of supporting high-level adventures even today – their stories and images delighted and amazed readers as far away as London and New York City. And in their honour, Mount Munday is named for them, and Baby Munday Peak is named for Edith.

Aerial Ice

Throughout British Columbia's mountains, thousands of glaciers – although, like everywhere, shrinking – exist today. And many of them remain hidden from view except to those who expend the requisite energy to seek them out – climbers, ski mountaineers, heli-skiers and a few snowmobilers exploring as far as their gas tanks allow them. And pilots.

While travelling on foot opens a person to an intimate view of the mountain and glacial micro-world, the view from the air offers an altogether different perspective of icefields that fill immense basins cradled between the highest summits, and the glaciers that descend like octopus's arms from those icefields. John Scurlock knows this perspective well, perhaps better than anyone else in the US Northwest and Coast Mountains regions. A photographer, climber and pilot from Bainbridge Island in Washington State, Scurlock flies low, circuitous routes in his Van's RV-6 home-built airplane, photographing the expansive landscapes of his backyard Cascade Mountains, the Coast, Columbia and Canadian Rocky mountains north of the US–Canada border and other ranges from Alaska to California.

Having earned his pilot's licence by his mid-twenties, he developed a passion for remote terrain that led him to begin flying around volcanic Mount Baker, near his home in the Skagit Valley. He started out using a small film camera, then switched to digital in 2002.

His Baker photos caught the attention of Dr. Kevin Scott with the US Geological Survey's Cascades Volcano Observatory, who shared them with his colleagues. Scott became an advocate for Scurlock's work, which led to his collaborating with scientists from several state universities and the US National Park Service in the North Cascades, Mount Rainier, Glacier and Grand Teton parks.

Deep amidst the peaks and valleys of the Coast Mountains, Mount Waddington, the highest peak entirely within British Columbia, is wrapped with glaciers on every side. Photo John Scurlock

His images also caught the attention of climbers and skiers, and Scurlock began to realize that the North Cascades had rarely been seen in winter, so he gradually flew deeper and deeper into the range to photograph increasingly remote terrain. Cognizant that the quality of guidebook images before the digital era left a lot of potentially useful detail to be desired, he set out to improve on what was available.

"This all developed into an obsession to photograph the entire range during winter, which I did," he said. Over the years his range expanded to include mountains all over western North America, from Oregon to California to Idaho, Colorado, Montana, Alaska and British Columbia and Alberta.

In 2007, his reputation for capturing high-quality images of remote, seldom seen mountains led to his being engaged in a project to photograph all the glaciers in the North Cascades in co-operation with Dr. Andrew Fountain at Portland State University.

"This type of photography is fortunately grant-funded," Scurlock said, adding, "I could likely not afford to do it on my own."

Over the next 11 years the project expanded to include every glacier in the lower 48 states. Glacier photography, particularly for scientific purposes, he pointed out, is quite different from creative photography or the types of photos appreciated by climbers seeking new routes up unfamiliar faces and ridges.

"Glacier photography, specifically, is a different game," Scurlock explained. "The photography must be done in late season when there is no snow cover at all, so that scientists can see the actual ice margins. In several cases I've managed to photograph the glaciers on the day before a big fall storm came in and covered everything up."

Just an Interested Observer

A great many of his photos – his library now numbers some 200,000 digital images – show the glaciers of the Coast Mountains covered with a thick carpet of springtime snow, when the coverage is at its deepest and the surfaces at their smoothest. Springtime, he said, often provides him optimal flying conditions to explore and photograph the glaciers of the Coast, Columbia and Canadian Rocky mountains.

The scale and power of the immense landscape Scurlock's photos portray is staggering as they reveal dynamic forces at work. One image shows the gargantuan northern British Columbia Andrei Icefield spilling across the frame, Scud Glacier and its siblings carpeting the immense landscape wall to wall – including some of the walls. Other well-buried icefalls appear as ripples, as if a giant stubbed its toe and dragged the rug up into folds. Twin icefalls of Satsalla Glacier tumble down either side of a domed rock pyramid like the thick flowing wavy hair of a Norse goddess cascading over each shoulder. Images snapped on less sunny days impart a moodiness and sense of mystery, with low clouds clinging to jagged rock faces like gossamer cotton strips.

Sublime, imposing, haunting, daunting.

In some places, tiny remnant patches of ice appear sad and desolate, such as

Tucked in a remote, difficult-to-access region of the Canadian Rockies, Tusk Peak is one of hundreds of glaciated peaks John Scurlock has photographed. Photo John Scurlock

small pocket scraps of 12,000-year-old ice melting into the rock scape in Montana's Glacier National Park. While a few heavy snowfall winters have slowed the rate of melting in recent years, scientists estimate that with the current rate of increase in Earth's temperatures most of the 26 remaining glaciers of the 150 that existed within that park's boundaries – which border Canada's Waterton park – when it was established in 1910 will likely have melted and flowed downstream by the end of this century.

Having retired from his day job in 2015 after 35 years as a paramedic, Scurlock continues to fly, and to photograph western North America's remote mountains and their glaciers.

"I find glaciers highly compelling both scientifically and aesthetically, and luckily they are found typically in beautiful mountainous terrain," Scurlock said in an interview for this book. "Because of glacier photography I've been able to fly over and photograph many of the great ranges of the western mountains, an opportunity for which I'm profoundly grateful."

Flying up to 6400 metres elevation at 298 kilometres per hour, he slows down to 225 to aim his Canon 5D Mark IV 31 MP DSLR camera through a ¼-inch-thick Plexiglas canopy, a task that requires caution and careful judgment. Slowing down is critical; if he's too fast and too close the shots will be blurry, and he'll have wasted flight time. And, he added, each flight has two components – out and back.

"The primary challenges of doing this photography relate to weather – wind and clouds specifically," Scurlock said. "You have to be able to return home, so weather has to be accommodated both ways, and sometimes over periods of a number of days."

The opportunity, he added, leaves him with no doubt about the fact glaciers on both sides of the 49th parallel are decreasing in size.

"I always tell people, I'm not a scientist, just an interested observer," Scurlock stated. "In a few instances I've seen significant changes in glaciers I've photographed repeatedly. But the greater number of glaciers I've only visited once. I will say, though, in all my glacier photography I've not seen a single glacier that's advancing; the evidence for glacier retreat is plain and ubiquitous, even to a non-scientist."

5-2 BRUSHES TO ICE

Selling the Scenery

Before the camera, there was the paintbrush, the charcoal pencil, oils, watercolours, woodcuts. Today, add acrylics to the mix. As Europeans explored the land that would be Canada, "expedition artists" were sometimes included as members of the party to record a historic visual account of the journey. Those artists were usually amateurs and tended to be hardy folks who were up to the rigours of travelling for months by horse train and simple watercraft.

With the completion of the railway, well-trained professional artists travelled to the mountains eager to interpret the landscape in their own style. In contrast to the mountaineers who carried cameras along with them on their adventures, most of the artists viewed the landscape from the valleys near the railroad, and not too far from hotels and comfortable backcountry cabins. Helping to sell the scenery was their task, and glaciers were one element of the scenery to be admired, marvelled at. And painted.

The wild and rugged mountains, with glaciers swooping along their flanks and cleaving the valleys between pointed summits, presented dramatic and desirable subjects. They still do. Natural light in the mountains is constantly changing – somewhat on blue-sky sunny days, but even more so and with terrific drama on cloudy or stormy ones. While some of those who passed through the mountains painted some fine representations of the peaks and glaciers, it was those who were so captivated that they chose to live out years of their lives amidst their presence whose works best convey the sense of scale, the forces of nature and the wild and moving changes of the seasons. Among them was Ina D.D. Uhthoff, who opened a teaching school that served as the beginnings of the Victoria School of Art, on Vancouver Island. Her oil painting *Glacier and Moraine, 1934* shows a keen perception of the glacial environment, with tiered icefalls smoothly dropping down in the frame toward the viewer. The addition of a skeletal tree, solitary, bare and ravaged by the winds that so relentlessly sweep downward from icefields captures a true feeling of ice and wind and harshness.

Having lived for five years in South Africa and toiled as a newspaper reporter, diamond digger, lawyer's clerk and a roving trader, in 1940 Walter J. Phillips joined the faculty at what was then the Banff Summer School of Fine Arts. From 1936 onward he focused his work on the Canadian Rockies, with glaciers featured regularly in his painting. One such work, *Saskatchewan Glacier*, water colour 1950, starkly and cleanly conveys an imposing scale of ice spilling out from between rocky walls, the ice tongue broad and flat and wide. The details are sublime – shafts of golden rock, faint runnels striping the ice surface, shadows and stark sunlight highlighting the glacier with power in its simplicity.

Alfred C. Leighton, another British-born artist, also contributed to the Banff School of Fine Arts (now the Banff Centre for Arts and Creativity). Although he trained as an architect, he much preferred painting. After being injured while serving in the military, he ended up being hired by the Canadian Pacific Railway as chief commercial artist and came to Canada in 1924. He started a summer school and invited students to Kananaskis, on the Rockies' eastern slope, to study; the school became part of the Banff school's programs. His watercolour *Flow Lake, Marble Canyon, 1930* – the location of which is a 12-kilometre uphill hike from the trailhead – reveals intention and purpose with his choice of viewpoint from the far end of the lake. The towering cliff – each of its pillars wedged beside the next like the folds of an accordion – dominates the scene, with the glacier ice ringing the rock base like a necklace.

Leighton became known for his preferred habit of sitting at a location for an hour, even two, to study the scene before he began painting at the site. The act of painting would only take 20 minutes, and if the desired light changed during that time, he would leave his work unfinished. In this work, it's obvious all the elements aligned.

Unlike his contemporaries, Belmore Browne was a climber. Born in New York in 1880, he spent several years of his childhood in Europe. After a journey following the west coast north to Alaska, his family resettled in Washington State to run a lumber company. He studied at the New York School of Art and at Académie Julian in Paris. But his love of outdoor exploration and adventure led to him sign on as artist, hunter and specimen hunter on an expedition to the "North," sponsored by the American Museum of Natural History in 1902. In 1921 he settled in Banff, where he stayed until 1940. He left during the Second World War to serve as an advisor for cold weather survival but returned afterward to live in Kananaskis for a few years. Browne's undated oil *After September Snow* captures the stillness of new snow and the turbulence of unsettled clouds. Glacier ice arms frame the prow of Mount

Bow Glacier, oil on board, Belmore Browne, 1928. Whyte Museum of the Canadian Rockies, BwB.02.04. (Gift of Mary Hallock, Fort St. James, 1981)

Lefroy, and cap Mount Victoria with equal strength and softness, conveying presence, power, majesty.

Group of Seven

Of course, it was only natural that Canada's famed Group of Seven would find their way to the snow and ice of the country's west.

Founded in 1920, the original group consisted of Franklin Carmichael, A.Y. Jackson, Frank H. Johnston, Arthur Lismer, J.E.H. MacDonald, Frederick H. Varley, and arguably the best known of the group, Lawren S. Harris. They would be later joined by A.J. Casson, Edwin Holgate and Lionel LeMoine FitzGerald. Nearly all of them would visit or live in western Canada at some point. And each in his own style painted on themes that would ultimately help define the young country's evolving sense of identity. Through their work, they created a fresh, new Canadian sensibility and style. And that style included mountains, and the glaciers draping their flanks. Icy, cold, austere, yet beguiling.

While, on a 1914 visit, Jackson complained that the weather was unpredictable and the mountains tended to dominate his images, he returned a decade later with Harris to travel the countryside by canoe, by packhorse and by hiking, camping throughout the Maligne Lake area and the Tonquin and Athabasca valleys. Attracted by the higher elevations, Jackson wrote, "It was a weird and ancient country of crumbling mountains and big glaciers," where they found places "where we could look both up and down most satisfying for painting."

Where Jackson saw the mountains as rugged, imposing and not quite welcoming, J.E.H. MacDonald's *Mountain Solitude (Lake Oesa)*, painted at that gem-like glacier lake a short, steep hike above Lake O'Hara in 1932, is nothing short of sublime. Anyone who has ever sat quietly with their head tucked warmly inside the hood of a reliable foul-weather jacket during an autumn snowfall can feel that moment in his canvas. By the looks of this painting, when MacDonald died of stroke just weeks later, he left this world having experienced the magic, the wonder and the comfort of the high glaciated Rockies peaks.

While many artists who painted western Canada's mountain landscapes in the first half of the 20th century did a fine job of expressing the moods and whims of the glacier environment, it was Lawren Harris who saw things at a higher level. Born in 1885 in Brantford, Ontario, Harris studied in Berlin, Germany, and hiked in the Tyrol mountains between 1904 and 1907. His love of hiking high in the alpine stayed with him right into his senior years. He first visited the Canadian Rockies in 1924 and returned every summer through 1929. Then he was back from 1940 through 1957.

Harris was fortunate to enjoy the support of family money from their farm equipment business, which left him free to travel. And free to create art. To his credit, he shared some of his wealth with his Group of Seven comrades whose circumstances were much leaner.

Nearly a century later, Harris's uniquely personalized style is recognized the world over, and not only within the art community. While to a non-mountain person his exquisite angles and clean sweeping lines portray an elegance of abstract work that has endured, to anyone who knows the peaks of the Canadian Rockies, his individual subjects are easily recognized as their real selves.

Harris didn't just visit the mountains, he breathed them. They inhabited his senses. They spoke to him and he embraced their language. Some might see his works as imaginary, fantastic representations of the mountain landscapes, but to my eye, they are as real as mountains get. By choosing to portray them in an abstract style, Harris has pared down the peaks to nothing more than their pure, raw essence. He does this exceptionally well with the glaciers. *Isolation Peak*, circa 1931, oil on canvas, portrays the peak – likely Mont Des Poilus as seen from Whaleback Ridge, a stiff, rocky, rugged and steep hike from the Little Yoho Valley – as a stark triangle, a near-perfect representation of the real thing. Better, the swooping lines of glacier ice crawling down the valley floor express the movement and flow of the ice. His masterpiece, *Mount Lefroy, 1930*, oil on canvas, expresses its steep north face piercing the sky and draped with snow like reams of raw silk falling into the Death Trap below its cliff shelf. Moody, dark, brooding and haunting, *Mount Temple, 1925*, is instantly recognizable to those of us who know the mountain well. By then he had stopped signing his paintings so they would be judged on their artistic merit alone, and not by his reputation or the popularity of the location.

Alleuvial Fan, Bow Lake, oil on canvas, Peter Whyte, 1945–1960. Whyte Museum of the Canadian Rockies, WyP.01.245. (Gift of Catharine Robb Whyte, O. C., Banff, 1979)

In 1969, Harris was made a Companion of the Order of Canada for his contributions, including his key role in forming the Group of Seven and for his advocacy of art in Canadian culture. He died in 1970, but his paintings live on, commanding high prices at the most high-brow of auction houses; in 2016, his *Mountain Forms* sold for $11.2 million.

Wa-Che-Yo-Cha-Pa

They were the romance of the Rockies. They were also very fine artists and devoted mountain lovers. Naturally, more than a few glaciers found their way into their paintings, but Peter and Catharine Whyte didn't just paint the glaciers, they experienced them first-hand.

Born in Banff in 1905 to entrepreneur Dave White and his wife, Annie, Pete grew up skiing and exploring the woods and riverbanks. Not particularly gifted in the traditional subjects, he drew and sketched and enrolled in a cartooning class, and learned some basic art instruction from a postcard illustrator at Banff High School. With many fine artists spending time in Banff during the 1920s, young Pete was fortunate to learn from several of them, including through private lessons with Belmore Browne, and later with J.E.H. MacDonald and Carl Rungius. Art, however, was a career direction that did not please his father, so without family support Pete worked to support his passion, toiling as crew on a boat sailing from New York to California by way of Cuba and the Panama Canal, and guarding Chinese workers while travelling by train from Montreal to Vancouver. With this he financed his studies at the School of the Museum of Fine Arts in Boston.

The choice was destiny. It was there he met Catharine Robb, heir to a wealthy Massachusetts family. Over the next few years the two became close friends despite their different backgrounds. Prior to meeting Pete (who changed the spelling of his surname from White to Whyte during his years in Boston), she'd spent several years dating John D. Rockefeller III. Ah, but in addition to sharing her passion for art, Pete Whyte was an exceptionally good skier. They fell in love, and she moved to Banff to live the mountain life with him. She learned how to ski – sometimes while carrying a heavy pack to backcountry Skoki Lodge – how to stay warm around a campfire when they didn't reach their destination, and how to hike and scramble high above treeline amidst the glaciers.

And together, they painted.

Pete, whose brother Cliff was a key creator of the first ski hut on Mount Norquay and Skoki Lodge, painted terrific, lively scenes of skiers racing down slopes with powder billowing behind them. In *Skiing the High Country,* oil on canvas circa 1940, he perfectly melded adventure and art in the zipper track that's imprinted in the snow by skiers planting their poles to propel them, left, right, left, right. His *Skiers, Deception Pass,* shows skiers at the top of a pass, skis standing on end in the snowpack beside them during those moments while transitioning from skinning uphill to skiing down, moments familiar and cherished by those who ski up and over passes to make turns down the opposite side.

Crowfoot Glacier, oil on canvas, Catharine Robb Whyte, O.C., 1945–1955. Whyte Museum of the Canadian Rockies, WyC.01.202. (Gift of Catharine Robb Whyte, O. C., Banff, 1979)

Both painted fine, engaging portraits of some of the region's colourful characters, such as outfitter Tom Wilson (Peter) and Old Dan Wildman (Catharine), and both were moved and inspired by the local Stoney (Îyârhe Nakoda) First Nations peoples, with whom they nurtured strong friendships. Catharine's finest talents, though, were displayed in her landscapes. Small glaciers are tucked into protected north-facing cirques. Glacial arms cascade down from Snow Dome to spill onto the moraine below. Her *Yoho Peak*, oil on canvas circa 1935, features a peak not seen from any road; rather, it's a long hike deep into the wilderness to visit. Her scene *Bow Lake, Crowfoot Glacier* perfectly blends all the elements of a windy day at that place – a common occurrence – with the glacier filling the upper valley, ice merging with swirling clouds high above the turquoise lake, its waters glinting in the intermittent sunshine.

More than artists, though, Peter and Catharine Whyte were keen curators of the Rockies' unique culture. With her great wealth, after Pete died in 1966 Catharine enjoyed the last phase of her life as a busy surrogate parent and mentor to a group of young friends, including her nephew, poet, author and wordsmith extraordinaire Jon Whyte, and as benefactor of numerous philanthropic projects. Among those was the money for the construction of the original Bow and Peyto huts, which provide comfort on the Wapta Icefield.

In 1968 doors opened to a building designed by architect Philippe Delesalle, housing the Banff Public Library, the Archives of the Canadian Rockies and the Peter Whyte Gallery. Though it was Catharine who broke ground on construction, the facility was a project the two of them had dreamed of and worked toward for years, having long collected photographs, artefacts, manuscripts and other valuable materials. They established the Wa-Che-Yo-Cha-Pa Foundation, under which the museum, archives and library would operate, its name paraphrased from the words of their friend, George McLean, Walking Buffalo, meaning "where the good, the wise and the beautiful come together in harmony."

The Whyte Museum of the Canadian Rockies thrives as an exceptional facility dedicated to preserving and promoting the culture and history of the Canadian Rockies.

Its archives ooze in richness, with 1,300 motion pictures, 1,100 sound recordings, 5,500 books and about a half-million photographs. There are First Nations gloves and moccasins, skis, ice axes, a mountain rescue cable and dishes and silverware. And there are paintings by many prominent and talented artists, including Peter and Catharine, that celebrate the Rockies' rivers and lakes and wildflower meadows, the peaks and rock cliffs. And the glaciers.

Glen Boles, Alpine Artist

In the course of pursuing his passion for wild, remote places in western Canada's mountains, Glen Boles climbed more than 500 mountains, pioneered new routes and made 37 first ascents. He even helped name a few peaks.

Many knew him as a member of the fabled Grizzly Group, climbing companions who shared a rich and special camaraderie. Boles moved to Alberta from New Brunswick as a young man, and enjoyed a 36-year career with the City of Calgary's Waterworks Department, most of them as a draughtsman. Likeable, kind and good-natured, he volunteered for several outdoor groups and the local community foundation in Cochrane, west of Calgary, where he makes his home with his wife, Liz. He's an honorary member of the American Alpine Club and the Alpine Club of Canada, and in 2005 he received the Summit of Excellence Award for his contributions to the Canadian climbing community.

It's through his splendid photography, exquisitely detailed pen and ink drawings and acrylic paintings, though, that Boles became most widely known and appreciated. From the wondrously intricate curls of a bighorn sheep's horns to sculpted snow ridges, painstakingly stacked cliff bands and the spectacularly jumbled icefall tumbling into Mount Robson's Berg Lake, to climbers and non-climbers alike Boles' artwork expresses the exquisite beauty and magic of the mountain world.

Always carrying his camera along with his backpack, rope and ice axe – he forgot his camera just twice – he amassed an astounding collection including 42,000 slides and more than 20,000 black and white photographs. His images have appeared in numerous magazines, guidebooks and climbing books. He set up a darkroom at home to develop and print his own photos. "I really liked seeing some of these mountain pictures form in the developing solution," he said during an interview for *Alpine Artistry: The Mountain Life of Glen Boles*.

With Grizzly Group cohorts – they earned the moniker after a memorable encounter with an especially large grizzly bear – Boles explored the high mountains, from his first climb in 1957 through his last in 2004. Accessing by helicopter places few, if anyone, did, they would stay for a week or more before the machine came back to retrieve them.

Robson Glacier, acrylic painting, Glen Boles.

They camped amidst glacier-fed tarns at treeline, rose early to make ascents of unclimbed, sometimes unnamed peaks. Along the way they walked across glaciers, leapt across crevasses and explored maze-like routes through labyrinth icefalls.

The most amazing sight Boles recalled witnessing was a migration of thousands of moths at the head of the Stutfield Glacier. They once found a MacGillivray's warbler on the edge of a crevasse on the Columbia Icefield, that Simpson warmed in his hand.

Thankfully, in 2006 he published a beautiful hardcover coffee-table volume, *My Mountain Album: Art & Photography of the Canadian Rockies & Columbia Mountains*, loaded with 140 of his finest black and white images, which capture so deliciously the moods of the high peaks and sprawling icefields, and fine pen and ink drawings.

The book is more than just a visual album, however; nearly every image is accompanied by a light-hearted anecdote capturing the sense of camaraderie between Boles and his climbing partners, and reverence for his mountain surroundings. Glaciers were front of mind, and lens, often.

One closely cropped image, *The Edge of the West Sir Alexander Glacier*, focuses on a broad, shell-like scoop of glacial ice, striations resembling a tree trunk split open. Boles and his friends spent five days in the area making first ascents of obscure, remote peaks. "The northeastern fringe of the West Sir Alexander Glacier shows each year's layer of snow. It is interesting to see the fluctuations."

Describing how water from the David Glacier drains into the Rausch River and eventually empties in the Pacific Ocean, with *Drainage Patterns on the David Glacier*, where thousands of ripples imprinted by running water fan out like a giant peacock's tail, he wrote, "Glacial patterns have always intrigued me, for they always follow the fall line."

Page after page, the images mesmerize, the massive expanse of creased and fractured ice in the Hooker Icefield area showing a jaw-dropping sense of scale. Like fins of ice stacked one beside the next, thicker at their bases and tapering to knife-edge at their

Death Trap, pen and ink drawing, Glen Boles.

crest, ice ridges at the toe of the East Lyell Glacier reach toward the viewer like a serpent's claws.

With a tiny person walking under mounds of ice and rock towering above him, Boles describes *Snout of the Commander Glacier*: "The person in the picture gives one an idea of the size of the ice hummocks. This photo was taken in 1971, and when I returned to the area in 1988 I couldn't believe how much the glacier had retreated."

His drawings expose a stupendous level of detail, evident as a deeply experienced labour of love. With tiered shelves of rock and ice, cascading glacier tongues creeping down vertical canyon walls, bergschrunds opening to release the ice from the mountain face, seracs perched to tumble off the cliff edges, *Abbot Pass*, he admitted, posed his greatest artistic challenge.

"This drawing was copied from a photo taken from Popes Peak looking across the North Victoria Glacier to Mt. Lefroy, Abbot Pass and Mt. Victoria. The intricate nature of the crevasses and rock in the lower part of the picture posed the biggest challenge I have ever had in a drawing."

As always, Boles rose to the challenge.

Glacier: A Journey

"Now you see why I love coming to places like this," said Jan Kabatoff as we each fired off another dozen shots with our cameras.

Six hours after we had hiked onto the Athabasca Glacier, the early evening light was soft and muted, casting a gentle glow on a serpentine stream of water coursing along the twisting groove it had worn into the ice surface as it raced toward the glacier's toe. Pale blue, the stream was framed by a border of white slushy-textured ice, which in turn was surrounded by a field of ice speckled with coffee-coloured rock dust.

I had to agree. I had long delighted in exploring glaciers up close, whether as the approach to climbing to a summit or skiing untracked powder blanketing the ice. But on that day, I was experiencing a new way to explore a glacier: walking slowly for a long afternoon for the sole purpose of strolling on the ancient ice, for the purpose of seeing and taking photos.

Unlike many of my friends and peers, Kabatoff discovered glaciers not from a mountaineer's perspective but rather from that of a trained artist who learned to walk in crampons specifically so she could peer down into swirling millwells. She learned to dress in layers and be prepared for the sudden, inevitable snow squalls that envelop glaciers even in the middle of summer so she could study crystal-clear cylindrical cryoconite holes cradling clusters of black dots, the result of rocks on the ice conducting more of the sun's heat and melting down at a faster rate than the rest of the ice.

"It's the compositions that I see in nature that are so stunningly beautiful that it's hard to replicate as an artist, as a painter. The best I can do is to take the best photographs I can to capture it," she said with a shrug.

Kabatoff's photographs, though, were just the beginning. Back in her studio as artist in residence at the Banff Centre, she created three-dimensional installations and encaustic – melted wax mixed with pigments – paintings inspired by the natural beauty she witnessed in the myriad ice formations: sunlight glinting through a slit as long and lean as a sword blade melted through a standing sheet of ice; a perfect bird's beak sculpted from ice by wind and sunlight; charcoal etchings sprayed by windblown rock dust.

A West Kootenay native who moved to Alberta in 1972, Kabatoff did not have her first experience on a glacier for another 30 years, while on a creative outing with Banff-based photographer Roy Andersen. While he was trying to impart the fundamentals of composition and landscape photography, she was focused on the minutiae of the glacier.

Artist Jan Kabatoff photographs crevasses on the Athabasca Glacier to use in her studio to create artworks for an exhibit on glaciers. Photo Lynn Martel

"That is when I absolutely fell in love with the glacier," Kabatoff gushed. "I was leaning into millwells, falling in love. It's a wonder I didn't fall in head-first! I was awestruck."

A graduate of the Alberta College of Art and Design, she raised her children on an acreage in Bragg Creek in the foothills west of the city where she ran the Two Pine Gallery for three years in the 1980s. Then when she moved to Canmore in 2000, Kabatoff was awakened to a new way of seeing wilderness.

"I was not looking at the view of the mountains, now I was *living* in the view of the mountains," she explained. "I became acutely aware of what was happening in the mountains, and especially how they were being affected by climate change. I was dumbfounded by the idea that humans could have an impact on the glaciers."

When Kabatoff sold her Canmore condo to ACMG mountain guide Helen Sovdat, Sovdat noticed one of her botanical prints hanging on a wall and suggested she might throw one in to sweeten the deal. In turn, Kabatoff suggested trading her print for Sovdat's guiding services. Before setting out with Sovdat, however, Kabatoff experienced her first technical mountain adventure with ACMG alpine guide Sharon Wood (another collector of her botanical prints), who led her on a rope across challenging terrain in British Columbia's Bugaboos.

"It was my first time walking across a talus field, being roped up, walking in crampons," Kabatoff recalled. "What was I doing being cramponed up a glacier? I was a fair-weather day hiker! It was exhilarating and frightening at the same time. Then when we hit the ridge and I looked across to the [Bugaboo] glacier, I was moved to tears. It looked like the womb of Mother Earth. And I thought about how we are not respecting the glaciers or the water the glaciers are storing for us."

That experience evolved into her feeling a calling to create art that would encourage people to think about glaciers. She joined Sovdat on a trip to Mongolia, and while Sovdat led three other clients up a mountain, Kabatoff stayed at a lower camp with other hikers, creating art. While there, she met a glaciologist who told her the glacier he was studying was shrinking – six metres annually. Spurred on, she travelled to Yukon for a two-month artist residency, and again, with Sovdat, to Patagonia to collect more images and inspiration toward her multi-media show, *Glacier: A Journey*, which ran at Banff's Whyte Museum for two months in autumn 2009. Among the earliest Canadian artists to address the effects of climate change on glaciers, she filled the Whyte Museum's main gallery with heavily textured encaustic paintings (which use beeswax pigmented with coloured dyes), deliberately composed photographs, hand-dyed silk rubbings and mould reliefs. Her installations were beautiful, delicate and mysterious – a lot like glaciers.

One of them, *Glacier Chorus*, incorporated audio recordings of glacier sounds – water dripping inside crevasses, splashing over rocks and ice, rushing in rivulets and burbling into streams. Her nearly three-square-metre panels titled *Bergy Bits* were created by building up layer upon layer of beeswax mixed with white pigment, aptly

Jan Kabatoff focuses her camera on the fine details of ice sculpted by wind and sun in the lower icefall of the Athabasca Glacier to use as models for her encaustic paintings. Photo Lynn Martel

mirroring the layered composition of glacial ice created as season upon season of snowfall compresses into many-hued striations of blues, greys, white.

Commanding attention, *Mass Balance* featured 4,000 samples of glacier melt from the Canadian Arctic. The vials were glued together with meticulous care to create 200 rods of varying sizes, which were attached in concentric rows and suspended from the ceiling like chandeliers. The scientifically labelled vials contained actual samples from the Prince of Wales Ice Sheet on Ellesmere Island in Nunavut, donated by the University of Calgary.

Two years after her Whyte Museum exhibit, though, Kabatoff admitted she didn't feel her work was nearly done, or that the message that glaciers worldwide were under threat from warming global temperatures and in need of protection was being heard nearly well enough. And that was why she was walking in crampons, tolerating knee-wobbling winds and finger-numbing cold in the middle of August with Sovdat guiding her, taking more photos to inspire pieces for her show, which continued to travel.

"The only way you can truly appreciate what nature has to offer is to spend a day being intimate with it. To really know a place, you have to immerse yourself. Let it hurt you, inspire you, motivate you," Kabatoff said.

"Glaciers are special entities. They're extremely important to water reserves on the planet and science is telling us they are shrinking very rapidly due to climate change. As an artist, I hope people will fall in love with the beauty as I have and it will inspire them to be more protective and want to work harder to find alternative energy sources. I feel it's my duty as a global citizen to do my part in some way."

Ice in Plein Air

For decades before Kabatoff's ground-breaking glacier exhibit, Canadian artists embarked on their own journeys, interpreting glaciers and their place in the landscape and as part of the ecosystem in their works.

In 1997 and '98, the Columbia Icefield Centre invited local artists to participate in week-long residencies. The artists were based out of the "Ice Palace," as the on-site

Canmore, Alberta artist Donna Jo Massie appreciated the opportunity to participate in artist residencies at the Athabasca and Bow Glaciers. Painting the mountains, she said, is personal. "Every time you go, you grow a friendship with the mountains, and it gets deeper and deeper." Watercolour, Donna Jo Massie

not-so-glamorous staff accommodation buildings are called, where they were gifted the use of a couple of extra staff rooms that weren't occupied. Canmore artist Donna Jo Massie recalled packing along her easel, stool, brushes and watercolours and bunking in one room with her good friend, glass artist Susan Gottselig, while a second room served as their studio – the bathroom linked the two rooms. Being close to the Athabasca Glacier early in the morning and into the evening after all the tourists had moved on to their hotels and campsites for the night created a special atmosphere, she said.

"It was a wonderful opportunity to stay in that place for a week and get to see the sunrise and the sunset day after day," Massie said. "There's a really different feel to the place when you get to see it in its primal state, without all the people and activity."

For Massie, the glaciers provided exquisite contrast as she painted the lines of the ridges and gullies and subtle light of the shadows cast on the rocky ice-clad peaks. "Every time you go, you grow a friendship with the mountains, and it gets deeper and deeper." She also enjoyed a similar artist resident opportunity in the same era at Num-Ti-Jah Lodge, even painting in Jimmy Simpson's original cabin. Such generosity on behalf of the handful of businesses along the Icefields Parkway has grown increasingly scarce, as marketing efforts have succeeded and every available accommodation for miles is filled to the brim through the summer months. Still painting on location into her seventies – with a pocket-size easel and paint set – Massie now wonders if she'll be able to secure a seat on the busy shuttle bus to Lake Louise for the autumn colours.

As a glass artist, Gottselig was especially attracted to the Athabasca glacier and its naturally sculpted forms.

"Ice is visually much like glass in colour and how it is affected by light," she said. "I discovered that the higher I went on the glacier, the more sculptural and 3D it became. The large abstract shapes that resulted from the effects of weather and melting were most inspirational for my sculptural work with hot glass."

Gottselig was also fascinated with the inclusions found in the glaciers, some of them hundreds of years old. Those details, she decided, were what she wanted to capture in her glass work – the colour of glacier ice in a smooth upright shape. To do so, she first cast bluish glass in her kiln, then broke it up in pieces to use as inclusions in hot molten glass to create her sculpture.

"It was interesting to consider the temperature extremes between molten glass and frozen, hard, glacier ice," she said.

Living on the West Coast, contemporary artist Brent Lynch includes glaciated places among his subjects, painting with broad, swift strokes that convey the energy embodied in wild alpine environments. He often paints outdoors, and his connection to the landscape is evident in his *Edith Cavell, Jasper National Park*, oil on prepared board, expressing the power of a large place with a small man leaning against a massive boulder and facing the Cavell pond, a shelf of multi-layered glacier ice sitting in its turquoise melt pool.

Inspired by the Group of Seven, Vancouver artist Charlie Easton frequently paints high alpine landscapes, including glaciers. With sweeping brush strokes his uncluttered style captures the essence of Lake Louise, with her backdrop Victoria Glacier, and Garibaldi in his home neighbourhood Coast Mountains. In a striking abstract style reminiscent of Lawren Harris, Kenneth T. Harrison's paintings capture a stillness and serenity, often with snow-draped peaks reflected in the impossibly clear alpine lakes at their bases. His *Stunning Mount Assiniboine*, oil on canvas, is just that: jaw-dropping.

Another Vancouver-based artist, Argentinean-born Lucas Kratochwil, reveals an obvious affection for glacier ice and the ever-changing shapes and shadows of the high alpine landscape. Black Tusk, Garibaldi and the lesser-known but exceptionally dramatic Serratus – glacial features of the Coast Mountains figure prominently and powerfully in his project to create a collection of large-scale oil paintings of the Pacific Northwest's prominent geographical landmarks. Through his paintings, Kratochwil hopes to raise public awareness of the vital need for people to interact with nature and connect with the importance of preserving these "natural treasures."

With glaciers making headlines around the world in these times, an exhibit at Banff's Canada House Gallery in the winter of 2019 showcased the work of painters Cameron Bird, Rod Charlesworth and Mike Svob, who spent several days the previous summer in the Cariboo Mountains with glass artist Ryan Bavin. The project was the result of a partnership between the gallery and CMH Heli-Skiing & Summer Adventures, the Banff Art & Culture Committee, the Banff Centre for Arts and Creativity and Banff Lake Louise Tourism Bureau.

"Painting en plein air lends an authenticity to landscape work," the gallery explained as part of its promotion of the resulting artworks. "As an artist breathes in the air, feels the atmosphere, watches the light and shadows move across the scene they understand that place in a truly authentic way that informs their work."

Their excellent impressionist paintings are vividly coloured, no doubt a reflection of the natural palette of the wildflowers that grow in the high alpine meadows amidst a backdrop of glacial ice shimmering in midsummer sunlight. Splashes of vibrant oranges, golds, emerald greens and deep turquoise frame rocky peaks as glittering ice chunks float in jewel-toned pro-glacial lakes, expressing well the energy of the natural alpine environment. The work is luscious and highly desirable.

The project, while successful in its endeavour to produce beautiful mountain-inspired paintings in the tradition of the early 20th century railway-invited artists, also punctuates the reality that Canada's first, and its most visited, national park continues to promote the selling of the scenery ahead of embracing any learning opportunities about the natural environment its mandate demands it preserve and protect. While the paintings were commissioned by several organizations based within, and at least partially supported by Canada's premier national park, there was no mention at all connected to the artwork of how Canada's glaciers are melting, and how that melting is being accelerated by Earth's warming climate, which is at least partially driven by human actions, particularly the burning of fossil fuels. The business of selling Canada's glaciers, without any reference to their state of diminishment, remains a profitable one.

Glaciogenic Art

Art is at its best when it makes the viewer think. Many a creative, from Banksy to Barry Lopez to Bruce Cockburn, has stimulated discussion and raised awareness on important social issues through their art.

As an artist and a scientist from the northeastern United States, Jill Pelto (sister of Ben Pelto, page 223) endeavours to do the same. She holds bachelor degrees in studio art and Earth and climate science, and a master's of science that focused on the sensitivity of the Antarctic ice sheet to changes in Earth's climate system. Through her "Glaciogenic Art" Pelto successfully challenges the notion that scientific charts and graphs are dull and of interest only to other scientists.

With bold, sharp angles, the outlines of her peaks and valleys are formed with the contours of scientific graph lines. Each piece tells a thoughtful story of nature, of climate change and of human relationships with Earth. Her colour palette embraces

Scientist and artist Jill Pelto intertwines graph lines with watercolours to create art that shares a true message and inspires viewers to think. Watercolour Jill Pelto

realistic earth tones and to-scale representations of the glaciated landscape, intermingled with scientific research. The result is captivating, and certainly provocative.

And it works.

Her piece *Landscape of Change* incorporates graph lines to depict sea-level rise, another line revealing glacier volume decline, and others increasing global temperatures and the increasing use of fossil fuels. The landscape is balanced with a big, bright sun shining down on watercolour hues of blues and greys melting, rising and being licked by red and orange flames.

"These data lines compose a landscape shaped by the changing climate, a world in which we are now living," Pelto said.

Moments of Observation is at once provocative and meditative, with the glacier image in one panel reflected in the sunglasses of four observers in the other panel.

"I believe that spending extensive time in nature encourages the development of observation," Pelto explained. "Within the sunglasses you can see the image of the glacier landscape, reflecting the graphical lines that denote where the glacier used to extend only several decades ago. The figures are taking the time to look and to reflect. Each of them may be noticing a different change in the glacier, but they are all taking in its retreat. It is important to pay attention to what is happening on our world; be aware, open to learning and understanding."

Constructing new ways to communicate science through art is her passion. Actual scientific research and data fuel her designs, and while a whimsical quality draws the viewer closer, her message of the environmental degradation, human impacts on nature, and threatened species is balanced with the beauty, the fragility and enchanting qualities of the natural world.

"Art is a uniquely articulate and emotional lens," Pelto said. "Through it I can address environmental concerns to raise awareness and inspire people to take action. My love of nature drives me to creatively communicate information about environmental issues with a broad audience."

Painting Glaciers for Conservation

Growing up on a ten-acre property on the glacier-fed Kicking Horse riverbank ignited a strong connection to nature for Regan Johnston, who spent his days exploring the forest looking for bugs and anything else that moved.

When their home burned down his family moved into Golden, a 20-minute drive away, and other than a few years in Europe – where he pursued a modelling career in his late twenties – Johnston has called that Columbia Valley town his home. Living with his wife, Christa, and their dog, Slayer, he works from home as a full-time artist.

As an avid backcountry explorer, Johnston has little interest in visiting, or painting, places easily viewed from the road. The journey is an essential part of the appeal. He maps out routes to remote areas, drives up logging roads and then bushwhacks uphill through mossy old-growth valley bottom forests to where the canopy opens into the sparser trees of the subalpine.

"There's nothing easy about hiking a week's worth of food and gear up a mountainside with no information on where I'm going," he said. "But living in an altered landscape really makes me appreciate seeing nature undisturbed. When I'm in the wilderness I feel like I've gone home, and I'm connected to the earth. "

And seeing glaciers is always a highlight.

"The most exciting goal for me is to see glaciers. The highest and most rugged areas of these ranges [surrounding Golden] still have massive glaciers from the last ice age. Even though they're receding each year, many of them are immense. A glaciated landscape reminds me of how ancient our world is and how the ecosystems of my home have evolved with glaciers. They also remind me how important they are for all the ecosystems they interact with, from the mountain peak to where the river flows into the ocean."

By hiking far into the backcountry on multi-day trips, Regan Johnston imparts a deep sense of wilderness and wonder on his canvasses. *The Monarch, Robson Glacier*, acrylic on canvas, Regan Johnston

It's with this awareness in mind that Johnston paints glaciers, often working on a painting for weeks in an effort to convey the feeling of what he's witnessed.

"Glaciers are beautiful and terrifying," he said. "They're covered in crevasses that add texture and show the most beautiful blue colours, but to fall in one could be death. They really are natural ice sculptures that are always changing. I love how the light affects them. Sometimes I'll choose to just paint

For Golden, British Columbia, artist Regan Johnston, glaciers are beautiful and terrifying. Painting ReganJohnston

part of the glacier to really show how interesting and unique these ice sculptures can be."

Spending so much time in wilderness means he spends a lot of time thinking about nature, and conservation. He aims to travel in the backcountry as ethically as possible, observing the landscape while trying not to disturb it, something he's always trying to improve on.

"The only way to have zero impact is by not going," he said. "Maybe some areas are best left alone? The idea of areas that nobody goes to is actually pretty cool. Then there's always a place to imagine."

But another reason he paints glaciers is to help bring attention to the fact they are melting, and fast.

"This ice is melting at an alarming rate," Johnston said. "The climate crisis affects every living thing on Earth, and even though it's not pleasant to talk about, it is very much our reality. The paintings I make will always keep the memory alive for how the glacier looked when I saw it."

In spring of 2019, after donating a painting of a wolverine with all the proceeds going to wolverine research, he was invited to fly in a helicopter for a day visiting a dozen remote research locations. And that got him thinking too.

"It was cool going to some areas I had been, but also seeing new zones was great. But it did make me think about if I would ever go heli-hiking knowing what kind of impact it has. Glacier recession is a side effect of the fact that our planet is heating up. This is the biggest threat that humankind has ever faced and it's important that we become more mindful about how our everyday choices affect this planet. It's also so important that we elect governments that are going to act on preventing further climate change. We need to transition away from burning fossil fuels and using our natural resources to clean renewable energy and renewable resources. Nature is everything and we need to protect it."

"It's important to me that I do my part and do what I can by either donating artwork to causes I believe in or spreading awareness through my paintings and media. And that's what I'll continue to do."

5–3 CELLULOID ICE

Hollywood on Ice

With the shakiness of the dusty black and white footage that is the telltale clue to the era, a party sets off on horseback following a trail around a picturesque lake, riding toward a spectacular glacier clinging like outstretched arms across a steep cliff face.

Likely shot in the 1920s, the film features a setting easily recognizable as Lake Louise and its stunning backdrop, Victoria Glacier. Interspersed with scenes of villages in Switzerland's Alps – to which the Canadian Rockies are cheekily compared as reminiscent of "old Europe" – a trio of climbers slowly and carefully ascends wild ridges and swales of sculpted glacier ice.

Bookended by one Swiss guide leading the rope and another taking the tail, pipes puffing in their mouths and long, wooden-shafted alpenstocks in their hands, they lead their client, Mrs. Outing. Sporting the latest in bloomers and leather boots, our heroine follows as they wind a route through a maze of caves and grottoes and ice canyons and sculpted glacier walls, the camera occasionally panning downward to peer into the deep, dark chasms. Slowing for a moment, the guides chop steps in a steep section of striated ice, layer upon layer of previous seasons' snowfall compressed and piled one atop the other like a gargantuan layer cake. When Mrs. Outing loses her footing, her guides haul her up the steep slope with all the grace and delicacy of reeling in a large freshly caught fish.

"She lost her head and her feet with fascinating frequency, but her smile stayed put," says the narration screen in this, one of the earliest motion pictures shot on a Canadian glacier.

To adventurous filmmakers, the glaciers of the Canadian Rockies radiated star quality. And from the early days of celluloid, having railroad tracks leading to within a couple of hours' horse and foot travel made them easy to work with, too.

Since the first film to feature a Canadian glacier as its backdrop was shot (likely on the Victoria Glacier, but the film has not survived) in 1910, more than 100 feature films have chosen the Rockies as a location. Until the 1970s, with 90 per cent of Hollywood films made in Canada being shot there, the region became known as Hollywood North.

Made in 1929, *Eternal Love* starred John Barrymore and Camilla Horn. A scene near the end of the film – and right before the big climactic avalanche finale – features the pair on Victoria Glacier. *Silent Barriers* (1937) was the first "talkie" that was filmed partially in Banff National Park. Released to theatres worldwide, the film featured an exciting scene of an avalanche crashing down from the front edge of a glacier, again most likely shot at Victoria Glacier with Swiss guides using dynamite to trigger the avalanche. In *Son of Lassie*, which hit theatres in 1945, one exciting scene captured skiers schussing down Victoria Glacier.

It was as a scout for such photogenic locations that Bruno Engler found a calling that would employ him for years. Guiding was not a reliable source of income in the years following the Second Word War, but as a trained photographer and certified mountain guide, Engler possessed some valuable skills. In 1953, he landed his big break. Universal Studios came to film a movie titled *The Far Country*, starring some of the big names of the day – Jimmy Stewart, Walter Brennan, Ruth Roman. Engler was assigned to assist in the production as location scout and mountain safety advisor. It was a full extravaganza. The crew pretty much invaded the small, subdued town of Jasper. Gregarious and enthusiastic, Engler fit right in.

One day, the entire production moved south to the Columbia Icefield Centre. The plan was to film a short scene on the lower Athabasca Glacier in which hundreds of gold-hungry prospectors crawled up White Mountain Pass from Skagway, Alaska, to Yukon in the gold rush of 1898. One hundred and twenty extras had been recruited from as far away as Edmonton, and any crew members who weren't immediately busy – including Engler – were also roped in. Oh, and there was livestock too.

"We also had forty head of Texas longhorn cattle," Engler described in *A Mountain Life*. "The SPCA would not allow us to drive the cattle onto the ice. I thought that was probably a good idea."

While the director, Anthony Mann, and the camera crew were transported up the glacier by snowmobile, Engler hauled a wooden sleigh loaded with sacks of hay. "The load was fairly light," he admitted, "but I had to act like it was heavy."

As the entire procession walked up the gradual incline of the glacier, Engler fell a bit behind. When he caught up, he was aghast to find the crew had set up the cameras atop the moraine bordering the south bank of the glacier, directly underneath the steep icefall cascading down the Andromeda Glacier (which nowadays has melted far enough back to pose little threat). While visually, the setting provided a

Hollywood director Ernst Lubitsch (right) explains his vision to a couple of actors on the Athabasca Glacier, circa 1929. Whyte Museum of the Canadian Rockies, Peter and Catharine Whyte Fonds (V683/II/A/pa-505)

spectacular backdrop, the location was also spectacularly dangerous. If that wasn't bad enough, Engler arrived in time to watch the assistant director instruct some of the extras – on foot and on horseback – to traverse the snow chute that had been formed by ice and snow falling from above.

Engler couldn't believe his eyes. Dropping his sleigh, he rushed right to the director and demanded the men and horses be moved down from there immediately.

"They're in the icefall chute!" Engler pleaded. "That nice white slope with the ice clumps in it is created by the falling ice that comes off the ice wall up there."

Mann, the director, wasn't convinced of any threat. "That ice has been there since the last ice age," Mann said with a shrug. "It won't come down now."

Engler stood his ground. Massive chunks of ice, he insisted, could break off at any time. Wasting no time, Engler directed the extras and crew away from the moraine ridge and over to the safer flat surface of the glacier far from the fall zone.

With that somewhat settled, Mann resumed charge and directed his extras and to stand where they were and look up to the slope and watch as an imaginary avalanche came crashing down. As that happened, they were to crowd around the saloon owner and "Queen of the Klondike" played by Roman.

Again, Engler disagreed with the director, not for safety reasons but in consideration of human nature. Bypassing Mann, he explained to the assistant director that in such a location, if a real avalanche was to crash down the slope, everyone would be running for their own lives in all directions. Poo-pooing his concerns, the assistant director assured Engler the audience would never know the difference.

The gods were on Engler's side that day. During the second take the fractured ice walls began to shiver. Chunks

It's not only Hollywood making movies on western Canada's glaciers. Pro skier Trevor Petersen shows his 1989-era ski skill jumping a serac wall for a RAP Productions film shot from Selkirk backcountry ski lodge. Trevor died in 1996, but his son, Kye, born in 1990, has followed his footsteps as a pro skier and is also a POW – Protect Our Winters – ambassador (see page 301). Photo Scott Rowed

of ice shifted and slid and, right on cue, a tumultuous avalanche came thundering down. As Engler predicted, the extras did not run to protect their heroine; they scattered in panic in all directions. Never one to turn down an opportunity to assist a damsel in distress, Engler ran to Roman and wrapped his strong arms around her, shielding her as they were swallowed by a billowing cloud of ice and snow dust.

Turning to the two camera positions, Mann called up. "Did you get it? Did you get the shot?"

"No," came the reply, "we took cover behind some rocks."

Collecting himself, Mann – whom Engler had last seen running across the flat glacier with his trench coat flapping behind him as he jumped across a small crevasse in a desperate search for safety – reached into his pocket and pulled out a $100 bill.

"Bruno, you're worth your weight in gold," he said, handing Engler the bill.

Hollywood Northwest

While Engler would continue to scout great locations over the coming decades, including for the award-winning Walt Disney nature documentary *White Wilderness* (1958), for which he spent three days patiently waiting by himself to capture footage of an avalanche bursting down from Victoria Glacier, Canada's glaciers have continued to provide settings for a range of film productions. A CBC documentary on David Thompson filmed scenes at the Athabasca in the late 1990s. Scenes from the 1981 *Superman II* movie were also shot on the Athabasca Glacier to represent the superhero's North Pole "home." Shamefully, this was accomplished without Parks' permission. *Last of the Dogmen*, filmed in and around Canmore in 1994, featured one scene for which ACMG mountain guides Barry Blanchard and Troy Kirwan climbed the rock route up the cliffs left of Takakkaw Falls, which gush down meltwater from the Daly Glacier in Yoho National Park. Then from the top they tossed a dummy off the waterfall.

In recent decades, professional mountain guides have worked behind the scenes on many a production filmed amidst glaciers. In 1991, Tiedemann Glacier in the Mount Waddington area of the Coast Mountains doubled – quite effectively – for the massive glaciers of Pakistan's Karakoram range for a Hollywood production called *K2*. Spending three and a half weeks camping in tents took its toll on the cast and crew, more accustomed to sleeping in warm hotel beds after long shooting days than enduring minus 24 Celsius temperatures and howling winds blasting snow around their set. While the Rockies' glaciers are much smaller, a Canadian production released in 1986 titled *The Climb* chose to use glaciers in the Columbia Icefield area to double as K2. For filming of the sobering drama titled *Alive* (1993), which recounts the story of Uruguayan rugby team members who survived a plane crash in the Andes by resorting to cannibalism, the Delphine Glacier in the Purcell Mountains marked one of the few times a glacier was used as a primary set location. That, of course, doesn't count the reams of footage shot for ski and snowboard films on and around western Canada's glaciers.

Carving Landscapes

"The glaciers must be measured, and I shall hope to use the camera seriously, and get all I can," wrote Mary Vaux in a letter to her husband, paleontologist Charles Doolittle Walcott.

The first time Revelstoke, British Columbia–based filmmaker Agathe Bernard saw a photograph of Mary Vaux standing next to a towering wall of glacial ice wearing the proper attire of the early 20th century, Bernard was gobsmacked. Having worked for years as a geologist spending long days out with only her high-tech clothing protecting her from rain, snow, wind and cold, Bernard imagined the effort it would have taken Mary to visit the glaciers of Rogers Pass wearing a ground-length skirt made of heavy fabric.

"I was born in the era of Gore-Tex," Bernard said. "When I saw the photo of Mary standing right in front of the glacier, I couldn't believe she was dressed like this. I mean, her dedication!"

She was out there every year – pure passion. I wanted to know more."

Bernard began reading. She learned about Mary and her brothers' studies on the Illecillewaet Glacier in 1904. That she didn't marry until she was 54 – and then despite the wishes of her father, who expected her to care for him – and spent her honeymoon studying the glacier, a passion she followed until she died at 80. That her flower illustration work was published by the Smithsonian Institution. Bernard knew she had the ideal subject for a film.

"The story of Mary Vaux inspired me in many ways to pursue my work as an earth scientist and as a filmmaker/photographer," she said. "In the process of bringing this project to life, I found myself incredibly inspired by her tenacity and motivation. Being a woman in sciences or in visual media is not the easiest road to adventure on. Managing this inferno drive bubbling inside, the physical requirements and limitations, the passion of creativity and curiosity while managing the obligations of the everyday family life is to say the least very challenging."

To play the role of Mary, Bernard hired Liliane Lambert, an ACMG ski guide. "I needed an actor who would be comfortable rapelling into a crevasse in a skirt!" she said with a laugh.

Playing the role of Mary Vaux, Liliane Lambert stands near the toe of the Illecillewaet Glacier, which is now about 600 metres higher up the valley than when the Vaux siblings initiated Canada's first glacier studies in 1904. Photo Agathe Bernard

But she also learned that Lambert, like Mary, had lost a brother (William Vaux died in 1908). And, it turned out, Lambert hadn't visited the Illecillewaet Glacier for several years since becoming a mother and was astonished at the extent of the melting. Lambert connected to her role more than Bernard could have imagined.

As an independent filmmaker, Bernard applied and received funding from the Columbia Basin Trust, and also set up a site for a Story Hive grant so she could pay her crew. Shooting in VR (virtual reality) format was new for her, and she produced two versions of the film, which she named *Carving Landscapes*, one in 3D. The film has toured with several festivals, and Bernard presents it at schools too.

"Lots of kids will never get a chance to stand on a glacier," she said.

Originally from Quebec, Bernard fell in love with glaciers while living in her mother's native Switzerland as a teenager. Then while working on her master's in environmental communication she began searching for ways to spark curiosity and communication about climate change without causing people to feel depressed.

"I want people to be inspired about preserving our environment, not depressed by it, but feeling energy," Bernard said. "I want people to feel empowered despite their gender, or what they're wearing, or what they think they can do. To appreciate there's lots of beauty around us. The film gives us perspective on some of the battles women had to

For many years the Vaux siblings photographed the Illecillewaet Glacier from the same location, a spot that came to be known as Photographer's Rock. Playing the role of Mary Vaux, Liliane Lambert aims an antique camera (similar to the one the Vauxes used) from that spot toward the glacier, now more than half a kilometre farther up-valley. Photo Agathe Bernard

endure in the Victorian era but also reminds us to stay true to our nature and persevere."

"I thought Mary's story was a good story."

The Big Bow Float

In more recent decades, large-scale productions have been denied permission from Parks Canada to film on the glaciers or pretty much anywhere in the Rockies parks beyond the Banff town limits or at the ski resorts. With tourists now numbering more than four million annually, this is a good thing. Applications to film within the park boundaries are now considered on a case-by-case basis, and the call is made depending on whether or how the project fits in with the park "message." But with growing public awareness of climate change and environmental degradation, film projects featuring glaciers have entered a different genre. The Big Bow Float was just such a project.

Over five weeks in 2005, Danielle Droitsch and her paddling partner, Jim Kievet, a retired teacher from Canmore, paddled their canoe the entire 650-kilometre length of the Bow River. Launching from Bow Lake inside Banff's park boundary, they floated past glaciated peaks into rolling foothills, right through Calgary's urban sprawl and beyond, moving with the current through fertile farm and ranch land. They pulled out at the southern Alberta hamlet of Grassy Lake, where the Bow joins the Oldman River to form the South Saskatchewan River flowing north into Hudson Bay. One component of the outreach part of their project was a film they made to share with audiences at presentations around the region.

As Bow Riverkeeper, Droitsch was the public advocate assigned by the Waterkeeper Alliance – co-founded by US environmental lawyer Robert F. Kennedy, Jr. – to protect and restore the Bow watershed. Her journey didn't begin on water, though. First, she hiked up to Bow Hut to spend a few days exploring the Wapta Icefield with several friends, with ACMG mountain guide Kirsten Knechtel keeping everyone safe. I had tagged along for the first day and night at the hut, then hiked back out the next morning on my own.

Walking up from the hut to the glacier's toe with Droitsch, who was experiencing a glacier up close for the first time, opened my eyes to an entirely new way of seeing the many-thousand-year-old ice. Until then, the glacier had been, for me, like other glaciers – cool, fascinating places to have fun and exciting adventures. But Droitsch saw more. She realized she was sitting in the very nucleus of a watershed. Through her eyes, I saw that we were experiencing the true beginnings of the Bow River.

"There is a tremendous amount of water stored up," Droitsch said. "I wish that everybody had the opportunity to see how beautiful and how critical it is. That ocean of snow – for everyone to make a connection to how important it is to have a healthy snowpack and intact glaciers. I think most people don't feel connected to or affected by climate change."

After descending from the Icefields, Droitsch and Kievit launched their canoe into Bow Lake's luminous turquoise waters and paddled south. Near Lake Louise several members of the Siksika First Nation joined the canoeists in a raft. The Siksika, who have made a formal claim to land at Castle Mountain – and the section of the Bow that flows through there – would join the paddlers again when they passed through the Siksika reserve on their journey to where the Bow joins the Oldman River.

Paddling through the transition zones at eye level with the flowing current allowed Droitsch to experience how the mountain river becomes a prairie river. In the lower reaches of the Bow, water use – much of it for land irrigation – leaves water levels 75 to 90 per cent lower than they would be if left natural. By the time Droitsch and Kievet reached Bassano in early August, flows were down to one-quarter of the river's natural levels. Overall, a full 75 per cent of the river's water is diverted. By the time they reached the end of their journey, temperatures were in the thirties Celsius and lawns were drying up in an area where cactus grows. While water is available in reliable abundance in the mountain towns of Banff and Canmore, communities downstream, she pointed out, don't have the same luxury.

Activism for Ice

Alberta is Canada's driest province.

The southern half of Alberta, where 88 per cent of its four million (as of 2016) inhabitants live, is where only 13 per cent of its freshwater resources are found. Alberta's real water supply is inconveniently located in the far north. And in the south, river flow is highly variable from one season to the next. Barely a year after Droitsch paddled the Bow, the Province halted all new surface water allocations from the South Saskatchewan River basin – which includes the Bow, Oldman, Red Deer and South Saskatchewan rivers – except for the Red Deer. The river basin of the

Don van Hout paddles on the Athabasca River near its confluence with the Sunwapta River at the start of his 1060-kilometre journey all the way to Fort Chipewyan on the eastern edge of Wood Buffalo National Park. Photo Lynn Martel

fastest-growing region of the province was officially over-allocated.

A message of water conservation was top of mind for Droitsch throughout their journey, and through her many outreach efforts. The future of the Bow River, she pointed out to reporters and audiences at schools and town halls, is connected to and affected by Earth's warming temperatures. A fistful of snow scooped up from the Wapta Icefields is the water supply for Banff and Canmore and Calgary and dozens of communities downstream. A reduced snowpack is one of the projected effects of our changing climate, and precipitation that falls as snow during the winter months is stored water that will be released when it melts in the spring. A low snowpack year, or spring runoff happening earlier in the season as temperatures rise, can result in a water shortage for people living in the lower reaches of the river.

"In terms of volume, reduced snowpack is a real problem," Droitsch explained. "We have to plan. Canadians are some of the highest per capita users of water anywhere in the world. The whole purpose of this trip is to talk about the value of the water in this river."

After their journey ended, footage captured by Droitsch and a friend, Don van Hout, was edited. The previous summer, van Hout had paddled the Athabasca River from its confluence with the Whirlpool River, following its course beyond the Jasper park boundary north all the way to Fort Chipewyan on the eastern edge of Wood Buffalo National Park. Covering nearly 45,000 square kilometres, Canada's largest national park, located in Alberta's sparsely populated northeast corner, Wood Buffalo is one of North America's most significant migratory bird paths and what is likely the last stand of free-ranging bison still engaged in a natural predator/prey relationship with wolves.

Big Bow Float: Journey Down the Emerald Thread, was produced by the professional filmmaking team of Doug Latimer and Rachel Gauk, and their Shadow Light Productions. The 22-minute film blended a documentary-style account of the voyage with the adventure of paddling through eight distinct eco-zones. Footage from the river was interspersed with conversations with water conservation experts, including outspoken, straight-shooting University of Alberta Killam Memorial professor of ecology David Schindler, who reflected on the scientifically proven value of healthy river flows and the necessary water quantity for river health.

The entire project involved four months of planning, five weeks on the river and a lot of time spent organizing, maintaining a website, coordinating with other groups and communicating with media. Through it all, Droitsch said she learned how important it was to see the river from the perspective of a canoe.

"The diversity is extraordinary, in terms of personality of the river," she said. "I knew it was glacially fed from the mountains to the prairies, but to actually see that diversity – the geography, topography, the ecology, the wildlife, how much water is in the river, how fast it moves, its size – you wouldn't know it's the same river."

People tend to think of the river, any river, in terms of individual segments, she suggested. But a river, she emphasized, is a *single* entity. While segmented, it is a continuum. And in western Canada, a great many rivers originate, as the Bow does, with a glacier. Even as many downstream communities live on the verge of water shortages, the film revealed how people living in the region and dependent on the river are often wary of conservation talk.

"One question I had to answer over and over – we are not about shutting down irrigation in southern Alberta," Droitsch said. "It's always a matter of what is a sustainable balance. What is the maximum amount we can draw from the river and still meet our ecological needs?"

And while residents upstream in the mountain communities may never have a problem, their water consumption will likely become a problem for people downstream. Everybody should take a minute to think about the river in its entirety, Droitsch suggested, not just the little section that flows through their own backyards or towns.

"You can't just point to the other guy," she said. "Everyone needs to take responsibility for their own water use."

White Water, Black Gold

Efforts to use documentary films to convey a message of prioritizing long-term conservation over short-term economic gain inspired by the Rockies' glaciers didn't end with *Big Bow Float*.

In October 2006, David Lavallée was sharing a conversation during a field trip to the Athabasca Glacier when he asked himself a question. The outing was part of a workshop organized by the Alpine Club of Canada to look at climate change impacts on the alpine ecosystem, and he'd been discussing climate change–induced glacial recession with one of the guest speakers, University of Calgary glaciologist and climatologist Dr. Shawn Marshall. As an ACMG-certified hiking guide and keen mountaineer, Lavallée was drawn to learn more about how climate change was affecting the region's glaciers. As the conversation came around to the subject of how water from the Athabasca Glacier flows all the way to Fort McMurray, where it is used in large quantities to facilitate oil production, a question popped into his mind.

"While government and industry are looking out for the economy, is anyone looking out for the river and the ecosystem it is part of?" Lavallée wondered. "What's happening to the glaciers, and what's happening to our water supply? How are these resources being managed? Are our institutions on the job?"

Within hours, Lavallée's question had evolved into a full-blown multi-faceted project. He would ski onto the Columbia Icefield and then paddle the length of the Athabasca River some 1500 kilometres right through Fort McMurray – his journey mirroring that of a single drop of water flowing from the cloud-hugging summit of Snow Dome all the way to where the Athabasca drains into the Peace-Athabasca Delta south of Fort Chipewyan in Alberta's northeastern corner.

His project experienced a bumpy start; Lavallée was a family counsellor and a hiking guide, not a filmmaker. Regardless, he did ski to the summit of Snow Dome and back down, then rafted the Athabasca from Sunwapta Falls as far as Hinton, east of the Jasper park boundary. Then he got his lucky break. While attending a reception at the Banff World Television Festival he met veteran filmmaker Alan Bibby. An avid mountain adventurer himself, Bibby has a son, Ken, who is also an ACMG ski guide. Lavallée described his project and Bibby enthusiastically jumped on board as director and director of photography.

Filmmaker David Lavallée lines up his shot on the banks of the Athabasca River during the filming of *White Water, Black Gold*, in which he followed the journey made by water that originates from the Columbia Icefield as it flows to northern Alberta, where it is a necessary element used in the production of synthetic crude oil – and other industries along the way. Photo Lynn Martel

"I met up with Alan and started all over again," Lavallée said. "He's a fantastic director. He brought the experience base that I needed to make my film real."

Together the men participated in a protest flotilla on the Athabasca from Fort McMurray to Fort McKay, along with canoeists, environmentalists and politicians, including then Alberta Liberal environment critic Dr. David Swann, who had publicly and persistently questioned the harmful effects of Fort McMurray's oil sands developments on First Nations populations living downstream, where the fish they eat were found deformed and growing tumours. Witnessing a broad-based co-alition of Albertans coming together to protest how their water resources were being managed helped reassure Lavallée that his project was a film that needed to be made.

Digging deeper, Lavallée returned to the Columbia Icefield with Alan and Ken Bibby, and Ken's brother, Andrew, to collect more footage, some of which turned out to be a little more graphic than anticipated.

"Everything went off pretty well without a hitch except for the crevasse fall," Lavallée said. "I fell about 30 feet. I had lots of time to ponder and think, hanging on the rope. I was unharmed, so my main concern was that Alan was getting the shot."

A consummate professional, Bibby got the shot. Ken and Andrew performed the rescue.

Producing the film turned into a non-stop learning experience for Lavallée. It was also time-consuming and expensive. He took leave from his counsellor job and worked as a substitute teacher. He maxed out his credit cards and applied for funding everywhere he could. And in addition to discovering a Pandora's Box worth of facts about the impacts of climate change and oil sands production on the natural environment of Alberta and beyond, he learned plenty about documentary filmmaking too.

"I learned it's a heck of a lot of work," Lavallée said. "You really have to stay open to ideas. It's like a scientific experiment, you start out working on a hypothesis, then your hypothesis gets challenged. Once your initial research is done you find you're not just scratching the surface – there's always more to learn, more layers to dig through. You keep learning there's more you don't know."

But overall, he learned more than he ever could have hoped for or wished to about the life of a drop of water flowing from a Rockies glacier to Alberta's oil sands industry hub. An area of worldwide importance on the energy reserve map, the oil sands development site covers an immense section of land the size of New Brunswick and employs many thousands. The highly toxic tailings ponds created in the aftermath of extracting bitumen from the clay, sand and water that make up the oil sands form man-made lakes so large they can be seen from space. Birds who mistakenly land in them don't survive, so now the ponds are ringed with scarecrows to keep them away. There's long been a saying in Alberta that the oil sands would not have been developed the way they have been if the Athabasca flowed south, through Calgary.

The filmmaking team spoke with scientists, policy makers, local residents, tribal elders and other stakeholders of the Athabasca ecosystem to gain their perspectives on how the oil sands operations affect them and the natural environment. Lavallée's commitment to his project continued to deepen, as did his fondness for and efforts to advocate for the glaciers.

"The mountain glaciers and snowpack are threatened – all the places I love to play in are at risk," Lavallée said. "We tend to take it for granted that the glaciers will always be there. I think it's really important that Canadians from all parts of the country, from all walks of life, understand our heritage is threatened by climate change, and our economy is threatened. I hope people will think about how what appears to be a plentiful short-term source of income needs to be balanced with the long-term consequences."

Moving Hearts and Minds

White Water, Black Gold was released in 2010 and screened at film festivals across North America. It caught the attention of audiences as well as jury members, winning Best Canadian Film at the Vancouver International Mountain Film Festival, the John Muir Award at the Yosemite International Film Festival and the Platinum Award at the Oregon Film Awards.

Looking back on his first film more than a decade after he optimistically followed his passion, Lavallée said he saw many ways he could have done it better.

"I really feel like I could have made a more powerful film by focusing less on the science," he said. "A rock solid empirically supported argument does not move hearts and minds – I mean, Trump is president, right? The truth is simply unimportant today. If you want to move hearts and minds you need something more than the truth. What that something more is, I'm not sure."

River beauties bloom in the gravel outwash flats of the Sunwapta River downstream from its source, the Athabasca Glacier, as sunset kisses Mount Athabasca. Photo Lynn Martel

Right. Facts are dull. But you'd think at some point, people would see enough of them they'd want to act. I mean really, what if all those facts turn out to be exactly that, facts? A federal study published in 2016 showed Alberta's oil sands contribute more air pollution daily than the country's largest city, Toronto. The oil sands operations in Alberta continue to be among Canada's largest contributors to globally rising carbon dioxide levels, which passed 415 parts per million in May 2019 for the first time since humans have lived on Earth. Eighteen of the 19 warmest years ever recorded on Earth have happened since 2001. Canada's climate is warming twice as fast as the average for the rest of the world. While that warming is not uniform across the country, those who live in Canada's north are watching and feeling the permafrost melting under their houses, under their feet.

Hindsight, they say, is 20/20. When I look back on the days when I first began interviewing scientists and activists about how Earth's climate is warming, and how human actions are accelerating that warming, and then consider how every attempt at global consensus on how best to act and to set hard timelines in which to take action has pretty much failed, I'd say in my province of Alberta, hearts and minds have definitely been moved.

Sadly, though, the collective decision by various groups advocating for improved environmental health to demonize the oil industry, with an especially large bull's eye on Alberta's oil sands, moved a lot of hearts and minds in a different way, to create angry, defensive opponents of people whose co-operation is so necessary on the road toward a more environmentally sustainable energy and economic model. And I don't blame any of those mothers and fathers working to provide food and shelter and comfortable lives for their families for getting their backs up about being so publicly blamed and shamed for what is becoming a climate crisis.

But we can and must do better.

Lavallée, for his part, hasn't given up on trying to raise awareness about climate change, and he is still making films.

Released in 2017, *To the Ends of the Earth* follows concerned citizens who live at the frontiers of what he calls "extreme oil and gas extraction" and are calling for human ingenuity to rebuild society and embrace a future beyond the current resource-dependent pyramid. He followed that with a short film, *Wildfire Warriors*, which looks at the steadily escalating numbers of wildfires burning each year in British Columbia at times of the year and in places they historically weren't expected to. With the frequency and intensity of wildfires exacerbated by Earth's warming temperatures – July 2019 was the hottest month ever recorded on Earth, but that's a moving target – and with well-forested British Columbia an absolute hot spot for such fires, the film examines yet another issue at least partly linked to climate warming.

Now living in Vancouver, Lavallée recently revisited the site that inspired his first film, and he compared what he saw to what he remembered.

"I went to visit the Athabasca a few years ago, I went for a hike across it," Lavallée said. "What I remember is not so much the length of it, how much it had shrunk, but the volume of it – how much higher the moraines were, how much lower the ice was.

It was like I was standing in the bottom of a huge pit. It's staggering, the exponential-ity of the changes happening right now. And yet we are being told by our prime min-ister that we need a pipeline to solve this problem. The sheer insanity of trickle-down economics boggles the mind. Let's put cigarettes in the cancer ward while we are at it – that will generate revenues for research."

Protect Our Winters

The world is getting hotter, and it's our fault.

Such is the slogan of POW – Protect Our Winters. Founded in the United States in 2007 by pro snowboarder Jeremy Jones, POW works to turn passionate outdoorspeople into effective climate advocates. Since then the not-for-profit organization has grown to en-compass a worldwide network of more than 130,000 supporters who include an all-star roster of professional snow sport athletes, plus thinkers and progressive business lead-ers, all working to effect systemic solutions to climate change.

Funded by partners that include some of the biggest names in North American ski re-sorts and outdoor gear and clothing companies, as well as individuals and private foun-dations, POW is encouraging a social movement, working to create the political will on behalf of state, provincial and federal policy makers to take meaningful action.

For skiers and snowboarders and ice climbers and any snow sport enthusiasts, the ef-fects of a warming climate are simple: warmer temperatures equal less snow and ice as snow levels rise and the winter season begins later and ends earlier.

The movement encourages snow lovers to join its ranks, and to act through education with recommended podcasts, websites and reading, including *Eaarth* by Bill McKibben, Tim Flannery's *The Weather Makers* and Naomi Klein's *This Changes Everything: Capitalism vs. The Climate*. Members are also en-couraged to become politically involved by voting, and by contacting elected rep-resentatives on specific matters. Other suggestions include fundraising, and "Be The Change" actions such as installing solar panels, driving energy-efficient ve-hicles, taking transit, shorter showers and energy-smart appliances. The site in-cludes steps to reduce one's carbon foot-print, complete with a carbon footprint calculator and meat-free calculator.

Self-propelled adventure advocate Greg Hill skis down Mount Athabasca's steep north face. Hill is one of POW's professional athlete ambassadors. Photo Anthony Bonello

Revelstoke ski-athlete Greg Hill takes a break against the electric car he drove to reach 100 adventure destinations in one year, captured in the film *Electric Greg*. His electric adventure continues. Photo Anthony Bonello

Another action involves inviting a HOT PLANET COOL ATHLETES representative to speak at schools and events.

"We believe educating and empowering the next generation to be future environmental leaders is one of the most important things we can be doing to address climate change," states POW.

"Our key formula for engaging 60 million+ outdoor sports enthusiasts globally: relevance and authenticity. Though we can dress up for meetings, in the end we are pro athletes, dirtbags and diehards; for us, winter is not just a passion, but a way of life."

Canadian POW athletes include Olympic ski cross medalist Ashleigh McIvor, self-propelled adventure athlete Chris Rubens, Paralympian Joshua Dueck and ski mountaineering über athlete Greg Hill. As part of his commitment to sharing the POW message, Hill sold his F-350 pickup truck and his snowmobile, retired from guiding for heli-ski companies and now travels to all his mountain adventures from his Revelstoke home in an electric car. Thus far he's climbed more than 100 peaks without using fossil fuels.

"As those who enjoy nature and find happiness there it is up to us to be stewards for what we love most," Hill said when asked why he chose to help share the POW message. "If we are not willing to stand up and protect it then who will? POW is a way to raise our collective voice and to create a movement of concerned citizens that ideally will be able to help create change."

We All Need Winter. Give a Flake!

5 – 4 WORDS FOR ICE

Carried by the Sub-Glacial Ice

The story has blossomed into mountain legend.

Like so many young people do, Bob Sandford left his hometown – in his case, Calgary – to take a summer job as a park naturalist in the Rocky Mountains that beckon on the city's western horizon. Just 20 years old – or as it then appeared to him, a mature and fully prepared 20 years old – he had it all figured out.

"I had my life all worked out," Sandford described. "I was going to graduate. I had picked a wife. I had picked a house. There would be a dog. There would be children. I would drive a wood-panelled station wagon. I was prepared, indeed, for the good life."

But first, he would go for the hike that would influence his choices for the rest of his days.

After viewing a "dizzying array" of slides projected on a wall by a friend depicting scene after scene of mountain-climbing adventures in the most beguiling of settings, Sandford knew what he needed. He had to become a mountaineer.

Naturally, he would go full-in. He only had two days off work, and he had never been backpacking before, but two days should be plenty of time to walk across the Columbia Icefield in the middle of summer. After all, he reasoned, how big can an icefield be?

His adventure progressed smoothly for the first day. He and three friends had successfully navigated a route up the Saskatchewan Glacier to Castleguard Meadows, Sandford wearing crampons fixed to his cowboy boots. Leaving camp the next morning, Sandford and one friend headed back down the long, gradually descending ice tongue. Inexperienced and unprepared, they were not roped together. The day began to drag on.

"I was so tired that I had given up trying to avoid the big meltwater streams that coursed across the glacier's broken surface," he recalled. "I was cold and wet and worn out and all I wanted to do was get down."

Like all glacier surfaces on a hot summer's day, the Saskatchewan was coursing with meltwater creeks. Tiny trickles, babbling brooks of just-thawed glacier water and gushing streams merged and multiplied around Sandford like Medusa's hair, all flowing down toward the glacier's toe.

Exhausted and depleted – a state commonly experienced by most young people on that first hike that is three times longer and more difficult than they should have bitten off – he decided to take a shortcut through the maze of running streams.

And he slipped.

"The power of the icy water lifted me up and carried me to the mouth of a huge crevasse," he recalled. "One moment I was looking at the sun-sparkle of splashing water, a moment later I was in the centre of a waterfall plunging into complete darkness beneath the ice."

There was no time to think, or to act. Helpless, he was along for the ride. The water carried him along as the torrent cascaded down a series of ice steps and drops and then flushed him into the river that flowed beneath the glacier.

"Never before, or since, have I heard from everywhere around me so many of the

Photographer Kahli April Hindmarsh readies her tripod near the entrance of a deep glacial ice cave in the Canadian Rockies. Photo Paul Zizka

different sounds that water makes," he said. "Here I was inside a planetary artery examining first-hand what water does to the world."

It wasn't the smoothest of rides. The space between the surging river and the ceiling of the glacier's underbelly amounted to mere inches. In the darkness, he ricocheted like a pinball off boulders and pillars of ice studded with rocks. As the shock and wonder of finding himself in such unimaginable circumstances began to evaporate and his calm began to escalate to sheer terror, the most amazing things happened.

"The ice above began to glow," he described. "At first it was a faint green. As the sub-glacial river swept me onward, the glow intensified. Green gradually merged into a pale blue. I noticed then that rocks were hanging out of a ceiling made entirely of light."

Swoosh!

Published in 1982, *The Great Glacier and Its House*, by respected mountaineer and author William Lowell "Bill" Putnam, is a rich and full account of the Illecillewaet Glacier and its many-faceted role as a place of adventure, science, the tourism business, First Nations peoples and the railway workers who were indispensable in making this fascinating place easily accessible.

As abruptly as he fell into the glacier netherworld, he was unceremoniously flushed back out into the midsummer sunshine.

And ever since that day when he heaved himself onto the moist, rocky moraine bank of the North Saskatchewan River, he's been writing about Canada's mountains, and the ice and water that flow from them.

Ice Prose

Glaciers have been appearing in books written in and about western Canada since the first Europeans set eyes on them nearly three centuries ago. In particular, climbers and mountaineers included glaciers and icefields in their descriptions of rugged adventures and bold explorations in personal letters, newspaper and magazine articles and in books. Explorers and surveyors too described glaciers in their reports. On the written page, glaciers have reliably provided writers – of fiction and non-fiction and poetry – with intriguing, enticing and deliciously foreboding background settings.

Some publications, however, elevate the cameo appearances by glaciers to starring roles.

One of these is William Lowell Putnam III's treasured 1982 coffee-table book *The Great Glacier and Its House: The Story of the First Center of Alpinism in North America, 1885–1925*. Published by the American Alpine Club, his is a rich and full story of how a glacier, the Illecillewaet of Canada's Glacier National Park, came to hold deep meaning and value not only to climbers but to a lengthy cast including mountain guides relocated from their native Swiss Alps, railway labourers, hotel staff, explorers, surveyors, First Nations peoples, tourists and inquisitive scientists. With Glacier House Hotel so deliberately located within walking distance of the "Great Glacier," the establishment and the glacier itself worked in partnership to inspire visitors with alternating moods of comfort and cool adventure. Within the book's covers are dozens of historical black and white photographs that celebrate and preserve the intertwined roles the glacier and the hotel played for the people who spent days, months or even years of their lives in this place. Putnam includes raw scientific data, tables of measurements taken on the Illecillewaet by members of the Vaux family in 1899, and some of the early maps of the towering peaks and deep valleys that make up the geography of Rogers Pass. It is a magnificent tribute.

Of course, Putnam, who died in 2014 at the age of 90, admitted the book was personal. A passionate mountaineer, he was an honorary member of the Alpine Club of Canada, the American Alpine Club, the UIAA (International Climbing and Mountaineering Federation), the Association of Canadian Mountain Guides and the Appalachian Mountain Club (North America's oldest mountaineering club). He was also a prolific author, devoted backcountry hut builder and constructor of legendary cairns. Founder, president and CEO of the Springfield Television Corporation, he managed three TV stations and in 2001 was inducted into the American Broadcasting Hall of Fame. Born to a prominent New England family, he was the sole trustee of the Lowell Observatory, the world's largest private astronomical research observatory.

And he loved western Canada's mountains.

"This narrative no doubt reflects a *personal* nostalgic admiration for the House, the Railroad, the Selkirk Mountains, and the early explorers," he wrote. "My own serious alpine experiences began after I stepped off the train and camped on the old Glacier House lawn."

In full and grand view of the glacier.

Lyrical Ice

In his novel *Icefields*, published in 1995, Thomas Wharton doesn't just set his story on the Athabasca Glacier and the little lodge near its toe at the turn of the 20th century; he weaves the glacier into the story like a mysterious, haunting, powerful character. And

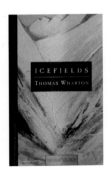

In his novel *Icefields*, Thomas Wharton weaves the fictional Arcturus Glacier into the story like a mysterious, haunting and powerful character.

in the writing of this historical novel, Wharton, who lives near Edmonton, displays an intimacy with the ice that can only come from hours spent sitting, standing, walking and gazing deeply into crevasses. Communing with a glacier.

"Glacial ice is not a liquid, nor is it a solid," Wharton writes. "It flows like lava, like melting wax, like honey. Supple glass. Fluid stone."

His story of love, of searching, and of loss slipping through fingers like icy meltwater earned him the Commonwealth Writer's Prize for Best First Book, and the 1995 Banff Mountain Book Festival's Grand Prize. Exquisitely lyrical, his vivid observations unfurl a world of natural miracles only experienced through intimate moments with ancient bodies of ice.

"When the temperature drops at dusk to below zero, all the streams on the glacier surface cease to flow. Everywhere the ice bristles up with glittering frost needles as the melted and now refreezing surface water dilatates. A garden of tiny ice flowers seems to be growing all around me."

It is delicate prose such as this that touches readers, inviting them to feel the faintest wisp of breeze breathing down the ice tongue, cradling ghosts.

In other books, Canadian authors portray glaciers with a bit of humour, as does Ben Gadd in his delightfully whimsical and at times seat-of-your-pants suspenseful *Raven's End*. Although there are cameos by squirrels and other mountain critters, the colourful, lively characters driving this story are all ravens, the protagonist named Colin. After a long flight, Colin stops to take a break on the Athabasca Glacier, where he discovers himself standing on his raven legs amidst an absolute feast on the ice. Then he proceeds to gobble partly frozen and numbed but still alive, and very, very tasty, flies and beetles and moths and mosquitoes.

In his 2009 novel *Hooker & Brown*, Jerry Auld, like Gadd a long-time Rockies resident, exhibits the richness acquired through his own plentiful travels on glaciers in describing his characters' surroundings deep in the backcountry of Jasper's Whirlpool River.

"A glacier descends beside us, washing us with cold drafts. It grows from the Divide, touching down in an agony of split crevasses, like a giant wrinkled hand, fingers dropped into a lake of their own ice blood."

Gives me goosebumps.

Living Ice

Over the decades, plenty of textbooks and academic publications, not to mention piles of mountaineers' guidebooks, have examined, exposed and extolled the size, composition and evolution and exploration of glaciers. Scientists, mountaineers or scholars: one thing those who write about glaciers and icefields undoubtedly share is a deep love, an unbridled passion for those frozen entities.

Glaciologist Mike Demuth is no exception. Now retired after a long, respected career with Natural Resources Canada, in 2012 he published *Becoming Water: Glaciers in a Warming World*. This compact hardcover serves up all anyone needs to know about glaciers – how they form, how they grow, how they melt and plenty more in between – in language that is accessible and readable. Despite being a respected authority on glaciers, however, Demuth doesn't hesitate to step a little beyond the dry, cold facts of science as he enlarges the world of glaciers for lay readers.

"By this point in our journey," he wrote, "we can all agree that *a glacier is not a glacier is not a glacier*. Glaciers are complex expressions of cold and warm on the landscape; while they are cold in some places, they are the source of water in others. Their forms are as variable as the landscapes they are confined by, overrun or carve. These Great Carvers are not static but alive – places of spirits."

Demuth is certainly not the first, nor the last – writer or otherwise – to refer to glaciers as more than static mounds of ice laying on a landscape. Many a climber, skier, scientist or thinker views a glacier as a living being. For my part, I see glaciers and icefields as alive the way a tree is alive, or more completely, as an old-growth forest teeming with 800-year-old trees is alive and supporting an intricate ecosystem.

Through history, though, glaciers have been viewed from many different perspectives. In medieval Europe, glaciers were feared and dreaded as they were believed to harbour evil spirits, even seen as ice-dragons advancing to devour people and livestock. Given that glaciers repeatedly surged downslope so forcefully during the Little Ice Age that they would plow right over farmland and demolish homes, prompting terrified villagers to approach glacial caves with their swords at the ready, the perception seems entirely reasonable.

In her brilliant book *Do Glaciers Listen? Local Knowledge, Colonial Encounters, & Social Imagination*, Julie Cruikshank brings alive the glaciers that spill down toward the Pacific from the apex of peaks where British Columbia, Yukon and Alaska converge, through mesmerizing stories told by elders in their native Tlingit, Tagish, Ahtna and Southern Tutchone languages.

Cruikshank, professor emerita in the Department of Anthropology at the

University of British Columbia, contrasts the perspectives on glaciers as expressed by the European colonizers who dropped their anchors into the bays of that coastal region with those of the First Nations peoples who had already lived intimately with the glaciers there for thousands of years.

While those European explorers viewed glaciers as inanimate, and from perspectives that ranged from intriguing natural phenomena to specimens of the sublime to resources that should be measured and employed toward the advancement of "civilization," the local Indigenous Peoples recognized and understood glaciers to be sentient. The glaciers in their neighbourhood were part of the continuum of life, along with the wildflowers, bears, fish, ravens and people. Though the elders' stories differ in their fine details, they are fundamentally similar, and they all see the glaciers as entities capable of interacting with human social groups. In response, those people conducted themselves with the glacier's sensibilities in mind – one repeatedly cited rule warned against cooking with grease in the presence of a glacier, lest the glacier be angered. In retaliation for such a transgression, the glacier was fully expected to surge or to swallow people travelling across it deep into its crevasses.

"If that ice smells grease, he doesn't like it," described elder Kitty Smith. "Should be people just boil meat. If he smells grease, that's the time he starts."

Glaciers speak. They whisper in a trickle of meltwater and roar in gushing creeks flowing of their own lifeblood. They sing in drips and drops and plunks. They grumble and groan and rumble and growl, then shout with crashing serac ice bursting into pieces on the slopes below. In winter they sleep peacefully blanketed in soothing, nourishing snow, then thrash to life during storms, snoring like ogres chased by howling nightmares.

To explore a glacier is to immerse yourself in a world of mystery and surprises as the surface dips into a basin, rises over a mound, or at the toe reveals iron blended into solid rock cradling an aqua-green tarn. Glaciers mesmerize, slit open with gashes and gaping holes. They guard secrets of the ages now being exposed and peeled away like layers of skin from a vital organ.

Mountains 101

What defines a mountain?

How do people adapt to living at high altitudes?

How do animals live in mountain environments?

What is a glacier?

Why do mountains matter?

Answers to these questions, and many, many more, make up the content of Mountains 101, a MOOC – Massive Open Online Course – created by professors at the University of Alberta in Edmonton. And while the course is situated in the Canadian Rockies, its global perspective and lessons have made it among the most popular MOOCs of all time.

Launched in January 2017, the course provides a comprehensive and interdisciplinary overview of mountain studies, focusing on the physical, biological and human dimensions of mountain places in Alberta, and around the world.

The MOOC grew from an introduction to mountains class taught at the university by several professors, including David Hik. Now a professor in the Department of Biological Sciences at Simon Fraser University, Hik studies the structure and dynamics of plant and animal populations and how they interact in the context of landscape and climate variability, particularly in arid and mountain environments. He's especially knowledgeable about the collared pika, a tiny mammal from the Lagomorpha order (which includes rabbits) that lives in small spaces amidst boulders at high elevations and is threatened by rising temperatures at those elevations. Drawing 60 students from eight different faculties, Hik and his colleagues – from the Faculties of Science and Kinesiology, Sport and Recreation – realized interest in mountains was high, and widespread amongst students from a range of backgrounds and focuses of study. But while the on-campus course was popular, the number of students they could fit into a classroom was limited.

So Hik and several colleagues applied for funding and began creating their Mountains 101 MOOC. It's been successful beyond their dreams, drawing students from more than 170 different countries around the world. The majority are from Canada, then the United States, but also from the United Kingdom, Greece and Turkey, Switzerland, Australia and Pakistan.

From left, David Hik, Lael Parrot (Alpine Club of Canada Access & Environment VP) and Zac Robinson. Hik and Robinson's MOOC, Mountains 101, is among the most popular Massive Open Online Courses of all time. Photo Zac Robinson Collection

"A lot of people take it on Sunday morning after their coffee," Hik said.

To create an interesting and captivating MOOC, Hik and his co-host and colleague Zac Robinson, University of Alberta associate professor in the Faculty of Kinesiology, Sport, and Recreation, invited a variety of professionals to share segments of the content. In partnership with Parks Canada, some segments were shot outside on location with guest faculty. Tech tips are presented by staff members from Mountain Equipment Co-op, sharing info such as how to dress for mountain weather or how to pitch a tent.

The course encompasses 12 lessons, each 60 minutes long, which incorporate video and reading materials designed to be completed one lesson per week, but which can be followed at one's own pace. Lessons focus on topics such as climate, biodiversity of plants and animals and even human imagination.

Lesson Five focuses on mountains as water towers, while Lesson Six is devoted to glaciers: different types of glaciers, the physical dynamics of glaciers, including how they grow and how they melt, how crevasses form and how features and forms caused by ice sculpting are different from those created by running water are all covered. University of Alberta glaciologist Martin Sharp appears as a guest presenter, as does ACMG mountain guide Matt Peter, who demonstrates how to rescue a person who has fallen into a crevasse. Subtitles and translations make the course accessible to people from anywhere, including countries with mountains and those without. And it's free, so anyone can get into glaciers!

The Whale Dying on the Mountain

Nowhere in western Canada today does the perspective of glaciers as alive and intertwined with local history and culture match that of Queneesh. While so many of British Columbia's glaciers are tucked up high behind steep rock ridges and thick coastal forest out of view from valley-bottom roads and towns and patios, the Vancouver Island city of Comox is located right under the sprawling cloak of many-thousand-year-old ice.

The local name for the glacier is Queneesh. According to the K'ómoks First Nation, the name comes from an origin story in which two men, named Koai'min and He'k'ten, descended from the sky and from them the PE'ntlatc (Pentlatch) people grew. At some time in their lives, the water retreated far from the shores of eastern Vancouver Island, which they had called the Land of Plenty, and the seabed remained dry for a long time. He'k'ten was concerned the water would one day return, so to prepare for that time he made a long rope of cedar branches and tied four boats together. When the water did flow back to the land, he tied one end of the rope to a large rock in the mouth of the PE'ntlatc River and the other end to the boats. The two chief families boarded the boats and floated about. Other people begged to be allowed on board, but they turned them away with poles.

When, finally, the water level dropped, the two chief families found their home again, and the other people were scattered around the world. And up high on the mountain a whale remained stranded near PE'ntlatc Lake. The location is so high that the water froze, leaving the whale unable to swim away. That whale can still be seen for miles and that's why the glacier in the PE'ntlatc Valley is called K'one-is, or Queneesh.

Like most oral histories, the story is told in differing versions. Sometimes the boats are fastened to a giant white whale, and then as the waters recede, the whale beaches itself across the top of the mountain and is transformed into a glacier. Regardless of the fine print, the meaning of the name Queneesh remains the Great White Whale.

In his book *Beyond Nootka*, a comprehensive history of the mountain regions of Vancouver Island, local mountaineer and historian Lindsay Elms relates a longer, more intricate version, finishing with these words: "So honoured is Queneesh that on the tribal grounds by the Comox estuary he is symbolized in paint on the front of one of the remaining long houses. Here the people assemble, dance and sing in the shadow of Queneesh. For many people these mountains are nothing more than rock and ice, a frigid cold place where no one lives. But as we can see from these stories told by indigenous people, they are the homes of animals and mythical creatures, maybe we too can see the spirits they talk about and honour."

Today, the glacier's presence is felt throughout Comox. There is Glacier View Lodge. Glacier Greens Golf Course. The local hockey team is called the Glacier Kings. Comox is also home to Queneesh Mobile Home Park, Queneesh Elementary School and Queneesh Road. Clearly, the whale on the mountain is welcome as an everyday element of life in the region.

In his award-winning article "The Whale Dying on the Mountain," published in *Hakai Magazine* in 2016, Vancouver writer J.B. MacKinnon asks how it is possible, as the realities of climate change become increasingly pressing, that far too many people around the world don't seem to care or even be mildly interested in the most urgent issue of our times. Answers, and lessons, he suggests, can be gained from the Comox Glacier.

"Flood stories like the legend of Queneesh are widespread on the BC coast, and the geological record, too, is marked with the devastating floods that accompanied the great melt at the end of the Ice Age," MacKinnon wrote. "There are harrowing tales of heroes who paddled their canoes through tunnels in the glaciers, risking their lives in hopes of finding greener pastures on the other side. There are stories that recall the arrival of salmon in streams and rivers newly released from the grip of the Ice Age."

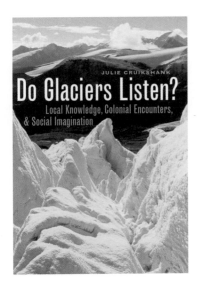

Thinking of the stories in Cruikshank's *Do Glaciers Listen*, MacKinnon suggests how one explanation for the warnings that people not cook with grease near a glacier could be related to how animal tallow could be seen to resemble glacial ice – a solid white mass that melts to liquid when it's heated. But, he suggested, there's more to it than that.

"Cruikshank also acknowledges that the academic urge to 'figure things out' could get in the way of more important insights, such as the way that such traditions keep glaciers in mind and entangle human behavior in their fates. Is it absurd to point out that the 'casual hubris and arrogance' Cruikshank spoke of has surely played a role in the melting of glaciers today? Can we see nothing but coincidence in the fact that we have caused the melting by burning oil?"

While the burning of fossil fuels is one of numerous factors causing glaciers around the world to melt at an accelerated rate, there is no denying: the great white whale is most certainly melting in its own blubber on that mountain.

With that, MacKinnon introduced the concept of solastalgia, coined by Australian environmental philosopher Glenn Albrecht to describe symptoms of distress among the inhabitants of a valley where 15 per cent of the landscape had so swiftly, over just 20 years, been decimated by open-pit mining.

"The comfort – the solace – that the locals had derived from a place they knew and loved was being taken from them." MacKinnon wrote. "They were, Albrecht said, 'homesick without leaving home.'"

This question comes up repeatedly with the long-term Comox residents he interviews.

"If there is no glacier, is it still Queneesh?"

Soul of Wilderness

In western Canada, we are truly fortunate that the headwaters of the Bow, the South and North Saskatchewan, the Athabasca and the Columbia rivers flow from icefields and glaciers that are located within the boundaries of Banff and Jasper national parks. The same goes for the Illecillewaet River splashing down from the ancient ice tongues of Glacier National Park in the Selkirk Mountains. Establishing laws protecting our headwaters – and, ideally, but sadly not entire rivers and oceans – is about the most basic and sensible decision humans can make. Water is life. We need it to be clean and uncontaminated to grow food. And to grow trees, which in turn provide us clean air to breathe. Water flows in the blood of our veins. Hundreds of western Canada's glaciers and dozens of major icefields, however, mostly in British Columbia, but a few in Alberta's Rockies too, are not protected by any environmental regulations. One of these areas is the expanse of peaks and glaciers that make up the headwaters of the Stikine River in the far northwest corner of British Columbia.

This region is the poster child for the term *remote*. That attribute, of course, is what attracted Vancouver-based adventurer and photographer John Baldwin. In May 2009, he and his wife, Linda Bily, and six others embarked on a three-week ski traverse with a plan to cross the glaciers between the Stikine and Iskut Rivers. First, they made the 1859-kilometre drive to the tiny village of Telegraph Creek, then loaded their gear into canoes and kayaks to paddle down the Stikine River, its banks still lined with late-spring ice chunks. Slipping in under the weight of their bulging packs, they started off hiking – carrying their skis too – until they were able to switch to that smoother, more efficient and enjoyable mode of travel. After three days they reached the head of the valley and skied up a gentle glacier. This, Baldwin described

A skier passes under enormous seracs on the Ring Glacier in British Columbia's Lillooet Icefield area. Photo Linda Bily

in his gorgeous coffee-table book, *Soul of Wilderness*, "was like a gateway to a different world." For the next two weeks, this would be their only world.

"Day after day we moved south through this serene landscape. The terrain was perfect for travel on skis: long glaciers threaded their way through steep mountains and each river of ice connected to the next."

To travel in a world devoid of human infrastructure is to experience constant awe, immeasurable wonder. It also means navigating sections of physically and mentally demanding terrain, such as they experienced side slipping with huge weight on their backs down a 40-degree-steep jumbled icefall. And it means, even days away from the nearest flush toilet, that evidence of Earth's warming climate is clear and obvious.

"From a peak south of Mount Hickman we got a view of the most stunning contrast between the brown, dirt-scarred headwaters of Schaft Creek to the northeast and the glistening white maze of glaciated summits to the southwest. All of the glaciers had high trim lines along their lower reaches, marking how high the glaciers had once been. Many of the glaciers had lost over 100m of ice since the 1970s."

Their next discovery, however, was unexpected, and unwelcome. As they enjoyed a long, easy ski down a low-angle glacier right to its snout at the head of Sphaler Creek, they suddenly skied right onto a snow-covered road.

"We were shocked to see a road in the midst of this remote wilderness," Baldwin wrote. It was part of a nearly 90-kilometre-long road being built to access a proposed mine. The developer had begun building separate sections of the road, using heavy-lift helicopters to fly in the machinery. When the price of minerals dropped, construction had halted and piles of culverts and machinery had been left there, abandoned for years.

"The planned road would slice through seven major tributaries of the Stikine watershed to reach right into the heart of this untouched wilderness," Baldwin described. "It was disturbing to see this pure wilderness in the process of being ripped open."

Today, plans to have the Galore Creek mine operational are ongoing. Since 2007, 50 per cent ownership of the project has been held by mining giant Teck Resources. In 2011 and 2012 a resource and geotechnical drill program was carried out, as were "minor safety improvements" on the access road. In 2012, exploration drilling was completed, resulting in the discovery of a new zone, which the following year proved to be significantly fertile. With a new partner since 2018, a feasibility study is underway, with expectations it will be completed by 2021 or 2022.

Baldwin's dismay at the discovery of this operation bulldozing its way into the headwaters of the Stikine is not without foundation.

In 2016, Teck was fined a combined $3.4 million under Canada's federal Fisheries Act and under provincial legislation for more than a dozen instances of discharging wastewater contaminated with illegally high levels of copper, zinc, ammonia, chlorine and cadmium in southern British Columbia over a period of just 15 months. Those fines came on the heels of other fines in 2011, 2013, 2014 and 2017 totalling $2.013

million for leaching mercury and sodium hydroxide and killing numerous fish downstream of its operations. Add to that, in 2018 a judgment made by a lower court was upheld, fining Teck Metals, a subsidiary of Teck Resources, $8.25 million for discharging solid and liquid waste containing heavy metals including lead, mercury, zinc and arsenic that flowed down the Columbia River through Washington. A total of 9.97 tons of slag were discharged between 1930 and 1995.

Clearly, a warming climate is just one threat to the health of glaciers and all they provide for us. And, Baldwin writes, the entire wilderness region that encompasses the Stikine, Iskut and Spatsizi Rivers is under threat of disruption and destruction from more than a half-dozen large-scale industrial projects.

"This is a rare and irreplaceable wilderness – one of the few intact wilderness areas left in North America, and the kind of precious wilderness that no longer exists in any other part of the world."

With their hearts trampled, the group skied on. Stopping on the ice of the massive Andrei Icefield, they pitched their tents and fired up their cookstoves. And sitting there, immersed in a remote land of snow and ancient ice, they were privy to a rare treat. A wolverine – an animal so elusive that those who devote their lives to studying them hardly ever see one – came running down the glacier and passed within 200 metres of their camp.

"When you travel slowly through the mountains day after day, week after week, you realize that behind the thunder of falling seracs and the roar of waterfalls there is a powerful silence, and you begin to feel the beauty and rhythm of this wilderness deep within your soul," Baldwin wrote.

"You feel the energy of the wilderness inside of you, filling your whole being. There is a feeling of joy and an awareness of the miracle of life. It's as if the wilderness – its life, its soul – is actually within us. Part of the wilderness is in us and we are part of it. Without any concrete thought we come to believe that the wild summits and icefields are alive, that the earth is alive. Not walking, talking alive, but they have a spirit, a soul."

Our Vanishing Glaciers

Though Bob Sandford's experience of being flushed through the arteries of the Saskatchewan Glacier lasted only minutes, the profound effect has lasted a lifetime.

Following a successful career as a Parks interpreter that evolved into his becoming a respected mountain historian, his prodigious talents for igniting people's enthusiasm led to his coordinating regional celebrations and awareness initiatives, including the Year of the Great Bear in 2001 and the United Nations' International Year of Mountains in 2002. One desirable result of these initiatives was the realization that unlikely partners sharing opposing perspectives could indeed work together productively. Then he turned his attention to water.

He published his first book on the topic, *Water and Our Way of Life*, in 2003 in his role as chair of the Canadian arm of the United Nations International Year of Fresh Water and Wonder of Water Initiative. On those pages he introduced readers to a journey through water, from how different cloud types form and transport water from one place to another, to sizes, shapes and velocity of raindrops as they fall to the earth. The pages floated down rivers and streams, discussing the lives of birds, bees, beavers and squirrels in relation to the water that sustains their lives and everything else's. He explained why fish don't freeze and how frogs freeze on purpose. He related how the voyageurs and fur traders helped shape Canada's cultural identity by exploring our vast country in birchbark canoes. And he wrote of Canadians' personal relationships with water through the seasons, saying, "What winter does to water is the essence of what the world imagines when they think of Canada. In many ways it is the wonder of water in winter that makes us Canadian."

He also rocked the boat, revealing how, when it comes to water, Canadians have a few reasons to feel embarrassed and ashamed. He listed more than a dozen threats to the country's drinking water and aquatic ecosystem health, including waterborne pathogens, algal toxins, pesticides, persistent pollutants – including mercury – acid rain, municipal water effluents and the effects of industrial, agricultural and forestry practices. He pointed out that two provincial capitals – Victoria, BC, and St. John's, Newfoundland – discharge raw sewage directly into the ocean at their doorsteps (a situation since improved, but not entirely remedied), and how Canadian toilets consume nearly one-quarter of all our municipal water supply. He wrote about the water in our showers, our clothes, our food and our lawns, and how water is used in virtually every step of car manufacturing (and virtually all manufacturing), from rubber tires to steering wheel to the roof. We even use it as a trashcan.

"Over the last century our riverbanks have become our back alley – the out-of-sight back road where we store what we no longer need or want. As is often the custom of wealthy people, we have, over time, lost touch with the source and true nature of our wealth."

Canada, however, is a microcosm of what is happening to water all over the world, he said then, and still does today.

"We have to protect our water. Because in the end, what we do to water, we do to ourselves."

By 2005, Canada was the first country to develop its own program in support of the United Nations' international decade for action, with Sandford at the helm of the national platform. Along with that, he was the first Canadian to be appointed to the permanent advisory committee of the respected Rosenberg International Forum on Water Policy and was instrumental behind Canada hosting the forum for the first time in 2006. Through the following decade, he collaborated with scientists and policy advisors across the country and internationally in an effort to tackle long-term water quality and availability issues in response to climate change.

He's also written some 35 books on the natural history and cultural heritage of the Canadian west, including more than 15 books on water, climate change and related topics. Topics have included ethical water, saving (choked with bacteria) Lake Winnipeg, flood risk as a component of climate change in Canada, water and climate security in a changing world, climate change in the "Age of Trump" and, in 2018, the Canada-China water crisis.

As Chair in Water and Climate Security at the United Nations University Institute for Water, Environment and Health, Sandford has remained at the forefront of public awareness and policy discussions with various levels of government concerning freshwater issues for the past two decades. In 2011 he was appointed senior water advisor to the Interaction Council, a global public policy forum composed of nearly three dozen former heads of state, including Canadian Prime Minister Jean Chrétien, US President Bill Clinton and Norwegian Prime Minister Gro Brundtland. This esteemed group mobilizes the experience, energy and international contacts of its members to work together to foster international co-operation in three principal areas – peace and security; revitalization of the world economy and the nexus between development, population and environment; and universal ethics.

At the core, a key part of Sandford's work is to translate scientific research outcomes into language decision makers can use to craft timely and meaningful public policy. His resume is long, his mission never-ending.

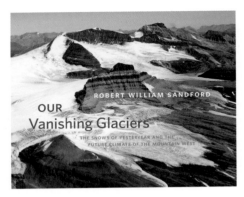

R.W. "Bob" Sandford's *Our Vanishing Glaciers: The Snows of Yesteryear and the Future Climate of the Mountain West* won the Lane Anderson Award for the best science writing in Canada in 2017.

A Book about Hope

Among Sandford's book titles, his splendid *Our Vanishing Glaciers: The Snows of Yesteryear and the Future Climate of the Mountain West* stands out. Deservedly, it earned him the Lane Anderson Award for the best science writing in Canada in 2017.

Lavishly accompanied by full-colour images, the hardcover volume is an absolute ode to glaciers. Focused on the Columbia Icefield, with aerial surveys, thermal imaging and 40 years of Sandford's own personal observations all anchored by the findings of some of the world's most respected snow and glacier scientists, the book graphically outlines the projected rate of glacial recession in western Canada's mountains over the remainder of this century. It also poignantly explains and illustrates the profound and crucial role water – as liquid, as snow and as glacial ice – plays in making life on Earth, and in the Canadian West, possible.

Despite the title, and the realities of diminishing glaciers worldwide, it is, he insisted during a conversation we shared, a book about hope.

"What inspired me to write this book – and to keep going on it year after year – was my love of these monumental landscapes," Sandford said. "Everything I have written has been informed by a deep sense of place."

"A second and very powerful inspiration for writing this book was the passion and sacrifice I observed among the scientists who so generously included me in what they were doing and unselfishly shared everything they learned so that others might see what they are seeing happening to the glaciers of the mountain West. We undervalue the important work of these people; and I wanted this book to honour their dedication, commitment and vision. I also wanted people to pay attention to the urgency of what they are so calmly trying to tell us."

The message has been clear, and has been repeated with increasing urgency in the pages of the Intergovernmental Panel on Climate Change assessment reports, written and prepared by thousands of scientists from all over the globe sharing their findings in a large range of climate-related studies since 1990.

Sunrise casts a warm glow on Mount Balfour's glaciated east-facing upper slopes. Photo Lynn Martel

Earth is warming. Fast.

If we don't make significant changes, the effects – floods, hurricanes fuelled by increasingly warm oceans, wildfires exacerbated by hot, dry weather, will continue to worsen. Melting glaciers are just the tip of the iceberg, pun intended. With each subsequent report, changes are happening faster than they were expected to, and with effects occurring that weren't expected. And, the reports state, we have a decade in which to act in substantial and meaningful ways.

Since Sandford's own first encounters with glaciers – and the underbelly of the Saskatchewan Glacier – more than four decades ago, the Columbia Icefield area has come to represent a touchstone that has guided him through his career. And it's only after a lifetime that he has come to fully realize the extent to which his experiences in places he finds deeply enriching and endlessly remarkable have inspired not just direction but purpose in his life.

"What makes the glaciers of Canada's western mountains unique is their relative accessibility. In places you can literally get out of your car, and in a few moments, walk directly back into the Pleistocene, a colder epoch in the Earth's history when much of North America was buried beneath two kilometres of ice. Epiphany is possible here, a sense of aesthetic arrest. A shudder runs through your soul as you realize, suddenly, what an Ice Age really means."

That, he said, was the feeling he hoped readers would take away from his book. And, on a practical level, he added that he hoped readers would allow glaciers to not only remind us of our past but inspire our future as human habits affect and alter the planet's natural cycles.

"There has probably never been a time in history when making science understandable to a vastly diverse public has been more important," Sandford said. "We are also at a bottleneck in the evolutionary history of our species where failing to understand and act appropriately on what we know could have devastating impacts on future generations, and potentially catastrophic effects on Earth system function for the rest of time."

Working day after day, year after year to do his best, he admitted his part in communicating this message has its ups and downs. But in the end, Sandford makes sure to find his way back to glowing green-blue glacial light.

"This book is about hope. Not just wishful thinking – but the genuine hope we can have if we pay attention to what we know and act on that knowledge in the service of creating a better world and a more secure future for all who come after us."

Writing books during his brief time home from an exhausting travel and speaking schedule that is the envy of no one (yes, he thinks about his carbon footprint), I could hear the tiredness in his voice, and suggested he might take some time off, take a break from his work.

"I sure don't need the money," he said with a shrug. "But this is urgent. It would be irresponsible."

Then, with a deep breath, he added, "I'd give anything to not have to do this work."

Sunset casts a rosy glow on Mount Robson's glaciers high in the Canadian Rockies.
Photo Paul Zizka

6 SPIRITUAL ICE

The Earth does not belong to man, man belongs to the Earth. All things are connected, like the blood that unites us all. Man did not weave the web of life, he is but a strand in it; whatever he does to the web, he does to himself.

—Chief Seattle

Old, Familiar Neighbourhood

"Are you going skiing?" the woman asked, looking at my clothing.

We were at Laggan's bakery in Lake Louise, paying for our purchases.

"Yes, we're going up onto the glaciers for four days."

"On the glaciers!" Her deep brown, almost burgundy eyes opened wide and her brown face lit right up. "You're going on the glaciers?"

I described how we would ski with packs on our backs and skins on our skis enabling us to travel uphill, up one glacier, over a col and down the next to reach a small hut where we would sleep for three nights. It was clear she had never imagined people might do such an outlandish thing.

I asked about her group of about a dozen, half of whom were sitting on the bench outside, smoking, laughing. They were First Nations elders from Saskatchewan on a trip to Banff, to the mountains. Her eyes twinkled; this was a special trip for them. They planned to soak in the hot springs in Banff.

I told her about Barry Blanchard, one of Canada's best-known mountain climbers, and that he is of Métis heritage from the Qu'Appelle Valley region of Saskatchewan and proudly wears his hair in a long silver ponytail.

"Blanchard – I know lots of Blanchards at home," she said, adding, "Climbing – ha, we're pretty limited in our activities. We'll go shopping and we eat too!" she said with a laugh and a pat of her round belly, a feature shared by her companions. The smell of cigarettes permeated her jacket. Her smile was infectious. We laughed together. She told me she was 68. With a bit of trepidation, I told her the two men in our party were in their mid-60s, and I 57. She laughed harder, amused by these mountain people. We bid each other a great day. After three decades, I never tire of asking our tourists where they are from and wishing them an enjoyable vacation in my world.

A fresh skiers' track leads up the Vulture Glacier with Balfour Glacier in the background. Fifteen minutes later a squall reduced visibility to a few metres for half an hour before the clouds parted. Photo Lynn Martel

Barely an hour later we had parked at Bow Lake, switched into ski boots and were gliding slowly across the solidly frozen snow-plastered lake. Shifting under the weight of my backpack, I knew I was in for a long day of skiing uphill under the strain of safety gear, sleeping bag and food for four days, significantly more weight than I'd carried any other day that season. For all the discomfort and labour, before long I moved into the rhythm of sliding my left ski, my right ski, my left. After 20-plus trips to the Wapta Icefields over the past 20 or so years, I absorbed the familiar terrain like visiting a friend in an old familiar neighbourhood. Ski across the lake, along the gravel flats veering around rocks covered by a mere few inches of wind-hammered snow, up into the trees and over the hump – with the first avalanche hazard of the trip above us – down the hard-packed opposite side of the hump and into the canyon.

On this day, I was delighted to find a snow-covered but still distinguishable wolverine track following along through the entire length of the canyon, winding around open pools of sparkling meltwater running under the snowpack to the next open spot downstream.

Up and out of the canyon, through the last trees and onto the moraine, Bow Hut, our halfway point for the day, was in full view on the rocky bench above us. Over to the headwall, sticking close to the rock band on our right to avoid the massive cliffs of Vulture Peak looming on the left, from which serac chunks and avalanches break off to land like ice boulders on the valley floor. At the three-hour mark, we stepped out of our skis and gathered inside the hut's common cooking and living area, boiled water for tea and savoured a few minutes with the gorillas off our backs. As usual, Bow Hut was alive with skiers, day-trippers passing through and a few overnight visitors dumping their loads in the sleeping dorm before heading up higher to bag peaks and make ski turns on glacier slopes.

Refreshed, we hoisted our packs and clicked into our ski bindings. Just ten minutes up the hill we glided smoothly from snow-covered moraine onto the glacier, any sign of crevasses buried in two metres of well-packed snow. For two hours we inched our way uphill on a gradual track set by previous skiers, and while my pack tugged at my shoulders and hips like a sack of potatoes, my mind drifted off into the peaceful, meditative state that comes with skiing slowly up consistently rising, not-too-steep glacier slope. The Zen of skinning.

Moving through the landscape at a human pace, a ridge, a row of rock pillars, ledges or a gully appeared on one side, or a new peak poked up above the horizon on the other, mountain features slid in and out of view to the pace of my breath. Same, same, yet always just slightly different until you realize one feature has drifted from view and a new one has emerged. On this day we were blessed: the sky was cloudless, there was no wind. The peace was mesmerizing.

I thought about the first time I drove up to Bow Lake with my mom some 35 years earlier. My sister, Daisy, and I had been living and working service industry jobs in Banff for a few months, and Mom was out visiting from Montreal. We were there to hike to Bow Falls, a popular half-day trail. As we walked across the gravel parking lot toward the lake, four bearded, unkempt-looking men walked toward us. They carried big backpacks, and more remarkably to me, a new-to-the-mountains city girl, they each had a pair of skis strapped to the sides of their packs like dual flagpoles strapped together near the tips. Wow! Where had these guys been that they needed skis in July? Skiing wasn't an activity I could manage with even a minor level of proficiency at that time, but the seed was planted. Someday I needed to go where they had been.

With memories of many of my trips onto the Wapta blending one into the other, and my body at 57 standing an inch shorter than it used to, I wondered how many more times I would be able to carry the load required for a three-night trip. Maybe next year, I told myself, I would hire a porter, some young, strong mountaineer keen to improve his or her fitness for a few dollars.

As we finally crested the incline, the glacier flattened and familiar rocky peaks ringed the horizon, growing taller as the track stretched ahead on the main icefield, a massive field of snow heaped upon glacial ice stretching for kilometres in each direction. In winter, due to their higher elevation, the Wapta and Waputik icefields – which combined cover an area several times the size of Canmore, where I live – have not lost nearly as much of their size as the glaciers extending down from them. Immersed in that sea of white, I felt grateful to know skiers could still easily travel from the icefields up the slopes of Mounts Rhondda, Habel, Collie, Des Poilus, and up and over the col that separates Mount Olive and Saint Nicholas Peak, where we were headed. Far from view of any of the tiny huts, as I ascended the ramp to the col with my companions ahead of me, I surveyed the expanse of white below, a handful of ski tracks crisscrossing the surface like tiny roadways leading to their destinations, with not one other sign of human presence. I felt profoundly, utterly content.

Over the col we skied down a ramp of fluffy powder snow, then groaned as the glacier curved to the south, leaving us to endure sun-crusted snow that felt like skiing through thick toast for three long, low-angled kilometres all the way to the hut.

The next day we skied around to the west side of Mount Balfour to the Diablerets Glacier, a massive expanse of unblemished snow untracked since the previous week's snowfall. Skinning up, we sliced a new track into a surface of ten centimetres of fresh snow, the trough feeling firm yet ever-so-slightly spongy underfoot, a sensation only experienced on a glacier topped with a full winter's snowpack. Reaching a broad col capped with a patch of bare rock, we soaked in the panorama of peaks, relaxing in the springtime temperatures on a windless, cloudless day, grateful for what we all knew is a rarity on the Wapta. Playing "name that peak" we identified the Bugaboos' Howser Towers, Hungabee, The Goodsirs, Forbes far to the north – summits some of our group had stood on. The 300-metre run down was pure bliss, and with little discussion we skinned back up for another hour to do it again. The four of us had the entire glacier to ourselves for the whole afternoon. It was a perfect day.

Delicate Balance

The stellar spring weather drew lots of skiers to the Wapta that weekend. While I was happy to have the painfully frozen fingers of a seriously cold February behind me, I was also relieved that the 20-degree summer-like temperatures of two weeks earlier had cooled. Safe travel in avalanche terrain requires overnight freezes. It's a delicate balance.

On a rainy September day, the toe of the Asulkan Glacier in Glacier National Park is at its thinnest, a sorry bedraggled sight as John McIsaac walks on moraine rocks freshly exposed after being buried by glacial ice for thousands of years. Photo Lynn Martel

If there's anything I've learned from three decades of outdoor adventures it's that Earth's natural systems function in a delicate balance. Every single thing in nature is connected. And there is always a tipping point at which it all unravels like a snow slope giving way to an avalanche.

I've also learned that things that are the most worthwhile often require some effort. The national park regulations set many decades ago mean there is only one way to ski the Diablerets and any glaciers of the Rockies' Wapta,

Columbia and other protected icefields. Beyond hiring a porter to help carry a few pounds, no amount of money can buy an easier way to experience these places than skinning uphill under your own sweat. For hours. Knowing this gives me joy, relief and hope.

While Earth warms, Canada is warming twice as fast as most places. This is not good news for most of our far northern populations who count on winter to sustain their way of life. Neither is it good news for those of us who live to experience the quiet, sprawling snowfields unmarked by humans save for a few delicate, ephemeral swooping S-turns etched on the surface to be swept away by tomorrow's wind or snow. Even though I'm not sure my body will be able to continue these trips more than a decade from now, it breaks my heart to think younger generations might miss out on these unmatched enriching experiences.

When I began interviewing glaciologists and snow hydrologists in the early 2000s, they all told me climate change would be a bumpy ride, that storms would grow bigger, more powerful, that weather extremes would become the new norm. Everything they predicted is happening.

The spring glacier-skiing season is a brief magical window in western Canada's high mountains, as it has been for centuries. But when I first lived in Banff, summers in the mountains were shocking. Coming from the muggy heat of Montreal, where you grew accustomed to being glued to yourself, snow blowing sideways in July was not imaginable. Over the years I grew to love the Rockies' summers and the variety of weather they brought. I learned not to pack away my winter jackets, because there really wasn't a season when I might not need them. I learned to pack a toque and gloves on just about every hike, and that a summer sleeping bag should be rated at least minus 7 Celsius. I learned to love the minus 30 spells in the dead of winter: such a perfect time to stay home and bake. I learned to love bundling up, just like I did as a kid excavating caves inside giant snow piles in Montreal in the 1960s and '70s.

But now, in the Rockies, I don't look forward to summer quite the way I used to. The summers of 2017 and '18 brought weeks of forest fire smoke from blazes a nerve-wracking few valleys away and hundreds more burning across British Columbia, clogging the valley between my windows and the mountains hemming the other side of town just a bike ride away. While I loved the cool, rainy 2019 summer – like old times – I have no idea how to learn to love weeks of dense wildfire smoke.

Three gorgeous sunny days on the Wapta at the end of March, though, gave me hope. At night I walked to the outhouse breathless with awe at the explosion of stars spilling across the inky black sky. While my companions set off to climb Mount

Ice sculpted by sun and wind frames the entrance to a large cave at the toe of the Bow Glacier, Banff National Park. Photo Lynn Martel

Balfour, I chose to spend our second morning doing chores in the hut before exploring the nearby rolling moraine hills for the afternoon. With all the previous night's hut guests either out for a day-ski or skiing over the high col and across the Daly Glacier to spend their next night at Scott Duncan Hut before finishing their traverse at Sherbrooke Lake, I savoured a few quiet hours before the first visitors arrived like pilgrims on a quest. Five skiers from Calgary, young and fit and including one woman, had departed the Peyto Glacier parking lot at 5:30 a.m. Arriving at Balfour Hut at noon marked their halfway point to completing the entire "classic" Wapta traverse in a single day. Soon after they skied away on their ambitious adventure, the next group arrived, three young men from Ireland working in Banff on visitor's visas and undertaking a glacier journey leaps and bounds greater in difficulty and commitment than any they'd previously experienced. That night a group of four staying at the hut included a young woman from Revelstoke who was days away from taking her ACMG apprentice ski guide's exam.

On the first of our mornings at the hut, I had woken early as a crew of four filled their packs and readied their gear for the two-hour climb to the Balfour high col. One of them was Zbigniew Lisiecki, a keen ski mountaineer from Calgary whom I'd previously met in another Rockies hut. Recently retired from a long career with the City of Calgary's urban forestry department, he was strong and fitter than most people half his age after a winter of many mountain trips, skiing across glaciers and icefields and up and down snow-capped peaks.

"Why do you come here, up to the icefields, again and again?" I asked him.

A tear squeezed out and rolled down his sun-bronzed cheek.

"I always find it's a cleansing experience for most of us to be up in the mountains," he replied. "I come to be up in the mountains with my own thoughts. It's where I feel I have my best moments. It's a spiritual experience."

Yes, Zbigniew, it is.

EPILOGUE

Be the Change You Want to See

Canmore, February 2020

The year I was born, 1961, Earth's population was 3 billion, 92 million. Today it's 7.7 billion. That's more than double. If that wasn't enough, that time period has generated astounding, and perpetually increasing, levels of energy consumption and waste.

Between the 1960s and the 1990s, virtually all packaging and drink containers were switched from glass to plastic. Sadly, most of that plastic is never recycled, and it does not biodegrade. As a teen I bought clothes that were manufactured in Montreal's hip factories, not shipped from China. Yes, they cost more, and we bought fewer items. The neighbourhood shoemaker resoled our shoes. Diapers were made of cloth and laundered at home or, for those with more money, by a service. Granted, in the 1960s it was publicly acceptable to toss cigarette butts and gum wrappers down the sewer grate, teachers were permitted to whack students with a yardstick and people smoked in airplanes, so life wasn't all rosy and perfect.

But somewhere along the line, it became not only acceptable but encouraged for people to fly in airplanes as often as their credit cards allowed, with points systems further urging them to the point we now have 200,000 aircraft spewing jet fuel around our little planet on any given day. Giant shopping malls with giant parking lots replaced locally owned mom and pop stores you could walk to. And I remember the "Save a Tree" campaign that implored us to switch from paper grocery bags to plastic. Plastic, of course, is made from fossil fuels. Now I wonder who was behind that campaign.

Then in the 1990s, computers and cellphones moved into all our homes and back pockets, none of them designed to last much more than three years. These items, now necessities to function in our social and work world, are not recyclable, not biodegradable. Seven billion phones and laptops being tossed into landfills every three years?

Industrial farming practices have depleted our soils and poisoned our water. Virtually every industrial activity depends on the same water we need for our food and beer, plus what our waters and lakes need to remain healthy. And every aspect of our modern lives is governed by an economic system that necessitates endless growth. Endless consumption. Endless waste.

But Earth is not growing. Our little home is finite. The amount of freshwater, arable soil, breathable air, it's all finite. Our human population is projected to grow to 9 billion by 2050. Meanwhile, all our current consumptive practices are causing the very ecosystem upon which all our lives depend to collapse. Our melting glaciers are just one component of the massive web of climate change. Yup, it's big stuff.

When things go sideways during a five-month ski traverse – as they almost inevitably do – ignoring the problem doesn't make it go away. Does anybody really want to be the dead body left to slowly rot inside a glacier crevasse? Hell no!

But this is no time for despair. It's time to spring to action. These are exciting times!

There is so much work to be done and so much teamwork required to initiate the changes we have to make. It's time for us to do what humans do well – improve, innovate, invent. It's time to embrace this challenge and completely overhaul our energy delivery system. Out with the old – fossil fuels – and in with the new – solar and wind technology. There is so much to learn, to explore, to discover, to accomplish. There's even money to be made. And the problems coming our way will cost a whole lot more to manage if we don't confront them now.

And to those who say, "What can I do, I'm just one person?" The answer is, Stop Being Just One Person. Find a climate action group in your neighbourhood, town, city. Join one online. Canada has all the brains and expertise to be a leader in green technology and the heart to lead the green transition – and build a resilient, sustainable economy while we're at it.

So, get excited, get to work. Greening our world is a grand adventure!

A kayaker (in an inflatable kayak he and the photographer lugged for hours on foot to reach that spot) paddles the freshly melted waters at the toe of Des Poilus Glacier, a lake that barely exists on my 1996 map, but which has expanded to be among the largest in Yoho National Park today. "Glaciers are complex expressions of cold and warm on the landscape," writes glaciologist Mike Demuth. "These Great Carvers are not static but alive – places of spirits." Photo Nick Fitzhardinge

ACKNOWLEDGEMENTS

It really does take a community to write a book about a place and the myriad smaller towns and valleys and rivers and lakes that make up the larger neighbourhood. I owe tremendous gratitude to all those adventurers, professional guides, business owners, scientists and creatives who have, over the years, shared their stories with me so I might write articles for readers to experience those stories. Extra thanks go to these people (in no particular order) for taking the time to answer my questions and read through my chapters on their adventures and projects: Robert Maiman, Paul Geddes, Jocelyn Hirose, Gioachino Roberti, Tannis Dakin, Alison Criscitiello, Matt Beedle, Ben Pelto, Jill Pelto, John Scurlock, Arnor Larson, Meredith Hamstead, Pat Morrow, Lisa Paulson, Dr. Mike Demuth, Dr. John Pomeroy, John Baldwin, Darcy Monchak, Isabel Budke, Regan Johnston, Martina Halik, Rupert Wedgwood, Brian Patton, David Lavallée, Brad Harrison, Alpine Club of Canada, Dr. Martin Sharp, Dr. Gwenn Flowers, Dr. Brian Luckman, Karl Ricker, John Ford, Pierre Friele, Mike Mokievsky-Zubok, Janet Fischer, Mark Olson, and Scott Rowed for his digital image wizardry, Andrea Lustenberger/HeliCat Canada Association, Laura Coulson/Parks Canada, Salina Riemer/CMH Heli-Skiing & Summer Adventures, Anne Ewan and Lindsay Stokalko/Whyte Museum of the Canadian Rockies, and Rick Gardiner/Alpine Club of Canada. A very special thank you to Bob Sandford for his bottomless encouragement, his sharp mind and his always sage advice.

And a heartfelt thank you to my copy editor Peter Enman for his polishing skills, to Chyla Cardinal for her exquisite design skills that make this book look gorgeous, and to Gorman and Rocky Mountain Books for believing in these Stories of Ice.

If there's anyone I've forgotten, please accept my apologies, and my thanks!

SELECT BIBLIOGRAPHY

Alpine Club of Canada. The Alpine Club of Canada 2019 State of the Mountains Report.

Atkinson, Chris, and Marc Piché. *The Bugaboos: One of the World's Great Rockclimbing Centres*. Squamish, BC: Elaho Publishing, 2003.

Baile, Lisa. *John Clarke: Explorer of the Coast Mountains*. Madeira Park, BC: Harbour Publishing, 2012.

Baldwin, John. *Exploring the Coast Mountains on Skis: A Guide to Ski Mountaineering*. 3rd ed. Vancouver: John Baldwin, 2009.

———. *Mountains of the Coast: Photographs of Remote Corners of the Coast Mountains*. Madeira Park, BC: Harbour Publishing, 1999.

Baldwin, John, and Linda Bily. *Soul of Wilderness: Mountain Journeys in Western BC and Alaska*. Madeira Park, BC: Harbour Publishing, 2015.

Boles, Glen. *My Mountain Album: Art & Photography of the Canadian Rockies & Columbia Mountains*. Surrey, BC: Rocky Mountain Books, 2006.

Boles, Glen, Roger W. Laurilla and William L. Putnam. *Canadian Mountain Place Names: The Rockies and Columbia*. Victoria, BC: Rocky Mountain Books, 2006.

Bridge, Kathryn. *Phyllis Munday: Mountaineer*. Montreal: XYZ Publishing, 2002.

Calvert, Kathy, and Dale Portman. *Guardians of the Peaks: Mountain Rescue in the Canadian Rockies and Columbia Mountains*. Victoria, BC: Rocky Mountain Books, 2008.

Chapman, C. "The Garibaldi District." *Canadian Alpine Journal* 8 (1917): 97–101. Available at http://library.alpine-clubofcanada.ca:8009/book-acc.php?id=CAJ008-1-1917%22%20\l%20%22page/97/mode/1up#page/1/mode/1up.

Coleman, A.P. *The Canadian Rockies: New and Old Trails*. Calgary, AB: Rocky Mountain Books, 2011.

Corbett, Bill. *The 11,000ers of the Canadian Rockies*. 2nd ed. Victoria, BC: Rocky Mountain Books, 2016.

Demuth, Michael. *Becoming Water: Glaciers in a Warming World*. Victoria, BC: Rocky Mountain Books, 2012.

Demuth, Michael, D.S. Munro and G.J. Young. *Peyto Glacier: One Century of Science*. Saskatoon, SK: National Water Research Institute, 2006.

Dougherty, Sean. *Selected Alpine Climbs in the Canadian Rockies*. Rev. ed. Calgary, AB: Rocky Mountain Books, 2009.

Edwards, Guy. "The Traverse—The First Complete Coast Mountain Ski." *Canadian Alpine Journal* 85 (2002): 4–13.

Ehlers, J., P.L. Gibbard and P.D. Hughes, eds. *Quaternary Glaciations – Extent and Chronology: A Closer Look*. Developments in Quaternary Science 15. Amsterdam: Elsevier, 2011.

Elms, Lindsay. *Beyond Nootka: A Historical Perspective of Vancouver Island Mountains*. Courtenay, BC: Misthorn Press, 1996.

Environment and Climate Change Canada. Canada's Changing Climate Report. April 2019. https://changingclimate.ca/CCCR2019/.

Gmoser, Hans. *The CMH Gallery: A Visual Celebration of CMH Heli Skiing and Heli Hiking*. Banff, AB: Canadian Mountain Holidays, 1996.

———. "High Level Ski Route from Lake Louise to Jasper." *Canadian Alpine Journal* 44 (1961): 11–22. Available at http://library.alpine-clubofcanada.ca:8009/book-acc.php?id=CAJ044-1-1961#page/11/mode/1up.

Gmoser, Hans, and Jon Whyte. *25 years of CMH Heli Skiing: A Photographic Celebration*. Banff, AB: Canadian Mountain Holidays, 1991.

Gooch, Jane Lytton. *Artists of the Rockies: Inspiration of Lake O'Hara*. Fernie, BC: Alpine Club of Canada and The Rockies Network, 2003.

Green, William Spotswood. *Among the Selkirk Glaciers: Being the Account of a Rough Survey in the Rocky Mountain Regions of British Columbia*. London: MacMillan, 2018. First published 1890.

Haberl, Keith. *Alpine Huts: A Guide to the Facilities of the Alpine Club of Canada*. 2nd ed. Canmore, AB: Alpine Club of Canada, 1997.

Harmon, Carole, and Bart Robinson. *Byron Harmon Mountain Photographer*. Canmore, AB: Altitude Publishing, 1999.

Jones, David P. *Rockies Central: The Climbers Guide to the Rocky Mountains of Canada*. Squamish, BC: High Col Publishing, 2015.

Kariel, Herb, and Pat Kariel. *Alpine Huts in the Rockies, Selkirks and Purcells*. Banff, AB: Alpine Club of Canada, 1986.

Kaufman, Andrew J., and William L. Putnam. *The Guiding Spirit*. Revelstoke, BC: Footprint Publishing, 1986.

Kivi, K. Linda, ed. *The Purcell Suite: Upholding the Wild*. Nelson, BC: Maa Press, 2007.

Martel, Lynn. *Alpine Artistry: The Mountain Life of Glen Boles*. Canmore, AB: Alpine Club of Canada, 2014.

Mastin, Catharine M., ed. *The Group of Seven in Western Canada*. Toronto: Key Porter Books, 2002.

Matrasova-Engler, Vera, and Susan Engler Potts. *Bruno Engler Photography: Sixty Years of Mountain Photography in the Canadian Rockies*. Calgary, AB: Rocky Mountain Books, 2001.

Patton, Brian. *Hollywood in the Canadian Rockies*. Kindle e-book. Summerthought, 2019.

———, ed. *Tales from the Canadian Rockies*. Toronto: McClelland & Stewart, 2012.

Pole, Graeme. *Canadian Rockies*. Rev. ed. Canmore, AB: Altitude Publishing, 2004.

Powter, Geoff. *Inner Ranges: An Anthology of Mountain Thoughts and Mountain People*. Victoria, BC: Rocky Mountain Books, 2018.

Pullan, Brandon. *The Bold and Cold: A History of 25 Classic Climbs in the Canadian Rockies*. Victoria, BC: Rocky Mountain Books, 2016.

Putnam, William Lowell. *The Great Glacier and Its House: The Story of the First Center of Alpinism in North America, 1885–1925*. New York: American Alpine Club, 1982.

Putnam, William Lowell, and Glen W. Boles. *Climber's Guide to the Rocky Mountains of Canada: South*. 6th ed. New York: American Alpine Club, 1973.

Reichwein, Pearlann. *Climber's Paradise: Making Canada's Mountain Parks 1906–1974*. Edmonton, AB: University of Alberta Press, 2014.

Render, Lorne E. *The Mountains and The Sky*. Calgary, AB: Glenbow-Alberta Institute, 1974.

Ricker, Karl. "The All Canadian Mt. Logan Expedition." *Canadian Alpine Journal* 43 (1960): 11–34. Available at http://library.alpineclubofcanada.ca:8009/book-acc.php?id=CAJ043-1-1960%22%20\l%20%22page/11/mode/1up#page/4/mode/1up.

Rowat, Lena. "Over the Top." *Canadian Alpine Journal* 86 (2003): 16–25. Available at http://library.alpineclubofcanada.ca:8009/book-acc.php?id=CAJ086-1-2003%22%20\l%20%22page/17/mode/1up#page/1/mode/1up.

Sandford, Robert W. *The Canadian Alps: The History of Mountaineering in Canada, Vol. 1.* Canmore, AB: Altitude Publishing, 1990.

———. *The Columbia Icefield*, 3rd ed. Victoria, BC: Rocky Mountain Books, 2016.

———. *Con Bravura: The Remarkable Mountaineering Life of Peter Fuhrmann.* Canmore, AB: Alpine Club of Canada, 2014.

———. *Ecology & Wonder in the Canadian Rocky Mountain Parks World Heritage Site.* Edmonton, AB: Athabasca University Press, 2010.

———. *A Mountain Life: The Stories and Photographs of Bruno Engler.* Canmore, AB: Alpine Club of Canada, 1997.

———. *Our Vanishing Glaciers: The Snows of Yesteryear and the Future Climate of the Mountain West.* Victoria, BC: Rocky Mountain Books, 2017.

Sanford, Emerson, and Janice Beck. *Life of the Trail 3: The Historic Route From Old Bow Fort to Jasper.* Surrey, BC: Rocky Mountain Books, 2009.

Scott, Chic. *Deep Powder and Steep Rock: The Life of Mountain Guide Hans Gmoser.* Victoria, BC: Rocky Mountain Books, 2015.

———. *A Life in the Wild: the Story of Mountain Explorer John Baldwin.* Canmore, AB: Alpine Club of Canada, 2019.

———. *Powder Pioneers: Ski Stories from the Canadian Rockies and Columbia Mountains.* Victoria, BC: Rocky Mountain Books, 2005.

———. *Pushing the Limits: The Story of Canadian Mountaineering.* Calgary, AB: Rocky Mountain Books, 2009.

Scott, Chic, and Mark Klassen. *Summits and Icefields 1: Alpine Ski Tours in the Canadian Rockies.* Victoria, BC: Rocky Mountain Books, 2012.

———. *Summits and Icefields 2: Alpine Ski Tours in the Columbia Mountains.* Victoria, BC: Rocky Mountain Books, 2015.

Scott, Jim. *Backcountry Huts and Lodges of the Rockies and Columbias.* Calgary, AB: Johnson Gorman Publishers, 2002.

Stutfield, Hugh, and J. Norman Collie. *Climbs & Exploration in the Canadian Rockies.* Vancouver: Rocky Mountain Books, 2008.

Townsend, Nancy. *Art Inspired by the Canadian Rockies, Purcell Mountains and Selkirk Mountains 1809–2012.* Calgary, AB: Bayeux Arts, 2012.

University of British Columbia Varsity Outdoor Club. *A Century of Antics, Epics & Escapades: The Varsity Outdoor Club 1917–2017.*

Vaux, Henry Jr. *Legacy in Time: Three Generations of Mountain Photography in the Canadian West.* Victoria, BC: Rocky Mountain Books, 2014.

Whyte, Jon. *Indians in the Rockies.* Banff, AB: Altitude Publishing, 1985.